PHILIP'S ROAD ATLAS

DRIVER'S BRITAIN

D0256392

James Osmond / Alamy

www.philips-maps.co.uk

First published in 2006 by Philip's
a division of Octopus Publishing Group Ltd,
Endeavour House, 189 Shaftesbury Avenue
London WC2H 8JY
www.octopus-publishing.co.uk
An Hachette UK company
www.hachette.co.uk

Seventh edition 2014
First impression 2014

ISBN 978-1-84907-336-3

Cartography by Philip's
Copyright © 2014 Philip's

Tourist information

✝	Abbey, cathedral or priory	⬚	House and garden
🏛	Ancient monument	▦	Motor racing circuit
⬂	Aquarium	⬚	Museum
🏛	Art gallery	Ⓐ	Picnic area
⬎	Bird collection or aviary	🚂	Preserved railway
🏰	Castle	⬎	Race course
⛪	Church	⬎	Roman antiquity
⬚	Country park England and Wales Scotland	⅄	Safari park
🐎	Farm park	⬚	Theme park
✿	Garden	*i*	Tourist information centre open all year
⛴	Historic ship	*i*	open seasonally
⬚	House	🐘	Zoo
		✦	Other place of interest

Route-finding system

Town names printed in yellow on a green background are those used on Britain's signposts to indicate primary destinations. To find your route quickly and easily, simply follow the signs to the primary destination immediately beyond the place you require.
Below Driving from St Ives to Camborne, follow the signs to Redruth, the first primary destination beyond Camborne. These will indicate the most direct main route to the side turning for Camborne.

Speed Cameras

Fixed camera locations are shown using the 40 symbol.

In congested areas the 40 symbol is used to show that there are two or more cameras on the road indicated.

Due to the restrictions of scale the camera locations are only approximate and cannot indicate the operating direction of the camera. Mobile camera sites, and cameras located on roads not included on the mapping are not shown. Where two or more cameras are shown on the same road, drivers are warned that this may indicate that a SPEC system is in operation. These cameras use the time taken to drive between the two camera positions to calculate the speed of the vehicle.

Road map scales

4·18 miles to 1 inch • 1: 265 000

0 1 2 3 4 5 6 miles

0 2 4 6 8 10 km

Parts of Scotland

5.24 miles to 1 inch • 1: 332 000

0 1 2 3 4 5 6 7 8 miles

0 2 4 6 8 10 12 km

Orkney and Shetland Islands 1:400 000, 6.31 miles to 1 inch

Relief

	Feet	metres
	3000	914
	2600	792
	2200	671
	1800	549
	1400	427
	1000	305
	0	0

Road map symbols

M6	Motorway, toll motorway
4 5	Motorway junction – full, restricted access
S S	Motorway service area – full, restricted access
= = = =	Motorway under construction
A453	Primary route – dual, single carriageway
S	Service area, roundabout, multi-level junction
4 5	Numbered junction – full, restricted access
- - - -	Primary route under construction
	Narrow primary route
Derby	Primary destination
A34	A road – dual, single carriageway
- - - - -	A road under construction, narrow A road
B2135	B road – dual, single carriageway
- - - - -	B road under construction, narrow B road
	Minor road – over 4 metres, under 4 metres wide
- - - - - - -	Minor road with restricted access
2	Distance in miles
	Scenic route
40 40	Speed camera – single, multiple
TOLL	Toll, steep gradient – arrow points downhill
= = = =	Tunnel
	National trail – England and Wales
	Long distance footpath – Scotland
	Railway with station
	Level crossing, tunnel
	Preserved railway with station
- - - -	National boundary
- - - - -	County / unitary authority boundary
⬂ ⬂	Car ferry, catamaran
⬚ ⬚	Passenger ferry, catamaran
⬚	Hovercraft
CALAIS	Ferry destination
Ferry	Car ferry – river crossing
✈ ⊕	Principal airport, other airport
	National park
	Area of Outstanding Natural Beauty – England and Wales National Scenic Area – Scotland forest park / regional park / national forest
	Woodland
	Beach
	Linear antiquity
- - - -	Roman road
⬚ ⚔ 1066	Hillfort, battlefield – with date
⬚ ♣ ▲795	Viewpoint, nature reserve, spot height – in metres
⚑ ▲ ⬚	Golf course, youth hostel, sporting venue
⬚ ⬚ ⬚	Camp site, caravan site, camping and caravan site
🛒 ▲ P&R	Shopping village, park and ride
29	Adjoining page number – road maps

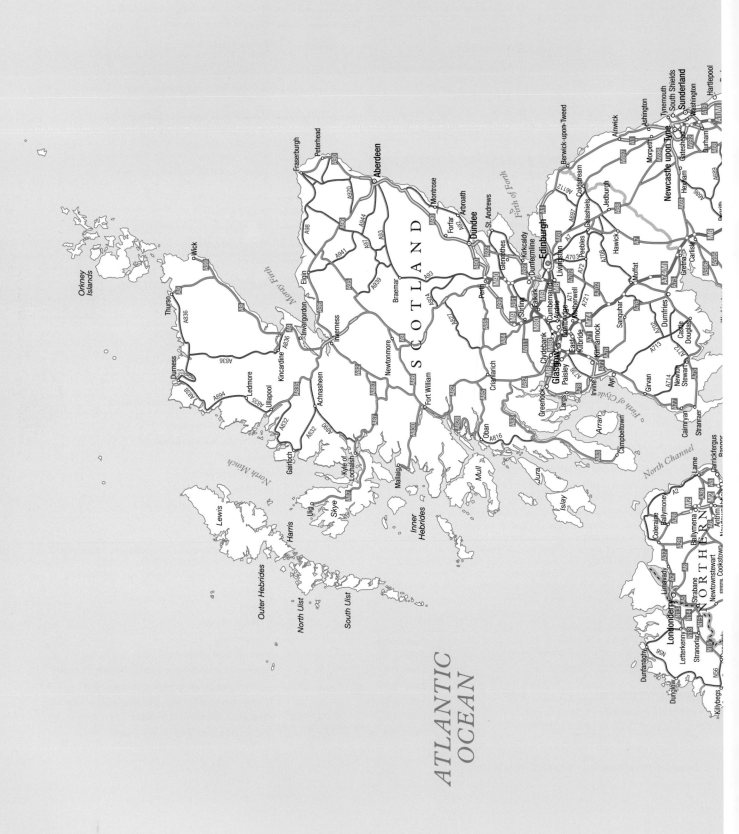

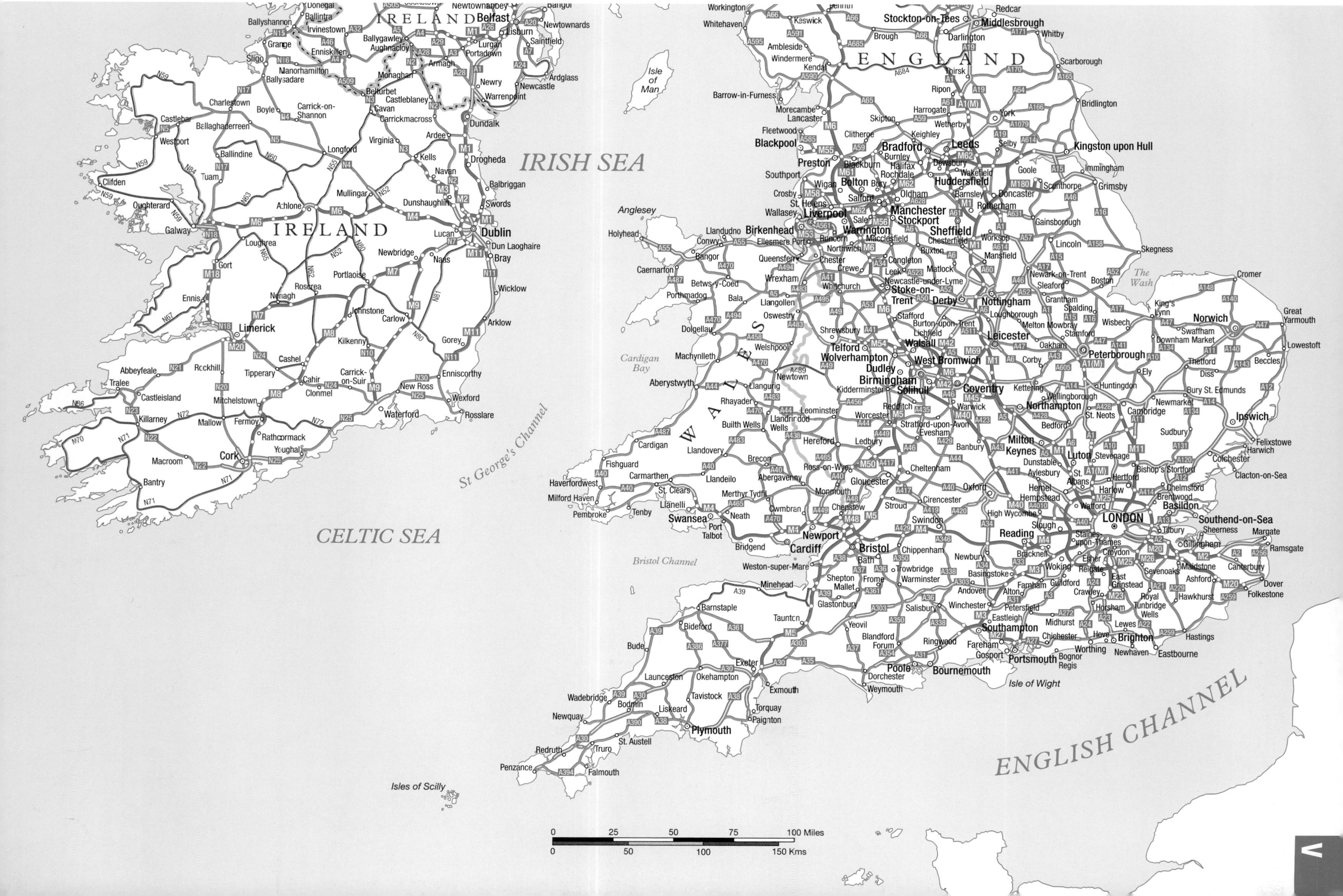
IRISH SEA
CELTIC SEA
ENGLISH CHANNEL
St George's Channel
Bristol Channel
Cardigan Bay
The Wash
Isle of Man
Anglesey
Isle of Wight
Isles of Scilly
IRELAND
N. IRELAND
ENGLAND
WALES
Belfast
Dublin
Limerick
Cork
Galway
Waterford
Liverpool
Manchester
Leeds
Sheffield
Birmingham
Nottingham
Leicester
Coventry
Bristol
Cardiff
Swansea
Newport
Plymouth
Southampton
Portsmouth
Brighton
LONDON
Norwich
Ipswich
Peterborough
Kingston upon Hull
Middlesbrough
Stockton-on-Tees
0
25
50
75
100 Miles
0
50
100
150 Kms

London approaches

Scale

1:100 000, 1cm = 1km, 1 inch = 1.58 miles

Distance table

How to use this table

Distances are shown in miles and, in *italics*, kilometres.
For example, the distance between Aberdeen and Bournemouth is 564 miles or *908* kilometres.

Map labels:
John o' Groats · Kyle of Lochalsh · Inverness · Aberdeen · Braemar · Fort William · Dundee · Oban · Edinburgh · Glasgow · Ayr · Berwick-upon-Tweed · Stranraer · Carlisle · Newcastle upon Tyne · York · Kingston upon Hull · Blackpool · Leeds · Manchester · Doncaster · Liverpool · Sheffield · Lincoln · Holyhead · Nottingham · Norwich · Great Yarmouth · Shrewsbury · Leicester · Birmingham · Aberystwyth · Cambridge · Fishguard · Gloucester · Oxford · Harwich · Swansea · Cardiff · Bristol · London · Dover · Southampton · Brighton · Exeter · Bournemouth · Portsmouth · Plymouth · Land's End

Supporting **THINK!**

Travel safe – Don't drive tired

Distance table (miles / *kilometres*)

City	Distances (miles top line, *km* bottom line)
London	—
Aberdeen	517 / *832*
Aberystwyth	445 211 / *716 340*
Ayr	317 183 394 / *510 295 634*
Berwick-upon-Tweed	134 311 182 352 / *216 501 293 567*
Birmingham	274 289 114 420 117 / *441 465 183 676 188*
Blackpool	123 181 180 153 308 226 / *198 291 290 246 496 364*
Bournemouth	270 147 412 436 207 564 107 / *435 237 663 702 333 908 172*
Braemar	524 281 385 148 143 405 59 482 / *843 452 620 238 230 652 95 776*
Brighton	534 92 286 163 409 446 253 573 52 / *859 148 460 262 658 718 407 922 84*
Bristol	147 477 82 204 81 362 370 125 493 122 / *237 768 132 328 130 583 595 201 793 196*
Cambridge	169 116 438 154 208 100 306 357 214 471 54 / *272 187 705 248 335 161 493 575 344 758 87*
Cardiff	190 45 182 483 117 209 103 368 382 105 505 157 / *306 72 293 778 188 336 166 592 615 169 813 253*
Carlisle	289 264 277 370 196 343 87 196 87 93 224 221 301 / *465 425 446 596 316 552 140 315 140 150 360 356 484*
Doncaster	142 209 116 175 236 310 235 99 44 184 235 176 344 171 / *229 336 187 282 380 499 378 151 151 296 378 283 554 275*
Dover	242 389 238 125 202 82 553 174 312 194 424 478 297 588 71 / *390 626 383 201 325 132 890 280 502 312 683 769 478 947 114*
Dundee	523 275 152 441 406 430 517 52 495 239 349 113 117 376 67 448 / *724 443 245 710 654 692 832 84 797 385 562 182 188 605 108 721*
Edinburgh	56 462 219 96 385 345 373 456 91 439 183 292 57 73 320 125 390 / *90 744 352 154 620 555 600 734 146 707 295 470 92 117 515 201 628*
Exeter	450 518 248 251 353 121 249 76 184 550 82 282 157 428 446 201 569 181 / *724 834 399 404 568 195 401 122 296 885 132 454 253 689 718 323 916 291*
Fishguard	230 399 460 331 247 297 112 270 154 291 493 222 209 170 371 373 56 504 260 / *370 642 740 533 398 478 180 435 248 468 794 357 336 274 597 600 90 811 418*
Fort William	486 560 144 127 596 357 206 485 479 486 575 125 539 296 392 190 133 430 149 510 / *782 901 232 204 959 575 332 781 771 782 926 201 867 476 631 306 214 692 240 821*
Glasgow	101 376 449 44 83 385 372 373 468 110 439 183 292 101 33 320 145 397 / *163 605 723 71 134 786 401 154 620 599 600 753 177 707 295 470 163 53 515 233 639*
Gloucester	346 454 153 111 349 410 191 150 247 56 123 35 159 443 99 174 56 318 330 102 468 109 / *557 731 246 179 562 660 307 241 398 90 198 56 256 713 159 280 90 512 531 164 753 175*
Great Yarmouth	225 419 527 366 335 386 484 185 160 527 366 284 82 275 180 477 240 252 180 477 294 517 128 / *362 674 848 589 539 621 779 298 269 515 457 132 443 290 768 386 406 290 555 647 473 832 206*
Harwich	82 196 432 543 337 279 413 469 125 194 336 246 67 217 128 504 187 275 167 372 425 281 535 76 / *132 316 695 874 542 449 665 755 201 312 541 396 108 349 206 811 301 443 269 599 684 452 861 122*
Holyhead	349 334 191 330 438 167 282 333 396 360 181 231 216 270 206 334 426 288 141 148 331 305 111 439 269 / *562 538 307 531 705 269 454 536 634 580 291 372 348 435 332 538 686 463 227 238 501 491 179 707 433*
Inverness	474 569 553 504 166 66 542 618 158 132 622 383 262 549 505 539 617 75 597 348 458 215 199 486 105 550 / *763 916 890 811 267 106 872 995 254 212 1001 617 422 884 813 867 993 121 961 560 737 346 320 782 169 885*
John o' Groats	129 603 693 677 628 295 195 671 744 285 259 746 507 391 680 630 668 741 202 724 478 573 340 328 601 232 663 / *208 970 1116 1090 1011 475 314 1080 1197 459 417 1201 816 629 1094 1014 1075 1193 325 1165 769 924 550 528 967 373 1067*
Kingston upon Hull	518 394 231 196 207 169 254 369 280 309 234 295 256 47 158 244 139 233 245 327 264 127 134 185 251 223 364 184 / *834 634 372 316 333 272 409 594 451 497 377 475 412 76 254 393 224 375 394 526 425 204 216 298 404 359 586 296*
Kyle of Lochalsh	445 189 84 514 611 602 528 179 79 567 628 216 186 457 432 275 564 455 552 551 159 618 372 471 263 212 499 189 586 / *716 304 135 827 983 969 850 288 127 913 1011 348 299 1080 695 443 908 893 888 1048 256 995 599 758 423 341 803 304 943*
Land's End	763 421 868 741 405 390 446 235 573 686 353 123 574 642 381 374 477 245 374 200 308 665 205 405 281 552 570 313 692 297 / *1228 678 1397 1193 652 628 718 378 922 1104 568 198 924 1033 613 602 768 394 602 322 496 1070 330 652 452 888 917 504 1114 478*
Leeds	405 394 55 487 360 176 223 196 174 215 329 237 270 260 202 119 232 145 156 260 293 175 72 113 156 212 160 327 189 / *652 634 89 784 579 283 359 315 280 346 530 381 435 325 415 418 47 192 373 233 312 419 472 410 116 182 251 341 272 526 304*
Leicester	95 320 500 102 588 461 190 147 140 85 314 422 209 196 296 349 185 74 206 154 68 120 166 389 158 140 39 252 299 153 414 97 / *153 515 805 164 947 742 306 237 225 137 505 679 336 315 476 562 298 119 332 248 109 193 267 626 254 225 63 406 481 246 666 156*
Lincoln	51 68 371 476 44 149 159 291 399 272 247 258 314 202 39 191 88 183 197 216 155 128 159 59 224 274 199 383 131 / *82 109 597 766 71 892 687 348 249 206 256 468 642 438 398 415 505 325 63 307 308 135 295 317 575 336 206 145 360 441 320 616 211*
Liverpool	129 130 75 361 407 130 511 382 102 265 240 140 216 329 160 237 216 286 299 86 120 169 194 161 272 318 234 49 93 219 213 104 341 202 / *208 209 121 581 655 209 822 615 164 427 386 225 348 530 257 381 348 460 481 138 193 272 312 259 438 512 377 79 150 352 343 167 549 325*
Manchester	35 84 92 40 361 406 195 529 311 73 20 246 149 328 620 811 552 496 589 679 98 119 295 266 259 414 512 365 77 129 315 341 208 547 298 / *56 135 148 64 581 654 153 805 600 200 367 341 203 346 530 317 380 346 459 444 98 119 295 266 259 414 512 365 77 129 315 341 208 547 298*
Newcastle upon Tyne	132 168 159 187 92 498 318 132 395 268 272 308 281 266 148 253 329 364 110 166 358 114 57 325 241 299 352 201 347 129 207 64 149 257 235 286 / *212 270 256 301 148 802 512 212 636 431 438 496 452 428 238 407 529 586 177 267 576 183 92 523 388 481 567 323 558 208 333 103 240 414 378 460*
Norwich	264 185 220 105 119 176 421 582 149 654 529 73 20 266 262 147 289 252 175 248 465 422 100 406 282 735 344 373 166 528 615 444 798 183 / *425 298 354 169 192 283 678 937 240 1053 852 501 117 32 328 620 811 552 496 589 679 280 237 465 422 100 406 282 735 344 373 166 528 615 444 798 183*
Nottingham	130 157 73 98 35 25 70 345 479 90 557 430 185 150 153 110 293 401 220 221 262 328 205 90 194 172 83 145 193 353 183 111 50 221 274 164 393 122 / *209 253 118 158 56 40 113 555 771 145 896 692 298 241 246 177 472 646 354 356 422 528 330 69 312 277 134 233 311 568 295 179 80 356 441 264 633 196*
Oban	390 492 233 308 387 419 307 665 128 346 244 117 195 248 309 177 248 385 384 180 34 412 178 79 774 884 198 188 942 556 303 768 768 748 910 227 853 459 618 290 151 663 286 803 / *628 792 375 494 496 623 674 494 1070 206 557 393 188 687 843 829 710 148 79 774 884 198 188 942 556 303 768 768 748 910 227 853 459 618 290 151 663 286 803*
Oxford	462 109 145 260 144 172 137 73 168 274 550 192 656 532 238 145 200 52 356 472 205 156 372 433 141 260 108 83 74 108 465 90 187 64 324 353 154 483 57 / *744 175 233 418 232 277 221 117 270 441 885 309 1056 856 383 233 322 84 573 760 330 251 599 697 227 233 418 174 134 119 174 749 145 301 103 521 568 248 777 92*
Plymouth	199 587 267 344 410 307 308 365 157 445 595 264 46 496 582 264 74 798 888 483 478 642 269 293 122 196 361 945 206 528 327 763 792 382 990 351 / *320 945 430 552 660 455 455 472 389 509 143 1085 571 1271 1069 528 497 588 253 797 595 264 74 798 888 483 478 642 269 77 293 122 196 361 945 206 528 327 763 792 382 990 351*
Portsmouth	176 77 545 191 207 337 236 254 201 162 257 259 633 269 737 613 311 166 221 119 448 555 251 135 453 514 130 234 348 142 144 97 48 547 52 264 141 401 430 222 560 70 / *283 124 877 307 333 542 380 409 323 261 414 417 1019 433 1186 987 501 267 356 192 721 893 404 217 729 827 209 377 560 229 232 156 77 881 84 425 227 645 692 357 901 113*
Sheffield	230 283 135 399 220 60 235 201 61 116 74 100 53 581 687 105 837 632 270 301 267 203 399 560 346 381 378 468 394 29 245 312 193 259 364 515 348 138 122 306 394 256 579 256 / *370 455 217 546 60 235 201 61 116 74 100 53 581 687 105 837 632 270 301 267 203 399 560 346 381 378 468 394 29 245 312 193 259 364 515 348 138 122 306 394 256 579 256*
Shrewsbury	82 207 225 106 364 93 205 201 69 58 133 84 93 303 451 169 567 438 113 240 225 77 272 382 145 179 274 330 251 109 176 111 159 45 265 269 77 399 160 / *132 333 362 171 586 150 330 323 111 93 214 135 175 488 726 272 912 705 182 386 362 124 438 615 233 288 441 531 404 175 283 179 256 72 426 433 124 642 258*
Southampton	185 199 21 151 64 530 176 324 220 228 218 105 438 500 109 859 256 723 598 305 164 220 105 433 541 225 105 438 500 149 209 324 121 148 76 61 531 31 251 128 387 417 200 547 77 / *298 320 34 243 103 853 283 332 521 356 385 328 220 373 367 995 412 1164 963 492 264 354 169 697 871 361 169 705 805 230 336 521 195 238 122 98 856 50 404 206 624 671 323 880 124*
Stranraer	445 277 263 461 500 379 148 290 403 158 220 221 298 330 220 585 263 259 379 262 318 410 426 343 84 195 392 454 124 167 496 257 101 390 379 378 475 194 444 188 297 170 51 325 228 402 / *716 446 423 742 805 610 238 467 649 254 354 356 480 531 354 942 423 417 610 422 544 660 686 552 135 314 631 731 200 269 798 414 309 628 610 608 765 312 715 303 478 274 82 523 367 647*
Swansea	417 161 182 301 248 194 187 195 233 177 248 369 164 86 227 85 222 505 167 216 119 383 337 274 309 89 409 496 67 161 412 473 274 232 309 16 227 85 222 505 167 216 119 383 337 274 309 / *671 259 190 349 293 332 227 815 309 485 559 301 314 375 285 399 459 594 264 696 572 132 296 430 530 143 658 798 108 259 663 761 441 373 497 26 365 137 357 813 269 348 192 616 610 117 816 312*
York	272 222 258 133 52 278 333 181 309 77 181 84 64 99 75 108 24 411 407 37 479 352 204 228 201 189 217 330 261 287 194 250 282 34 121 244 165 252 275 285 269 96 130 148 214 195 319 207 / *438 357 415 214 84 448 536 291 497 124 291 135 103 159 121 174 39 661 655 60 771 566 328 367 323 304 349 531 420 462 312 402 454 55 195 393 266 357 443 459 433 154 209 238 344 314 513 333*

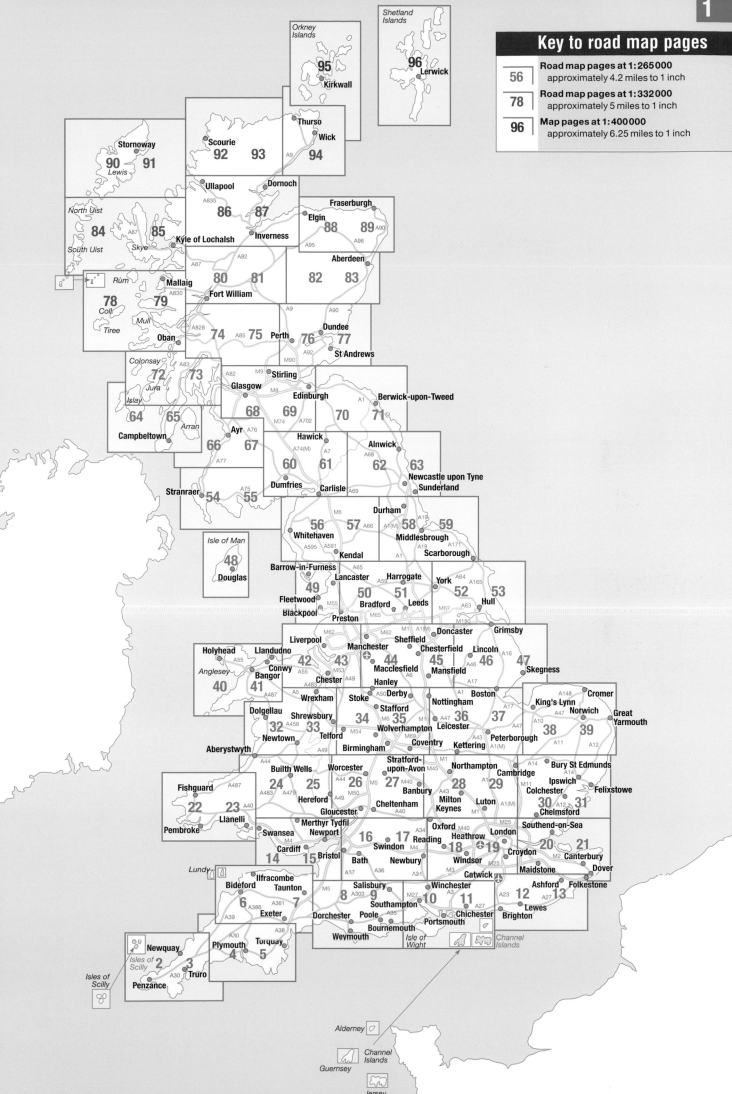

1

Key to road map pages

56	**Road map pages at 1:265 000** approximately 4.2 miles to 1 inch
78	**Road map pages at 1:332 000** approximately 5 miles to 1 inch
96	**Map pages at 1:400 000** approximately 6.25 miles to 1 inch

Orkney Islands

95 Kirkwall

Shetland Islands

96 Lerwick

Stornoway
90 Lewis **91**

Thurso
Scourie
92 **93** Wick **94**
A9

North Uist
Ullapool Dornoch
A835
86 **87**
South Uist
84 **85** Kyle of Lochalsh Inverness
Skye A87 A82

Fraserburgh
Elgin
88 **89** A90
A95 A96
Aberdeen
82 **83**

Rùm
Mallaig
A830
78 **79** Fort William
Coll **80** **81**
Mull A9 A90
Tiree A828
Oban **74** **75** Perth Dundee
Colonsay A85 A92 St Andrews
A83 **76** **77**
72 **73** M90
Jura
Islay A82 M9 Stirling
64 **65** Glasgow M8 Edinburgh Berwick-upon-Tweed
Campbeltown Arran M74 **68** **69** A702 **70** **71** A1
Ayr A76
66 **67** Hawick Alnwick
A77 **60** **61** A7 **62** A68 **63**
Stranraer Dumfries Carlisle Newcastle upon Tyne
54 **55** A69 Sunderland
A75 Durham
M6 **56** **57** A1(M) **58** A19 **59**
Whitehaven A66 Middlesbrough A171
A595 A591 Kendal A19 Scarborough
Isle of Man A1
48 Barrow-in-Furness A65 Harrogate York A64 A165
Douglas Lancaster A59 **52** **53** Hull
49 **50** **51** Leeds A63
Fleetwood Bradford M62 A62
Blackpool M55 M65 Grimsby
Preston M62 A1(M) Doncaster M180
Holyhead Llandudno Liverpool Sheffield Lincoln
Anglesey A55 Conwy Manchester Chesterfield A16
40 **41** Bangor **42** **43** Macclesfield **44** Mansfield **45** **46** Skegness **47**
A55 M53 A6
Chester A49 Hanley A17
A483 Wrexham Stoke Derby A1 Boston Cromer A148
A5 Nottingham King's Lynn Norwich
Dolgellau Shrewsbury Stafford **36** **37** A17 Great Yarmouth
32 **33** **34** **35** Leicester A47 **38** **39** A12
Newtown Telford Wolverhampton A47 Peterborough A10
M54 M6 M69 A1(M) A11
Aberystwyth A458 Birmingham Coventry Kettering
A49 Northampton A14 Bury St Edmunds
A44 Stratford- M1 Cambridge Ipswich
Builth Wells Worcester upon-Avon **28** **29** Colchester A14 Felixstowe
22 **24** **25** **26** **27** M45 Banbury A43 **30** **31**
Fishguard A487 Hereford M5 M40 A1(M) Luton Chelmsford A12
23 A483 A479 Gloucester Cheltenham Milton A43 Southend-on-Sea
Pembroke A40 Cheltenham Keynes M1 London **20** **21**
Llanelli A49 M50 Oxford M40 M25 Croydon Canterbury
Swansea Merthyr Tydfil Newport **16** **17** Reading Heathrow **18** **19** Maidstone Dover
14 **15** Swindon M4 Windsor M25 A2
Cardiff Bath Newbury M3 Catwick A23 Ashford Folkestone
Lundy Bristol A36 A34 Winchester **12** **13**
Ilfracombe A37 Salisbury A3 **10** **11** Lewes
Bideford Taunton M5 A303 Southampton M27 A27 Brighton
6 **7** **8** **9** Portsmouth Chichester
A386 A361 Dorchester Poole Isle of Channel
Exeter Weymouth Bournemouth A35 Wight Islands
A39 A38
Isles of Scilly Newquay Plymouth Torquay
2 **3** **4** **5**
A30 Truro
Penzance

Alderney

Channel Islands
Guernsey

Jersey

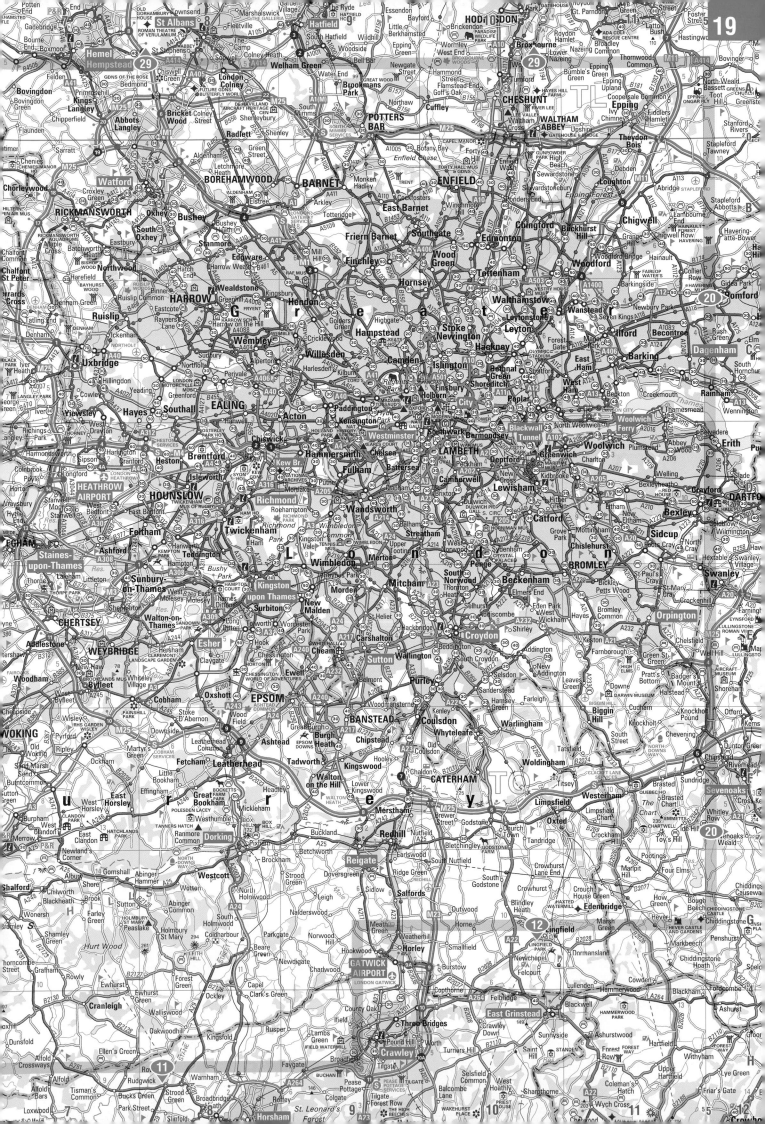

Worcestershire

Herefordshire

Gloucestershire

Kidderminster · **Bewdley** · **Stourport on Severn** · **Droitwich Spa** · **Worcester** · **Bromsgrove** · **Aston Fields** · **Catshill**

Ludlow · **Tenbury Wells** · **Leominster** · **Bromyard** · **Broadwas** · **Great Malvern** · **Malvern Link** · **West Malvern** · **Malvern Wells** · **Pershore**

Hereford · **Ledbury** · **Upton upon Severn** · **Tewkesbury** · **Bishop's Cleeve** · **Cheltenham** · **Charlton Kings**

Ross-on-Wye · **Newent** · **Gloucester** · **Huccleclote** · **Churchdown**

Monmouth (Trefynwy) · **Coleford** · **Cinderford** · **Lydney** · **Frampton on Severn** · **Stonehouse** · **Stroud** · **Chalford**

FOREST OF DEAN

MALVERN HILLS

River Severn · River Wye · River Teme · River Leadon

0 1 2 3 4 5 6 miles
0 1 2 3 4 5 6 7 8 9 10km

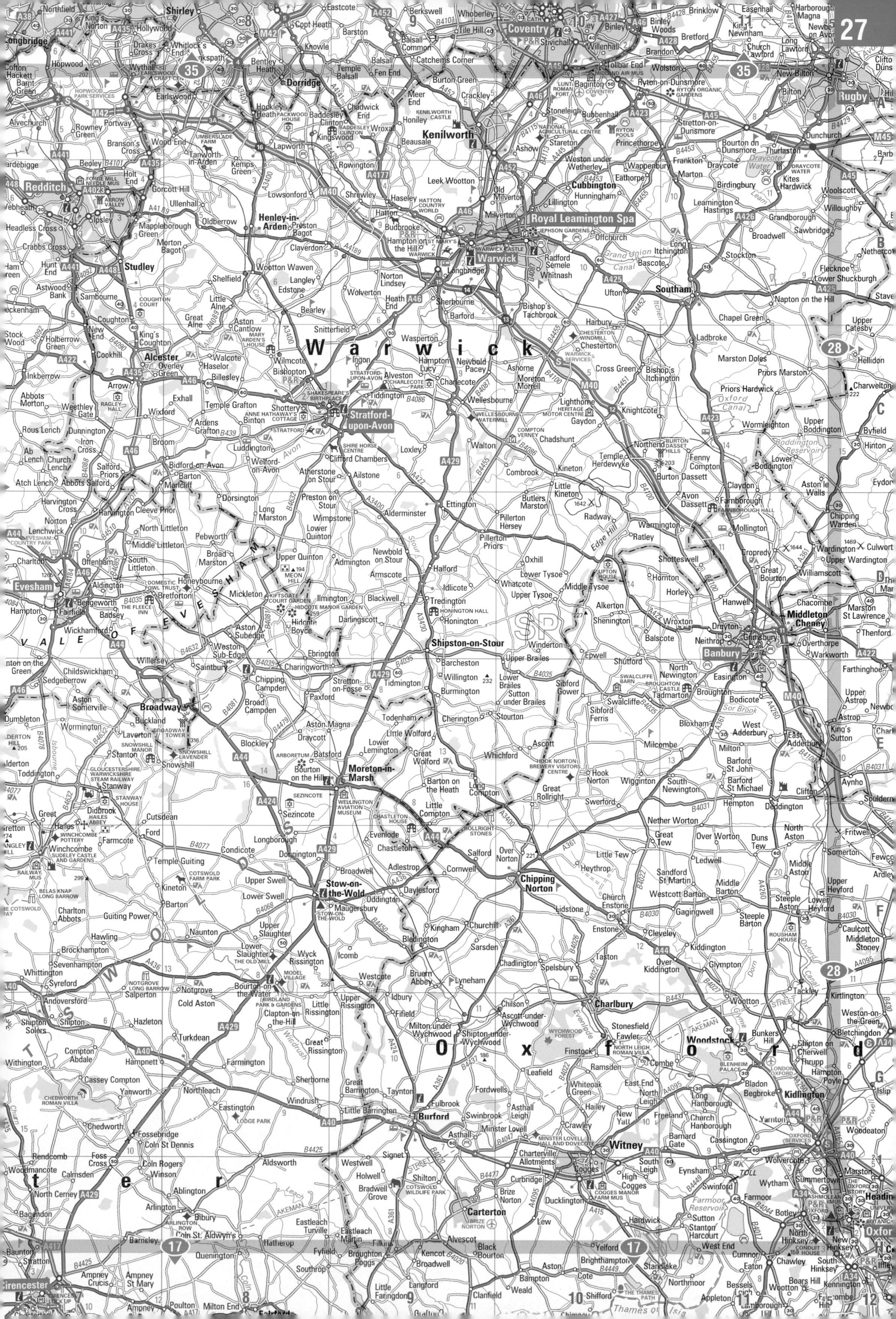

Warwick

Coventry
Rugby
Kenilworth
Royal Leamington Spa
Warwick
Southam
Banbury
Stratford-upon-Avon
Alcester
Redditch
Studley
Henley-in-Arden
Dorridge
Shirley
Evesham
Broadway
Shipston-on-Stour
Moreton-in-Marsh
Stow-on-the-Wold
Chipping Norton
Chipping Campden
Bourton-on-the-Water
Burford
Witney
Woodstock
Kidlington
Oxford
Charlbury
Middleton Cheney
Cirencester

WARWICKSHIRE
VALE OF EVESHAM
GLOUCESTERSHIRE
COTSWOLDS
OXFORDSHIRE

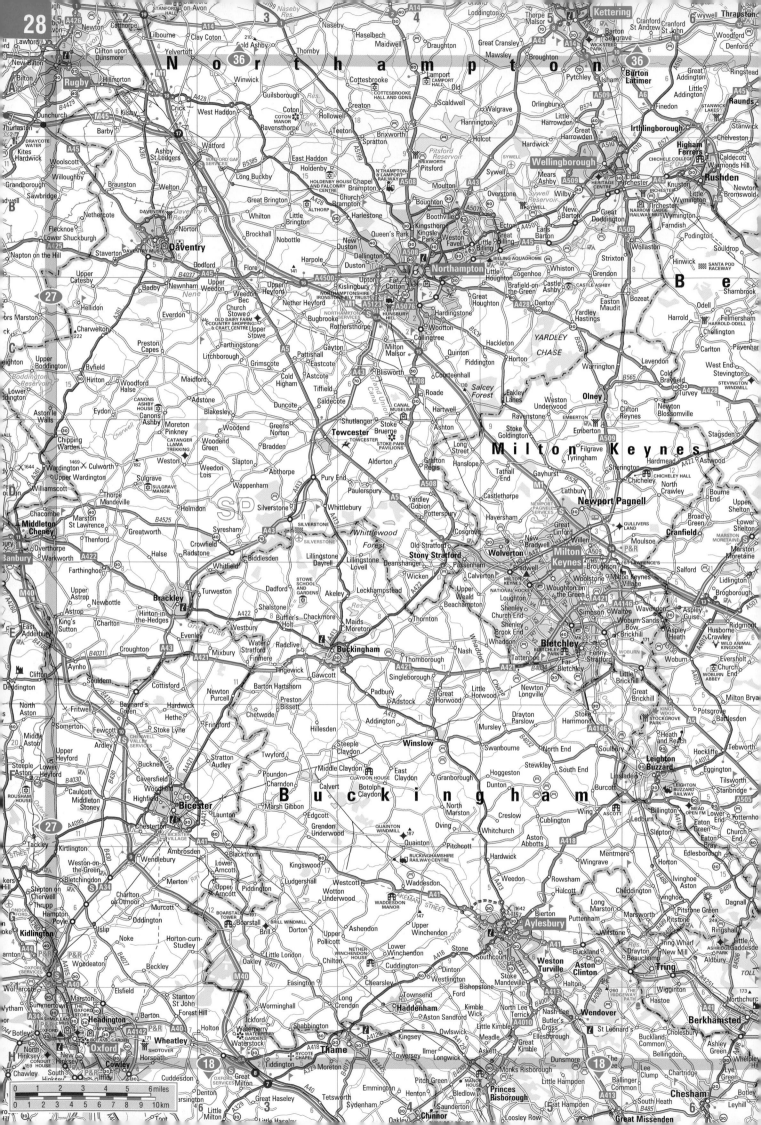

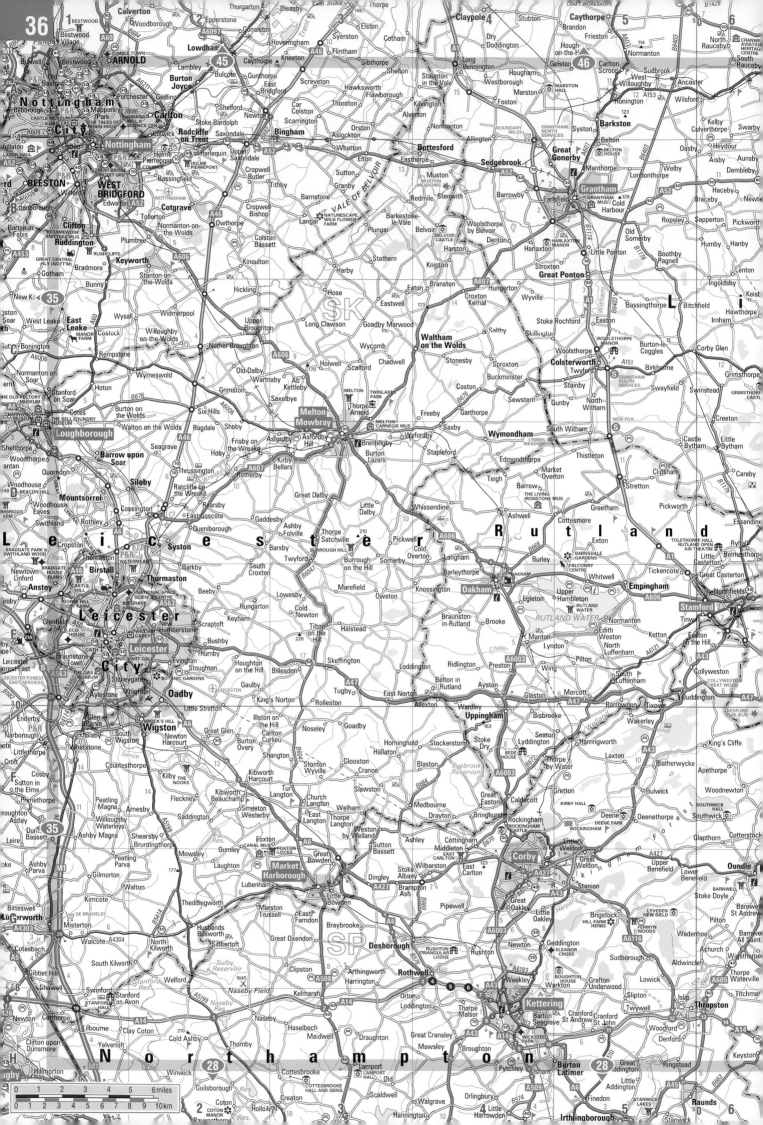

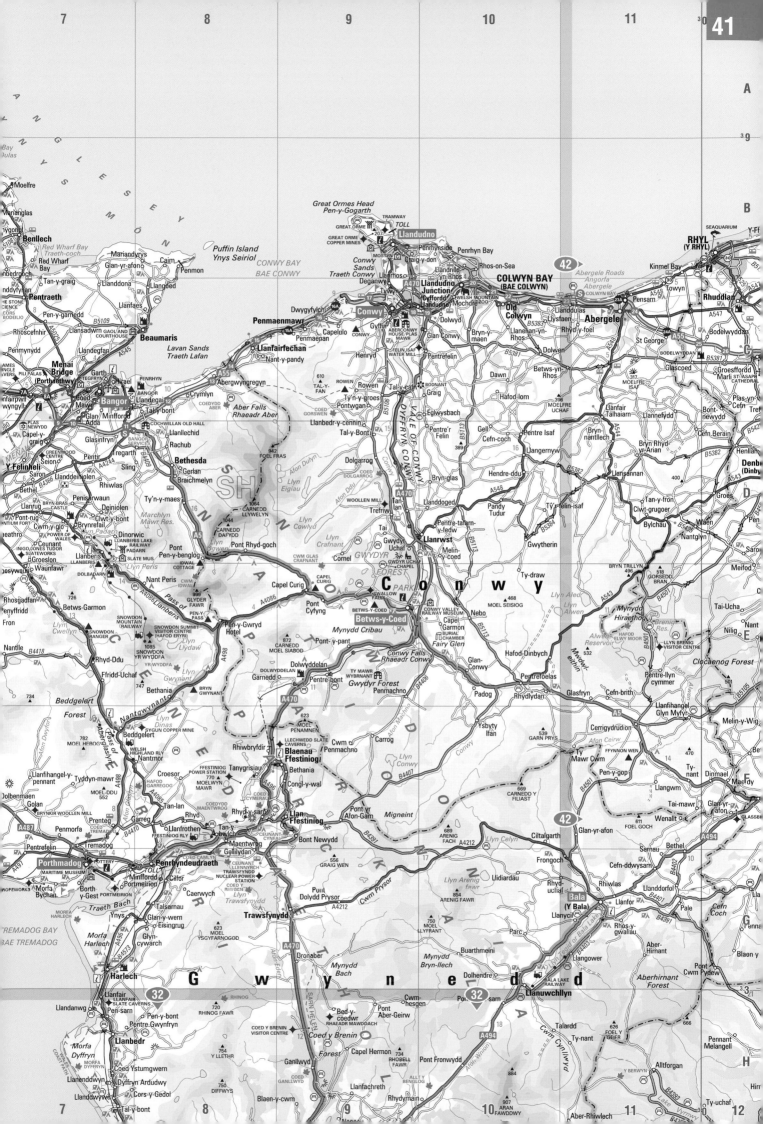

NX

I R I S H

S E A

POINT OF AYRE

Rue Pt.   The Ayres

Glentruan   Cranstal
The Lhen   Dhowin   Bride
A10   A19   B6   A17   A16
A10   A10
B3
Andreas   A9
MANX CROSSES   Jurby
Jurby Head   Jurby   East   MANX
          South   Sandygate   CROSSES   Regaby
Ballasalla   Jurby   B7
          West   Dhoor
The Cronk   St   A15
          Judes   RAMSEY BAY
          Ballaugh   Sulby   B14
Orrisdale   A3   Ramsey   MANX ELECTRIC
          9   Churchtown   RAILWAY
          T.T. Course   CURRAGHS   Grove   Port e Vullen
          WILDLIFE PARK   MUSEUM   Maughold
Rhencullen   30   Glen   A15   Maughold Head
          Ravensdale   Auldyn   Dreemskerry   MANX CROSSES
Kirk   CELTIC   565   Ballajora
MANX CROSSES   Michael   CRAFT CENTRE   NORTH   Corrany
          I   s   l   BARRULE   A2   Cornaa
          Balleleigh   SNAEFELL   Glen Mona
          Barregarrow   Res.   e   9   Dhoon
          B10   Druidale   o   SNAEFELL   Agneash   LAXEY WHEEL
          Knocksharry   MURRAYS   f   MOUNTAIN   AND MINES   Bulgham Bay
MANX TRANSPORT MUSEUM   MOTORCYCLE MUSEUM   RAILWAY   Ballaquine   Laxey
          Cronk-y-Voddy   544   LAXEY   Old Laxey
St Patrick's I.   7   487   BALLALHEANNAGH   WOOLLEN MILLS   Laxey Head
PEEL   COLDEN   GARDENS   Fairy Cottage
Peel   A20   Res.   Laxey Bay
HOUSE OF MANANNAN   A1   M   a   n   Ballacannel
Contrary Head   TYNWALD   Baldwin   Creg-ny-Baa   Baldrine
KIPPER MUSEUM   CRAFT CENTRE   B22   B12   Clay Head
          TYNWALD HILL   B20
          St John's   A23   MANX CROSSES
Patrick   A30   Greeba   T.T.
Glenmaye   333   Baldwin   Strang   Course   Onchan   GROUDLE GLEN
          8   Crosby   Tromode   RAILWAY   HEYSHAM
Dalby Pt.   Lower Foxdale   Glen Vine   A1   ONCHAN PLEASURE PARK   LARNE
          Foxdale   Union Mills   Spring   Douglas   (TT race period only)
Niarbyl   Dalby   A24   B36   Braaid   Valley   Douglas Bay
Niarbyl Bay   A3   B35   Cooil   Ellenbrook   Douglas   LIVERPOOL
          483   B37   A5   Head   (March-Nov)
          SOUTH   222   Ballaveare   CAMERA OBSCURA   LIVERPOOL
          BARRULE   A6   Little Ness   (Winter only)
Fleshwick Bay   Ballamodha   B39   Close   St Mark's   A25   ISLE OF MAN
Lingague   B30   Clark   Newtown   11   STEAM RAILWAY
Bradda Head   Surby   Ronague   Grenaby   A34   Santon Head
Bradda   B44   Colby   Ballabeg   Ballasalla   Port
Port Erin   B40   RUSHEN   B25   Greenaugh
RAILWAY MUS   Four Roads   ABBEY   ISLE OF MAN
The Howe   BILLOWN   Santon Head
Cregneash   Castletown   Derbyhaven   BELFAST (April-Sept)
          A31   CASTLE RUSHEN   DUBLIN (June-Sept)
          NAUTICAL MUS   St Michael's I.
          128   SCARLETT   OLD
          VISITOR CENTRE   HOUSE OF KEYS
Calf of Man   CREGNEASH VILLAGE   Port   Scarlett   Dreswick Pt.
          FOLK MUSEUM   St Mary   Point
Spanish Head
Chicken Rock

0 1 2 3 4 5 6 miles
0 1 2 3 4 5 6 7 8 9 10km

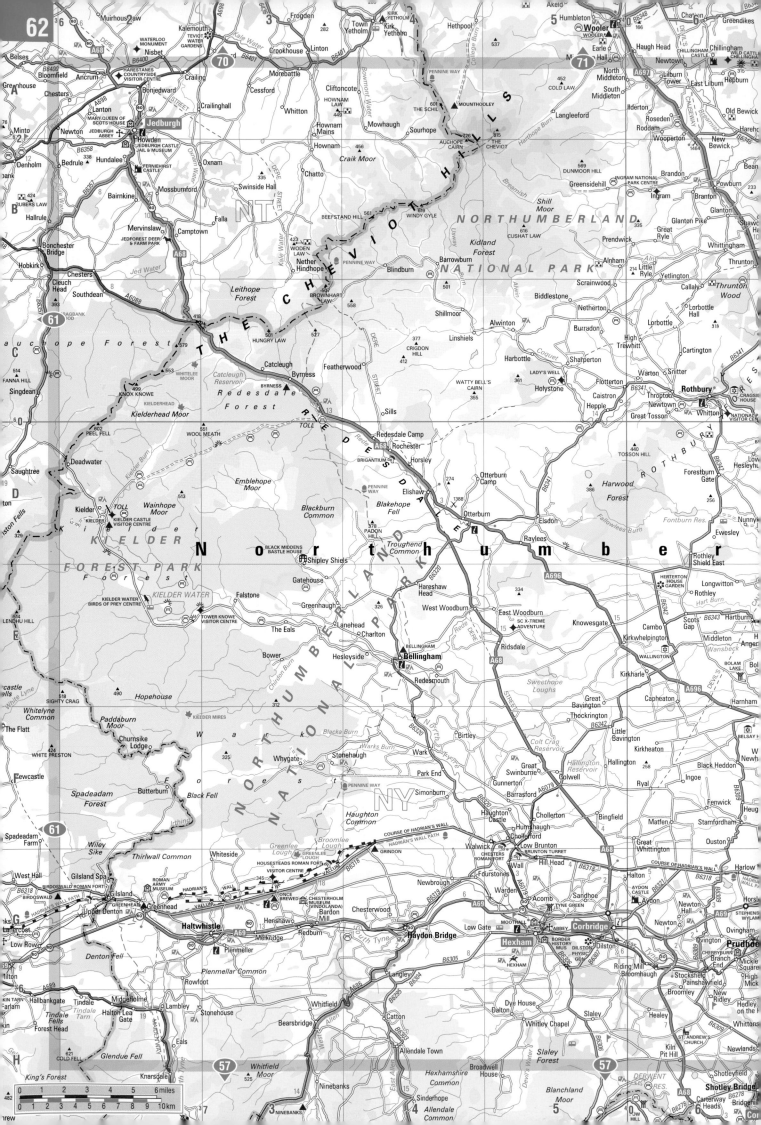

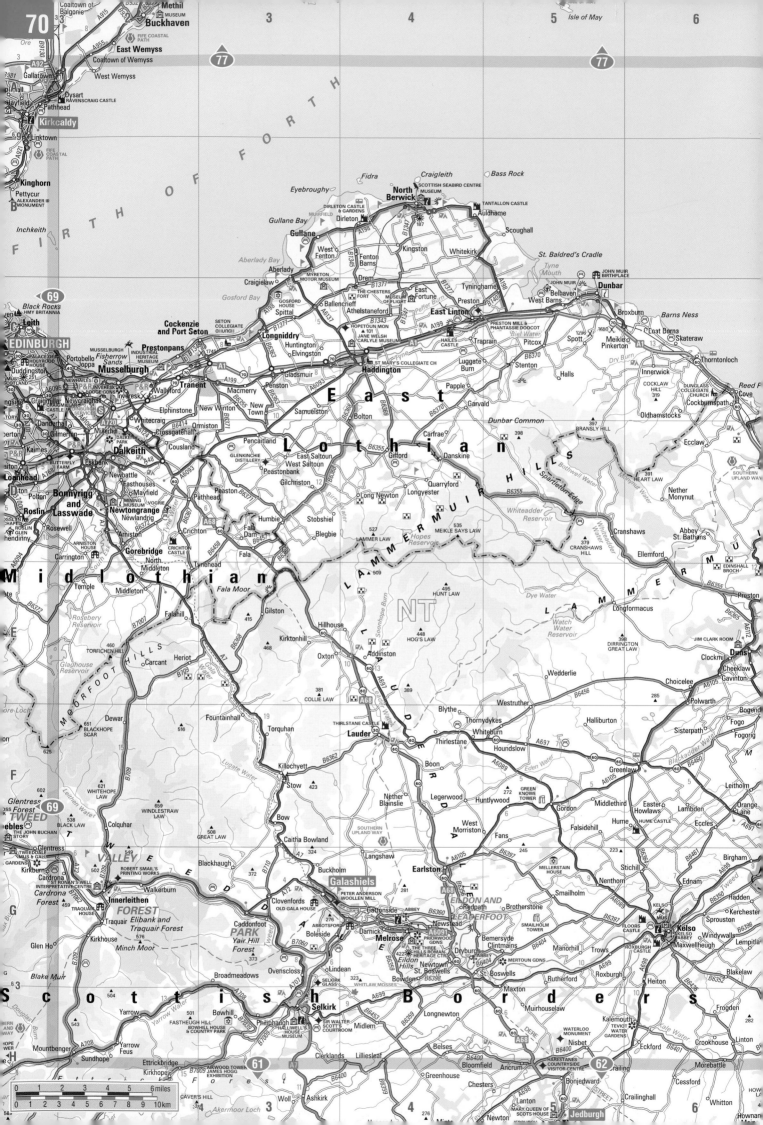

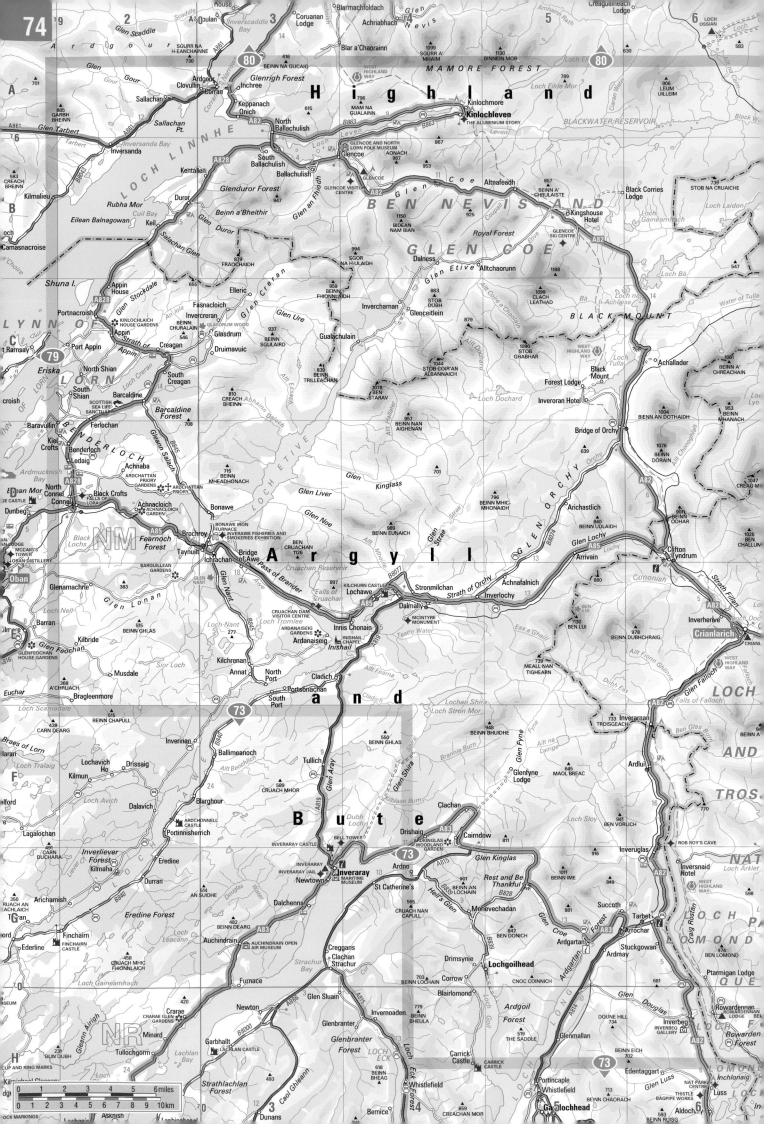

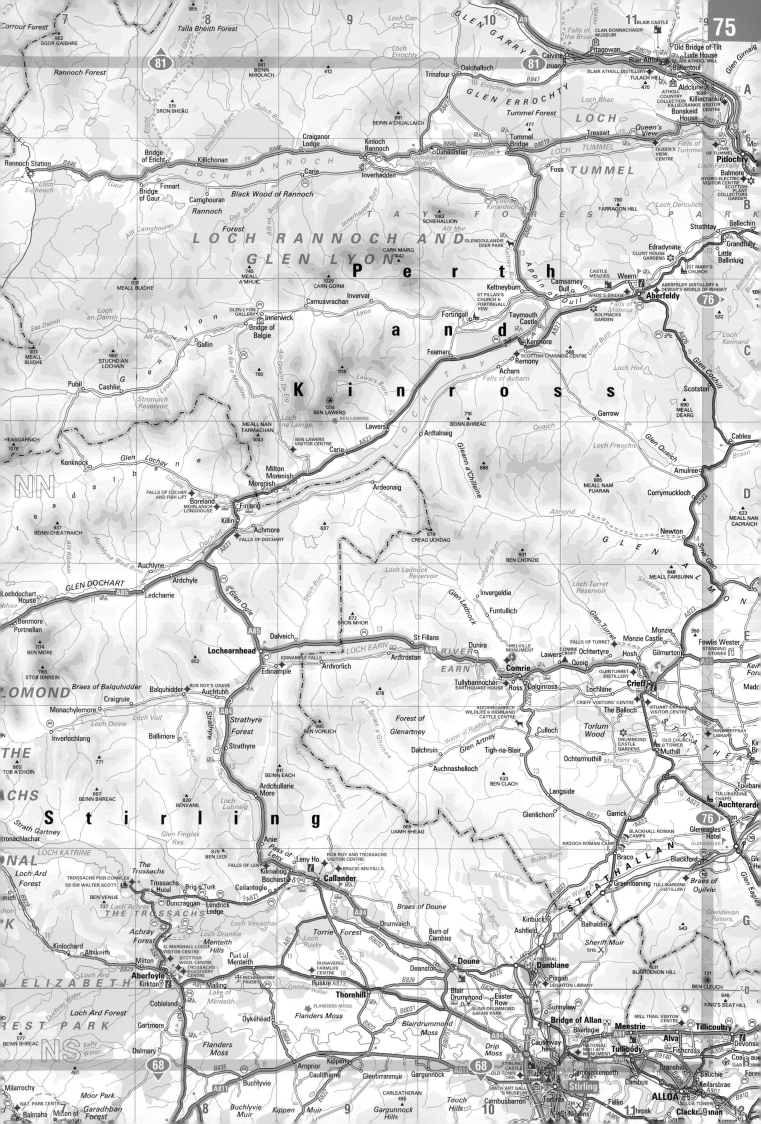

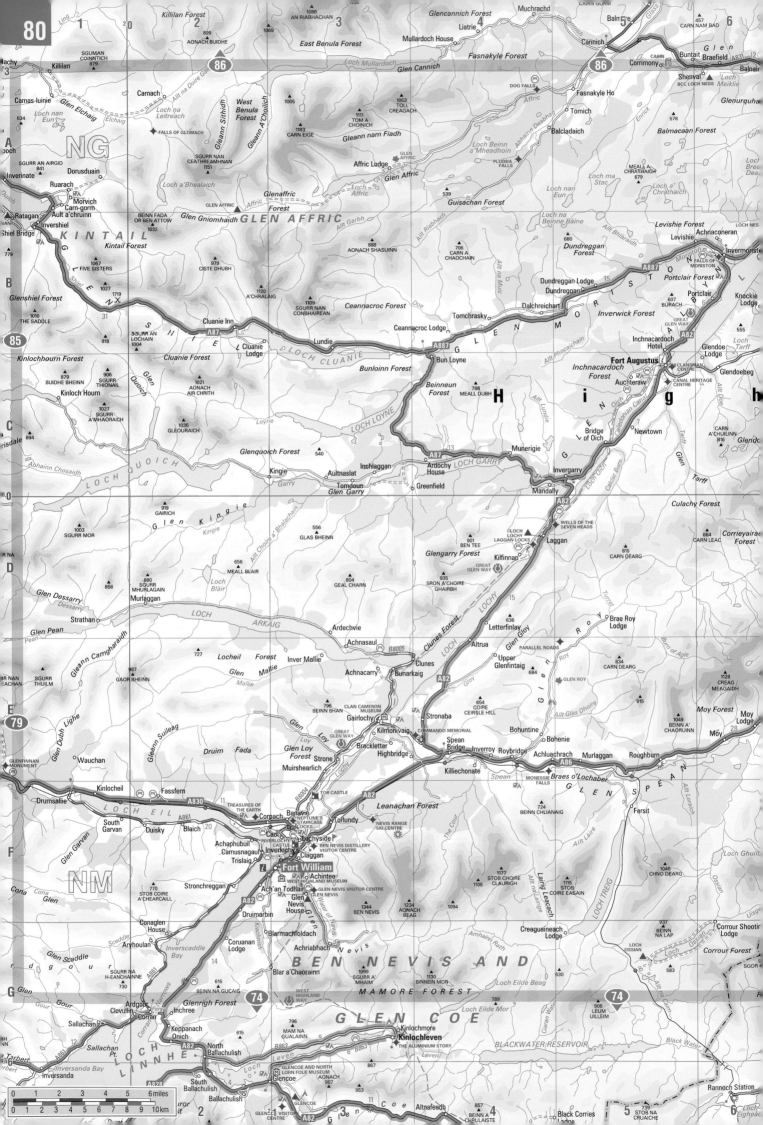

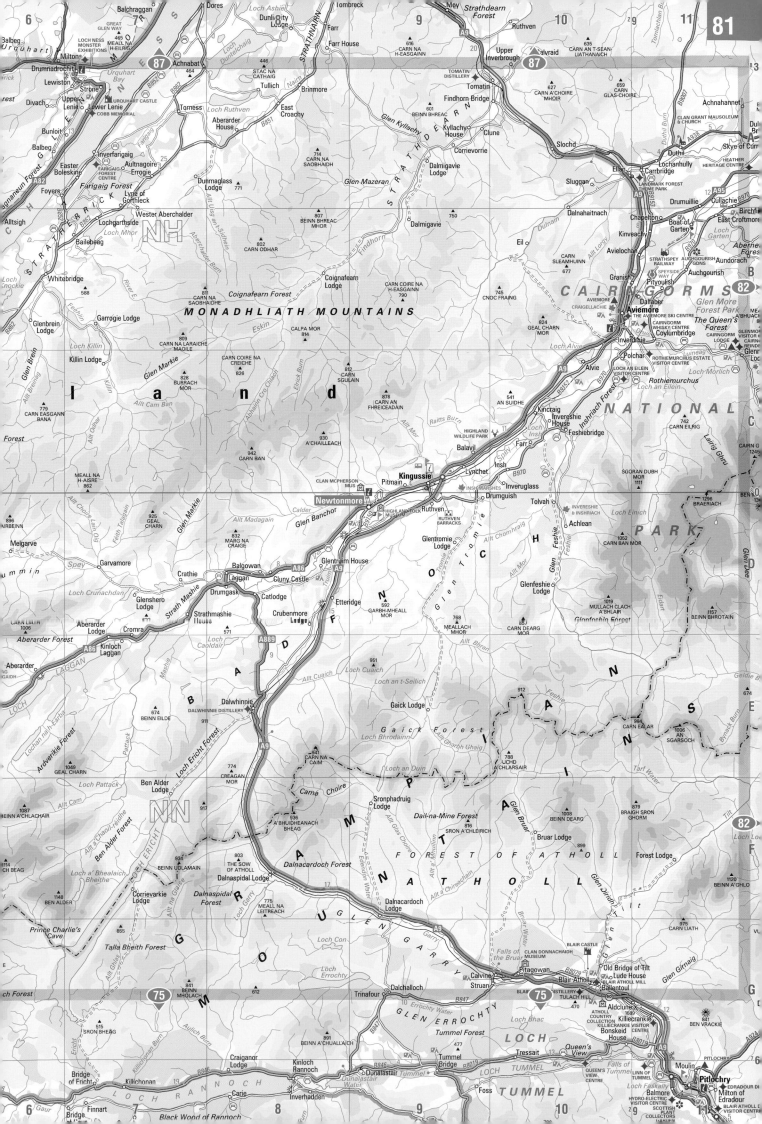

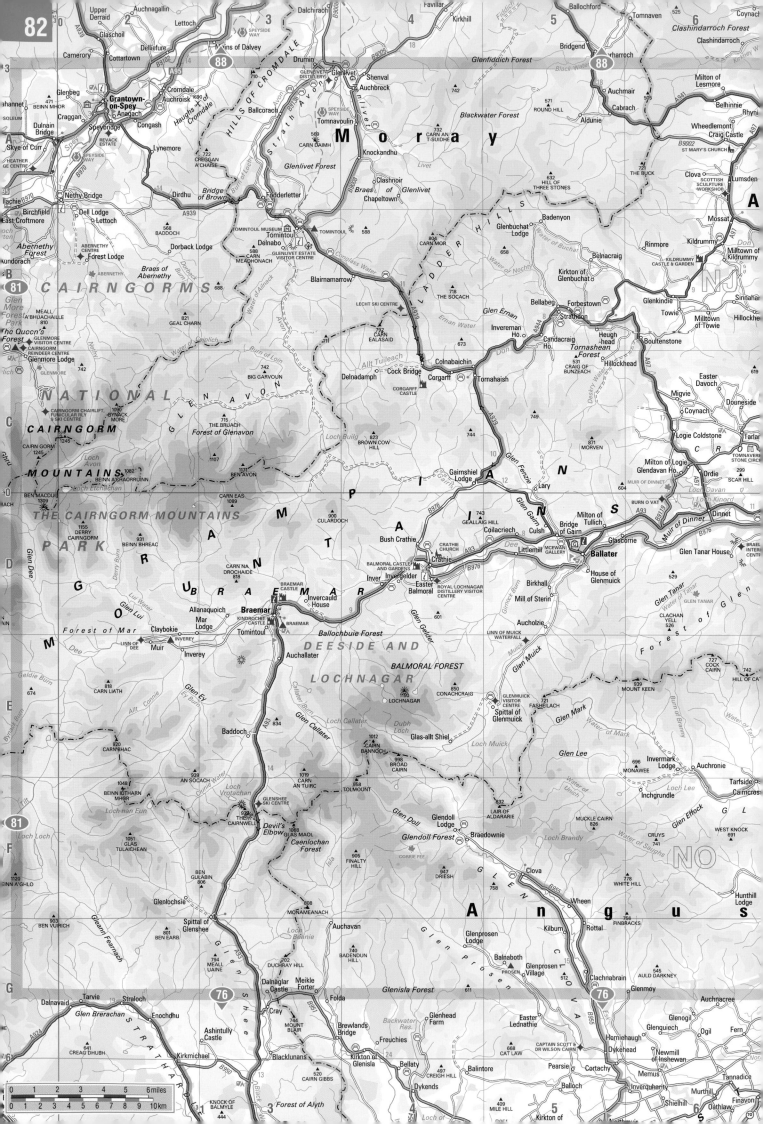

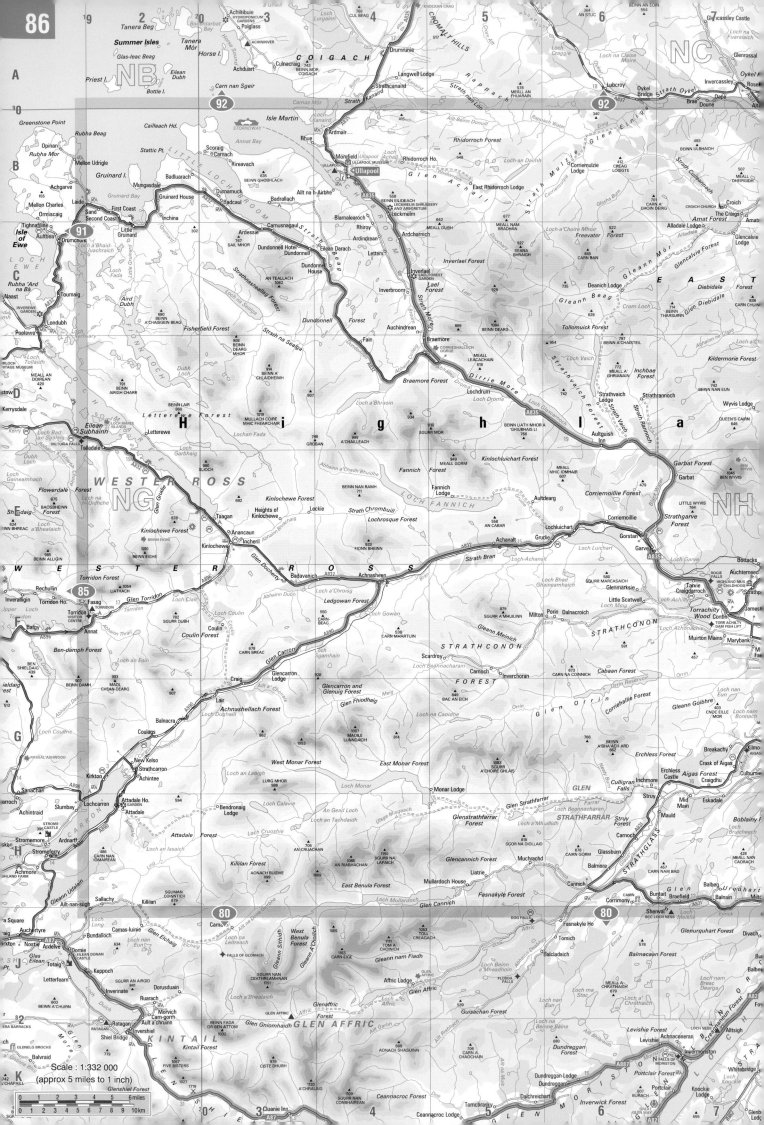

St. Kilda

NA

NF

NA

ST KILDA

Boreray
384

CNOC
GLAS
376
Soay
Loch a'
Ghlinne

CONACHAIR
376

MULLACH BI
358
ST KILDA

St Kilda or Hirta
(Hiort)

Bagh a
Bhaile
Dun

NA

NF

Na h-Eileanan Flannach

I s l e s

W e s t e r n

NF

Na Gearrannan
Siabost bho Thuath
SHAWBOST NORSE MILL
Siabost bho Dheas
Siabost bho Dheas
Bàgh Dhail Beag
Pa
Shia
GEARRANNAN
BLACKHOUSE VILLAGE
GARENIN
Dail Beag
Dail Mòr
Borghastan
Campay
Loch Chàrlabhaigh
Cairbhig
Floday
AN CAOLAS
Little
Bernera
Dun
Charlabhaigh
IRON AGE HOUSE
GEARRANNAN
An Galan Uigeach
Aird Uig
Pabay
Mòr
Tolastadh a Chaolais
Vacsay
BERNERA
Breacleit
Great Bernera
Keava
Breasclete
Cliobh
Miabhig
Riof
Vuia Mòr
Barraglom
Eilean
Kearstay
Keava
Timsgearraidh
Cradhlastadh
Uigen
DUN CARLOWAY
BROCH
Circebost
Tobhtarol
CALANAIS VISITOR
CENTRE
Càrnais
Cairisiadar
Floday
Vuia Beag
Crulabhig
CALANAIS
STANDING
STONES
Calanais
Gearraidh
h-Aibhne
Mangurstadh
Eadar Dha
Fhadhail
SUAINAVAL
429
Geisiadar
256
Linsiadar
Ard More Mangersta
Loch
Suaineabhal
Loch Ròg
Loch
Tungabhat
Aird Fenish
574
MEALISVAL
Islibhig
Einacleite
Aird Brenish
Loch Ròg
Breanais
Loch
Grunabhat
Giosla
Loch Airigh
na h-Airde
397
BEINN MHEADHONACH
Loch
Chaolartan
Loch Fuaroil
Loch
Morsgail
Mealasta Island
Caolas an Eilean
Loch Cro
Criosdaig
Loch
Coirigerod
Loch
Beiniseabhal
Morsgail
Forest
Loch Langabhat
Loch
Bòdabhat
Loch
Strandabhat
Ceann
Tarabhaigh
A859
Airidh
Bhruai
Kearstay
Braighe
Mòr
308
Aird an
Troim
Loch Tealasabhaigh
Loch Crabhadail
Scarp
Gaisgeir
Huisinis
489
679
TIRGA MOR
659
ULLAVAL
SOUTH LEWIS,
STULAVAL
570
Aline Lodge
572
BEINN Mb
Hushinish Pt.
Bàgh Huisinis
Caolas
Aird a' Mhulaidh
Seaforth I
Gobhaig
Forest of Harris
UISGNAVAL
MORE
729
Horsanish
Abhainn Suidhe
Arda Mòra
Cliasmol
B887
HARRIS AND
17
Maraig
Taransay Glorigs
Soay Beag
Miabhag
CUSHAM
799
CEANN A TUATH NA
HEARADH
Soay Mòr
Bun Abhainn
Eadarra
A859
Camus an
t-suithean
OLD WHALING STATION
559
449
Tarasaigh
(Taransay)
Isay
Aird Asaig
NORTH UIST
436
BEN LUSKENTYRE
'Lochan
Lacasdail
Rhenigidale
Loch Trollamarig
99
Paible
Losgaintir
467
Tairbeart
(Tarbert)
Urgha
Carragraich
Rubha Sgeirigin
South Harris
Forest
Caolas Scalpaigh
Carnach
Luskentyre
Beach
Loch Ceann
Dibig
Miabhag
Sgeotasaigh
Rubha Cra
Caolas Tharasaigh
Seilebost
A859
Loch
an Tairbeart
Scalpay
Eile
Sca
(Sc
Borve Lodge
Buirgh
23
Drinisiadar
Kennacley
Greosabhagh
Plocropol Pt.
Toe Head
BORVE
386
Leac a Li
Plocrapol
Scadabhagh
Coppay
Aird Mhighe
Liceasto
Rubha
Bhocaig
CHAIPAVAL
365
Sgarasta Mhòr
Geocrab
Cluthar
Caolas
Stocinis
Shillay
Little Shillay
Rubha'an Teampuill
398
BLEAVAL
NA HEARADH
(HARRIS)
Beacrabhaic
Stockinish Is.
Sound of Shillay
Brenish Pt.
Taobh Tuath
SEALLAM!
Fleoideabhagh
Aird
Mhighe
UIG
Pabaidh
(Pabbay)
Quinish
A859
Loch
Steiseabhat
An t-Ob (Leverburgh)
Fionnsbhagh
Aird
Mhighe
Boirseam
Lingreabhagh
Sound of Spuir
Ensay
Carminish Is.
Roineabhal
Cuidhtinis
Lingarabay I.
Spuir
Killegray
Cairinis
Srannda
Roghadal
Eilean
Bhearnaraigh
(Berneray)
Ruisigearraidh
ST CLEMENT'S
CHURCH
Haskeir I.
Borgh
BERNERAY
Baile
Valley
Renish Pt.
Haskeir Eagach
Boreray
Langay

Aird a'Mhòrain
Groay
Gilsay
Lingay
Scaravay

Scale : 1:332 000
(approx 5 miles to 1 inch)

0 1 2 3 4 5 6 miles
0 1 2 3 4 5 6 7 8 9 10km

Veilish Pt.
Griminish Pt.
Valley
Lingay
Port nan Long
Sursay
Opsay
Tahay

A865
Scolpaig
Valley
Strand
Oronsay
A865
B893
Baile Mhic Phail
Baile Mhartainn
Malacleit
Solas
Greinetobht
Trumaisgearraidh
180
Hermetray

Scolpaig
Malacleit
Amhlsaraigh

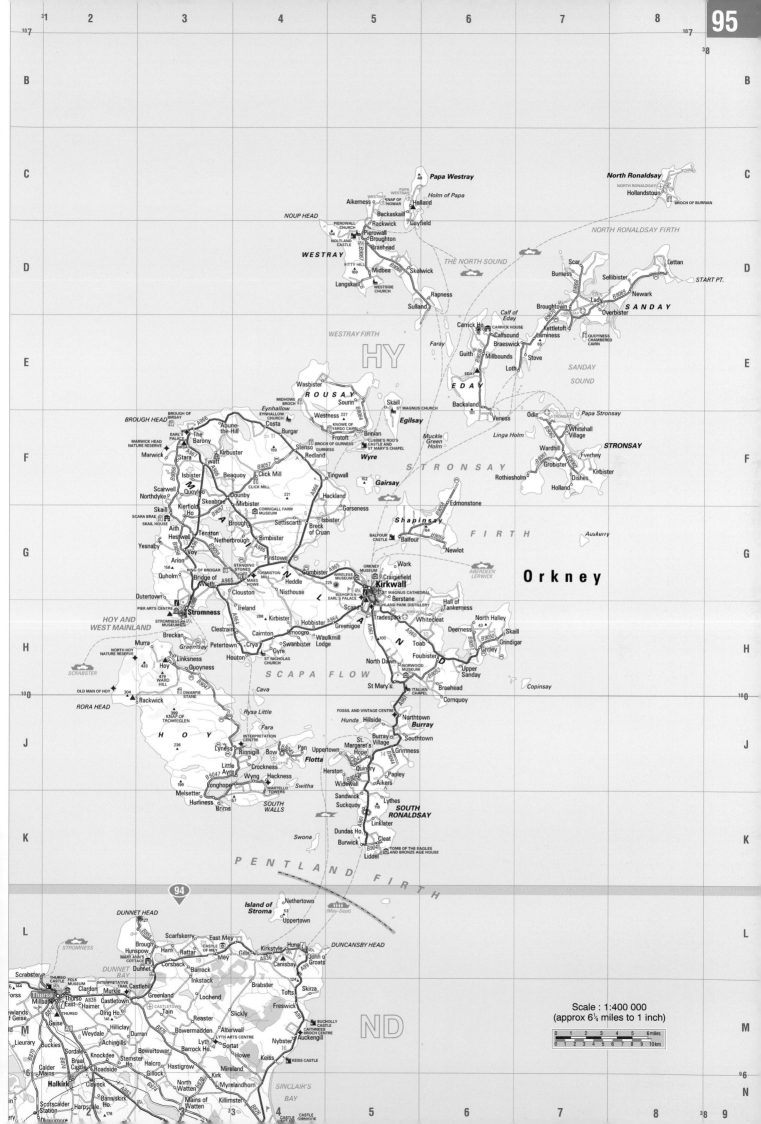

95

B

C

Papa Westray
North Ronaldsay
NORTH RONALDSAY
Hollandstoun
BROCH OF BURRIAN
Holm of Papa
Aikerness
WESTRAY
KNAP OF HOWAR
PAPA WESTRAY
Helland
NOUP HEAD
Backaskaill
Rackwick
Gayfield
PIEROWALL CHURCH
Pierowall
Broughton
Scar
Lettan
NOLTLAND CASTLE
Braehead
Burness
Sellibister
THE NORTH SOUND
NORTH RONALDSAY FIRTH

D

WESTRAY
FITTY HILL
Midbea
Skelwick
START PT.
169
Broughtown
Lady
Newark
Langskaill
WESTSIDE CHURCH
Rapness
SANDAY
Sulland
Overbister
Calf of Eday
WESTRAY FIRTH
Carrick Ho.
CARRICK HOUSE
Calfsound
Kettletoft
Laminess
QUOYNESS CHAMBERED CAIRN
HY
Faray
Braeswick
65
Guith
Millbounds
Stove
SANDAY
EDAY
Loth
SOUND

E

Wasbister
ROUSAY
Skaill
ST MAGNUS CHURCH
Veness
Papa Stronsay
MIDHOWE BROCH
Sourin
Backaland
STRONSAY
Whitehall
EYNHALLOW
Westness
101
Odie
Village
EYNHALLOW CHURCH
KNOWE OF YARSO CAIRN
Brinian
Linga Holm
Wardhill
Fverhay
BROUGH HEAD
Abune-the-Hill
Costa
Burgar
Egilsay
Muckle
STRONSAY
BROUGH OF BIRSAY
CUBBIE ROO'S CASTLE AND ST MARY'S CHAPEL
Green
Grobister
EARL'S PALACE
The Barony
Frotoft
Wyre
Holm
Kirbister
MARWICK HEAD NATURE RESERVE
BIRSAY
Stenso
Redland
Rothiesholm
Dishes

F

Marwick
Stara
Twatt
159
GAIRSAY
Holland
Isbister
Beaquoy
Click Mill
Tingwall
102
Scarwell
CLICK MILL
FIRTH
Northdyke
Dounby
Hackland
Edmonstone
Skaill
Kierfield Ho.
Mirbister
221
SHAPINSAY
Auskerry
SCARA BRAE
Skeabrae
Brough
Gorseness
64
SKAIL HOUSE
CORRIGALL FARM MUSEUM
Settiscarth
Breck of Cruan
BALFOUR CASTLE
Aith
Netherbrough
6
Balfour
Orkney

G

Hestwall
Tenston
Bimbister
Newlot
Yesnaby
Voy
Finstown
STANDING STONES
Gorn
WORK
Arion
Cairston
Heddle
ORKNEY MUSEUM
158
RING OF BROGAR
TORMISTON MILL
WIRELESS MUSEUM
Craigiefield
ABERDEEN LERWICK
Quholm
Bridge of Waith
MAES HOWE
325
Nisthouse
KIRKWALL
Clouston
ST MAGNUS CATHEDRAL
HOY AND WEST MAINLAND
Outertown
A965
Ireland
Berstane
BISHOP'S AND EARL'S PALACE
Hall of Tankerness
PIER ARTS CENTRE
Scapa
HIGHLAND PARK DISTILLERY

H

Stromness
Kirbister
Hobbister
Greenigoe
KIRKWALL
North Halley
STROMNESS MUSEUM
Clestrain
Smoogro
Tradespark
Whitecleat
Deerness
43
Murra
Breckan
Cairnton
WAULKMILL LODGE
Toab
Skaill
NORTH HOY NATURE RESERVE
Graemsay
Petertown
Crya
Gyre
NORWOOD MUSEUM
Grindigar
Linksness
Houton
ST NICHOLAS CHURCH
North Dawn
Foubister
Gritley
SCRABSTER
Hoy
Quoyness
SCAPA FLOW
Upper Sanday
433
479 WARD HILL
Cava
St Mary's

J/100

OLD MAN OF HOY
Rackwick
DWARFIE STANE
ITALIAN CHAPEL
Braehead
304
399 KNAP OF TROWIEGLEN
Copinsay
RORA HEAD
Rysa Little
Cornquoy
FOSSIL AND VINTAGE CENTRE
Northtown
Hunda
Hillside
HOY
Fara
236
Burray
INTERPRETATION CENTRE
BURRAY
Lyness
Burray Village
St.
Southtown
Rinnigill
Bow
Pan
Uppertown
Margaret's
Little Ayre
FLOTTA
Hope
Grimness
Crockness
Flotta
Quindry
Papley
Longhope
Wyng
Hackness
Herston
Aikers
199
MARTELLO TOWERS
Widewall
Melsetter
Swatha
Sandwick
Lythes
Hurliness
Brims
SOUTH WALLS
Suckquoy
SOUTH RONALDSAY
Swona

K

PENTLAND
Dundas Ho.
Linklater
Burwick
Cleat
Liddel
TOMB OF THE EAGLES AND BRONZE AGE HOUSE
FIRTH

94

DUNNET HEAD
Island of Stroma
Nethertown
Uppertown
(May-Sept)
DUNCANSBY HEAD

L

127
Brough
Scarfskerry
East Mey
Huna
STROMNESS
Hunspow
Ham
Rattar
CASTLE OF MEY
Kirkstyle
John o'Groats
MARY ANN'S COTTAGE
Corsback
Mey
Canisbay
DUNNET BAY
Dunnet
19
Gills
A99
DUNNET HEAD
INTERPRETATIVE TRAIL
Barrock
Inkstack
Skirza
Scrabster
CASTLEHILL
124
THURSO CASTLE
Greenland
Tofts
THURSO FOLK MUSEUM
Castletown
Lochend
Brabster
Clardon
Murkle
Tain
Freswick

M

Thurso
Milbank
Haimer
Castletown
Reaster
Slickly
East
Olrig Ho.
141
Durran
Hilliclay
Alterwall
BUCHOLLY CASTLE
Geise
Weydale
LYTH ARTS CENTRE
CAITHNESS BROCH CENTRE
Lieurary
Buckies
Sordale
Bowermadden
Lyth
Auckengill
ND
Sortat
Nybster
Calder Mains
Braal Castle
Knockdee
Bowertower
16
Howe
Keiss
Stemster Ho.
Halcro
KEISS CASTLE
Halkirk
Cloyock
Gillock
Mireland
SINCLAIR'S
Scotscalder Station
Bannskirk Ho.
North Watten
Myrelandhorn
BAY
176
Harpsdale
Kirk
Mains of Watten
CASTLE GIRNIGOE

Scale : 1:400 000
(approx 6¼ miles to 1 inch)

0 1 2 3 4 5 6 miles
0 1 2 3 4 5 6 7 8 9 10km

Town plan symbols

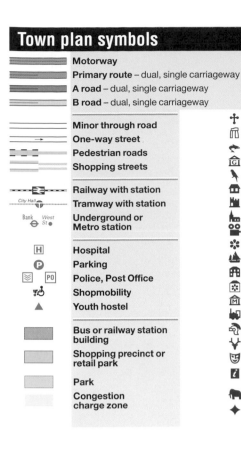

Motorway

Primary route – dual, single carriageway

A road – dual, single carriageway

B road – dual, single carriageway

Minor through road

One-way street

Pedestrian roads

Shopping streets

Railway with station

Tramway with station

Underground or Metro station

Hospital

Parking

Police, Post Office

Shopmobility

Youth hostel

Bus or railway station building

Shopping precinct or retail park

Park

Congestion charge zone

✝ Abbey or cathedral

Ancient monument

Aquarium

Art gallery

Bird collection or aviary

Building of interest

Castle

Church of interest

Cinema

Garden

Historic ship

House

House and garden

Museum

Preserved railway

Roman antiquity

Safari park

Theatre

ℹ Tourist information centre

Zoo

✦ Other place of interest

Aberdeen

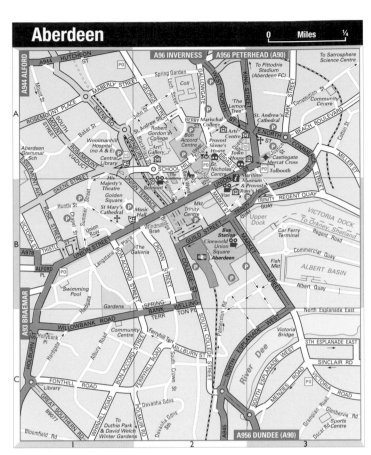

0 Miles ¼

Bath

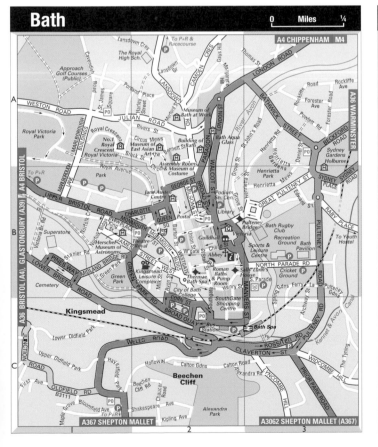

0 Miles ¼

Blackpool

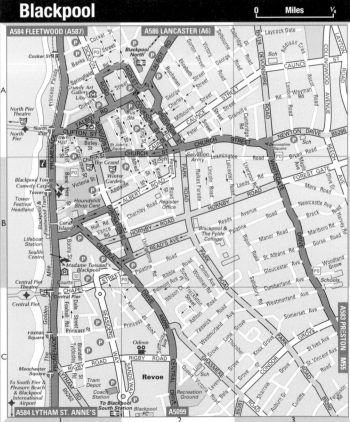

0 Miles ¼

Birmingham

0 Miles ¼

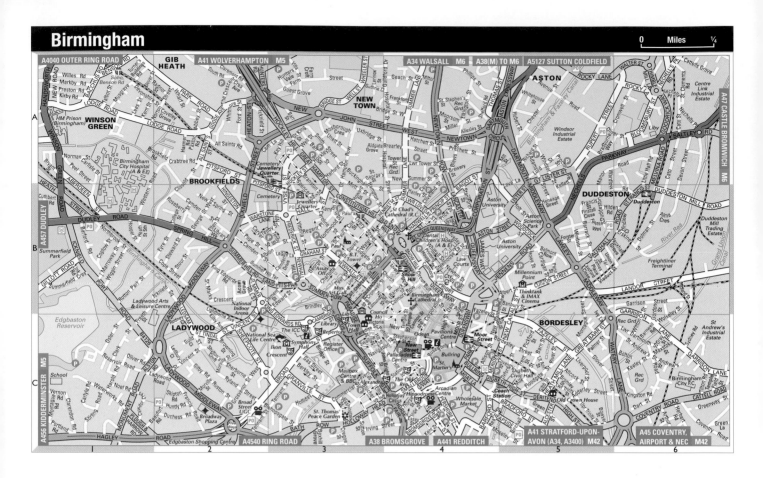

Bournemouth

0 Miles ¼

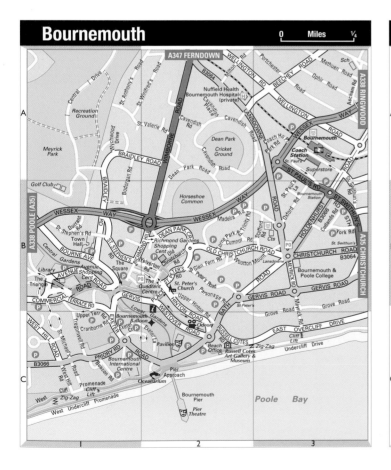

Bradford

0 Miles ¼

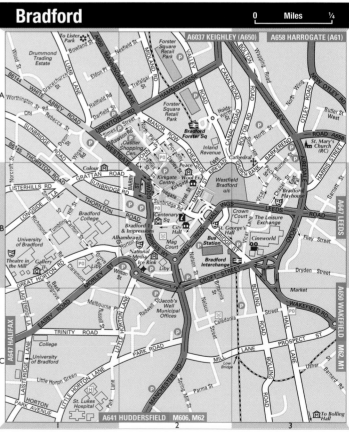

Bristol

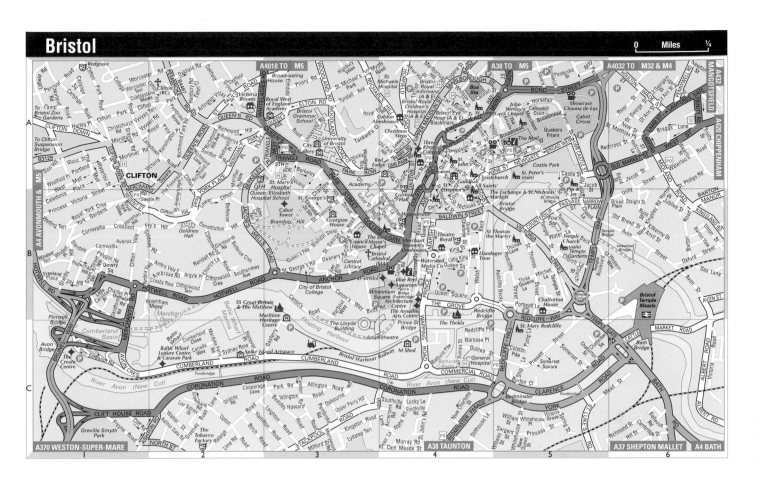

Brighton

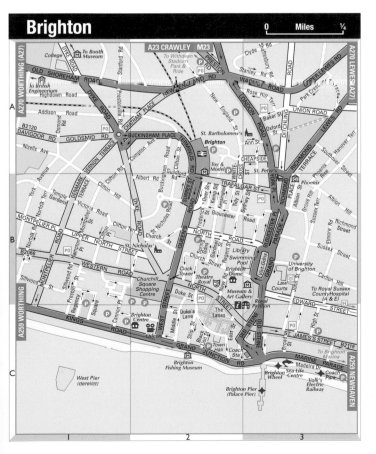

Cambridge

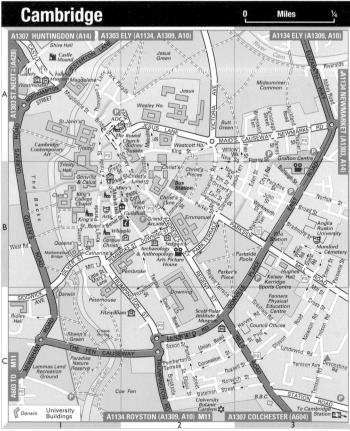

Canterbury

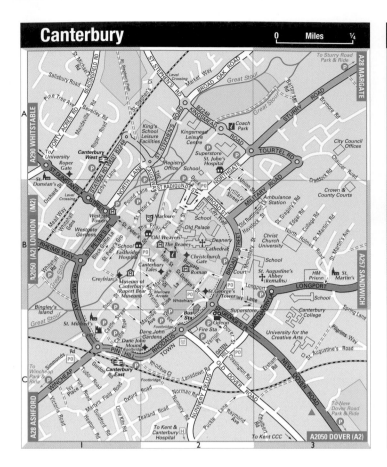

Cardiff / Caerdydd

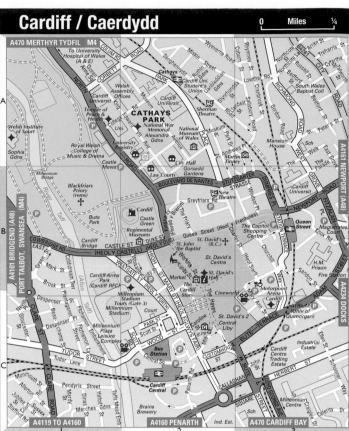

Cheltenham

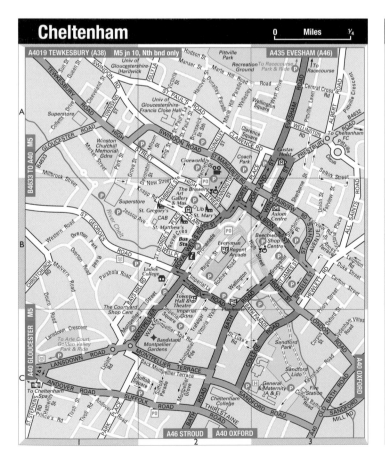

Chester

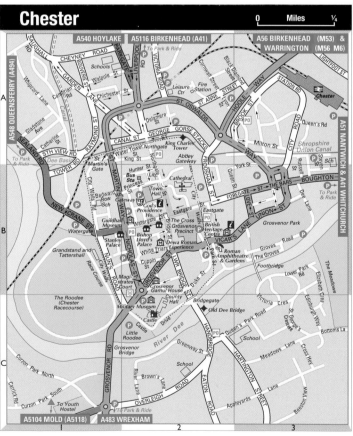

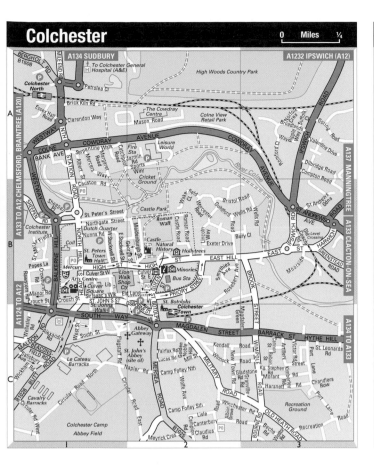

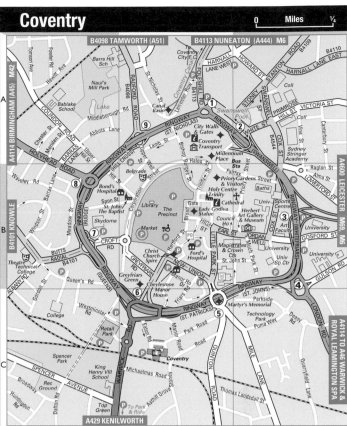

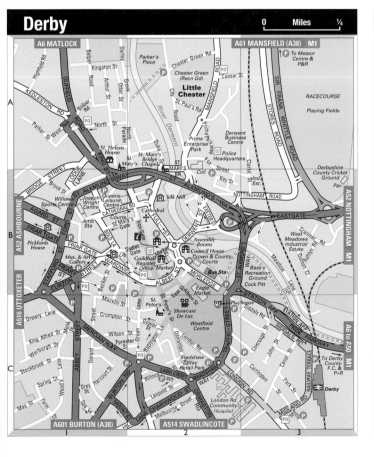

Edinburgh

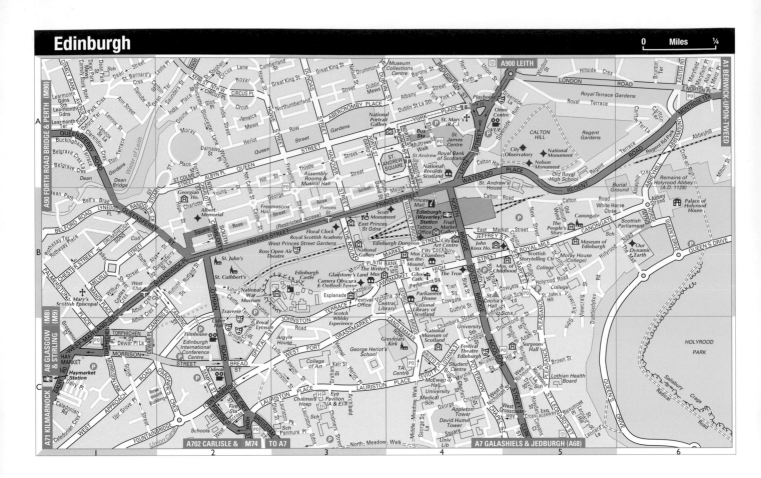

Exeter

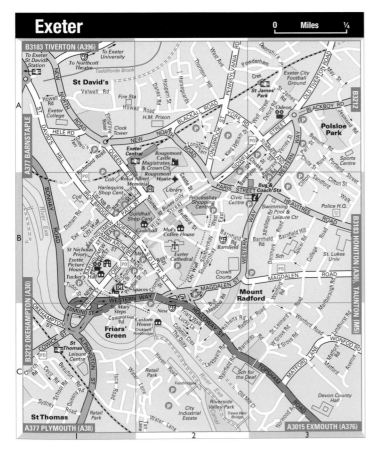

Gloucester

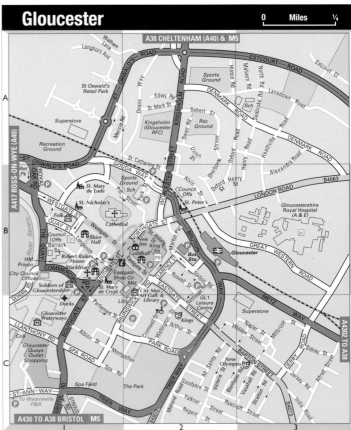

Glasgow

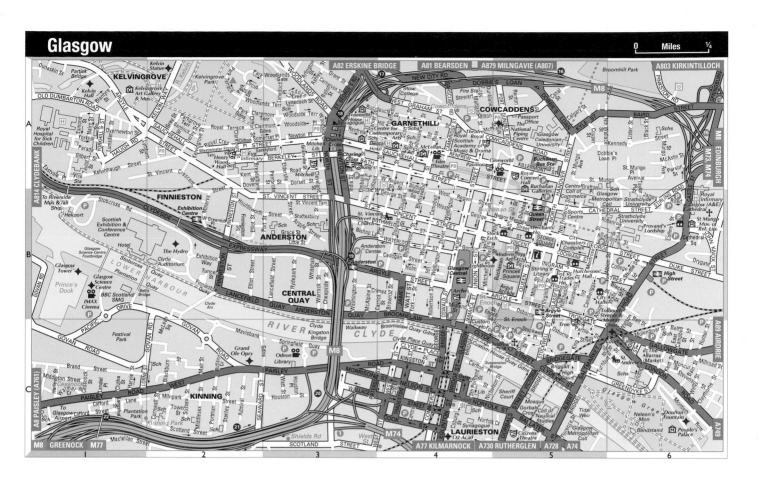

Hull

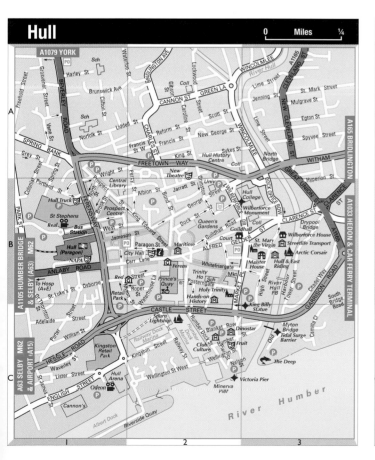

Ipswich

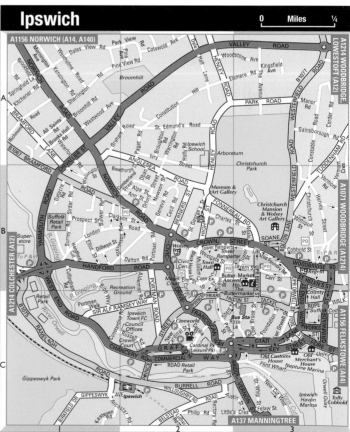

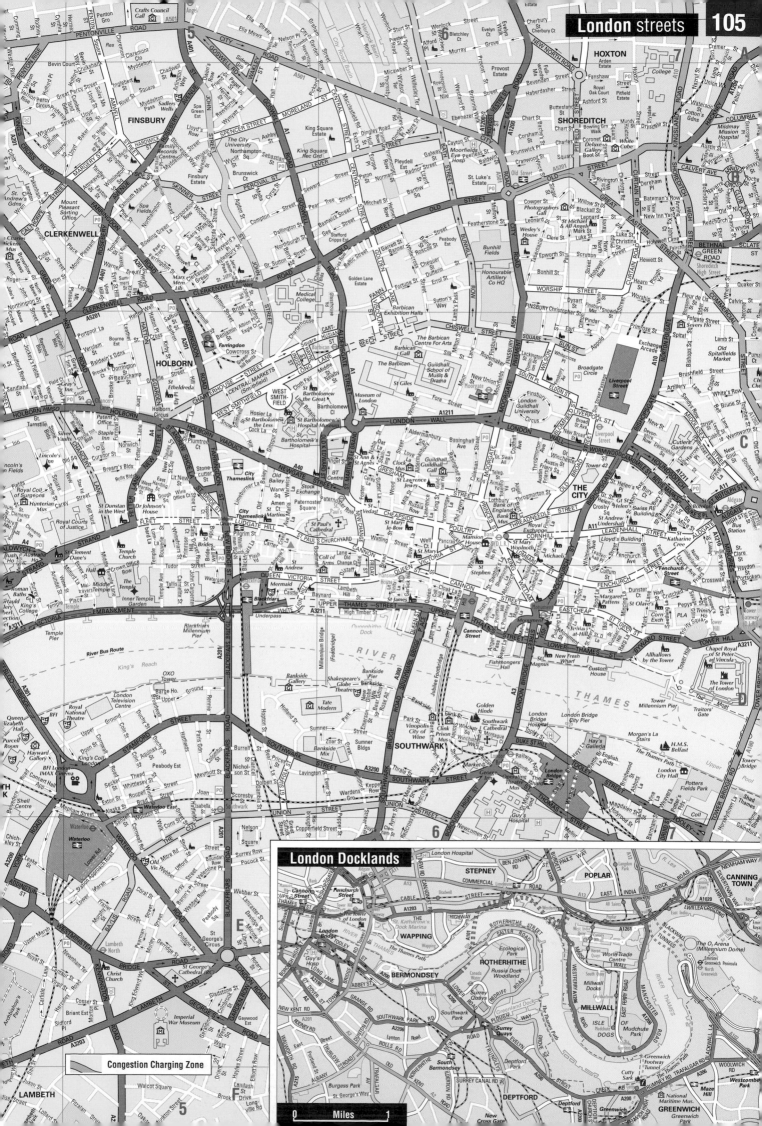

Congestion Charging Zone

London Docklands

0 Miles 1

Leeds

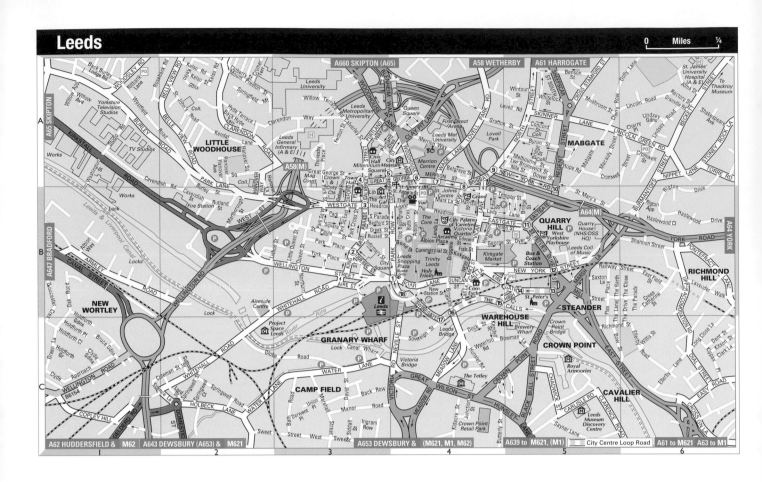

Leicester

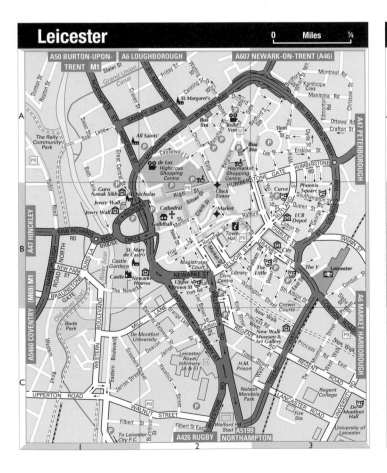

Lincoln

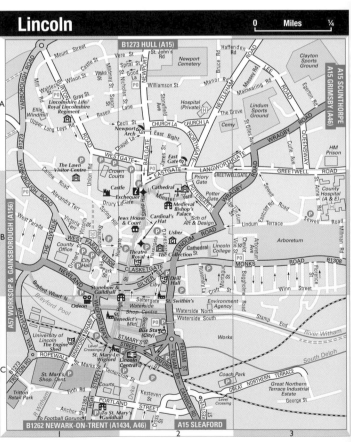

Liverpool

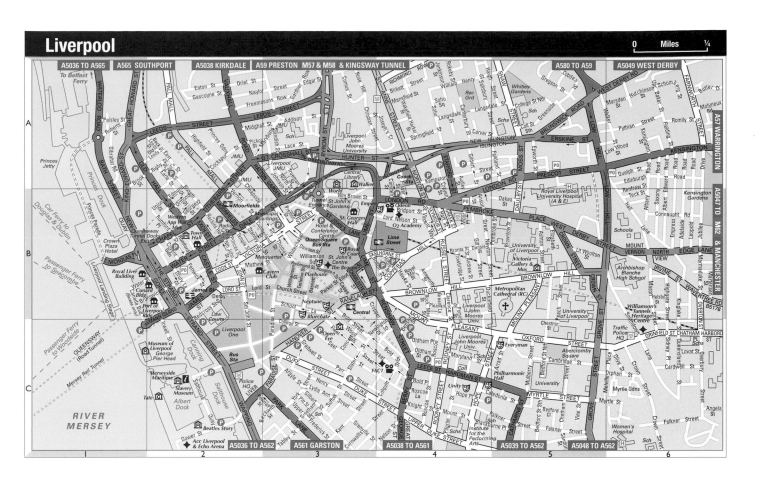

Manchester

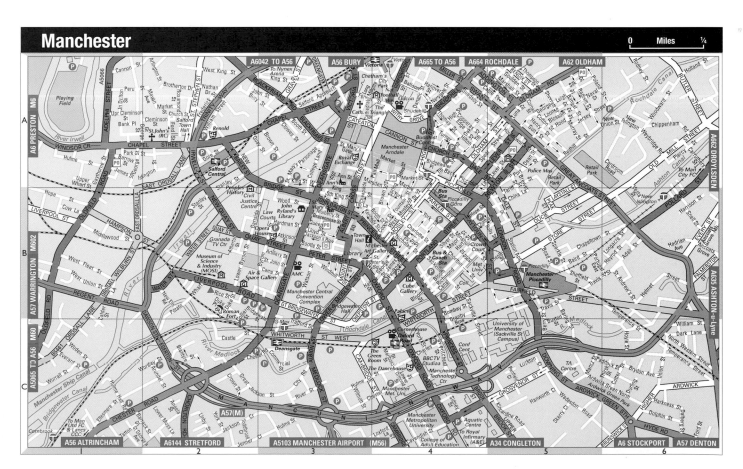

Middlesbrough

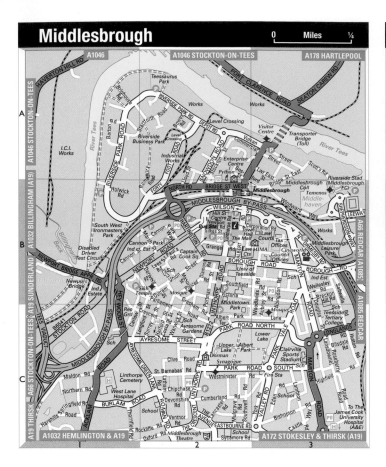

Newcastle upon Tyne

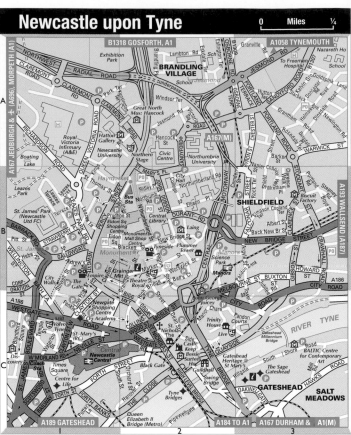

Northampton

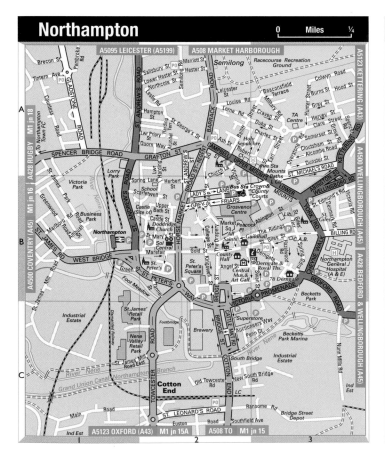

Norwich

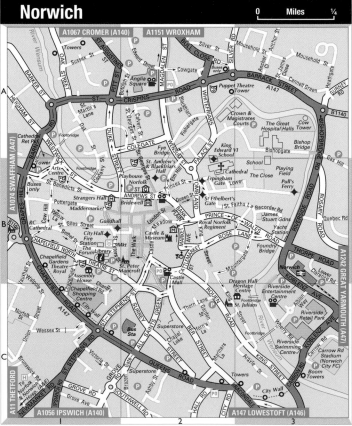

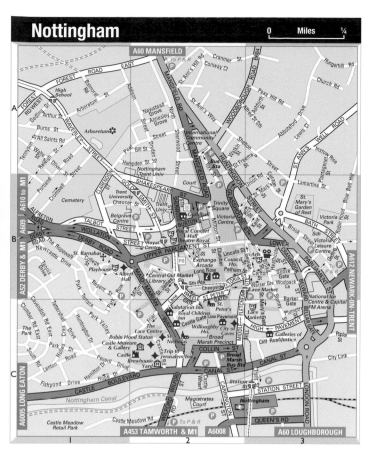

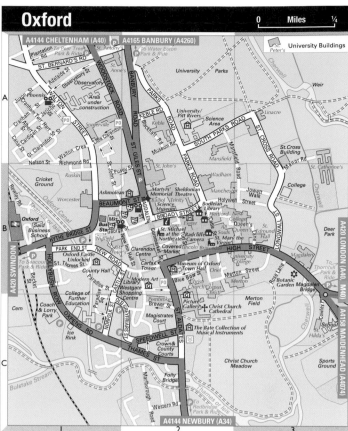

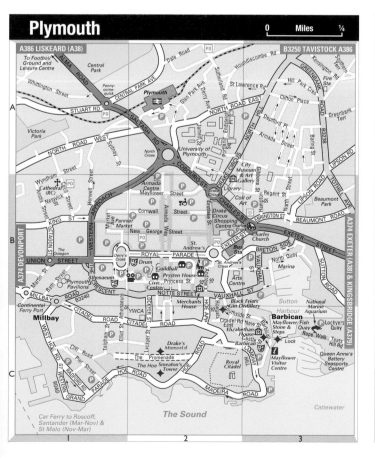

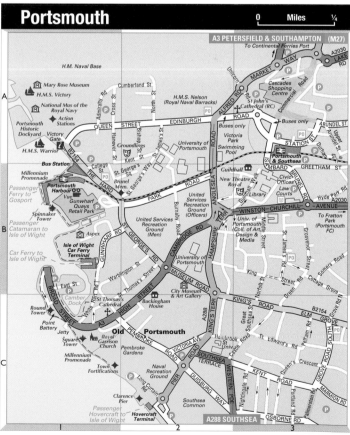

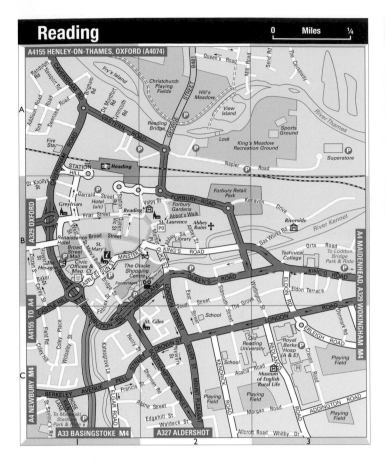

Reading

0 — Miles — ¼

Salisbury

0 — Miles — ¼

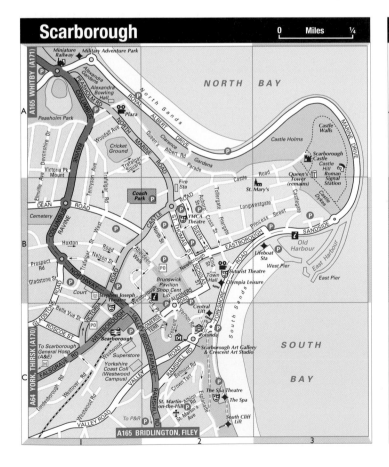

Scarborough

0 — Miles — ¼

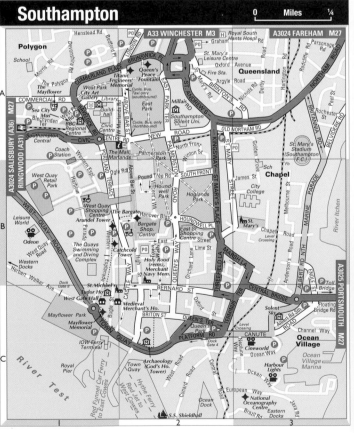

Southampton

0 — Miles — ¼

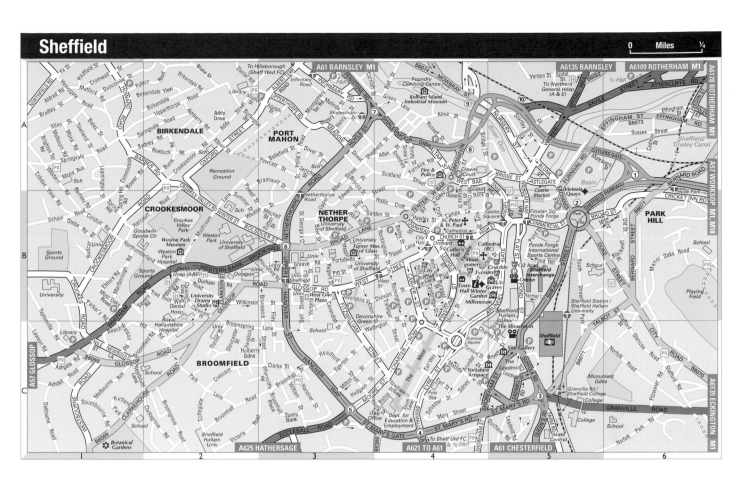

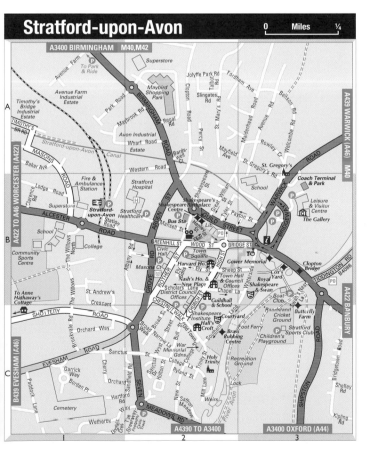

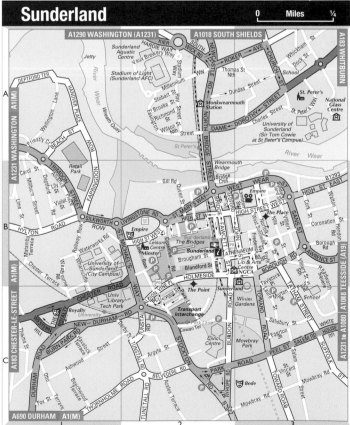

Swansea / Abertawe

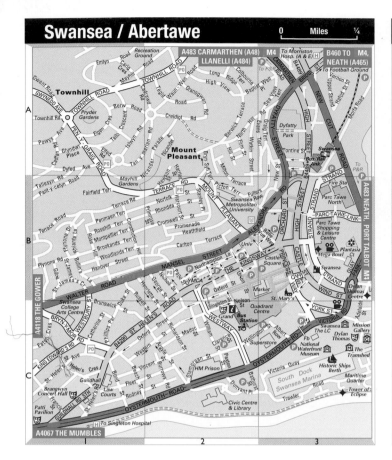

Winchester

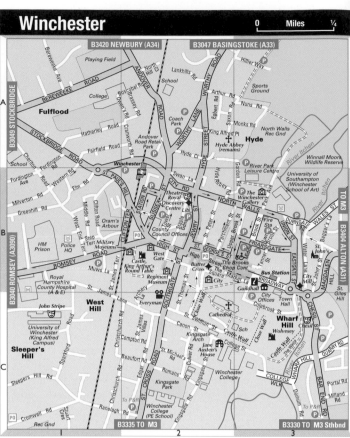

Worcester

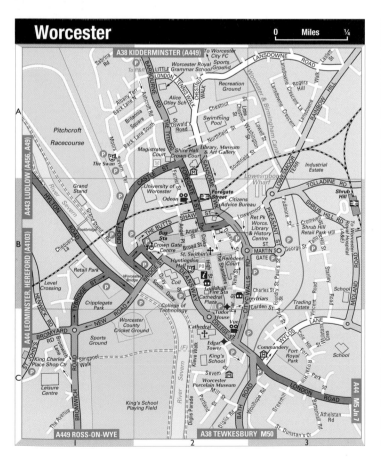

York

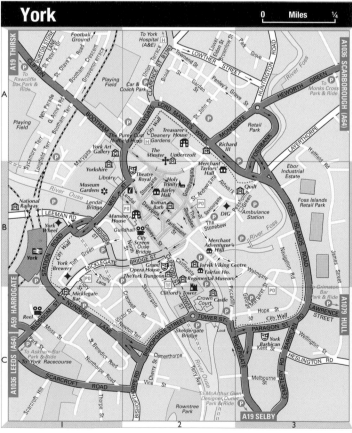

Abbreviations used in the index

Aberdeen	**Aberdeen City**	
Aberds	**Aberdeenshire**	
Ald	**Alderney**	
Anglesey	**Isle of Anglesey**	
Angus	**Angus**	
Argyll	**Argyll and Bute**	
Bath	**Bath and North East Somerset**	
Bedford	**Bedford**	
Bl Gwent	**Blaenau Gwent**	
Blackburn	**Blackburn with Darwen**	
Blackpool	**Blackpool**	
Bmouth	**Bournemouth**	
Borders	**Scottish Borders**	
Brack	**Bracknell**	
Bridgend	**Bridgend**	
Brighton	**City of Brighton and Hove**	
Bristol	**City and County of Bristol**	
Bucks	**Buckinghamshire**	
C Beds	**Central Bedfordshire**	
Caerph	**Caerphilly**	
Cambs	**Cambridgeshire**	
Cardiff	**Cardiff**	
Carms	**Carmarthenshire**	
Ceredig	**Ceredigion**	
Ches E	**Cheshire East**	
Ches W	**Cheshire West and Chester**	
Clack	**Clackmannanshire**	
Conwy	**Conwy**	
Corn	**Cornwall**	
Cumb	**Cumbria**	
Darl	**Darlington**	
Denb	**Denbighshire**	
Derby	**City of Derby**	
Derbys	**Derbyshire**	
Devon	**Devon**	
Dorset	**Dorset**	
Dumfries	**Dumfries and Galloway**	
Dundee	**Dundee City**	
Durham	**Durham**	
E Ayrs	**East Ayrshire**	
E Dunb	**East Dunbartonshire**	

E Loth	**East Lothian**
E Renf	**East Renfrewshire**
E Sus	**East Sussex**
E Yorks	**East Riding of Yorkshire**
Edin	**City of Edinburgh**
Essex	**Essex**
Falk	**Falkirk**
Fife	**Fife**
Flint	**Flintshire**
Glasgow	**City of Glasgow**
Glos	**Gloucestershire**
Gtr Man	**Greater Manchester**
Guern	**Guernsey**
Gwyn	**Gwynedd**
Halton	**Halton**
Hants	**Hampshire**
Hereford	**Herefordshire**
Herts	**Hertfordshire**
Highld	**Highland**
Hrtlpl	**Hartlepool**
Hull	**Hull**
IoM	**Isle of Man**
IoW	**Isle of Wight**
Invclyd	**Inverclyde**
Jersey	**Jersey**
Kent	**Kent**
Lancs	**Lancashire**
Leicester	**City of Leicester**
Leics	**Leicestershire**
Lincs	**Lincolnshire**
London	**Greater London**
Luton	**Luton**
M Keynes	**Milton Keynes**
M Tydf	**Merthyr Tydfil**
Mbro	**Middlesbrough**
Medway	**Medway**
Mers	**Merseyside**
Midloth	**Midlothian**
Mon	**Monmouthshire**
Moray	**Moray**
N Ayrs	**North Ayrshire**
N Lincs	**North Lincolnshire**
N Lanark	**North Lanarkshire**
N Som	**North Somerset**
N Yorks	**North Yorkshire**

NE Lincs	**North East Lincolnshire**
Neath	**Neath Port Talbot**
Newport	**City and County of Newport**
Norf	**Norfolk**
Northants	**Northamptonshire**
Northumb	**Northumberland**
Nottingham	**City of Nottingham**
Notts	**Nottinghamshire**
Orkney	**Orkney**
Oxon	**Oxfordshire**
Pboro	**Peterborough**
Pembs	**Pembrokeshire**
Perth	**Perth and Kinross**
Plym	**Plymouth**
Poole	**Poole**
Powys	**Powys**
Ptsmth	**Portsmouth**
Reading	**Reading**
Redcar	**Redcar and Cleveland**
Renfs	**Renfrewshire**
Rhondda	**Rhondda Cynon Taff**
Rutland	**Rutland**
S Ayrs	**South Ayrshire**
S Glos	**South Gloucestershire**
S Lanark	**South Lanarkshire**
S Yorks	**South Yorkshire**
Scilly	**Scilly**
Shetland	**Shetland**
Shrops	**Shropshire**
Slough	**Slough**
Som	**Somerset**

Soton	**Southampton**
Staffs	**Staffordshire**
Southend	**Southend-on-Sea**
Stirling	**Stirling**
Stockton	**Stockton-on-Tees**
Stoke	**Stoke-on-Trent**
Suff	**Suffolk**
Sur	**Surrey**
Swansea	**Swansea**
Swindon	**Swindon**
T&W	**Tyne and Wear**
Telford	**Telford and Wrekin**
Thurrock	**Thurrock**
Torbay	**Torbay**
Torf	**Torfaen**
V Glam	**The Vale of Glamorgan**
W Berks	**West Berkshire**
W Dunb	**West Dunbartonshire**
W Isles	**Western Isles**
W Loth	**West Lothian**
W Mid	**West Midlands**
W Sus	**West Sussex**
W Yorks	**West Yorkshire**
Warks	**Warwickshire**
Warr	**Warrington**
Wilts	**Wiltshire**
Windsor	**Windsor and Maidenhead**
Wokingham	**Wokingham**
Worcs	**Worcestershire**
Wrex	**Wrexham**
York	**City of York**

How to use the index

Example

Trudoxhill Som **16 G4**
└ grid square
└ page number
└ county or unitary authority

Index to road maps of Britain

Anstruther Wester Fife 77 G8
Ansty Hants 18 G4
Ansty W Sus 12 D1
Ansty Warks 35 G9
Ansty Wilts 9 B8
Anthill Common Hants 10 C5
Anthorn Cumb 61 H7
Antingham Norf 39 B8
Anton's Gowt Lincs 46 H6
Antonshill Falk 69 B7
Antony Corn 4 F4
Anwick Lincs 46 G5
Anwoth Dumfries 55 D8
Aoradh Argyll 64 B3
Apes Hall Cambs 38 F1
Apethorpe Northants 36 F6
Apeton Staffs 34 D4
Apley Lincs 46 E5
Apperknowle Derbys 45 E7
Apperley Glos 26 F5
Apperley Bridge W Yorks 51 F7
Appersett N Yorks 57 G10
Appin Argyll 74 C2
Appin House Argyll 74 C2
Appleby N Lincs 46 A3
Appleby-in-Westmorland Cumb 57 D8
Appleby Magna Leics 35 E9
Appleby Parva Leics 35 E9
Applecross Highld 85 D12
Applecross Ho. Highld 85 D12
Appledore Devon 6 C3
Appledore Devon 7 E9
Appledore Kent 13 D8
Appledore Heath Kent 13 C8
Appleford Oxon 18 B2
Applegarthtown Dumfries 61 E7
Appleshaw Hants 17 G10
Applethwaite Cumb 56 D4
Appleton Halton 43 D8
Appleton Oxon 17 A11
Appleton-le-Moors N Yorks 59 H8
Appleton-le-Street N Yorks 52 B3
Appleton Roebuck N Yorks 52 E1
Appleton Thorn Warr 43 D9
Appleton Wiske N Yorks 58 F4
Appletreehall Borders 61 B11
Appletreewick N Yorks 51 C6
Appley Som 7 D9
Appley Bridge Lancs 43 B8
Apse Heath IoW 10 F4
Apsley End C Beds 29 E8
Apuldram W Sus 11 D7
Aquhythie Aberds 83 B9
Arabella Highld 87 D11
Arbeadie Aberds 83 D8
Arberth = Narberth Pembs 22 E6
Arbirlot Angus 77 C9
Arboll Highld 87 C11
Arborfield Wokingham 18 E4
Arborfield Cross Wokingham 18 E4
Arborfield Garrison Wokingham 18 E4
Arbour-thorne S Yorks 45 D7
Arbroath Angus 77 C9
Arbuthnott Aberds 83 F9
Archiestown Moray 88 D2
Arclid Ches E 43 F10
Ard-dhubh Highld 85 D12
Ardachu Highld 93 J9
Ardalanish Argyll 78 K6
Ardanaiseig Argyll 74 E3
Ardaneaskan Highld 85 E13
Ardanstur Argyll 73 B7
Ardargie House Hotel Perth 76 F3
Ardarroch Highld 85 E13
Ardbeg Argyll 64 D5
Ardbeg Argyll 73 E10
Ardcharnich Highld 86 C4
Ardchiavaig Argyll 78 K6
Ardchullarie More Stirling 75 F8
Ardchyle Stirling 75 E8
Arddleen Powys 33 D8
Ardechvie Highld 80 D3
Ardeley Herts 29 F10
Ardelve Highld 85 F13
Arden Argyll 68 B2
Ardens Grafton Warks 27 C8
Ardentinny Argyll 73 E10
Ardentraive Argyll 73 F9
Ardeonaig Stirling 75 D9
Ardersier Highld 87 F10
Ardessie Highld 86 C3
Ardfern Argyll 73 C7
Ardgartan Argyll 74 G5
Ardgay Highld 87 B8
Ardgour Highld 74 A3
Ardheslaig Highld 85 C12
Ardiecow Moray 88 B5
Ardindrean Highld 86 C4
Ardingly W Sus 12 D2
Ardington Oxon 17 C11
Ardlair Aberds 83 A7
Ardlamont Ho. Argyll 73 G8
Ardleigh Essex 31 F7
Ardler Perth 76 C5
Ardley Oxon 28 F2
Ardlui Argyll 74 F6
Ardlussa Argyll 72 E5
Ardmair Highld 86 B4
Ardmay Argyll 74 G5
Ardminish Argyll 65 D7
Ardmolich Highld 79 D10
Ardmore Argyll 79 J10
Ardmore Highld 87 C10
Ardmore Highld 92 D5
Ardnacross Argyll 79 G8
Ardnadam Argyll 73 F10
Ardnagrask Highld 87 G8
Ardnarff Highld 85 E13
Ardnastang Highld 79 E11
Ardnave Argyll 64 A3
Ardno Argyll 73 C10
Ardo Aberds 89 E8
Ardo Ho. Aberds 89 F9
Ardoch Perth 76 D3
Ardochy House Highld 80 C4
Ardoyne Aberds 83 A8
Ardpatrick Argyll 72 G6
Ardpatrick Ho. Argyll 72 H6
Ardpeaton Argyll 73 E11
Ardrishaig Argyll 73 E7
Ardross Fife 77 G8
Ardross Highld 87 D9
Ardross Castle Highld 87 D9
Ardrossan N Ayrs 66 B5
Ardshealach Highld 79 E9
Ardsley S Yorks 45 B7
Ardslignish Highld 79 E8
Ardtalla Argyll 64 C5
Ardtalnaig Perth 75 D10
Ardtoe Highld 79 D9
Ardtrostan Perth 75 E9
Arduaine Argyll 72 B6
Ardullie Highld 87 E8
Ardvasar Highld 85 H11
Ardvorlich Perth 75 E9
Ardwell Dumfries 54 E4
Ardwell Mains Dumfries 54 E4
Ardwick Gtr Man 44 C2
Areley Kings Worcs 26 A5
Arford Hants 18 H5
Argoed Caerph 15 B7
Argoed Mill Powys 24 B6
Arichamish Argyll 73 C8
Arichastlich Argyll 74 D5
Aridhglas Argyll 78 J6
Arileod Argyll 78 F4
Arinacrinachd Highld 85 C12
Arinagour Argyll 78 F5
Arion Orkney 95 G3
Arisaig Highld 79 C9
Ariundle Highld 79 E11
Arkendale N Yorks 51 C9
Arkesden Essex 29 E11
Arkholme Lancs 50 B1
Arkle Town N Yorks 58 F1
Arkleton Dumfries 61 D9
Arkley London 19 B9
Arksey S Yorks 45 B9
Arkwright Town Derbys 45 E8
Arle Glos 26 F6
Arlecdon Cumb 56 E2
Arlesey C Beds 29 E8
Arleston Telford 34 D2
Arley Ches E 43 D9
Arlingham Glos 26 G4
Arlington Devon 6 B5
Arlington E Sus 12 F4
Arlington Glos 27 H8
Armadale Highld 93 C10
Armadale W Loth 69 D8
Armadale Castle Highld 85 H11
Armathwaite Cumb 57 B7
Arminghall Norf 39 E8
Armitage Staffs 35 D6
Armley W Yorks 51 F8
Armscote Warks 27 D9
Armthorpe S Yorks 45 B10
Arnabost Argyll 78 F5
Arncliffe N Yorks 50 B5
Arncroach Fife 77 G8
Arne Dorset 9 F8
Arnesby Leics 36 F2
Arngask Perth 76 F4
Arnisdale Highld 85 G13
Arnish Highld 85 D10
Arniston Engine Midloth 70 D2
Arnol W Isles 91 C8
Arnold E Yorks 53 E7
Arnold Notts 45 H9
Arnprior Stirling 68 A5
Arnside Cumb 49 B4
Aros Mains Argyll 79 G8
Arowry Wrex 33 B10
Arpafeelie Highld 87 F9
Arrad Foot Cumb 49 A3
Arram E Yorks 52 E6
Arrathorne N Yorks 58 G3
Arreton IoW 10 F4
Arrington Cambs 29 C10
Arrivain Argyll 74 D5
Arrochar Argyll 74 G5
Arrow Warks 27 C7
Arthington W Yorks 51 E8
Arthingworth Northants 36 G3
Arthog Gwyn 32 D2
Arthrath Aberds 89 E9
Arthurstone Perth 76 C5
Artrochie Aberds 89 E10
Arundel W Sus 11 D9
Aryhoulan Highld 80 G2
Asby Cumb 56 D2
Ascog Argyll 73 G10
Ascot Windsor 18 E6
Ascott Warks 27 E10
Ascott-under-Wychwood Oxon 27 G10
Asenby N Yorks 51 B9
Asfordby Leics 36 D3
Asfordby Hill Leics 36 D3
Asgarby Lincs 46 H5
Asgarby Lincs 47 F7
Ash Kent 20 E2
Ash Kent 21 F9
Ash Som 8 B3
Ash Sur 18 F5
Ash Bullayne Devon 7 F6
Ash Green Warks 35 G9
Ash Magna Shrops 34 B1
Ash Mill Devon 7 D6
Ash Priors Som 7 D10
Ash Street Suff 31 D7
Ash Thomas Devon 7 E9
Ash Vale Sur 18 F5
Ashampstead W Berks 18 D2
Ashbocking Suff 31 C8
Ashbourne Derbys 44 H5
Ashbrittle Som 7 D9
Ashburton Devon 5 E8
Ashbury Devon 6 G4
Ashbury Oxon 17 C9
Ashby N Lincs 46 B3
Ashby by Partney Lincs 47 F8
Ashby cum Fenby NE Lincs 46 B6
Ashby de la Launde Lincs 46 G4
Ashby-de-la-Zouch Leics 35 D9
Ashby Folville Leics 36 D3
Ashby Magna Leics 36 F1
Ashby Parva Leics 35 G11
Ashby Puerorum Lincs 47 E7
Ashby St Ledgers Northants 28 B2
Ashby St Mary Norf 39 E9
Ashchurch Glos 26 E6
Ashcombe Devon 5 D10
Ashcott Som 15 H10
Ashdon Essex 30 D2
Ashe Hants 18 G2
Asheldham Essex 20 A6
Ashen Essex 30 D4
Ashendon Bucks 28 G4
Ashfield Carms 24 F3
Ashfield Stirling 75 G10
Ashfield Suff 31 B9
Ashfield Green Suff 31 A9
Ashfold Crossways W Sus 11 B11
Ashford Devon 6 C4
Ashford Hants 9 C10
Ashford Kent 13 B9
Ashford Sur 19 D7
Ashford Bowdler Shrops 26 A2
Ashford Carbonell Shrops 26 A2
Ashford Hill Hants 18 E2
Ashford in the Water Derbys 44 F5
Ashgill S Lanark 68 F6
Ashill Devon 7 E9
Ashill Norf 38 E4
Ashill Som 8 C2
Ashingdon Essex 20 B5
Ashington Northumb 63 E8
Ashington Som 8 B4
Ashington W Sus 11 C10
Ashintully Castle Perth 76 A4
Ashkirk Borders 61 A10
Ashlett Hants 10 D3
Ashleworth Glos 26 F5
Ashley Cambs 30 B3
Ashley Ches E 43 D10
Ashley Devon 6 E5
Ashley Dorset 9 D10
Ashley Glos 16 B6
Ashley Hants 10 A2
Ashley Hants 10 E1
Ashley Northants 36 F3
Ashley Staffs 34 B3
Ashley Green Bucks 28 H6
Ashley Heath Dorset 9 D10
Ashley Heath Staffs 34 B3
Ashmanhaugh Norf 39 C9
Ashmansworth Hants 17 F11
Ashmansworthy Devon 6 E2
Ashmore Dorset 9 C8
Ashorne Warks 27 C10
Ashover Derbys 45 F7
Ashow Warks 27 A10
Ashprington Devon 5 F9
Ashreigney Devon 6 E5
Ashtead Sur 19 F8
Ashton Ches W 43 F8
Ashton Corn 2 G5
Ashton Hants 10 C4
Ashton Hereford 26 B2
Ashton Invclyd 73 F11
Ashton Northants 28 D4
Ashton Northants 37 G6
Ashton Common Wilts 16 F5
Ashton-In-Makerfield Gtr Man 43 C8
Ashton Keynes Wilts 17 B7
Ashton under Hill Worcs 26 E6
Ashton-under-Lyne Gtr Man 44 C3
Ashton upon Mersey Gtr Man 43 C10
Ashurst Hants 10 C2
Ashurst Kent 12 C4
Ashurst W Sus 11 C10
Ashurstwood W Sus 12 C3
Ashwater Devon 6 G2
Ashwell Herts 29 E9
Ashwell Rutland 36 D4
Ashwell Som 8 C2
Ashwellthorpe Norf 39 F7
Ashwick Som 16 G3
Ashwicken Norf 38 D3
Ashybank Borders 61 B11
Askam in Furness Cumb 49 B2
Askern S Yorks 45 A9
Askerswell Dorset 8 E4
Askett Bucks 28 H5
Askham Cumb 57 D7
Askham Notts 45 E11
Askham Bryan York 52 E1
Askham Richard York 51 E11
Asknish Argyll 73 D8
Askrigg N Yorks 57 G11
Askwith N Yorks 51 E7
Aslackby Lincs 37 B6
Aslacton Norf 39 F7
Aslockton Notts 36 B3
Asloun Aberds 83 B7
Aspatria Cumb 56 B3
Aspenden Herts 29 F10
Asperton Lincs 37 B8
Aspley Guise C Beds 28 E6
Aspley Heath C Beds 28 E6
Aspull Gtr Man 43 B9
Asselby E Yorks 52 G3
Asserby Lincs 47 E8
Assington Suff 30 E6
Assynt Ho. Highld 87 E8
Astbury Ches E 44 F2
Astcote Northants 28 C3
Asterley Shrops 33 E9
Asterton Shrops 33 F9
Asthall Oxon 27 G9
Asthall Leigh Oxon 27 G10
Astley Shrops 33 D11
Astley Warks 35 G9
Astley Worcs 26 B4
Astley Abbotts Shrops 34 F3
Astley Bridge Gtr Man 43 A10
Astley Cross Worcs 26 B5
Astley Green Gtr Man 43 C10
Aston Ches E 43 H9
Aston Ches W 43 E8
Aston Derbys 44 D5
Aston Hereford 25 A11
Aston Herts 29 F9
Aston Oxon 17 A10
Aston S Yorks 45 D8
Aston Shrops 33 C11
Aston Staffs 34 A3
Aston Telford 34 E2
Aston W Mid 35 G6
Aston Wokingham 18 C4
Aston Abbotts Bucks 28 F5
Aston Botterell Shrops 34 G2
Aston-By-Stone Staffs 34 B5
Aston Cantlow Warks 27 C8
Aston Clinton Bucks 28 G5
Aston Crews Hereford 26 F3
Aston Cross Glos 26 E6
Aston End Herts 29 F9
Aston Eyre Shrops 34 F2
Aston Fields Worcs 26 B6
Aston Flamville Leics 35 F10
Aston Ingham Hereford 26 F3
Aston juxta Mondrum Ches E 43 G9
Aston le Walls Northants 27 C11
Aston Magna Glos 27 E8
Aston Munslow Shrops 33 G11
Aston on Clun Shrops 33 G9
Aston-on-Trent Derbys 35 C10
Aston Rogers Shrops 33 E9
Aston Rowant Oxon 18 B4
Aston Sandford Bucks 28 H4
Aston Somerville Worcs 27 E7
Aston Subedge Glos 27 D8
Aston Tirrold Oxon 18 C2
Aston Upthorpe Oxon 18 C2
Astrop Northants 28 E2
Astwick C Beds 29 E9
Astwood M Keynes 28 D6
Astwood Worcs 26 C5
Astwood Bank Worcs 27 B7
Aswarby Lincs 37 B6
Aswardby Lincs 47 E7
Atch Lench Worcs 27 C7
Atcham Shrops 33 E11
Athelhampton Dorset 9 E6
Athelington Suff 31 A9
Athelney Som 8 B2
Athelstaneford E Loth 70 C4
Atherington Devon 6 D4
Atherstone Warks 35 F9
Atherstone on Stour Warks 27 C9
Atherton Gtr Man 43 B9
Atley Hill N Yorks 58 F3
Atlow Derbys 44 H6
Attadale Highld 86 H2
Attadale Ho. Highld 86 H2
Attenborough Notts 35 B11
Atterby Lincs 46 C3
Attercliffe S Yorks 45 D7
Attleborough Norf 38 F6
Attleborough Warks 35 F9
Attlebridge Norf 39 D7
Atwick E Yorks 53 D7
Atworth Wilts 16 E5
Aubourn Lincs 46 F3
Auchagallon N Ayrs 66 C1
Auchallater Aberds 82 E3
Aucharnie Aberds 89 D6
Auchattie Aberds 83 D8
Auchavan Angus 82 G3
Auchbreck Moray 82 A4
Auchenback E Renf 68 E4
Auchenbainzie Dumfries 60 D4
Auchenblae Aberds 83 F9
Auchenbrack Dumfries 60 D3
Auchenbreck Argyll 73 E9
Auchencairn Dumfries 55 D10
Auchencairn Dumfries 60 E5
Auchencairn N Ayrs 66 D3
Auchencrosh S Ayrs 54 B4
Auchencrow Borders 71 D7
Auchendinny Midloth 69 D11
Auchengray S Lanark 69 E8
Auchenhalrig Moray 88 B3
Auchenheath S Lanark 69 F7
Auchenlochan Argyll 73 F8
Auchenmalg Dumfries 54 D5
Auchensoul S Ayrs 66 G5
Auchentiber N Ayrs 67 B6
Auchertyre Highld 85 F13
Auchgourish Highld 81 B11
Auchincarroch W Dunb 68 B3
Auchindrain Argyll 73 C9
Auchindrean Highld 86 C4
Auchininna Aberds 89 D6
Auchinleck E Ayrs 67 D8
Auchinloch N Lanark 68 C5
Auchinroath Moray 88 C2
Auchintoul Aberds 83 B7
Auchiries Aberds 89 E10
Auchlee Aberds 83 D10
Auchleven Aberds 83 A8
Auchlochan S Lanark 69 G7
Auchlossan Aberds 83 C7
Auchlunies Aberds 83 D10
Auchlyne Stirling 75 E8
Auchmacoy Aberds 89 E9
Auchmair Moray 82 A5
Auchmantle Dumfries 54 C4
Auchmillan E Ayrs 67 D8
Auchmithie Angus 77 C9
Auchmuirbridge Fife 76 G5
Auchmull Angus 83 F7
Auchnacree Angus 77 A7
Auchnagallin Highld 87 H13
Auchnagatt Aberds 89 D9
Auchnaha Argyll 73 E8
Auchnashelloch Perth 75 F10
Aucholzie Aberds 82 D5
Auchrannie Angus 76 B5
Auchroisk Highld 82 A2
Auchronie Angus 82 E6
Auchterarder Perth 76 F2
Auchteraw Highld 80 C5
Auchterderran Fife 76 H5
Auchterhouse Angus 76 D6
Auchtermuchty Fife 76 F5
Auchterneed Highld 86 F7
Auchtertool Fife 69 A11
Auchtertyre Moray 88 C1
Auchtubh Stirling 75 E8
Auckengill Highld 94 D5
Auckley S Yorks 45 B10
Audenshaw Gtr Man 44 C3
Audlem Ches E 34 A2
Audley Staffs 43 G10
Audley End Essex 30 E5
Auds Aberds 89 B6
Aughton E Yorks 52 F3
Aughton Lancs 43 B6
Aughton Lancs 50 C1
Aughton S Yorks 45 D8
Aughton Wilts 17 F9
Aughton Park Lancs 43 B7
Auldearn Highld 87 F12
Aulden Hereford 25 C11
Auldgirth Dumfries 60 E5
Auldhame E Loth 70 B4
Auldhouse S Lanark 68 E5
Ault a'chruinn Highld 80 A1
Aultanrynie Highld 92 F6
Aultbea Highld 91 J13
Aultdearg Highld 86 E5
Aultgrishan Highld 91 J12
Aultguish Inn Highld 86 D6
Aultibea Highld 93 G13
Aultiphurst Highld 93 C11
Aultmore Moray 88 C4
Aultnagoire Highld 81 A7
Aultnamain Inn Highld 87 C9
Aultnaslat Highld 80 C3
Aulton Aberds 83 A8
Aundorach Highld 82 B1
Aunsby Lincs 36 B6
Auquhorthies Aberds 89 F8
Aust S Glos 16 C2
Austendike Lincs 37 C8
Austerfield S Yorks 45 C10
Austrey Warks 35 E8
Austwick N Yorks 50 C3
Authorpe Lincs 47 D8
Authorpe Row Lincs 47 E9
Avebury Wilts 17 E8
Aveley Thurrock 20 C2
Avening Glos 16 B5
Averham Notts 45 G11
Aveton Gifford Devon 5 G7
Avielochan Highld 81 B11
Aviemore Highld 81 B10
Avington Hants 10 A4
Avington W Berks 17 E10
Avoch Highld 87 F10
Avon Hants 9 E10
Avon Dassett Warks 27 D11
Avonbridge Falk 69 C8
Avonmouth Bristol 15 D11
Avonwick Devon 5 F8
Awbridge Hants 10 B2
Awhirk Dumfries 54 D3
Awkley S Glos 16 C2
Awliscombe Devon 7 F10
Awre Glos 26 H4
Awsworth Notts 35 A10
Axbridge Som 15 F10
Axford Hants 18 G3
Axford Wilts 17 D9
Axminster Devon 8 E1
Axmouth Devon 8 E1
Axton Flint 42 D4
Aycliff Kent 21 G10
Aycliffe Durham 58 D3
Aydon Northumb 62 G6
Aylburton Glos 16 A3
Ayle Northumb 57 B9
Aylesbeare Devon 7 G9
Aylesbury Bucks 28 G5
Aylesby NE Lincs 46 B6
Aylesford Kent 20 F4
Aylesham Kent 21 F9
Aylestone Leicester 36 E1
Aylmerton Norf 39 B7
Aylsham Norf 39 C7
Aylton Hereford 26 E3
Aymestrey Hereford 25 B11
Aynho Northants 28 E2
Ayot St Lawrence Herts 29 G8
Ayot St Peter Herts 29 G9
Ayr S Ayrs 66 D6
Aysgarth N Yorks 58 H1
Ayside Cumb 49 A3
Ayston Rutland 36 E4
Aythorpe Roding Essex 30 G2
Ayton Borders 71 D8
Aywick Shetland 96 E7
Azerley N Yorks 51 B8

B

Babbacombe Torbay 5 E10
Babbinswood Shrops 33 B9
Babcary Som 8 B4
Babel Carms 24 E5
Babell Flint 42 E4
Babraham Cambs 30 C2
Babworth Notts 45 D10
Bac W Isles 91 C9
Bachau Anglesey 40 B6
Back of Keppoch Highld 79 C9
Back Rogerton E Ayrs 67 D8
Backaland Orkney 95 E6
Backaskaill Orkney 95 C5
Backbarrow Cumb 49 A3
Backe Carms 23 E7
Backfolds Aberds 89 C10
Backford Ches W 43 E7
Backford Cross Ches W 43 E6
Backhill Aberds 89 E10
Backhill Aberds 89 E7
Backhill of Clackriach Aberds 89 D9
Backhill of Fortree Aberds 89 D9
Backhill of Trustach Aberds 83 D8
Backies Highld 93 J11
Backlass Highld 94 E4
Backwell N Som 15 E10
Backworth T&W 63 F9
Bacon End Essex 30 G3
Baconsthorpe Norf 39 B7
Bacton Hereford 25 E10
Bacton Norf 39 B9
Bacton Suff 31 B7
Bacton Green Suff 31 B7
Bacup Lancs 50 G4
Badachro Highld 85 A12
Badanloch Lodge Highld 93 F10
Badavanich Highld 86 F4
Badbury Swindon 17 C8
Badby Northants 28 C2
Badcall Highld 92 D5
Badcaul Highld 86 B3
Baddeley Green Stoke 44 G3
Baddesley Clinton Warks 27 A9
Baddesley Ensor Warks 35 F8
Baddidarach Highld 92 G3
Baddoch Aberds 82 E3
Baddock Highld 87 F10
Badenscoth Aberds 89 E7
Badenyon Aberds 82 B5
Badger Shrops 34 F3
Badger's Mount Kent 19 E11
Badgeworth Glos 26 G6
Badgworth Som 15 F9
Badicaul Highld 85 F12
Badingham Suff 31 B10
Badlesmere Kent 21 F7
Badlipster Highld 94 F4
Badluarach Highld 86 B2
Badminton S Glos 16 C5
Badnaban Highld 92 G3
Badninish Highld 87 B10
Badrallach Highld 86 B3
Badsey Worcs 27 D7
Badshot Lea Sur 18 G5
Badsworth W Yorks 45 A8
Badwell Ash Suff 30 B6
Bae Colwyn = Colwyn Bay Conwy 41 C10
Bag Enderby Lincs 47 E7
Bagby N Yorks 51 A10
Bagendon Glos 27 H7
Bagh a Chaisteil = Castlebay W Isles 84 J1
Bagh Mor W Isles 84 C3
Bagh Shiarabhagh W Isles 84 H2
Baghasdal W Isles 84 G2
Bagillt Flint 42 E5
Baginton Warks 27 A10
Baglan Neath 14 B3
Bagley Shrops 33 C10
Bagnall Staffs 44 G3
Bagnor W Berks 17 E11
Bagshot Sur 18 E6
Bagshot Wilts 17 E10
Bagthorpe Norf 38 B3
Bagthorpe Notts 45 G8
Bagworth Leics 35 E10
Bagwy Llydiart Hereford 25 F11
Bail Àrd Bhuirgh W Isles 91 B9
Bail' Iochdrach W Isles 84 C3
Bail Uachdraich W Isles 84 B3
Bail' Ur Tholastaidh W Isles 91 C10
Baildon W Yorks 51 F7
Baile W Isles 90 J4
Baile a Mhanaich W Isles 84 C2
Baile Ailein W Isles 91 E7
Baile an Truiseil W Isles 91 B8
Baile Boidheach Argyll 72 F6
Baile Glas W Isles 84 C3
Baile Mhartainn W Isles 84 A2
Baile Mhic Phail W Isles 84 A3
Baile Mor Argyll 78 J5
Baile Mor W Isles 84 B2
Baile na Creige W Isles 84 H1
Baile nan Cailleach W Isles 84 C2
Baile Raghaill W Isles 84 A2
Bailebeag Highld 81 B7
Baileyhead Cumb 61 F11
Bailiesward Aberds 88 E4
Baillieston Glasgow 68 D5
Bainbridge N Yorks 57 G11
Bainsford Falk 69 B7
Bainshole Aberds 88 E6
Bainton E Yorks 52 D5
Bainton Pboro 37 E6
Bairnkine Borders 62 B2
Baker Street Thurrock 20 C3
Baker's End Herts 29 G10
Bakewell Derbys 44 F6
Bala = Y Bala Gwyn 32 B5
Balachuirn Highld 85 D10
Balavil Highld 81 C9
Balbeg Highld 81 A6
Balbeg Highld 86 H7
Balbeggie Perth 76 E4
Balbithan Aberds 83 B9
Balbithan Ho. Aberds 83 B10
Balblair Highld 87 B8
Balblair Highld 87 E10
Balby S Yorks 45 B9
Balchladich Highld 92 F3
Balchraggan Highld 87 G8
Balchraggan Highld 87 H8
Balchrick Highld 92 D4
Balchrystie Fife 77 G7
Balcladaich Highld 80 A4
Balcombe W Sus 12 C2
Balcombe Lane W Sus 12 C2
Balcomie Fife 77 F9
Balcurvie Fife 76 G6
Baldersby N Yorks 51 B9
Baldersby St James N Yorks 51 B9
Balderstone Lancs 50 F2
Balderton Ches W 42 F6
Balderton Notts 46 G2
Baldhu Corn 3 E6
Baldinnie Fife 77 F7
Baldock Herts 29 E9
Baldovie Dundee 77 D7
Baldrine IoM 48 D4
Baldslow E Sus 13 E6
Baldwin IoM 48 D3
Baldwinholme Cumb 56 A5
Baldwin's Gate Staffs 34 A3
Bale Norf 38 B6
Balearn Aberds 89 C10
Balemartine Argyll 78 G2
Balephuil Argyll 78 G2
Balerno Edin 69 D10
Balevullin Argyll 78 G2
Balfield Angus 83 G7
Balfour Orkney 95 G5
Balfron Stirling 68 B4
Balfron Station Stirling 68 B4
Balgaveny Aberds 89 D6
Balgavies Angus 77 B8
Balgonar Fife 69 A9
Balgove Aberds 89 E8
Balgowan Highld 81 D8
Balgown Highld 85 B8
Balgrochan E Dunb 68 C5
Balgy Highld 85 C13
Balhaldie Stirling 75 G11
Balhalgardy Aberds 83 A9
Balham London 19 D9
Balhary Perth 76 C5
Baliasta Shetland 96 C8
Baligill Highld 93 C11
Balintore Angus 76 B5
Balintore Highld 87 D11
Balintraid Highld 87 D10
Balk N Yorks 51 A10
Balkeerie Angus 76 C6
Balkemback Angus 76 D6
Balkholme E Yorks 52 G3
Balkissock S Ayrs 54 A4
Ball Shrops 33 C9
Ball Haye Green Staffs 44 G3
Ball Hill Hants 17 E11
Ballabeg IoM 48 E2
Ballacannel IoM 48 D4
Ballachulish Highld 74 B3
Ballajora IoM 48 C4
Ballaleigh IoM 48 D3
Ballamodha IoM 48 E2
Ballantrae S Ayrs 54 A3
Ballaquine IoM 48 D4
Ballards Gore Essex 20 B6
Ballasalla IoM 48 C3
Ballasalla IoM 48 E2
Ballater Aberds 82 D5
Ballaugh IoM 48 C3
Ballaveare IoM 48 E3
Ballcorach Moray 82 A3
Ballechin Perth 76 B2
Balleigh Highld 87 C10
Ballencrieff E Loth 70 C3
Ballentoul Perth 81 G10
Ballidon Derbys 44 G6
Balliemore Argyll 73 E9
Balliemore Argyll 79 J11
Ballikinrain Stirling 68 B4
Ballimeanoch Argyll 73 B9
Ballimore Argyll 73 E8
Ballimore Stirling 75 F8
Ballinaby Argyll 64 B3
Ballindean Perth 76 E5
Ballingdon Suff 30 D5
Ballinger Common Bucks 18 A6
Ballingham Hereford 26 E2
Ballingry Fife 76 H4
Ballinlick Perth 76 C2
Ballinluig Perth 76 B2
Ballintuim Perth 76 B4
Balloch Angus 76 B6
Balloch Highld 87 G10
Balloch N Lanark 68 C6
Balloch W Dunb 68 B2
Ballochan Aberds 83 D7
Ballochford Moray 88 E3
Ballochmorrie S Ayrs 54 A5
Balls Cross W Sus 11 B8
Balls Green Essex 31 F7
Ballygown Argyll 78 G7
Ballygrant Argyll 64 B4
Ballyhaugh Argyll 78 F4
Balmacara Highld 85 F13
Balmacara Square Highld 85 F13
Balmaclellan Dumfries 55 B9
Balmacneil Perth 76 B2
Balmacqueen Highld 85 A9
Balmae Dumfries 55 E9
Balmaha Stirling 68 A3
Balmalcolm Fife 76 G6
Balmeanach Highld 85 D10
Balmedie Aberds 83 B11
Balmer Heath Shrops 33 B10
Balmerino Fife 76 E6
Balmerlawn Hants 10 D2
Balmichael N Ayrs 66 C2
Balmirmer Angus 77 D8
Balmore Highld 85 D7
Balmore Highld 86 H6
Balmore Highld 87 G11
Balmore Perth 76 B2
Balmule Fife 69 B11
Balmullo Fife 77 E7
Balmungie Highld 87 F10
Balnaboth Angus 82 G5
Balnabruaich Highld 87 E10
Balnabruich Highld 94 H3
Balnacoil Highld 93 H11
Balnacra Highld 86 G2
Balnafoich Highld 87 H9
Balnagall Highld 87 C11
Balnaguard Perth 76 B2
Balnahard Argyll 72 D3
Balnahard Argyll 78 H7
Balnain Highld 86 H7
Balnakeil Highld 92 C6
Balnaknock Highld 85 B9
Balnapaling Highld 87 E10
Balne N Yorks 52 H1
Balochroy Argyll 65 C8
Balone Fife 77 F7
Balornock Glasgow 68 D5
Balquharn Perth 76 D3
Balquhidder Stirling 75 E8
Balsall W Mid 35 H8
Balsall Common W Mid 35 H8
Balsall Hth. W Mid 35 G6
Balscott Oxon 27 D10
Balsham Cambs 30 C2
Baltasound Shetland 96 C8
Balterley Staffs 43 G10
Baltersan Dumfries 55 C7
Balthangie Aberds 89 C8
Baltonsborough Som 8 A4
Balvaird Highld 87 F8
Balvicar Argyll 72 B6
Balvraid Highld 85 G13
Balvraid Highld 87 H11
Bamber Bridge Lancs 50 G1
Bambers Green Essex 30 F2
Bamburgh Northumb 71 G10
Bamff Perth 76 B5
Bamford Derbys 44 D6
Bamford Gtr Man 44 A2
Bampton Cumb 57 E7
Bampton Devon 7 D8
Bampton Oxon 17 A10
Bampton Grange Cumb 57 E7
Banavie Highld 80 F3
Banbury Oxon 27 D11
Bancffosfelen Carms 23 E9
Banchory Aberds 83 D8
Banchory-Devenick Aberds 83 C11
Bancycapel Carms 23 E9
Bancyfelin Carms 23 E8
Bancyffordd Carms 23 C9
Bandirran Perth 76 D5
Banff Aberds 89 B6
Bangor Gwyn 41 C7
Bangor-is-y-coed Wrex 43 H6
Banham Norf 39 G6
Bank Hants 10 D1
Bank Newton N Yorks 50 D5
Bank Street Worcs 26 B3
Bankend Dumfries 60 G6
Bankfoot Perth 76 D3
Bankglen E Ayrs 67 E9
Bankhead Aberdeen 83 B10
Bankhead Aberds 83 C8
Banknock Falk 68 C6
Banks Cumb 61 G11
Banks Lancs 49 G3
Bankshill Dumfries 61 E7
Banningham Norf 39 C8
Banniskirk Ho. Highld 94 E3
Bannister Green Essex 30 F3
Bannockburn Stirling 69 A7
Banstead Sur 19 F9
Bantham Devon 5 G7
Banton N Lanark 68 C6
Banwell N Som 15 F9
Banyard's Green Suff 31 A10
Bapchild Kent 20 E6
Bar Hill Cambs 29 B10
Barabhas W Isles 91 C8
Barabhas Iarach W Isles 91 C8
Barabhas Uarach W Isles 91 B8
Barachandroman Argyll 79 J9
Barassie S Ayrs 66 C6
Baravullin Argyll 79 H11
Barbaraville Highld 87 D10
Barber Booth Derbys 44 D5
Barbieston S Ayrs 67 E7
Barbon Cumb 50 A2
Barbridge Ches E 43 G9
Barbrook Devon 6 B6
Barby Northants 28 A2
Barcaldine Argyll 74 C2
Barcheston Warks 27 E9
Barcombe E Sus 12 E3
Barcombe Cross E Sus 12 E3
Barden N Yorks 58 G2
Barden Scale N Yorks 51 D6
Bardennoch Dumfries 67 G8
Bardfield Saling Essex 30 F3
Bardister Shetland 96 F5
Bardney Lincs 46 F5
Bardon Leics 35 D10
Bardon Mill Northumb 62 G3
Bardowie E Dunb 68 C4
Bardrainney Invclyd 68 C2
Bardsea Cumb 49 B3
Bardsey W Yorks 51 E9
Bardwell Suff 30 A6
Bare Lancs 49 C4
Barfad Argyll 73 G7
Barford Norf 39 E7
Barford Warks 27 B9
Barford St John Oxon 27 E11
Barford St Martin Wilts 9 A9
Barford St Michael Oxon 27 E11
Barfrestone Kent 21 F9
Bargod = Bargoed Caerph 15 B7
Bargoed = Bargod Caerph 15 B7
Bargrennan Dumfries 54 B6
Barham Cambs 37 H7
Barham Kent 21 F9
Barham Suff 31 C8
Barharrow Dumfries 55 D9
Barhill Dumfries 55 C11
Barholm Lincs 37 D6
Barkby Leics 36 E2
Barkestone-le-Vale Leics 36 B3
Barkham Wokingham 18 E4
Barking London 19 C11
Barking Suff 31 C7
Barking Tye Suff 31 C7
Barkingside London 19 C11
Barkisland W Yorks 51 H6
Barkston Lincs 36 A5
Barkston N Yorks 51 F10
Barkway Herts 29 E10
Barlaston Staffs 34 B4
Barlavington W Sus 11 C8
Barlborough Derbys 45 E8
Barlby N Yorks 52 F2
Barlestone Leics 35 E10
Barley Herts 29 E10
Barley Lancs 50 E4
Barley Mow T&W 58 A3
Barleythorpe Rutland 36 E4
Barling Essex 20 C6
Barlow Derbys 45 E7
Barlow N Yorks 52 G2
Barlow T&W 63 G7
Barmby Moor E Yorks 52 E3
Barmby on the Marsh E Yorks 52 G2
Barmer Norf 38 B4
Barmoor Castle Northumb 71 G8
Barmoor Lane End Northumb 71 G9
Barmouth = Abermaw Gwyn 32 D2
Barmpton Darl 58 E4
Barmston E Yorks 53 D7
Barnack Pboro 37 E6
Barnacle Warks 35 G9
Barnard Castle Durham 58 E1
Barnard Gate Oxon 27 G11
Barnardiston Suff 30 D4
Barnbarroch Dumfries 55 D11
Barnburgh S Yorks 45 B8
Barnby Suff 39 G10
Barnby Dun S Yorks 45 B10
Barnby in the Willows Notts 46 G2
Barnby Moor Notts 45 D10
Barnes Street Kent 20 G3
Barnet London 19 B9
Barnetby le Wold N Lincs 46 B4
Barney Norf 38 B5
Barnham Suff 38 H4
Barnham W Sus 11 D8
Barnham Broom Norf 39 E6
Barnhead Angus 77 B9
Barnhill Ches W 43 G7
Barnhill Dundee 77 D7
Barnhill Moray 88 C1
Barnhills Dumfries 54 B2
Barningham Durham 58 E1
Barningham Suff 38 H5
Barnoldby le Beck NE Lincs 46 B6
Barnoldswick Lancs 50 E4
Barns Green W Sus 11 B10
Barnsley Glos 27 H7
Barnsley S Yorks 45 B7
Barnstaple Devon 6 C4
Barnston Essex 30 G3
Barnston Mers 42 D5
Barnstone Notts 36 B3
Barnt Green Worcs 27 A7
Barnton Ches W 43 E9
Barnton Edin 69 C10
Barnwell All Saints Northants 36 G6
Barnwell St Andrew Northants 36 G6
Barnwood Glos 26 G5
Barochreal Argyll 79 J11
Barons Cross Hereford 25 C11
Barr S Ayrs 66 G5
Barra Castle Aberds 83 A9
Barrachan Dumfries 54 E6
Barrack Aberds 89 D8
Barraglom W Isles 90 D6
Barrahormid Argyll 72 E6
Barran Argyll 79 J11
Barrapol Argyll 78 G2
Barras Aberds 83 E10
Barras Cumb 57 E10
Barrasford Northumb 62 F5
Barravullin Argyll 73 C7
Barregarrow IoM 48 D3
Barrhead E Renf 68 E3
Barrhill S Ayrs 54 A5
Barrington Cambs 29 D10
Barrington Som 8 C2
Barripper Corn 2 F5
Barrmill N Ayrs 67 A6
Barrock Highld 94 C4
Barrock Ho. Highld 94 D4
Barrow Lancs 50 F3
Barrow Rutland 36 D4
Barrow Suff 30 B4
Barrow Green Kent 20 E6
Barrow Gurney N Som 15 E11
Barrow Haven N Lincs 53 G6
Barrow-in-Furness Cumb 49 C2
Barrow Island Cumb 49 C1
Barrow Nook Lancs 43 B7
Barrow Street Wilts 9 A7
Barrow upon Humber N Lincs 53 G6
Barrow upon Soar Leics 36 D1
Barrow upon Trent Derbys 35 C9
Barroway Drove Norf 38 E1
Barrowburn Northumb 62 B4
Barrowby Lincs 36 B4
Barrowcliff N Yorks 59 H11
Barrowden Rutland 36 E5
Barrowford Lancs 50 F4
Barrows Green Ches E 43 G9
Barrows Green Cumb 57 H7
Barrow's Green Mers 43 D8
Barry Angus 77 D8
Barry = Y Barri V Glam 15 E7
Barry Island V Glam 15 E7
Barsby Leics 36 D2
Barsham Suff 39 G9
Barston W Mid 35 H8
Bartestree Hereford 26 D2
Barthol Chapel Aberds 89 E8
Barthomley Ches E 43 G10
Bartley Hants 10 C2
Bartley Green W Mid 34 G6
Bartlow Cambs 30 D2
Barton Cambs 29 C11
Barton Ches W 43 G7
Barton Glos 27 F8
Barton Lancs 42 B6
Barton Lancs 49 F5
Barton N Yorks 58 F3
Barton Oxon 28 H2
Barton Torbay 5 E10
Barton Warks 27 C8
Barton Bendish Norf 38 E3
Barton Hartshorn Bucks 28 E3
Barton in Fabis Notts 35 B11
Barton in the Beans Leics 35 E9
Barton-le-Clay C Beds 29 E7
Barton-le-Street N Yorks 52 B3
Barton-le-Willows N Yorks 52 C3
Barton Mills Suff 30 A4
Barton on Sea Hants 9 E11
Barton on the Heath Warks 27 E9
Barton St David Som 8 A4
Barton Seagrave Northants 36 H4
Barton Stacey Hants 17 G11
Barton Turf Norf 39 C9
Barton-under-Needwood Staffs 35 D7
Barton-upon-Humber N Lincs 52 G6
Barton Waterside N Lincs 52 G6
Barugh S Yorks 45 B7
Barway Cambs 37 H11
Barwell Leics 35 F10
Barwick Herts 29 G10
Barwick Som 8 C4
Barwick in Elmet W Yorks 51 F9
Baschurch Shrops 33 C10
Bascote Warks 27 B11
Basford Green Staffs 44 G3
Bashall Eaves Lancs 50 E2
Bashley Hants 9 E11
Basildon Essex 20 C4
Basingstoke Hants 18 F3
Baslow Derbys 44 E6
Bason Bridge Som 15 G9
Bassaleg Newport 15 C8
Bassenthwaite Cumb 56 C4
Bassett Soton 10 C3
Bassingbourn Cambs 29 D10
Bassingfield Notts 36 B2
Bassingham Lincs 46 F3
Bassingthorpe Lincs 36 C5
Basta Shetland 96 D7
Baston Lincs 37 D7
Bastwick Norf 39 D10
Baswick Steer E Yorks 53 E6
Batchworth Heath Herts 19 B7
Batcombe Dorset 8 D5
Batcombe Som 16 H3
Bate Heath Ches E 43 E9
Batford Herts 29 G8
Bath Bath 16 E4
Bathampton Bath 16 E4
Bathealton Som 7 D9
Batheaston Bath 16 E4
Bathford Bath 16 E4
Bathgate W Loth 69 D8
Bathley Notts 45 G11
Bathpool Corn 4 D3
Bathpool Som 8 B1
Bathville W Loth 69 D8
Batley W Yorks 51 G8
Batsford Glos 27 E8
Battersby N Yorks 59 F6
Battersea London 19 D9
Battisborough Cross Devon 5 G6
Battisford Suff 31 C7
Battisford Tye Suff 31 C7
Battle E Sus 12 E6
Battle Powys 25 E7
Battledown Glos 26 F6
Battlefield Shrops 33 D11
Battlesbridge Essex 20 B4
Battlesden C Beds 28 F6
Battlesea Green Suff 39 H8
Battleton Som 7 D8
Battram Leics 35 E10
Battramsley Hants 10 E2
Baughton Worcs 26 D5
Baughurst Hants 18 F2
Baulking Oxon 17 B10
Baumber Lincs 46 E6
Baunton Glos 17 A7
Baverstock Wilts 9 A9
Bawburgh Norf 39 E7
Bawdeswell Norf 39 C6
Bawdrip Som 15 H9
Bawdsey Suff 31 D10
Bawtry S Yorks 45 C10
Baxenden Lancs 50 G3
Baxterley Warks 35 F8
Baybridge Hants 10 B4

Bwl–Chu 117

Bwlchyddar Powys 33 C7
Bwlchygroes Pembs 23 C7
Byermoor T&W 63 H7
Byers Green Durham 58 C3
Byfield Northants 28 C2
Byfleet Sur 19 E7
Byford Hereford 25 D10
Bygrave Herts 29 E9
Byker T&W 63 G8
Bylchau Conwy 42 F2
Byley Ches W 43 F10
Bynea Carms 23 G10
Byrness Northumb 62 C3
Bythorn Cambs 37 H6
Byton Hereford 25 B10
Byworth W Sus 11 B8

C

Cabharstadh W Isles 91 E8
Cablea Perth 76 D2
Cabourne Lincs 46 B5
Cabrach Argyll 72 G3
Cabrach Moray 82 A5
Cabrich Highld 87 G8
Cabus Lancs 49 E4
Cackle Street E Sus 12 D3
Cadbury Devon 7 F8
Cadbury Barton Devon 6 E5
Cadder E Dunb 68 C5
Caddington C Beds 29 G7
Caddonfoot Borders 70 G3
Cade Street E Sus 12 D5
Cadeby Leics 35 E10
Cadeby S Yorks 45 B9
Cadeleigh Devon 7 F8
Cadgwith Corn 2 H6
Cadham Fife 76 G5
Cadishead Gtr Man 43 C10
Cadle Swansea 14 B2
Cadley Lancs 49 F5
Cadley Wilts 17 E9
Cadley Wilts 17 F9
Cadmore End Bucks 18 B4
Cadnam Hants 10 C1
Cadney N Lincs 46 B4
Cadole Flint 42 F5
Cadoxton V Glam 15 E7
Cadoxton-Juxta-Neath Neath 14 B3
Cadshaw Blackburn 50 H3
Cadzow S Lanark 68 E6
Caeathro Gwyn 41 D7
Caehopkin Powys 24 G5
Caenby Lincs 46 D4
Caenby Corner Lincs 46 D3
Caér-bryn Carms 23 E10
Caer Llan Mon 25 H11
Caerau Bridgend 14 B4
Caerau Cardiff 15 D7
Caerdeon Gwyn 32 D2
Caerdydd = Cardiff Cardiff 15 D7
Caerfarchell Pembs 22 D2
Caerffili = Caerphilly Caerph 15 C7
Caerfyrddin = Carmarthen Carms 23 D9
Caergeiliog Anglesey 40 C5
Caergwrle Flint 42 G6
Caergybi = Holyhead Anglesey 40 B4
Caerleon = Caerllion Newport 15 B9
Caerllion = Caerleon Newport 15 B9
Caernarfon Gwyn 40 D6
Caerphilly = Caerffili Caerph 15 C7
Caersws Powys 32 F6
Caerwedros Ceredig 23 A8
Caerwent Mon 15 B10
Caerwych Gwyn 41 G8
Caerwys Flint 42 E4
Caethle Gwyn 32 F2
Caim Anglesey 41 B8
Caio Carms 24 E3
Cairinis W Isles 84 B3
Cairisiadar W Isles 90 D5
Cairminis W Isles 90 J5
Cairnbaan Argyll 73 D7
Cairnbanno Ho. Aberds 89 D8
Cairnborrow Aberds 88 D4
Cairnbrogie Aberds 89 F8
Cairnbulg Castle Aberds 89 B10
Cairncross Angus 82 F6
Cairncross Borders 71 D7
Cairndow Argyll 74 F4
Cairness Aberds 89 B10
Cairneyhill Fife 69 B9
Cairnfield Ho. Moray 88 B4
Cairngaan Dumfries 54 F4
Cairngarroch Dumfries 54 E3
Cairnhill Aberds 89 E6
Cairnie Aberds 83 C10
Cairnie Aberds 88 D4
Cairnorrie Aberds 89 D8
Cairnpark Aberds 83 B10
Cairnryan Dumfries 54 C3
Cairnton Orkney 95 H4
Caister-on-Sea Norf 39 D11
Caistor Lincs 46 B5
Caistor St Edmund Norf 39 E8
Caistron Northumb 62 C5
Caitha Bowland Borders 70 F3
Calais Street Suff 30 E6
Calanais W Isles 90 D7
Calbost W Isles 91 F9
Calbourne IoW 10 F3
Calceby Lincs 47 E7
Calcot Row W Berks 18 D3
Calcott Kent 21 E8
Caldback Shetland 96 C8
Caldbeck Cumb 56 C5
Caldbergh N Yorks 58 H1
Caldecote Cambs 29 C10
Caldecote Cambs 37 G7
Caldecote Herts 29 E9
Caldecote Northants 28 C3
Caldecott Northants 28 B6
Caldecott Oxon 17 B11
Caldecott Rutland 36 F4
Calder Bridge Cumb 56 F2
Calder Hall Cumb 56 F2
Calder Mains Highld 94 E2
Calder Vale Lancs 49 E5
Calderbank N Lanark 68 D6
Calderbrook Gtr Man 50 H5
Caldercruix N Lanark 69 D7
Caldermill S Lanark 68 F5
Calderwood S Lanark 68 E5
Caldhame Angus 77 C7
Caldicot Mon 15 C10
Caldwell Derbys 35 D8
Caldwell N Yorks 58 E2
Caldy Mers 42 D5
Caledrhydiau Ceredig 23 A9
Calfsound Orkney 95 E6
Calgary Argyll 78 F6
Califer Moray 87 F13
California Falk 69 C8
California Norf 39 D11
Calke Derbys 35 C9
Callakille Highld 85 C11
Callaly Northumb 62 C6
Callander Stirling 75 G9
Callaughton Shrops 34 F2
Callestick Corn 3 D6
Calligarry Highld 85 H11
Callington Corn 4 E4
Callow Hereford 25 E11
Callow End Worcs 26 D5
Callow Hill Wilts 17 C7
Callow Hill Worcs 26 A4
Callows Grave Worcs 26 B2
Calmore Hants 10 C2
Calmsden Glos 27 H7
Calne Wilts 17 D7
Calow Derbys 45 E8
Calshot Hants 10 D3
Calstock Corn 4 E5
Calstone Wellington Wilts 17 E7
Calthorpe Norf 39 B7
Calthwaite Cumb 56 B6
Calton N Yorks 50 D5
Calton Staffs 44 G5
Calveley Ches E 43 G8
Calver Derbys 44 E6
Calver Hill Hereford 25 D10
Calverhall Shrops 34 B2
Calverleigh Devon 7 E8
Calverley W Yorks 51 F8
Calvert Bucks 28 F3
Calverton M Keynes 28 E4
Calverton Notts 45 H10
Calvine Perth 81 G10
Calvo Cumb 56 A3
Cam Glos 16 B4
Camas-luinie Highld 80 A1
Camasnacroise Highld 79 F11
Camastianavaig Highld 85 E10
Camasunary Highld 85 G10
Camault Muir Highld 87 G8
Camb Shetland 96 D7
Camber E Sus 13 E8
Camberley Sur 18 E5
Camberwell London 19 D10
Camblesforth N Yorks 52 G2
Cambo Northumb 62 E6
Cambois Northumb 63 E9
Camborne Corn 2 E5
Cambourne Cambs 29 C10
Cambridge Cambs 29 C11
Cambridge Glos 16 A4
Cambridge Town Southend 20 C6
Cambus Clack 69 A7
Cambusavie Farm Highld 87 B10
Cambusbarron Stirling 68 A6
Cambuskenneth Stirling 69 A7
Cambuslang S Lanark 68 D5
Cambusmore Lodge Highld 87 B10
Camden London 19 C9
Camelford Corn 4 C2
Camelsdale Sur 11 A7
Camerory Highld 87 H13
Camer's Green Worcs 26 E4
Camerton Bath 16 F3
Camerton Cumb 56 C2
Camerton E Yorks 53 G8
Camghouran Perth 75 B8
Cammachmore Aberds 83 D11
Cammeringham Lincs 46 D3
Camore Highld 87 B10
Camp Hill Warks 35 F9
Campbeltown Argyll 65 F8
Camperdown T&W 63 F8
Campmuir Perth 76 D5
Campsall S Yorks 45 A9
Campsey Ash Suff 31 C10
Campton C Beds 29 E8
Camptown Borders 62 B2
Camrose Pembs 22 D4
Camserney Perth 75 C11
Camster Highld 94 F4
Camuschoirk Highld 79 E10
Camuscross Highld 85 G11
Camusnagaul Highld 80 F2
Camusnagaul Highld 86 C3
Camusrory Highld 79 B11
Camusteel Highld 85 D12
Camusterrach Highld 85 D12
Camusvrachan Perth 75 C9
Canada Hants 10 C1
Canadia E Sus 12 E6
Canal Side S Yorks 45 A10
Candacraig Ho. Aberds 82 B5
Candlesby Lincs 47 F8
Candy Mill S Lanark 69 F9
Cane End Oxon 18 D3
Canewdon Essex 20 B5
Canford Bottom Dorset 9 D9
Canford Cliffs Poole 9 F9
Canford Magna Poole 9 E9
Canham's Green Suff 31 B7
Canholes Derbys 44 E4
Canisbay Highld 94 C5
Cann Dorset 9 B7
Cann Common Dorset 9 B7
Cannard's Grave Som 16 G3
Cannich Highld 86 H6
Cannington Som 15 H8
Cannock Staffs 34 E5
Cannock Wood Staffs 34 D6
Canon Bridge Hereford 25 D11
Canon Frome Hereford 26 D3
Canon Pyon Hereford 25 D11
Canonbie Dumfries 61 F9
Canons Ashby Northants 28 C2
Canonstown Corn 2 F4
Canterbury Kent 21 F8
Cantley Norf 39 E9
Cantley S Yorks 45 B10
Cantlop Shrops 33 E11
Canton Cardiff 15 D7
Cantraybruich Highld 87 G10
Cantraydoune Highld 87 G10
Cantraywood Highld 87 G10
Cantsfield Lancs 50 B2
Canvey Island Essex 20 C4
Canwick Lincs 46 F3
Canworthy Water Corn 4 B3
Caol Highld 80 F3
Caol Ila Argyll 64 A5
Caolas Argyll 78 G3
Caolas Scalpaigh W Isles 90 H7
Caolas Stocinis W Isles 90 H6
Capel Sur 19 G8
Capel Bangor Ceredig 32 G2
Capel Betws Lleucu Ceredig 24 C3
Capel Carmel Gwyn 40 H3
Capel Coch Anglesey 40 B6
Capel Curig Conwy 41 E9
Capel Cynon Ceredig 23 B8
Capel Dewi Carms 23 D9
Capel Dewi Ceredig 23 B9
Capel Dewi Ceredig 32 G2
Capel Garmon Conwy 41 E10
Capel-gwyn Anglesey 40 C5
Capel Gwyn Carms 23 D9
Capel Gwynfe Carms 24 F4
Capel Hendre Carms 23 E10
Capel Hermon Gwyn 32 C3
Capel Isaac Carms 23 D10
Capel Iwan Carms 23 C7
Capel le Ferne Kent 21 H9
Capel Llanilltern Cardiff 14 C6
Capel Mawr Anglesey 40 C6
Capel St Andrew Suff 31 D10
Capel St Mary Suff 31 E7
Capel Seion Ceredig 32 H2
Capel Tygwydd Ceredig 23 B7
Capel Uchaf Gwyn 40 F6
Capel-y-graig Gwyn 41 D7
Capelulo Conwy 41 C9
Capenhurst Ches W 42 E6
Capernwray Lancs 49 B5
Capheaton Northumb 62 E6
Cappercleuch Borders 61 A8
Capplegill Dumfries 61 C7
Capton Devon 5 F9
Caputh Perth 76 D3
Car Colston Notts 36 A3
Carbis Bay Corn 2 F4
Carbost Highld 85 D9
Carbost Highld 85 E8
Carbrook S Yorks 45 D7
Carbrooke Norf 38 E5
Carburton Notts 45 E10
Carcant Borders 70 E2
Carcary Angus 77 B9
Carclaze Corn 3 D9
Carcroft S Yorks 45 A9
Cardenden Fife 69 A11
Cardeston Shrops 33 D9
Cardiff = Caerdydd Cardiff 15 D7
Cardigan = Aberteifi Ceredig 22 B6
Cardington Bedford 29 D7
Cardington Shrops 33 F11
Cardinham Corn 4 E2
Cardonald Glasgow 68 D4
Cardow Moray 88 D1
Cardrona Borders 70 G2
Cardross Argyll 68 C2
Cardurnock Cumb 61 H7
Careby Lincs 36 D6
Careston Castle Angus 77 B8
Carew Pembs 22 F5
Carew Cheriton Pembs 22 F5
Carew Newton Pembs 22 F5
Carey Hereford 26 E2
Carfrae E Loth 70 D4
Cargenbridge Dumfries 60 F5
Cargill Perth 76 D4
Cargo Cumb 61 H9
Cargreen Corn 4 E5
Carham Northumb 71 G7
Carhampton Som 7 B9
Carharrack Corn 2 E6
Carie Perth 75 B9
Carie Perth 75 D9
Carines Corn 3 D6
Carisbrooke IoW 10 F3
Cark Cumb 49 B3
Carlabhagh W Isles 90 C7
Carland Cross Corn 3 D7
Carlby Lincs 37 D6
Carlecotes S Yorks 44 B5
Carlesmoor N Yorks 51 B7
Carleton Cumb 56 A6
Carleton Cumb 57 D7
Carleton Lancs 49 F3
Carleton N Yorks 50 E5
Carleton Forehoe Norf 39 E6
Carleton Rode Norf 39 F7
Carlin How Redcar 59 E8
Carlingcott Bath 16 F3
Carlisle Cumb 61 H10
Carlops Borders 69 E10
Carlton Bedford 28 C6
Carlton Cambs 30 C3
Carlton Leics 35 E9
Carlton N Yorks 51 A6
Carlton N Yorks 52 G2
Carlton N Yorks 58 E2
Carlton N Yorks 59 H7
Carlton Notts 36 A2
Carlton S Yorks 45 A7
Carlton Stockton 58 D4
Carlton Suff 31 B10
Carlton W Yorks 51 G9
Carlton Colville Suff 39 G11
Carlton Curlieu Leics 36 F2
Carlton Husthwaite N Yorks 51 B10
Carlton in Cleveland N Yorks 58 F6
Carlton in Lindrick Notts 45 D9
Carlton le Moorland Lincs 46 G3
Carlton Miniott N Yorks 51 A9
Carlton on Trent Notts 45 F11
Carlton Scroop Lincs 36 A5
Carluke S Lanark 69 E7
Carmarthen = Caerfyrddin Carms 23 D9
Carmel Anglesey 40 B5
Carmel Carms 23 E10
Carmel Flint 42 E4
Carmel Guern 11
Carmel Gwyn 40 E6
Carmont Aberds 83 E10
Carmunnock Glasgow 68 E5
Carmyle Glasgow 68 D5
Carmyllie Angus 77 C8
Carn-gorm Highld 80 A1
Carnaby E Yorks 53 C7
Carnach Highld 80 A2
Carnach Highld 86 B3
Carnach W Isles 90 H7
Carnachy Highld 93 D10
Càrnais W Isles 90 D5
Carnbee Fife 77 G8
Carnbo Perth 76 G3
Carnbrea Corn 2 E5
Carnduff S Lanark 68 F5
Carnduncan Argyll 64 B3
Carne Corn 3 F8
Carnforth Lancs 49 B4
Carnhedryn Pembs 22 D3
Carnhell Green Corn 2 F5
Carnkie Corn 2 F5
Carnkie Corn 2 F6
Carno Powys 32 F5
Carnoch Highld 86 F5
Carnoch Highld 86 H6
Carnock Fife 69 B9
Carnon Downs Corn 3 E6
Carnousie Aberds 89 C6
Carnoustie Angus 77 D8
Carnwath S Lanark 69 F8
Carnyorth Corn 2 F2
Carperby N Yorks 58 H1
Carpley Green N Yorks 57 H11
Carr S Yorks 45 C9
Carr Hill T&W 63 G8
Carradale Argyll 65 E9
Carragraich W Isles 90 H6
Carrbridge Highld 81 A11
Carrefour Selous Jersey 11
Carreg-wen Pembs 23 B7
Carreglefn Anglesey 40 B5
Carrick Argyll 73 E8
Carrick Fife 77 E7
Carrick Castle Argyll 73 D10
Carrick Ho. Orkney 95 E6
Carriden Falk 69 B9
Carrington Gtr Man 43 C10
Carrington Lincs 47 G7
Carrington Midloth 70 D2
Carrog Conwy 41 F9
Carrog Denb 33 A7
Carron Falk 69 B7
Carron Moray 88 D2
Carron Bridge Stirling 68 B6
Carronbridge Dumfries 60 D4
Carronshore Falk 69 B7
Carrshield Northumb 57 B10
Carrutherstown Dumfries 61 F7
Carrville Durham 58 B4
Carsaig Argyll 72 E6
Carsaig Argyll 79 J8
Carscreugh Dumfries 54 D5
Carse Gray Angus 77 B7
Carse Ho. Argyll 72 G6
Carsegowan Dumfries 55 D7
Carseriggan Dumfries 54 C6
Carsethorn Dumfries 60 H5
Carshalton London 19 E9
Carsington Derbys 44 G6
Carskiey Argyll 65 H7
Carsluith Dumfries 55 D7
Carsphairn Dumfries 67 G8
Carstairs S Lanark 69 F8
Carstairs Junction S Lanark 69 F8
Carswell Marsh Oxon 17 B10
Carter's Clay Hants 10 B2
Carterton Oxon 27 H9
Carterway Heads Northumb 58 A1
Carthew Corn 3 D9
Carthorpe N Yorks 51 A9
Cartington Northumb 62 C6
Cartland S Lanark 69 F7
Cartmel Cumb 49 B3
Cartmel Fell Cumb 56 H6
Carway Carms 23 F9
Cary Fitzpaine Som 8 B4
Cas-gwent = Chepstow Mon 15 B11
Cascob Powys 25 B9
Cashlie Perth 75 C7
Cashmoor Dorset 9 C8
Casnewydd = Newport Newport 15 C9
Cassey Compton Glos 27 G7
Cassington Oxon 27 G11
Cassop Durham 58 C4
Castell Denb 42 F4
Castell-Howell Ceredig 23 B9
Castell-Nedd = Neath Neath 14 B3
Castell Newydd Emlyn = Newcastle Emlyn Carms 23 B8
Castell-y-bwch Torf 15 B8
Castellau Rhondda 14 C6
Casterton Cumb 50 B2
Castle Acre Norf 38 D4
Castle Ashby Northants 28 C5
Castle Bolton N Yorks 58 G1
Castle Bromwich W Mid 35 G7
Castle Bytham Lincs 36 D5
Castle Caereinion Powys 33 E7
Castle Camps Cambs 30 D3
Castle Carrock Cumb 61 H11
Castle Cary Som 8 A5
Castle Combe Wilts 16 D5
Castle Donington Leics 35 C10
Castle Douglas Dumfries 55 C10
Castle Eaton Swindon 17 B8
Castle Eden Durham 58 C5
Castle Forbes Aberds 83 B8
Castle Frome Hereford 26 D3
Castle Green Sur 18 E6
Castle Gresley Derbys 35 D8
Castle Heaton Northumb 71 F8
Castle Hedingham Essex 30 E4
Castle Hill Kent 12 B5
Castle Huntly Perth 76 E6
Castle Kennedy Dumfries 54 D4
Castle O'er Dumfries 61 D8
Castle Pulverbatch Shrops 33 E10
Castle Rising Norf 38 C2
Castle Stuart Highld 87 G10
Castlebay = Bagh a Chaisteil W Isles 84 J1
Castlebythe Pembs 22 D5
Castlecary N Lanark 68 C6
Castlecraig Highld 87 E11
Castlefairn Dumfries 60 E3
Castleford W Yorks 51 G10
Castlehill Borders 69 G11
Castlehill Highld 94 D3
Castlehill W Dunb 68 C2
Castlemaddy Dumfries 67 H8
Castlemartin Pembs 22 G4
Castlemilk Dumfries 61 F7
Castlemilk Glasgow 68 E5
Castlemorris Pembs 22 C4
Castlemorton Worcs 26 E4
Castleside Durham 58 B1
Castlethorpe M Keynes 28 D5
Castleton Angus 76 C6
Castleton Argyll 73 E7
Castleton Derbys 44 D5
Castleton Gtr Man 44 A2
Castleton N Yorks 59 F7
Castleton Newport 15 C8
Castletown Ches W 43 G7
Castletown Highld 87 G10
Castletown Highld 94 D3
Castletown IoM 48 F2
Castletown T&W 63 H9
Castleweary Borders 61 C10
Castley N Yorks 51 E8
Caston Norf 38 F5
Castor Pboro 37 F7
Catacol N Ayrs 66 B2
Catbrain S Glos 16 C2
Catbrook Mon 15 A11
Catchall Corn 2 G3
Catchems Corner W Mid 35 H8
Catchgate Durham 58 A2
Catcleugh Northumb 62 C3
Catcliffe S Yorks 45 D8
Catcott Som 15 H9
Caterham Sur 19 F10
Catfield Norf 39 C9
Catfirth Shetland 96 H6
Catford London 19 D10
Catforth Lancs 49 F4
Cathays Cardiff 15 D7
Cathcart Glasgow 68 D4
Cathedine Powys 25 F8
Catherington Hants 10 C5
Catherton Shrops 34 H2
Catlodge Highld 81 D8
Catlowdy Cumb 61 F10
Catmore W Berks 17 C11
Caton Lancs 49 C5
Caton Green Lancs 49 C5
Catrine E Ayrs 67 D8
Cat's Ash Newport 15 B9
Catsfield E Sus 12 E6
Catshill Worcs 26 A6
Cattal N Yorks 51 D10
Cattawade Suff 31 E8
Catterall Lancs 49 E4
Catterick N Yorks 58 G3
Catterick Bridge N Yorks 58 G3
Catterick Garrison N Yorks 58 G2
Catterlen Cumb 57 C6
Catterline Aberds 83 F10
Catterton N Yorks 51 E11
Catthorpe Leics 36 H1
Cattistock Dorset 8 E4
Catton N Yorks 51 B9
Catton Northumb 62 H4
Catwick E Yorks 53 E7
Catworth Cambs 29 A7
Caudlesprings Norf 38 E5
Caulcott Oxon 28 F2
Cauldcots Angus 77 C9
Cauldhame Stirling 68 A5
Cauldmill Borders 61 B11
Cauldon Staffs 44 H4
Caulkerbush Dumfries 60 H5
Caulside Dumfries 61 E10
Caunsall Worcs 34 G4
Caunton Notts 45 G11
Causeway End Dumfries 55 C7
Causeway Foot W Yorks 51 F6
Causeway-head Stirling 75 H10
Causewayend S Lanark 69 G9
Causewayhead Cumb 56 A3
Causey Park Bridge Northumb 63 D7
Causeyend Aberds 83 B11
Cautley Cumb 57 G8
Cavendish Suff 30 D5
Cavendish Bridge Leics 35 C10
Cavenham Suff 30 B4
Caversfield Oxon 28 F2
Caversham Reading 18 D4
Caverswall Staffs 34 A5
Cavil E Yorks 52 F3
Cawdor Highld 87 F11
Cawkwell Lincs 46 E6
Cawood N Yorks 52 F1
Cawsand Corn 4 F5
Cawston Norf 39 C7
Cawthorne S Yorks 44 B6
Cawthorpe Lincs 37 C6
Cawton N Yorks 52 B2
Caxton Cambs 29 C10
Caynham Shrops 26 A2
Caythorpe Lincs 46 H3
Caythorpe Notts 45 H10
Cayton N Yorks 53 A6
Ceann a Bhaigh W Isles 84 B2
Ceann a Deas Loch Baghasdail W Isles 84 G2
Ceann Shiphoirt W Isles 91 F7
Ceann Tarabhaigh W Isles 90 F7
Ceannacroc Lodge Highld 80 B4
Cearsiadair W Isles 91 E8
Cefn Berain Conwy 42 F2
Cefn-brith Conwy 42 G2
Cefn Canol Powys 33 B8
Cefn-coch Conwy 41 D10
Cefn Coch Powys 33 C7
Cefn-coed-y-cymmer M Tydf 25 H7
Cefn Cribbwr Bridgend 14 C4
Cefn Cross Bridgend 14 C4
Cefn-ddwysarn Gwyn 32 B5
Cefn Einion Shrops 33 G8
Cefn-gorwydd Powys 24 D6
Cefn-mawr Wrex 33 A8
Cefn-y-bedd Flint 42 G6
Cefn-y-pant Carms 22 D6
Cefneithin Carms 23 E10
Cei-bach Ceredig 23 A9
Ceinewydd = New Quay Ceredig 23 A8
Ceint Anglesey 40 C6
Cellan Ceredig 24 D3
Cellarhead Staffs 44 H3
Cemaes Anglesey 40 A5
Cemmaes Powys 32 E4
Cemmaes Road Powys 32 E4
Cenarth Carms 23 B7
Cenin Gwyn 40 F6
Central Invclyd 73 F11
Ceos W Isles 91 E8
Ceres Fife 77 F7
Cerne Abbas Dorset 8 D5
Cerney Wick Glos 17 B7
Cerrigceinwen Anglesey 40 C6
Cerrigydrudion Conwy 42 H2
Cessford Borders 62 A3
Ceunant Gwyn 41 D7
Chaceley Glos 26 E5
Chacewater Corn 3 E6
Chackmore Bucks 28 E3
Chacombe Northants 27 D11
Chad Valley W Mid 34 G6
Chadderton Gtr Man 44 B3
Chadderton Fold Gtr Man 44 B2
Chaddesden Derby 35 B9
Chaddesley Corbett Worcs 26 A5
Chaddleworth W Berks 17 D11
Chadlington Oxon 27 F10
Chadshunt Warks 27 C10
Chadwell Leics 36 C3
Chadwell St Mary Thurrock 20 D3
Chadwick End W Mid 27 A9
Chadwick Green Mers 43 C8
Chaffcombe Som 8 C2
Chagford Devon 5 C8
Chailey E Sus 12 E2
Chain Bridge Lincs 37 A9
Chainbridge Cambs 37 E10
Chainhurst Kent 20 G4
Chalbury Dorset 9 D9
Chalbury Common Dorset 9 D9
Chaldon Sur 19 F10
Chaldon Herring Dorset 9 F6
Chale IoW 10 G3
Chale Green IoW 10 G3
Chalfont Common Bucks 19 B7
Chalfont St Giles Bucks 18 B6
Chalfont St Peter Bucks 19 B7
Chalford Glos 16 A5
Chalgrove Oxon 18 B3
Chalk Kent 20 D3
Challacombe Devon 6 B5
Challoch Dumfries 54 C6
Challock Kent 21 F7
Chalton C Beds 29 F7
Chalton Hants 10 C6
Chalvington E Sus 12 F4
Chancery Ceredig 32 H1
Chandler's Ford Hants 10 B3
Channel Tunnel Kent 21 H8
Channerwick Shetland 96 L6
Chantry Som 16 G4
Chantry Suff 31 D8
Chapel Fife 69 A11
Chapel Allerton Som 15 F10
Chapel Allerton W Yorks 51 F9
Chapel Amble Corn 3 B8
Chapel Brampton Northants 28 B4
Chapel Chorlton Staffs 34 B4
Chapel-en-le-Frith Derbys 44 D4
Chapel End Warks 35 F9
Chapel Green Warks 27 B11
Chapel Green Warks 35 G8
Chapel Haddlesey N Yorks 52 G1
Chapel Head Cambs 37 G9
Chapel Hill Aberds 89 E10
Chapel Hill Lincs 46 G6
Chapel Hill Mon 15 B11
Chapel Hill N Yorks 51 E9
Chapel Lawn Shrops 33 H9
Chapel-le-Dale N Yorks 50 B3
Chapel Milton Derbys 44 D4
Chapel of Garioch Aberds 83 A9
Chapel Row W Berks 18 E2
Chapel St Leonards Lincs 47 E9
Chapel Stile Cumb 56 F5
Chapelgate Lincs 37 C10
Chapelhall N Lanark 68 D6
Chapelhill Dumfries 60 D6
Chapelhill Highld 87 D11
Chapelhill N Ayrs 66 B5
Chapelhill Perth 76 D3
Chapelhill Perth 76 E5
Chapelknowe Dumfries 61 F9
Chapelton Angus 77 C9
Chapelton Devon 6 D4
Chapelton Highld 81 B11
Chapelton S Lanark 68 F5
Chapeltown Blackburn 50 H3
Chapeltown Moray 82 A4
Chapeltown S Yorks 45 C7
Chapmans Well Devon 6 G2
Chapmanslade Wilts 16 G5
Chapmore End Herts 29 G10
Chappel Essex 30 F5
Chard Som 8 D2
Chardstock Devon 8 D2
Charfield S Glos 16 B4
Charford Worcs 26 B6
Charing Kent 20 G6
Charing Cross Dorset 9 C10
Charing Heath Kent 20 G6
Charingworth Glos 27 E9
Charlbury Oxon 27 G10
Charlcombe Bath 16 E4
Charlecote Warks 27 C9
Charles Devon 6 C5
Charles Tye Suff 31 C7
Charlesfield Dumfries 61 G7
Charleston Angus 76 C6
Charleston Renfs 68 D3
Charlestown Aberdeen 83 C11
Charlestown Corn 3 D9
Charlestown Derbys 44 C4
Charlestown Dorset 8 G5
Charlestown Fife 69 B9
Charlestown Gtr Man 44 B2
Charlestown Highld 85 A13
Charlestown Highld 87 G9
Charlestown W Yorks 50 G5
Charlestown of Aberlour Moray 88 D2
Charlesworth Derbys 44 C4
Charleton Devon 5 G8
Charlton Hants 17 G10
Charlton Herts 29 F8
Charlton London 19 D11
Charlton Northants 28 E2
Charlton Northumb 62 E4
Charlton Som 16 F3
Charlton Telford 34 D1
Charlton W Sus 11 C7
Charlton Wilts 9 B8
Charlton Wilts 16 C6
Charlton Wilts 17 F8
Charlton Worcs 27 D7
Charlton Abbots Glos 27 F7
Charlton Adam Som 8 B4
Charlton-All-Saints Wilts 9 B10
Charlton Down Dorset 8 E5
Charlton Horethorne Som 8 B5
Charlton Kings Glos 26 F6
Charlton Mackerell Som 8 B4
Charlton Marshall Dorset 9 D7
Charlton Musgrove Som 8 B6
Charlton on Otmoor Oxon 28 G2
Charltons Redcar 59 E7
Charlwood Sur 19 G9
Charlynch Som 7 C11
Charminster Dorset 8 E5
Charmouth Dorset 8 E2
Charndon Bucks 28 F3
Charney Bassett Oxon 17 B10
Charnock Richard Lancs 50 H1
Charsfield Suff 31 C9
Chart Corner Kent 20 F4
Chart Sutton Kent 20 G5
Charter Alley Hants 18 F2
Charterhouse Som 15 F10
Charterville Allotments Oxon 27 G10
Chartham Kent 21 F8
Chartham Hatch Kent 21 F8
Chartridge Bucks 18 A6
Charvil Wokingham 18 D4
Charwelton Northants 28 C2
Chasetown Staffs 34 E6
Chastleton Oxon 27 F9
Chasty Devon 6 F2
Chatburn Lancs 50 E3
Chatcull Staffs 34 B3
Chatham Medway 20 E4
Chathill Northumb 71 H10
Chattenden Medway 20 D4
Chatteris Cambs 37 G9
Chattisham Suff 31 D7
Chatto Borders 62 B3
Chatton Northumb 71 H9
Chawleigh Devon 6 E6
Chawley Oxon 17 A11
Chawston Bedford 29 C8
Chawton Hants 18 H4
Cheadle Gtr Man 44 D2
Cheadle Staffs 34 A6
Cheadle Heath Gtr Man 44 D2
Cheadle Hulme Gtr Man 44 D2
Cheam London 19 E9
Cheapside Sur 19 F7
Chearsley Bucks 28 G4
Chebsey Staffs 34 C4
Checkendon Oxon 18 C3
Checkley Ches E 43 H10
Checkley Hereford 26 E2
Checkley Staffs 34 B6
Chedburgh Suff 30 C4
Cheddar Som 15 F10
Cheddington Bucks 28 G6
Cheddleton Staffs 44 G3
Cheddon Fitzpaine Som 8 B1
Chedglow Wilts 16 B6
Chedgrave Norf 39 F9
Chedington Dorset 8 D3
Chediston Suff 39 H9
Chedworth Glos 27 G7
Chedzoy Som 15 H9
Cheeklaw Borders 70 E6
Cheeseman's Green Kent 13 C9
Cheglinch Devon 6 B4
Cheldon Devon 7 E6
Chelford Ches E 44 E2
Chell Heath Stoke 44 G2
Chellaston Derby 35 B9
Chellington Bedford 28 C6
Chelmarsh Shrops 34 G3
Chelmer Village Essex 30 H4
Chelmondiston Suff 31 E9
Chelmorton Derbys 44 F5
Chelmsford Essex 30 H4
Chelsea London 19 D9
Chelsfield London 19 E11
Chelsworth Suff 30 D6
Cheltenham Glos 26 F6
Chelveston Northants 28 B6
Chelvey N Som 15 E10
Chelwood Bath 16 E3
Chelwood Common E Sus 12 D3
Chelwood Gate E Sus 12 D3
Chelworth Wilts 16 B6
Chelworth Green Wilts 17 B7
Chemistry Shrops 33 A11
Chenies Bucks 19 B7
Cheny Longville Shrops 33 G10
Chepstow = Cas-gwent Mon 15 B11
Chequerfield W Yorks 51 G10
Cherhill Wilts 17 D7
Cherington Glos 16 B6
Cherington Warks 27 E9
Cheriton Devon 7 B6
Cheriton Hants 10 B4
Cheriton Kent 21 H8
Cheriton Swansea 23 G9
Cheriton Bishop Devon 7 G6
Cheriton Fitzpaine Devon 7 F7
Cheriton or Stackpole Elidor Pembs 22 G4
Cherrington Telford 34 C2
Cherry Burton E Yorks 52 E5
Cherry Hinton Cambs 29 C11
Cherry Orchard Worcs 26 C5
Cherry Willingham Lincs 46 E4
Cherrybank Perth 76 E4
Chertsey Sur 19 E7
Cheselbourne Dorset 9 E6
Chesham Bucks 18 A6
Chesham Bois Bucks 18 B6
Cheshunt Herts 19 A10
Cheslyn Hay Staffs 34 E5
Chessington London 19 E8
Chester Ches W 43 F7
Chester-Le-Street Durham 58 A3
Chester Moor Durham 58 B3
Chesterblade Som 16 G3
Chesterfield Derbys 45 E7
Chesters Borders 62 A2
Chesters Borders 62 B2
Chesterton Cambs 29 B11
Chesterton Cambs 37 F7
Chesterton Glos 17 A7
Chesterton Oxon 28 F2
Chesterton Shrops 34 F3
Chesterton Staffs 44 H2
Chesterton Warks 27 C10
Chesterwood Northumb 62 G4
Chestfield Kent 21 E8
Cheston Devon 5 F7
Cheswardine Shrops 34 C3
Cheswick Northumb 71 F9
Chetnole Dorset 8 D5
Chettiscombe Devon 7 E8
Chettisham Cambs 37 G11
Chettle Dorset 9 C8
Chetton Shrops 34 F2
Chetwode Bucks 28 F3
Chetwynd Aston Telford 34 D3
Cheveley Cambs 30 B3
Chevening Kent 19 F11
Chevington Suff 30 C4
Chevithorne Devon 7 E8
Chew Magna Bath 16 E2
Chew Stoke Bath 16 E2
Chewton Keynsham Bath 16 E3
Chewton Mendip Som 16 F2
Chicheley M Keynes 28 D6
Chichester W Sus 11 D7
Chickerell Dorset 8 F5
Chicklade Wilts 9 A8
Chicksgrove Wilts 9 A8
Chidden Hants 10 C5
Chiddingfold Sur 18 H6
Chiddingly E Sus 12 E4
Chiddingstone Kent 19 G11
Chiddingstone Causeway Kent 20 G2
Chiddingstone Hoath Kent 12 B3
Chideock Dorset 8 E3
Chidham W Sus 11 D6
Chidswell W Yorks 51 G8
Chieveley W Berks 17 D11
Chignall St James Essex 30 H3
Chignall Smealy Essex 30 G3
Chigwell Essex 19 B11
Chigwell Row Essex 19 B11
Chilbolton Hants 17 H10
Chilcomb Hants 10 B4
Chilcombe Dorset 8 E4
Chilcompton Som 16 F3
Chilcote Leics 35 D8
Child Okeford Dorset 9 C7
Childer Thornton Ches W 42 E6
Childrey Oxon 17 C10
Child's Ercall Shrops 34 C2
Childswickham Worcs 27 E7
Childwall Mers 43 D7
Childwick Green Herts 29 G8
Chilfrome Dorset 8 E4
Chilgrove W Sus 11 C7
Chilham Kent 21 F7
Chilhampton Wilts 9 A9
Chilla Devon 6 F3
Chillaton Devon 4 C5
Chillenden Kent 21 F9
Chillerton IoW 10 F3
Chillesford Suff 31 C10
Chillingham Northumb 71 H9
Chillington Devon 5 G8
Chillington Som 8 C2
Chilmark Wilts 9 A8
Chilson Oxon 27 G10
Chilsworthy Corn 4 D5
Chilsworthy Devon 6 F2
Chilthorne Domer Som 8 C4
Chiltington E Sus 12 E2
Chilton Bucks 28 G3
Chilton Durham 58 D3
Chilton Oxon 17 C11
Chilton Cantelo Som 8 B4
Chilton Foliat Wilts 17 D10
Chilton Lane Durham 58 C4
Chilton Polden Som 15 H9
Chilton Street Suff 30 D4
Chilton Trinity Som 15 H8
Chilvers Coton Warks 35 F9
Chilwell Notts 35 B11
Chilworth Hants 10 C3
Chilworth Sur 19 G7
Chimney Oxon 17 A10
Chineham Hants 18 F3
Chingford London 19 B10
Chinley Derbys 44 D4
Chinley Head Derbys 44 D4
Chinnor Oxon 18 A4
Chipnall Shrops 34 B3
Chippenhall Green Suff 39 H8
Chippenham Cambs 30 B3
Chippenham Wilts 16 D6
Chipperfield Herts 19 A7
Chipping Herts 29 E10
Chipping Lancs 50 E2
Chipping Campden Glos 27 E8
Chipping Hill Essex 30 G5
Chipping Norton Oxon 27 F10
Chipping Ongar Essex 20 A2
Chipping Sodbury S Glos 16 C4
Chipping Warden Northants 27 D11
Chipstable Som 7 D9
Chipstead Kent 19 F11
Chipstead Sur 19 F9
Chirbury Shrops 33 F8
Chirk = Y Waun Wrex 33 B8
Chirk Bank Shrops 33 B8
Chirmorrie S Ayrs 54 B5
Chirnside Borders 71 E7
Chirnsidebridge Borders 71 E7
Chirton Wilts 17 F7
Chisbury Wilts 17 E9
Chiselborough Som 8 C3
Chiseldon Swindon 17 D8
Chiserley W Yorks 50 G6
Chislehampton Oxon 18 B2
Chislehurst London 19 D11
Chislet Kent 21 E9
Chiswell Green Herts 19 A8
Chiswick London 19 D9
Chiswick End Cambs 29 D10
Chisworth Derbys 44 C3
Chithurst W Sus 11 B7
Chittering Cambs 29 A11
Chitterne Wilts 16 G6
Chittlehamholt Devon 6 D5
Chittlehampton Devon 6 D5
Chittoe Wilts 16 E6
Chivenor Devon 6 C4
Chobham Sur 18 E6
Choicelee Borders 70 E6
Cholderton Wilts 17 G9
Cholesbury Bucks 28 H6
Chollerford Northumb 62 F5
Chollerton Northumb 62 F5
Cholmondeston Ches E 43 F9
Cholsey Oxon 18 C2
Cholstrey Hereford 25 C11
Chop Gate N Yorks 59 G6
Choppington Northumb 63 E8
Chopwell T&W 63 H7
Chorley Ches E 43 G8
Chorley Lancs 50 H1
Chorley Shrops 34 G2
Chorley Staffs 35 D6
Chorleywood Herts 19 B7
Chorlton cum Hardy Gtr Man 44 C2
Chorlton Lane Ches W 43 H7
Choulton Shrops 33 G9
Chowdene T&W 63 H8
Chowley Ches W 43 G7
Chrishall Essex 29 E11
Christchurch Cambs 37 F10
Christchurch Dorset 9 E10
Christchurch Glos 26 G2
Christchurch Newport 15 C9
Christian Malford Wilts 16 D6
Christleton Ches W 43 F7
Christmas Common Oxon 18 B4
Christon N Som 15 F9
Christon Bank Northumb 63 A8
Christow Devon 5 C9
Chryston N Lanark 68 C5
Chudleigh Devon 5 D9
Chudleigh Knighton Devon 5 D9
Chulmleigh Devon 6 E5
Chunal Derbys 44 C4
Church Lancs 50 G3
Church Aston Telford 34 D3
Church Brampton Northants 28 B4
Church Broughton Derbys 35 B8
Church Crookham Hants 18 F5
Church Eaton Staffs 34 D4
Church End C Beds 28 E6
Church End C Beds 28 F6
Church End C Beds 29 E8
Church End Cambs 37 E9
Church End Cambs 37 G8
Church End E Yorks 53 D6
Church End Essex 30 D2
Church End Essex 30 F4
Church End Hants 18 F3
Church End Lincs 37 B8
Church End Warks 35 F8
Church End Warks 35 F8
Church End Wilts 17 D7
Church Enstone Oxon 27 F10
Church Fenton N Yorks 51 F11
Church Green Devon 7 G10
Church Green Norf 39 F6
Church Gresley Derbys 35 D8
Church Hanborough Oxon 27 G11
Church Hill Ches W 43 F9
Church Houses N Yorks 59 G7
Church Knowle Dorset 9 F8
Church Laneham Notts 46 E2
Church Langton Leics 36 F3
Church Lawford Warks 35 H10
Church Lawton Ches E 44 G2
Church Leigh Staffs 34 B6
Church Lench Worcs 27 C7
Church Mayfield Staffs 35 A7
Church Minshull Ches E 43 F9
Church Norton W Sus 11 E7
Church Preen Shrops 33 F11
Church Pulverbatch Shrops 33 E10
Church Stoke Powys 33 F8
Church Stowe Northants 28 C3
Church Street Kent 20 D4
Church Stretton Shrops 33 F10
Church Town N Lincs 45 B11
Church Town Sur 19 F10
Church Village Rhondda 14 C6
Church Warsop Notts 45 F9
Churcham Glos 26 G4
Churchbank Shrops 33 H8
Churchbridge Staffs 34 E5
Churchdown Glos 26 G5
Churchend Essex 21 B7
Churchend Essex 30 F3
Churchend S Glos 16 B4
Churchfield W Mid 34 F6
Churchgate Street Essex 29 G11
Churchill Devon 6 B4
Churchill Devon 8 D2

Churchill N Som 15 F10
Churchill Oxon 27 F9
Churchill Worcs 26 C6
Churchill Worcs 34 H4
Churchinford Som 7 E11
Churchover Warks 35 G11
Churchstanton Som 7 E10
Churchstow Devon 5 G8
Churchtown Derbys 44 F6
Churchtown IoM 48 C4
Churchtown Lancs 49 E4
Churchtown Mers 49 H3
Churnsike Lodge Northumb 62 F2
Churston Ferrers Torbay 5 F10
Churt Sur 18 H5
Churton Ches W 43 G7
Churwell W Yorks 51 G8
Chute Standen Wilts 17 F10
Chwilog Gwyn 40 G6
Chyandour Corn 2 F3
Cilan Uchaf Gwyn 40 H4
Cilcain Flint 42 F4
Cilcennin Ceredig 24 B2
Cilfor Gwyn 41 G8
Cilfrew Neath 14 A3
Cilfynydd Rhondda 14 B6
Cilgerran Pembs 22 B6
Cilgwyn Carms 24 F4
Cilgwyn Gwyn 40 E6
Cilgwyn Pembs 22 C5
Ciliau Aeron Ceredig 23 A9
Cill Donnain W Isles 84 F2
Cille Bhrighde W Isles 84 G2
Cille Pheadair W Isles 84 G2
Cilmery Powys 25 C7
Cilsan Carms 23 D10
Ciltalgarth Gwyn 41 F10
Cilwendeg Pembs 23 C7
Cilybebyll Neath 14 A3
Cilycwm Carms 24 E4
Cimla Neath 14 B3
Cinderford Glos 26 G3
Cippyn Pembs 22 B6
Circebost W Isles 90 D6
Cirencester Glos 17 A7
Ciribhig W Isles 90 C6
City London 19 C10
City Powys 33 G8
City Dulas Anglesey 40 B6
Clachaig Argyll 73 E10
Clachan Argyll 72 B6
Clachan Argyll 72 H6
Clachan Argyll 74 F4
Clachan Argyll 79 G11
Clachan Highld 85 E10
Clachan W Isles 84 D2
Clachan na Luib W Isles 84 B3
Clachan of Campsie E Dunb 68 C5
Clachan of Glendaruel Argyll 73 E8
Clachan-Seil Argyll 72 B6
Clachan Strachur Argyll 73 C9
Clachaneasy Dumfries 54 B6
Clachanmore Dumfries 54 E3
Clachbreck Argyll 72 F6
Clachnabrain Angus 82 G5
Clachtoll Highld 92 G3
Clackmannan Clack 69 A8
Clacton-on-Sea Essex 31 G8
Cladach Chireboist W Isles 84 B2
Claddach-knockline W Isles 84 B2
Cladich Argyll 74 E3
Claggan Highld 79 G9
Claggan Highld 80 F3
Claigan Highld 84 C7
Claines Worcs 26 C5
Clandown Bath 16 F3
Clanfield Hants 10 C5
Clanfield Oxon 17 A9
Clanville Hants 17 G10
Claonaig Argyll 73 H7
Claonel Highld 93 J8
Clap Hill Kent 13 C9
Clapgate Dorset 9 D9
Clapgate Herts 29 F11
Clapham Bedford 29 C7
Clapham London 19 D9
Clapham N Yorks 50 C3
Clapham W Sus 11 D9
Clappers Borders 71 E8
Clappersgate Cumb 56 F5
Clapton Som 8 D3
Clapton-in-Gordano N Som 15 D10
Clapton-on-the-Hill Glos 27 G8
Clapworthy Devon 6 D5
Clara Vale T&W 63 G7
Clarach Ceredig 32 G2
Clarbeston Pembs 22 D5
Clarbeston Road Pembs 22 D5
Clarborough Notts 45 D11
Clardon Highld 94 D3
Clare Suff 30 D4
Clarebrand Dumfries 55 C10
Clarencefield Dumfries 60 G6
Clarilaw Borders 61 B11
Clark's Green Sur 19 H8
Clarkston E Renf 68 E4
Clashandorran Highld 87 G8
Clashcoig Highld 87 B9
Clashindarroch Aberds 88 E4
Clashmore Highld 87 C10
Clashmore Highld 92 F3
Clashnessie Highld 92 F3
Clashnoir Moray 82 A4
Clate Shetland 96 G7
Clathy Perth 76 F2
Clatt Aberds 83 A7
Clatter Powys 32 F5
Clatterford IoW 10 F3
Clatterin Bridge Aberds 83 F8
Clatworthy Som 7 C9
Claughton Lancs 49 E5
Claughton Lancs 50 C1
Claughton Mers 42 D6
Claverdon Warks 27 B8
Claverham N Som 15 E10
Clavering Essex 29 E11
Claverley Shrops 34 F3
Claverton Bath 16 E4
Clawdd-newydd Denb 42 G3
Clawthorpe Cumb 49 B5
Clawton Devon 6 G2
Claxby Lincs 46 C5
Claxby Lincs 47 E8
Claxton NYorks 52 C2
Claxton Norf 39 E9
Clay Common Suff 39 G10
Clay Coton Northants 36 H1
Clay Cross Derbys 45 F7
Clay Hill W Berks 18 D2
Clay Lake Lincs 37 C8
Claybokie Aberds 82 D2
Claybrooke Magna Leics 35 G10
Claybrooke Parva Leics 35 G10
Claydon Oxon 27 C11
Claydon Suff 31 C8
Claygate Dumfries 61 F9
Claygate Kent 12 B6
Claygate Sur 19 E8
Claygate Cross Kent 20 F3
Clayhanger Devon 7 D9
Clayhanger W Mid 34 E6
Clayhidon Devon 7 E10
Clayhill E Sus 13 D7
Clayhill Hants 10 D2
Clayock Highld 94 E3
Claypole Lincs 46 H2
Clayton S Yorks 45 B8
Clayton Staffs 34 A4
Clayton W Sus 12 E1
Clayton W Yorks 51 F7
Clayton Green Lancs 50 G1
Clayton-le-Moors Lancs 50 F3
Clayton-le-Woods Lancs 50 G1
Clayton West W Yorks 44 A6
Clayworth Notts 45 D11
Cleadale Highld 78 C7
Cleadon T&W 63 G9
Clearbrook Devon 4 E6
Clearwell Glos 26 H2
Cleasby N Yorks 58 E3
Cleat Orkney 95 K5
Cleatlam Durham 58 E2
Cleator Cumb 56 E2
Cleator Moor Cumb 56 E2
Clebrig Highld 93 F8
Cleckheaton W Yorks 51 G7
Clee St Margaret Shrops 34 G1
Cleedownton Shrops 34 G1
Cleehill Shrops 34 H1
Cleethorpes NE Lincs 47 B7
Cleeton St Mary Shrops 34 H2
Cleeve N Som 15 E10
Cleeve Hill Glos 26 F6
Cleeve Prior Worcs 27 D7
Clegyrnant Powys 32 E5
Clehonger Hereford 25 E11
Cleish Perth 76 H3
Cleland N Lanark 69 E7
Clench Common Wilts 17 E8
Clenchwarton Norf 38 C1
Clent Worcs 34 H5
Cleobury Mortimer Shrops 34 H2
Cleobury North Shrops 34 G2
Cleongart Argyll 65 E7
Clephanton Highld 87 F11
Clerklands Borders 61 A11
Clestrain Orkney 95 H4
Cleuch Head Borders 61 B11
Cleughbrae Dumfries 60 F6
Clevancy Wilts 17 D7
Clevedon N Som 15 D10
Cleveley Oxon 27 F10
Cleveleys Lancs 49 E3
Cleverton Wilts 16 C6
Clevis Bridgend 14 D4
Clewer Som 15 F10
Cley next the Sea Norf 38 A6
Cliaid W Isles 84 H1
Cliasmol W Isles 90 G5
Cliburn Cumb 57 D7
Click Mill Orkney 95 F4
Cliddesden Hants 18 G3
Cliff End E Sus 13 E7
Cliffburn Angus 77 C9
Cliffe Medway 20 D4
Cliffe N Yorks 52 F2
Cliffe Woods Medway 20 D4
Clifford Hereford 25 D9
Clifford W Yorks 51 E10
Clifford Chambers Warks 27 C8
Clifford's Mesne Glos 26 F4
Cliffsend Kent 21 E10
Clifton Bristol 16 D2
Clifton C Beds 29 E8
Clifton Cumb 57 D7
Clifton Derbys 35 A7
Clifton Lancs 49 F4
Clifton N Yorks 51 E7
Clifton Northumb 63 E8
Clifton Nottingham 36 B1
Clifton Oxon 27 E11
Clifton S Yorks 45 C9
Clifton Stirling 74 D6
Clifton Worcs 26 D5
Clifton York 52 D1
Clifton Campville Staffs 35 D8
Clifton Green Gtr Man 43 B10
Clifton Hampden Oxon 18 B2
Clifton Reynes M Keynes 28 C6
Clifton upon Dunsmore Warks 35 H11
Clifton upon Teme Worcs 26 B4
Cliftoncote Borders 62 A4
Cliftonville Kent 21 D10
Climaen gwyn Neath 24 H4
Climping W Sus 11 D9
Climpy S Lanark 69 E8
Clink Som 16 G4
Clint N Yorks 51 D8
Clint Green Norf 38 D6
Clintmains Borders 70 G5
Cliobh W Isles 90 D5
Clippesby Norf 39 D10
Clipsham Rutland 36 D5
Clipston Northants 36 G3
Clipstone Notts 45 F9
Clitheroe Lancs 50 E3
Cliuthar W Isles 90 H6
Clive Shrops 33 C11
Clivocast Shetland 96 C8
Clixby Lincs 46 B5
Clocaenog Denb 42 G3
Clochan Moray 88 B4
Clock Face Mers 43 C8
Clockmill Borders 70 E6
Cloddiau Powys 33 E8
Clodock Hereford 25 F10
Clola Aberds 89 D10
Clophill C Beds 29 E7
Clopton Northants 37 G6
Clopton Suff 31 C9
Clopton Corner Suff 31 C9
Clopton Green Suff 30 C4
Close Clark IoM 48 E2
Closeburn Dumfries 60 D4
Closworth Som 8 C4
Clothall Herts 29 E9
Clotton Ches W 43 F8
Clough Foot W Yorks 50 G5
Cloughton N Yorks 59 G11
Cloughton Newlands N Yorks 59 G11
Clousta Shetland 96 H5
Clouston Orkney 95 G3
Clova Aberds 82 A6
Clova Angus 82 F5
Clove Lodge Durham 57 E11
Clovelly Devon 6 D2
Clovenfords Borders 70 G3
Clovenstone Aberds 83 B9
Clovullin Highld 74 A3
Clow Bridge Lancs 50 G4
Clowne Derbys 45 E8
Clows Top Worcs 26 A4
Cloy Wrex 33 A9
Cluanie Inn Highld 80 B2
Cluanie Lodge Highld 80 B2
Clun Shrops 33 G9
Clunbury Shrops 33 G9
Clunderwen Carms 22 E6
Clune Highld 81 A9
Clunes Highld 80 E4
Clungunford Shrops 33 H9
Clunie Aberds 89 C6
Clunie Perth 76 C4
Clunton Shrops 33 G9
Cluny Fife 76 H5
Cluny Castle Highld 81 D8
Clutton Bath 16 F3
Clutton Ches W 43 G7
Clwt-grugoer Conwy 42 F2
Clwt-y-bont Gwyn 41 D7
Clydach Mon 25 G9
Clydach Swansea 14 A2
Clydach Vale Rhondda 14 B5
Clydebank W Dunb 68 C3
Clydey Pembs 23 C7
Clyffe Pypard Wilts 17 D7
Clynder Argyll 73 E11
Clyne Neath 14 A4
Clynelish Highld 93 J11
Clynnog-fawr Gwyn 40 E6
Clyro Powys 25 D9
Clyst Honiton Devon 7 G8
Clyst Hydon Devon 7 F9
Clyst St George Devon 5 C10
Clyst St Lawrence Devon 7 F9
Clyst St Mary Devon 7 G8
Cnoc Amhlaigh W Isles 91 D10
Cnwch-coch Ceredig 32 H2
Coachford Aberds 88 D4
Coad's Green Corn 4 D3
Coal Aston Derbys 45 E7
Coalbrookdale Telford 34 E2
Coalbrookvale Bl Gwent 25 H8
Coalburn S Lanark 69 G7
Coalburns T&W 63 G7
Coalcleugh Northumb 57 B10
Coaley Glos 16 A4
Coalhall E Ayrs 67 E7
Coalhill Essex 20 B4
Coalpit Heath S Glos 16 C3
Coalport Telford 34 E2
Coalsnaughton Clack 76 H2
Coaltown of Balgonie Fife 76 H5
Coaltown of Wemyss Fife 76 H6
Coalville Leics 35 D10
Coalway Glos 26 G2
Coat Som 8 B3
Coatbridge N Lanark 68 D6
Coatdyke N Lanark 68 D6
Coate Swindon 17 C8
Coate Wilts 17 E7
Coates Cambs 37 F9
Coates Glos 16 A6
Coates Lancs 50 E4
Coates Notts 46 D2
Coates W Sus 11 C8
Coatham Redcar 59 D6
Coatham Mundeville Darl 58 D3
Coatsgate Dumfries 60 C6
Cobbaton Devon 6 D5
Cobbler's Green Norf 39 F8
Coberley Glos 26 G6
Cobham Kent 20 E3
Cobham Sur 19 E8
Cobholm Island Norf 39 E11
Cobleland Stirling 75 H8
Cobnash Hereford 25 B11
Coburty Aberds 89 B9
Cock Bank Wrex 42 H6
Cock Bridge Aberds 82 C4
Cock Clarks Essex 20 A5
Cockayne N Yorks 59 G7
Cockayne Hatley Cambs 29 D9
Cockburnspath Borders 70 C6
Cockenzie and Port Seton E Loth 70 C3
Cockerham Lancs 49 D4
Cockermouth Cumb 56 C3
Cockernhoe Green Herts 29 F8
Cockfield Durham 58 D2
Cockfield Suff 30 C6
Cockfosters London 19 B9
Cocking W Sus 11 C7
Cockington Torbay 5 E9
Cocklake Som 15 G10
Cockley Beck Cumb 56 F4
Cockley Cley Norf 38 E3
Cockshutt Shrops 33 C10
Cockthorpe Norf 38 A5
Cockwood Devon 5 C10
Cockyard Hereford 25 E11
Codda Corn 4 D2
Coddenham Suff 31 C8
Coddington Ches W 43 G7
Coddington Hereford 26 D4
Coddington Notts 46 G2
Codford St Mary Wilts 16 H6
Codford St Peter Wilts 16 H6
Codicote Herts 29 G9
Codmore Hill W Sus 11 B9
Codnor Derbys 45 H8
Codrington S Glos 16 D4
Codsall Staffs 34 E4
Codsall Wood Staffs 34 E4
Coed Duon = Blackwood Caerph 15 B7
Coed Mawr Gwyn 41 C7
Coed Morgan Mon 25 G10
Coed-Talon Flint 42 G5
Coed-y-bryn Ceredig 23 B8
Coed-y-paen Mon 15 B9
Coed-yr-ynys Powys 25 F8
Coed Ystumgwern Gwyn 32 C1
Coedely Rhondda 14 C6
Coedkernew Newport 15 C8
Coedpoeth Wrex 42 G5
Coedway Powys 33 D9
Coelbren Powys 24 G5
Coffinswell Devon 5 E9
Cofton Hackett Worcs 34 H6
Cogan V Glam 15 D7
Cogenhoe Northants 28 B5
Cogges Oxon 27 H10
Coggeshall Essex 30 F5
Coggeshall Hamlet Essex 30 F5
Coggins Mill E Sus 12 D4
Coig Peighinnean W Isles 91 A10
Coig Peighinnean Bhuirgh W Isles 91 B9
Coignafearn Lodge Highld 81 B8
Coilacriech Aberds 82 D5
Coilantogle Stirling 75 G8
Coilleag W Isles 84 G2
Coillore Highld 85 E8
Coity Bridgend 14 C5
Col W Isles 91 C9
Col Uarach W Isles 91 D9
Colaboll Highld 93 H8
Colan Corn 3 C7
Colaton Raleigh Devon 7 H9
Colbost Highld 84 D7
Colburn N Yorks 58 G2
Colby Cumb 57 D8
Colby IoM 48 E2
Colby Norf 39 B8
Colchester Essex 31 F7
Colcot V Glam 15 E7
Cold Ash W Berks 18 E2
Cold Ashby Northants 36 H2
Cold Ashton S Glos 16 D4
Cold Aston Glos 27 G8
Cold Blow Pembs 22 E6
Cold Brayfield M Keynes 28 C6
Cold Hanworth Lincs 46 D4
Cold Harbour Lincs 36 B5
Cold Hatton Telford 34 C2
Cold Hesledon Durham 58 B5
Cold Higham Northants 28 C3
Cold Kirby N Yorks 51 A11
Cold Newton Leics 36 E3
Cold Northcott Corn 4 C3
Cold Norton Essex 20 A5
Cold Overton Leics 36 D4
Coldbackie Highld 93 D9
Coldbeck Cumb 57 F9
Coldblow London 20 D2
Coldean Brighton 12 F2
Coldeast Devon 5 D9
Colden W Yorks 50 G5
Colden Common Hants 10 B3
Coldfair Green Suff 31 B11
Coldham Cambs 37 E10
Coldharbour Glos 16 A2
Coldharbour Kent 20 F2
Coldharbour Sur 19 G8
Coldingham Borders 71 D8
Coldrain Perth 76 G3
Coldred Kent 21 G9
Coldridge Devon 6 F5
Coldstream Angus 76 D6
Coldstream Borders 71 G7
Coldwaltham W Sus 11 C9
Coldwells Aberds 89 D11
Coldwells Croft Aberds 83 A7
Coldyeld Shrops 33 F9
Cole Som 8 A5
Cole Green Herts 29 G9
Cole Henley Hants 17 F11
Colebatch Shrops 33 G9
Colebrook Devon 7 F9
Colebrooke Devon 7 G6
Coleby Lincs 46 F3
Coleby N Lincs 52 H4
Coleford Devon 7 F6
Coleford Glos 26 G2
Coleford Som 16 G3
Colehill Dorset 9 D9
Coleman's Hatch E Sus 12 C3
Colemere Shrops 33 B10
Colemore Hants 10 A6
Coleorton Leics 35 D10
Colerne Wilts 16 D5
Cole's Green Suff 31 B9
Coles Green Suff 31 D7
Colesbourne Glos 26 G6
Colesden Bedford 29 C8
Coleshill Bucks 18 B6
Coleshill Oxon 17 B9
Coleshill Warks 35 G8
Colestocks Devon 7 F9
Colgate W Sus 11 A11
Colgrain Argyll 68 B2
Colinsburgh Fife 77 G7
Colinton Edin 69 D11
Colintraive Argyll 73 F9
Colkirk Norf 38 C5
Collace Perth 76 D5
Collafirth Shetland 96 G6
Collaton St Mary Torbay 5 F9
College Milton S Lanark 68 E5
Collessie Fife 76 F5
Collier Row London 20 B2
Collier Street Kent 20 G4
Collier's End Herts 29 F10
Collier's Green Kent 13 C6
Colliery Row T&W 58 B4
Collieston Aberds 89 F10
Collin Dumfries 60 F6
Collingbourne Ducis Wilts 17 F9
Collingbourne Kingston Wilts 17 F9
Collingham Notts 46 F2
Collingham W Yorks 51 E9
Collington Hereford 26 B3
Collingtree Northants 28 C4
Collins Green Warr 43 C8
Colliston Angus 77 C9
Collycroft Warks 35 G9
Collynie Aberds 89 E8
Collyweston Northants 36 E5
Colmonell S Ayrs 66 H4
Colmworth Bedford 29 C8
Coln Rogers Glos 27 H7
Coln St Aldwyn's Glos 27 H8
Coln St Dennis Glos 27 G7
Colnabaichin Aberds 82 C4
Colnbrook Slough 19 D7
Colne Cambs 37 H9
Colne Lancs 50 E4
Colne Edge Lancs 50 E4
Colne Engaine Essex 30 E5
Colney Norf 39 E7
Colney Heath Herts 29 H9
Colney Street Herts 19 A8
Colpy Aberds 89 E6
Colquhar Borders 70 F2
Colsterdale N Yorks 51 A7
Colsterworth Lincs 36 C5
Colston Bassett Notts 36 B2
Coltfield Moray 87 E14
Colthouse Cumb 56 G5
Coltishall Norf 39 D8
Coltness N Lanark 69 E7
Colton Cumb 56 H5
Colton N Yorks 51 E11
Colton Norf 39 E7
Colton Staffs 35 C6
Colton W Yorks 51 F9
Colva Powys 25 C9
Colvend Dumfries 55 D11
Colvister Shetland 96 D7
Colwall Green Hereford 26 D4
Colwall Stone Hereford 26 D4
Colwell Northumb 62 F5
Colwich Staffs 34 C6
Colwick Notts 36 A2
Colwinston V Glam 14 D5
Colworth W Sus 11 D8
Colwyn Bay = Bae Colwyn Conwy 41 C10
Colyford Devon 8 E1
Colyton Devon 8 E1
Combe Hereford 25 B10
Combe Oxon 27 G11
Combe W Berks 17 E10
Combe Common Sur 18 H6
Combe Down Bath 16 E4
Combe Florey Som 7 C10
Combe Hay Bath 16 F4
Combe Martin Devon 6 B4
Combe Moor Hereford 25 B10
Combe Raleigh Devon 7 F10
Combe St Nicholas Som 8 C2
Combeinteignhead Devon 5 D10
Comberbach Ches W 43 E9
Comberton Cambs 29 C10
Comberton Hereford 25 B11
Combpyne Devon 8 E1
Combridge Staffs 35 B6
Combrook Warks 27 C10
Combs Derbys 44 E4
Combs Suff 31 C7
Combs Ford Suff 31 C7
Combwich Som 15 G8
Comers Aberds 83 C8
Comins Coch Ceredig 32 G2
Commercial End Cambs 30 B2
Commins Capel Betws Ceredig 24 C3
Commins Coch Powys 32 E4
Common Edge Blackpool 49 F3
Common Side Derbys 45 E7
Commondale N Yorks 59 E7
Commonmoor Corn 4 E3
Commonside Ches W 43 E8
Compstall Gtr Man 44 C3
Compton Devon 5 E9
Compton Hants 10 B3
Compton Sur 18 G5
Compton Sur 18 G6
Compton W Berks 18 D2
Compton W Sus 11 C6
Compton Wilts 17 F8
Compton Abbas Dorset 9 C7
Compton Abdale Glos 27 G7
Compton Bassett Wilts 17 D7
Compton Beauchamp Oxon 17 C9
Compton Bishop Som 15 F9
Compton Chamberlayne Wilts 9 B9
Compton Dando Bath 16 E3
Compton Dundon Som 8 A3
Compton Martin Bath 15 F11
Compton Pauncefoot Som 8 B5
Compton Valence Dorset 8 E4
Comrie Fife 69 B9
Comrie Perth 75 E10
Conaglen House Highld 80 G2
Conchra Argyll 73 E9
Concraigie Perth 76 C4
Conder Green Lancs 49 D4
Conderton Worcs 26 E6
Condicote Glos 27 F8
Condorrat N Lanark 68 C6
Condover Shrops 33 E10
Coney Weston Suff 38 H5
Coneyhurst W Sus 11 B10
Coneysthorpe N Yorks 52 B3
Coneythorpe N Yorks 51 D9
Conford Hants 11 A7
Congash Highld 82 A2
Congdon's Shop Corn 4 D3
Congerstone Leics 35 E9
Congham Norf 38 C3
Congl-y-wal Gwyn 41 F9
Congleton Ches E 44 F2
Congresbury N Som 15 E10
Congreve Staffs 34 D5
Conicavel Moray 87 F12
Coningsby Lincs 46 G6
Conington Cambs 29 B10
Conington Cambs 37 G7
Conisbrough S Yorks 45 C9
Conisby Argyll 64 B3
Conisholme Lincs 47 C8
Coniston Cumb 56 G5
Coniston E Yorks 53 F7
Coniston Cold N Yorks 50 D5
Conistone N Yorks 50 C5
Connah's Quay Flint 42 F5
Connel Argyll 74 D2
Connel Park E Ayrs 67 E9
Connor Downs Corn 2 F4
Conon Bridge Highld 87 F8
Conon House Highld 87 F8
Cononley N Yorks 50 E5
Conordan Highld 85 E10
Consall Staffs 44 H3
Consett Durham 58 A2
Constable Burton N Yorks 58 G2
Constantine Corn 2 G6
Constantine Bay Corn 3 B7
Contin Highld 86 F7
Contlaw Aberdeen 83 C10
Conwy Conwy 41 C9
Conyer Kent 20 E6
Conyers Green Suff 30 B5
Cooden E Sus 12 F6
Cooil IoM 48 E3
Cookbury Devon 6 F3
Cookham Windsor 18 C5
Cookham Dean Windsor 18 C5
Cookham Rise Windsor 18 C5
Cookhill Worcs 27 C7
Cookley Suff 39 H9
Cookley Worcs 34 G4
Cookley Green Oxon 18 B3
Cookney Aberds 83 D10
Cookridge W Yorks 51 E8
Cooksbridge E Sus 12 E3
Cooksmill Green Essex 30 H3
Coolham W Sus 11 B10
Cooling Medway 20 D4
Coombe Corn 3 D8
Coombe Corn 6 E1
Coombe Hants 10 B5
Coombe Wilts 17 F8
Coombe Bissett Wilts 9 B10
Coombe Hill Glos 26 F5
Coombe Keynes Dorset 9 F7
Coombes W Sus 11 D10
Coopersale Common Essex 19 A11
Cootham W Sus 11 C9
Copdock Suff 31 D8
Copford Green Essex 30 F6
Copgrove N Yorks 51 C9
Copister Shetland 96 F6
Cople Bedford 29 D8
Copley Durham 58 D1
Coplow Dale Derbys 44 E5
Copmanthorpe York 52 E1
Coppathorne Corn 4 A3
Coppenhall Staffs 34 D5
Coppenhall Moss Ches E 43 G10
Copperhouse Corn 2 F4
Coppingford Cambs 37 G7
Copplestone Devon 7 F6
Coppull Lancs 43 A8
Coppull Moor Lancs 43 A8
Copsale W Sus 11 B10
Copster Green Lancs 50 F2
Copston Magna Warks 35 G10
Copt Heath W Mid 35 H7
Copt Hewick N Yorks 51 B9
Copt Oak Leics 35 D10
Copthorne Shrops 33 D10
Copthorne Sur 12 C2
Copy's Green Norf 38 B5
Copythorne Hants 10 C2
Corbets Tey London 20 C2
Corbridge Northumb 62 G5
Corby Northants 36 G4
Corby Glen Lincs 36 C5
Cordon N Ayrs 66 C3
Coreley Shrops 26 A3
Cores End Bucks 18 C6
Corfe Som 7 E11
Corfe Castle Dorset 9 F8
Corfe Mullen Dorset 9 E8
Corfton Shrops 33 G10
Corgarff Aberds 82 C4
Corhampton Hants 10 B5
Corlae Dumfries 67 G9
Corley Warks 35 G9
Corley Ash Warks 35 G8
Corley Moor Warks 35 G8
Cornaa IoM 48 D4
Cornabus Argyll 64 D4
Cornel Conwy 41 D9
Corner Row Lancs 49 F4
Corney Cumb 56 G3
Cornforth Durham 58 C4
Cornhill Aberds 88 C5
Cornhill-on-Tweed Northumb 71 G7
Cornholme W Yorks 50 G5
Cornish Hall End Essex 30 E3
Cornquoy Orkney 95 J6
Cornsay Durham 58 B2
Cornsay Colliery Durham 58 B2
Corntown Highld 87 F8
Corntown V Glam 14 D5
Cornwell Oxon 27 F9
Cornwood Devon 5 F7
Cornworthy Devon 5 F9
Corpach Highld 80 F2
Corpusty Norf 39 C7
Corran Highld 74 A3
Corran Highld 85 H13
Corranbuie Argyll 73 G7
Corrany IoM 48 D4
Corrie N Ayrs 66 B3
Corrie Common Dumfries 61 E8
Corriecravie N Ayrs 66 D2
Corriemoillie Highld 86 E6
Corriemulzie Lodge Highld 86 B6
Corrievarkie Lodge Perth 81 F7
Corrievorrie Highld 81 A9
Corrimony Highld 86 H6
Corringham Lincs 46 C2
Corringham Thurrock 20 C4
Corris Gwyn 32 E3
Corris Uchaf Gwyn 32 E3
Corrour Shooting Lodge Highld 80 G6
Corrow Argyll 74 G4
Corry Highld 85 F11
Corry of Ardnagrask Highld 87 G8
Corrykinloch Highld 92 G6
Corrymuckloch Perth 75 D11
Corrynachenchy Argyll 79 G9
Cors-y-Gedol Gwyn 32 C1
Corsback Highld 94 C4
Corscombe Dorset 8 D4
Corse Aberds 88 D6
Corse Glos 26 F4
Corse Lawn Worcs 26 E5
Corse of Kinnoir Aberds 88 D5
Corsewall Dumfries 54 C3
Corsham Wilts 16 D5
Corsindae Aberds 83 C8
Corsley Wilts 16 G5
Corsley Heath Wilts 16 G5
Corsock Dumfries 60 F3
Corston Bath 16 E3
Corston Wilts 16 C6
Corstorphine Edin 69 C10
Cortachy Angus 76 B6
Corton Suff 39 F11
Corton Wilts 16 G6
Corton Denham Som 8 B5
Coruanan Lodge Highld 80 G2
Corunna W Isles 84 B3
Corwen Denb 33 A6
Coryton Devon 4 C5
Coryton Thurrock 20 C4
Cosby Leics 35 F11
Coseley W Mid 34 F5
Cosgrove Northants 28 D4
Cosham Ptsmth 10 D5
Cosheston Pembs 22 F5
Cossall Notts 35 A10
Cossington Leics 36 D2
Cossington Som 15 G9
Costa Orkney 95 F4
Costessey Norf 39 D7
Costock Notts 36 C1
Coston Leics 36 C4
Cote Oxon 17 A10
Cotebrook Ches W 43 F8
Cotehill Cumb 56 A6
Cotes Cumb 57 H6
Cotes Leics 36 C1
Cotes Staffs 34 B4
Cotesbach Leics 35 G11
Cotgrave Notts 36 B2
Cothall Aberds 83 B10
Cotham Notts 45 H11
Cothelstone Som 7 C10
Cotherstone Durham 58 E1
Cothill Oxon 17 B11
Cotleigh Devon 7 F11
Cotmanhay Derbys 35 A10
Cotmaton Devon 7 H10
Coton Cambs 29 C11
Coton Northants 28 A3
Coton Staffs 34 B5
Coton Staffs 34 C4
Coton Clanford Staffs 34 C4
Coton Hill Shrops 33 D10
Coton Hill Staffs 34 B5
Coton in the Elms Derbys 35 D8
Cott Devon 5 E8
Cottam E Yorks 52 C5
Cottam Lancs 49 F5
Cottam Notts 46 E2
Cottartown Highld 87 H13
Cottenham Cambs 29 B11
Cotterdale N Yorks 57 G10
Cottered Herts 29 F10
Cotteridge W Mid 34 H6
Cotterstock Northants 36 F6
Cottesbrooke Northants 28 A4
Cottesmore Rutland 36 D5
Cotteylands Devon 7 E8
Cottingham E Yorks 52 F6
Cottingham Northants 36 F4
Cottingley W Yorks 51 F7
Cottisford Oxon 28 E2
Cotton Staffs 44 H4
Cotton Suff 31 B7
Cotton End Bedford 29 D7
Cottown Aberds 83 A7
Cottown Aberds 83 B9
Cottown Aberds 89 D8
Cotwalton Staffs 34 B5
Couch's Mill Corn 4 F2
Coughton Hereford 26 F2
Coughton Warks 27 B7
Coulaghailtro Argyll 72 G6
Coulags Highld 86 G2
Coulby Newham Mbro 58 E6
Coulderton Cumb 56 F1
Coulin Highld 86 F3
Coull Aberds 83 C7
Coull Argyll 64 B3
Coulport Argyll 73 E11
Coulsdon London 19 F9
Coulston Wilts 16 F6
Coulter S Lanark 69 G9
Coulton N Yorks 52 B2
Cound Shrops 34 E1
Coundon Durham 58 D3
Coundon W Mid 35 G9
Coundon Grange Durham 58 D3
Countersett N Yorks 57 H11
Countess Wilts 17 G8
Countess Wear Devon 5 C10
Countesthorpe Leics 36 F1
Countisbury Devon 7 B6
County Oak W Sus 12 C1
Coup Green Lancs 50 G1
Coupar Angus Perth 76 C5
Coupland Northumb 71 G8
Cour Argyll 65 D9
Courance Dumfries 60 D6
Court-at-Street Kent 13 C9
Court Henry Carms 23 D10
Courteenhall Northants 28 C4
Courtsend Essex 21 B7
Courtway Som 7 C11
Cousland Midloth 70 D2
Cousley Wood E Sus 12 C5
Cove Argyll 73 E11
Cove Borders 70 C6
Cove Devon 7 E8
Cove Hants 18 F5
Cove Highld 91 H13
Cove Bay Aberdeen 83 C11
Cove Bottom Suff 39 H10
Covehithe Suff 39 G11
Coven Staffs 34 E5
Coveney Cambs 37 G10
Covenham St Bartholomew Lincs 47 C7
Covenham St Mary Lincs 47 C7
Coventry W Mid 35 H9
Coverack Corn 3 H6
Coverham N Yorks 58 H2
Covesea Moray 88 A1
Covington Cambs 29 A7
Covington S Lanark 69 G8
Cow Ark Lancs 50 E2
Cowan Bridge Lancs 50 B2
Cowbeech E Sus 12 E5
Cowbit Lincs 37 D8
Cowbridge Lincs 47 H7
Cowbridge Som 7 B8
Cowbridge = Y Bont-Faen V Glam 14 D5
Cowdale Derbys 44 E4
Cowden Kent 12 B3
Cowdenbeath Fife 69 A10
Cowdenburn Borders 69 E11
Cowers Lane Derbys 45 H7
Cowes IoW 10 E3
Cowesby N Yorks 58 H5
Cowfold W Sus 11 B11
Cowgill Cumb 57 H9
Cowie Aberds 83 E10
Cowie Stirling 69 B7
Cowley Devon 7 G8
Cowley Glos 26 G6
Cowley London 19 C7
Cowley Oxon 18 A2
Cowleymoor Devon 7 E8
Cowling Lancs 50 H1
Cowling N Yorks 50 E5
Cowling N Yorks 58 H3
Cowlinge Suff 30 C4
Cowpe Lancs 50 G4
Cowpen Northumb 63 E8
Cowpen Bewley Stockton 58 D5
Cowplain Hants 10 C5
Cowshill Durham 57 B10
Cowslip Green N Som 15 E10
Cowstrandburn Fife 69 A9
Cowthorpe N Yorks 51 D10
Cox Common Suff 39 G9
Cox Green Windsor 18 D5
Cox Moor Notts 45 G9
Coxbank Ches E 34 A2
Coxbench Derbys 35 A9
Coxford Norf 38 C4
Coxford Soton 10 C2
Coxheath Kent 20 F4
Coxhill Kent 21 G9
Coxhoe Durham 58 C4
Coxley Som 15 G11
Coxwold N Yorks 51 B11
Coychurch Bridgend 14 D5
Coylton S Ayrs 67 D7
Coylumbridge Highld 81 B11
Coynach Aberds 82 C6
Coynachie Aberds 88 E4
Coytrahen Bridgend 14 C4
Crabadon Devon 5 F8
Crabbs Cross Worcs 27 B7
Crabtree W Sus 11 B11
Crackenthorpe Cumb 57 D8
Crackington Haven Corn 4 B2
Crackley Warks 27 A9
Crackleybank Shrops 34 D3
Crackpot N Yorks 57 G11
Cracoe N Yorks 50 C5
Craddock Devon 7 E9
Cradhlastadh W Isles 90 D5
Cradley Hereford 26 D4
Cradley Heath W Mid 34 G5
Crafthole Corn 4 F4
Cragg Vale W Yorks 50 G6
Craggan Highld 82 A2
Craggie Highld 87 H10
Craggie Highld 93 H11
Craghead Durham 58 A3
Crai Powys 24 F5
Craibstone Moray 88 C4
Craichie Angus 77 C8
Craig Dumfries 55 B9
Craig Dumfries 55 C9
Craig Highld 86 G3
Craig Castle Aberds 82 A6
Craig-cefn-parc Swansea 14 A2
Craig Penllyn V Glam 14 D5
Craig-y-don Conwy 41 B9
Craig-y-nos Powys 24 G5
Craiganor Lodge Perth 75 B9
Craigdam Aberds 89 E8
Craigdarroch Dumfries 60 D3
Craigdarroch Highld 86 F7
Craigdhu Highld 86 G7
Craigearn Aberds 83 B9
Craigellachie Moray 88 D2
Craigencross Dumfries 54 C3
Craigend Perth 76 E4
Craigend Stirling 68 B6
Craigendive Argyll 73 E9
Craigendoran Argyll 68 B2
Craigends Renfs 68 D3
Craigens Argyll 64 B3
Craigens E Ayrs 67 E8
Craighat Stirling 68 B3
Craighead Fife 77 G9
Craighlaw Mains Dumfries 54 C6
Craighouse Argyll 72 G4
Craigie Aberds 83 B11
Craigie Dundee 77 D7
Craigie Perth 76 C4
Craigie Perth 76 E4
Craigie S Ayrs 67 C7
Craigiefield Orkney 95 G5
Craigielaw E Loth 70 C3
Craiglockhart Edin 69 C11
Craigmalloch E Ayrs 67 G7
Craigmaud Aberds 89 C8
Craigmillar Edin 69 C11
Craigmore Argyll 73 G10
Craignant Shrops 33 B8
Craigneuk N Lanark 68 D6
Craigneuk N Lanark 68 E6
Craignure Argyll 79 H10
Craigo Angus 77 A9
Craigow Perth 76 G3
Craigrothie Fife 76 F6
Craigroy Moray 87 F14
Craigruie Stirling 75 E7
Craigston Castle Aberds 89 C7
Craigton Aberdeen 83 C10
Craigton Angus 76 B6
Craigton Angus 77 D8
Craigton Highld 87 B9
Craigtown Highld 93 D11
Craik Borders 61 C9
Crail Fife 77 G9
Crailing Borders 62 A2
Crailinghall Borders 62 A2
Craiselound N Lincs 45 C11
Crakehill N Yorks 51 B10
Crakemarsh Staffs 35 B6
Crambe N Yorks 52 C3
Cramlington Northumb 63 F8
Cramond Edin 69 C10
Cramond Bridge Edin 69 C10
Cranage Ches E 43 F10
Cranberry Staffs 34 B4
Cranborne Dorset 9 C9
Cranbourne Brack 18 D6
Cranbrook Devon 7 G9
Cranbrook Kent 13 C6
Cranbrook Common Kent 13 C6
Crane Moor S Yorks 45 B7
Crane's Corner Norf 38 D5
Cranfield C Beds 28 D6
Cranford London 19 D8
Cranford St Andrew Northants 36 H5
Cranford St John Northants 36 H5
Cranham Glos 26 G5
Cranham London 20 C2
Crank Mers 43 C8
Crank Wood Gtr Man 43 B9
Cranleigh Sur 19 H7
Cranley Suff 31 A8
Cranmer Green Suff 31 A7
Cranmore IoW 10 F2
Cranna Aberds 89 C6
Crannich Argyll 79 G8
Crannoch Moray 88 C4
Cranoe Leics 36 F3
Cransford Suff 31 B10
Cranshaws Borders 70 D5
Cranstal IoM 48 B4
Crantock Corn 3 C6
Cranwell Lincs 46 H4
Cranwich Norf 38 F3
Cranworth Norf 38 E5
Craobh Haven Argyll 72 C6
Crapstone Devon 4 E6
Crarae Argyll 73 D8
Crask Inn Highld 93 G8
Crask of Aigas Highld 86 G7
Craskins Aberds 83 C7
Craster Northumb 63 B8
Craswall Hereford 25 E9
Cratfield Suff 39 H9
Crathes Aberds 83 D9
Crathie Aberds 82 D4
Crathie Highld 81 D7
Crathorne N Yorks 58 F5
Craven Arms Shrops 33 G10
Crawcrook T&W 63 G7
Crawford Lancs 43 B7
Crawford S Lanark 60 A5
Crawfordjohn S Lanark 60 A4
Crawick Dumfries 60 B3
Crawley Hants 10 A3
Crawley Oxon 27 G10
Crawley W Sus 12 C1
Crawley Down W Sus 12 C2
Crawleyside Durham 57 B11
Crawshawbooth Lancs 50 G4
Crawton Aberds 83 F10
Cray N Yorks 50 B5
Cray Perth 76 A4
Crayford London 20 D2
Crayke N Yorks 52 B1
Crays Hill Essex 20 B4
Cray's Pond Oxon 18 C3
Creacombe Devon 7 E7
Creag Ghoraidh W Isles 84 D2
Creagan Argyll 74 C2
Creaguaineach Lodge Highld 80 G5
Creaksea Essex 20 B6
Creaton Northants 28 A4
Creca Dumfries 61 F8
Credenhill Hereford 25 D11
Crediton Devon 7 F7
Creebridge Dumfries 55 C7
Creech Heathfield Som 8 B1
Creech St Michael Som 8 B1
Creed Corn 3 E8
Creekmouth London 19 C11
Creeting Bottoms Suff 31 C8
Creeting St Mary Suff 31 C7
Creeton Lincs 36 C6
Creetown Dumfries 55 D7
Creg-ny-Baa IoM 48 D3
Creggans Argyll 73 C9
Cregneash IoM 48 F1
Cregrina Powys 25 C8
Creich Fife 76 E6
Creigiau Cardiff 14 C6
Cremyll Corn 4 F5
Creslow Bucks 28 F5
Cressage Shrops 34 E1
Cressbrook Derbys 44 E5
Cresselly Pembs 22 F5
Cressing Essex 30 F4
Cresswell Northumb 63 D8
Cresswell Staffs 34 B5
Cresswell Quay Pembs 22 F5
Creswell Derbys 45 E9
Cretingham Suff 31 B9
Cretshengan Argyll 72 G6
Crewe Ches E 43 G10
Crewe Ches W 43 G7
Crewgreen Powys 33 D9
Crewkerne Som 8 D3
Crianlarich Stirling 74 E6
Cribyn Ceredig 23 A10
Criccieth Gwyn 40 G6
Crich Derbys 45 G7
Crichie Aberds 89 D9
Crichton Midloth 70 D2
Crick Mon 15 B10
Crick Northants 28 A2
Crickadarn Powys 25 D7
Cricket Malherbie Som 8 C2
Cricket St Thomas Som 8 D2
Crickheath Shrops 33 C8
Crickhowell Powys 25 G9
Cricklade Wilts 17 B8
Cricklewood London 19 C9
Cridling Stubbs N Yorks 51 G11
Crieff Perth 75 E11
Criggion Powys 33 D8
Crigglestone W Yorks 51 H9
Crimond Aberds 89 C10
Crimonmogate Aberds 89 C10
Crimplesham Norf 38 E2
Crinan Argyll 72 D6
Cringleford Norf 39 E7
Cringles W Yorks 50 E6
Crinow Pembs 22 E6
Cripplesease Corn 2 F4
Cripplestyle Dorset 9 C9
Cripp's Corner E Sus 13 D6
Croasdale Cumb 56 E2
Crock Street Som 8 C2
Crockenhill Kent 20 E2
Crockernwell Devon 7 G6
Crockerton Wilts 16 G5
Crocketford or Ninemile Bar Dumfries 60 F4
Crockey Hill York 52 E2
Crockham Hill Kent 19 F11
Crockleford Heath Essex 31 F7
Crockness Orkney 95 J4
Croes-goch Pembs 22 C3
Croes-lan Ceredig 23 B8

G

Glyndebourne E Sus 12 E3
Glyndyfrdwy Denb 33 A7
Glynedd = Glyn-neath Neath 24 H5
Glynogwr Bridgend 14 C5
Glyntaff Rhondda 14 C6
Glyntawe Powys 24 G5
Gnosall Staffs 34 C4
Gnosall Heath Staffs 34 C4
Goadby Leics 36 F3
Goadby Marwood Leics 36 C3
Goat Lees Kent 21 G7
Goatacre Wilts 17 D7
Goathill Dorset 8 C5
Goathland N Yorks 59 F9
Goathurst Som 8 A1
Gobernuisgach Lodge Highld 92 E7
Gobhaig W Isles 90 G5
Gobowen Shrops 33 B9
Godalming Sur 18 G6
Godley Gtr Man 44 C3
Godmanchester Cambs 29 A9
Godmanstone Dorset 8 E5
Godmersham Kent 21 F7
Godney Som 15 G10
Godolphin Cross Corn 2 F5
Godre'r-graig Neath 24 H4
Godshill Hants 9 C10
Godshill IoW 10 F4
Godstone Sur 19 F10
Godwinscroft Hants 9 E10
Goetre Mon 25 H10
Goferydd Anglesey 40 B4
Goff's Oak Herts 19 A10
Gogar Edin 69 C10
Goginan Ceredig 32 G2
Golan Gwyn 41 F7
Golant Corn 4 F2
Golberdon Corn 4 D4
Golborne Gtr Man 43 C9
Golcar W Yorks 51 H7
Gold Hill Norf 37 F11
Goldcliff Newport 15 C9
Golden Cross E Sus 12 E4
Golden Green Kent 20 G3
Golden Grove Carms 23 E10
Golden Hill Hants 10 E1
Golden Pot Hants 18 G4
Golden Valley Glos 26 F6
Goldenhill Stoke 44 G2
Golders Green London 19 C9
Goldhanger Essex 30 H6
Golding Shrops 33 E11
Goldington Bedford 29 C7
Goldsborough N Yorks 51 D9
Goldsborough N Yorks 59 E9
Goldsithney Corn 2 F4
Goldsworthy Devon 6 D2
Goldthorpe S Yorks 45 B8
Gollanfield Highld 87 F11
Golspie Highld 93 J11
Golval Highld 93 C11
Gomeldon Wilts 17 H8
Gomersal W Yorks 51 G8
Gomshall Sur 19 G7
Gonalston Notts 45 H10
Gonfirth Shetland 96 G5
Good Easter Essex 30 G3
Gooderstone Norf 38 E3
Goodleigh Devon 6 C5
Goodmanham E Yorks 52 E4
Goodnestone Kent 21 E7
Goodnestone Kent 21 F9
Goodrich Hereford 26 G2
Goodrington Torbay 5 F9
Goodshaw Lancs 50 G4
Goodwick = Wdig Pembs 22 C4
Goodworth Clatford Hants 17 G10
Goole E Yorks 52 G3
Goonbell Corn 2 E6
Goonhavern Corn 3 D6
Goose Eye W Yorks 50 E6
Goose Green Gtr Man 43 B8
Goose Green Norf 39 G7
Goose Green W Sus 11 C10
Gooseham Corn 6 E1
Goosey Oxon 17 B10
Goosnargh Lancs 50 F1
Goostrey Ches E 43 E10
Gorcott Hill Warks 27 B7
Gord Shetland 96 L6
Gordon Borders 70 F5
Gordonbush Highld 93 J11
Gordonsburgh Moray 88 B4
Gordonstoun Moray 88 B1
Gordonstown Aberds 88 C5
Gordonstown Aberds 89 E7
Gore Kent 21 F10
Gore Cross Wilts 17 F7
Gore Pit Essex 30 G5
Gorebridge Midloth 70 D2
Gorefield Cambs 37 D10
Gorey Jersey 11
Gorgie Edin 69 C11
Goring Oxon 18 C3
Goring-by-Sea W Sus 11 D10
Goring Heath Oxon 18 D3
Gorleston-on-Sea Norf 39 E11
Gornalwood W Mid 34 F5
Gorrachie Aberds 89 C7
Gorran Churchtown Corn 3 E8
Gorran Haven Corn 3 E9
Gorrenberry Borders 61 D10
Gors Ceredig 32 H2
Gorse Hill Swindon 17 C8
Gorsedd Flint 42 E4
Gorseinon Swansea 23 G10
Gorseness Orkney 95 G5
Gorsgoch Ceredig 23 A9
Gorslas Carms 23 E10
Gorsley Glos 26 F3
Gorstan Highld 86 E6
Gorstanvorran Highld 79 D11
Gorsteyhill Staffs 43 G10
Gorsty Hill Staffs 35 C7
Gortantaoid Argyll 64 A4
Gorton Gtr Man 44 C2
Gosbeck Suff 31 C8
Gosberton Lincs 37 B8
Gosberton Clough Lincs 37 C7
Gosfield Essex 30 F4
Gosford Hereford 26 B2
Gosforth Cumb 56 F2
Gosforth T&W 63 G8
Gosmore Herts 29 F8
Gosport Hants 10 E5
Gossabrough Shetland 96 E7
Gossington Glos 16 A4
Goswick Northumb 71 F9
Gotham Notts 35 B11
Gotherington Glos 26 F6
Gott Shetland 96 J6
Goudhurst Kent 12 C6
Goulceby Lincs 46 E6
Gourdas Aberds 89 D7
Gourdon Aberds 83 F10
Gourock Involyd 73 F11
Govan Glasgow 68 D4
Govanhill Glasgow 68 D4
Goveton Devon 5 G8
Govilon Mon 25 G9
Gowanhill Aberds 89 B10
Gowdall E Yorks 52 G2
Gowerton Swansea 23 G10
Gowkhall Fife 69 B9
Gowthorpe E Yorks 52 D3
Goxhill E Yorks 53 E7
Goxhill N Lincs 53 G7
Goxhill Haven N Lincs 53 G7
Goytre Neath 14 C3
Grabhair W Isles 91 F8
Graby Lincs 37 C6
Grade Corn 2 H6
Graffham W Sus 11 C8
Grafham Cambs 29 B8
Grafham Sur 19 G7
Grafton Hereford 25 E11
Grafton N Yorks 51 C10
Grafton Oxon 17 A9
Grafton Shrops 33 D10
Grafton Worcs 26 B2
Grafton Flyford Worcs 26 C6
Grafton Regis Northants 28 D4
Grafton Underwood Northants 36 G5
Grafty Green Kent 20 G5
Graianrhyd Denb 42 G5
Graig Conwy 41 C10
Graig Denb 42 E3
Graig-fechan Denb 42 G4
Grain Medway 20 D5
Grainsby Lincs 46 C6
Grainthorpe Lincs 47 C7
Grampound Corn 3 E8
Grampound Road Corn 3 D8
Gramsdal W Isles 84 C3
Granborough Bucks 28 F4
Granby Notts 36 B3
Grandborough Warks 27 B11
Grandtully Perth 76 B2
Grange Cumb 56 E4
Grange E Ayrs 67 C7
Grange Medway 20 E4
Grange Mers 42 D5
Grange Perth 76 E5
Grange Crossroads Moray 88 C4
Grange Hall Moray 87 E13
Grange Hill Essex 19 B11
Grange Moor W Yorks 51 H8
Grange of Lindores Fife 76 F5
Grange-over-Sands Cumb 49 B4
Grange Villa Durham 58 A3
Grangemill Derbys 44 G6
Grangemouth Falk 69 B8
Grangepans Falk 69 B9
Grangetown Cardiff 15 D7
Grangetown Redcar 59 D6
Granish Highld 81 B11
Gransmoor E Yorks 53 D7
Granston Pembs 22 C3
Grantchester Cambs 29 C11
Grantham Lincs 36 B5
Grantley N Yorks 51 C8
Grantlodge Aberds 83 B9
Granton Dumfries 60 C6
Granton Edin 69 C11
Grantown-on-Spey Highld 82 A2
Grantshouse Borders 71 D7
Grappenhall Warr 43 D9
Grasby Lincs 46 B4
Grasmere Cumb 56 F5
Grasscroft Gtr Man 44 B3
Grassendale Mers 43 D6
Grassholme Durham 57 D11
Grassington N Yorks 50 C6
Grassmoor Derbys 45 F8
Grassthorpe Notts 45 F11
Grateley Hants 17 G9
Gratwich Staffs 34 B6
Graveley Cambs 29 B9
Graveley Herts 29 F9
Gravelly Hill W Mid 35 F7
Gravels Shrops 33 E9
Graven Shetland 96 F6
Graveney Kent 21 E7
Gravesend Herts 29 F11
Gravesend Kent 20 D3
Grayingham Lincs 46 C3
Grayrigg Cumb 57 G7
Grays Thurrock 20 D3
Grayshott Hants 18 H5
Grayswood Sur 11 A8
Graythorp Hrtlpl 58 D6
Grazeley Wokingham 18 E3
Greasbrough S Yorks 45 C8
Greasby Mers 42 D5
Great Abington Cambs 30 D2
Great Addington Northants 28 A6
Great Alne Warks 27 C8
Great Altcar Lancs 42 B6
Great Amwell Herts 29 G10
Great Asby Cumb 57 E8
Great Ashfield Suff 30 B6
Great Ayton N Yorks 59 E6
Great Baddow Essex 20 A4
Great Bardfield Essex 30 E3
Great Barford Bedford 29 C8
Great Barr W Mid 34 F6
Great Barrington Glos 27 G9
Great Barrow Ches W 43 F7
Great Barton Suff 30 B5
Great Barugh N Yorks 52 B3
Great Bavington Northumb 62 E5
Great Bealings Suff 31 D9
Great Bedwyn Wilts 17 E9
Great Bentley Essex 31 F8
Great Billing Northants 28 B5
Great Bircham Norf 38 B3
Great Blakenham Suff 31 C8
Great Blencow Cumb 56 C6
Great Bolas Telford 34 C2
Great Bookham Sur 19 F8
Great Bourton Oxon 27 D11
Great Bowden Leics 36 G3
Great Bradley Suff 30 C3
Great Braxted Essex 30 G5
Great Bricett Suff 31 C7
Great Brickhill Bucks 28 E6
Great Bridge W Mid 34 F5
Great Bridgeford Staffs 34 C4
Great Brington Northants 28 B3
Great Bromley Essex 31 F7
Great Broughton Cumb 56 C2
Great Broughton N Yorks 59 F6
Great Budworth Ches W 43 E9
Great Burdon Darl 58 E4
Great Burgh Sur 19 F9
Great Burstead Essex 20 B3
Great Busby N Yorks 58 F6
Great Canfield Essex 30 G2
Great Carlton Lincs 47 D8
Great Casterton Rutland 36 E6
Great Chart Kent 13 B8
Great Chatwell Staffs 34 D3
Great Chesterford Essex 30 D2
Great Cheverell Wilts 16 F6
Great Chishill Cambs 29 E11
Great Clacton Essex 31 G8
Great Cliff W Yorks 51 H9
Great Clifton Cumb 56 D2
Great Coates NE Lincs 46 B6
Great Comberton Worcs 26 D6
Great Corby Cumb 56 A6
Great Cornard Suff 30 D5
Great Cowden E Yorks 53 E8
Great Coxwell Oxon 17 B9
Great Crakehall N Yorks 58 G3
Great Cransley Northants 36 H4
Great Cressingham Norf 38 E4
Great Crosby Mers 42 C6
Great Cubley Derbys 35 B7
Great Dalby Leics 36 D3
Great Denham Bedford 29 D7
Great Doddington Northants 28 B5
Great Dunham Norf 38 D4
Great Dunmow Essex 30 F3
Great Durnford Wilts 17 H8
Great Easton Essex 30 F3
Great Easton Leics 36 F4
Great Eccleston Lancs 49 E4
Great Edstone N Yorks 52 A3
Great Ellingham Norf 38 F6
Great Elm Som 16 G4
Great Eversden Cambs 29 C10
Great Fencote N Yorks 58 G3
Great Finborough Suff 31 C7
Great Fransham Norf 38 D4
Great Gaddesden Herts 29 G7
Great Gidding Cambs 37 G7
Great Givendale E Yorks 52 D4
Great Glemham Suff 31 B10
Great Glen Leics 36 F2
Great Gonerby Lincs 36 B4
Great Gransden Cambs 29 C9
Great Green Norf 39 G8
Great Green Suff 30 C6
Great Habton N Yorks 52 B3
Great Hale Lincs 37 A7
Great Hallingbury Essex 30 G2
Great Hampden Bucks 18 A5
Great Harrowden Northants 28 A5
Great Harwood Lancs 50 F3
Great Haseley Oxon 18 A3
Great Hatfield E Yorks 53 E7
Great Haywood Staffs 34 C6
Great Heath W Mid 35 G9
Great Heck N Yorks 52 G1
Great Henny Essex 30 E5
Great Hinton Wilts 16 F6
Great Hockham Norf 38 F5
Great Holland Essex 31 G9
Great Horkesley Essex 30 E6
Great Hormead Herts 29 F10
Great Horton W Yorks 51 F7
Great Horwood Bucks 28 E4
Great Houghton Northants 28 C4
Great Houghton S Yorks 45 B8
Great Hucklow Derbys 44 E5
Great Kelk E Yorks 53 D7
Great Kimble Bucks 28 H5
Great Kingshill Bucks 18 B5
Great Langton N Yorks 58 G3
Great Leighs Essex 30 G4
Great Lever Gtr Man 43 B10
Great Limber Lincs 46 B5
Great Linford M Keynes 28 D5
Great Livermere Suff 30 A5
Great Longstone Derbys 44 E6
Great Lumley Durham 58 B3
Great Lyth Shrops 33 E10
Great Malvern Worcs 26 D4
Great Maplestead Essex 30 E5
Great Marton Blackpool 49 F3
Great Massingham Norf 38 C3
Great Melton Norf 39 E7
Great Milton Oxon 18 A3
Great Missenden Bucks 18 A5
Great Mitton Lancs 50 F3
Great Mongeham Kent 21 F10
Great Moulton Norf 39 F7
Great Munden Herts 29 F10
Great Musgrave Cumb 57 E9
Great Ness Shrops 33 D9
Great Notley Essex 30 F4
Great Oakley Essex 31 F8
Great Oakley Northants 36 G4
Great Offley Herts 29 F8
Great Ormside Cumb 57 E9
Great Orton Cumb 56 A5
Great Ouseburn N Yorks 51 C10
Great Oxendon Northants 36 G3
Great Oxney Green Essex 30 H3
Great Palgrave Norf 38 D4
Great Parndon Essex 29 H11
Great Paxton Cambs 29 B9
Great Plumpton Lancs 49 F3
Great Plumstead Norf 39 D9
Great Ponton Lincs 36 B5
Great Preston W Yorks 51 G10
Great Raveley Cambs 37 G8
Great Rissington Glos 27 G8
Great Rollright Oxon 27 E10
Great Ryburgh Norf 38 C5
Great Ryle Northumb 62 B6
Great Ryton Shrops 33 E10
Great Saling Essex 30 F4
Great Salkeld Cumb 57 C7
Great Sampford Essex 30 E3
Great Sankey Warr 43 D8
Great Saxham Suff 30 B4
Great Shefford W Berks 17 D10
Great Shelford Cambs 29 C11
Great Smeaton N Yorks 58 F4
Great Snoring Norf 38 B5
Great Somerford Wilts 16 C6
Great Stainton Darl 58 D4
Great Stambridge Essex 20 B5
Great Staughton Cambs 29 B8
Great Steeping Lincs 47 F8
Great Stonar Kent 21 F10
Great Strickland Cumb 57 D7
Great Stukeley Cambs 29 A9
Great Sturton Lincs 46 E6
Great Sutton Ches W 43 E6
Great Sutton Shrops 33 G11
Great Swinburne Northumb 62 F5
Great Tew Oxon 27 F10
Great Tey Essex 30 F5
Great Thurkleby N Yorks 51 B10
Great Thurlow Suff 30 C3
Great Torrington Devon 6 E3
Great Tosson Northumb 62 C6
Great Totham Essex 30 G5
Great Totham Essex 30 G5
Great Tows Lincs 46 C6
Great Urswick Cumb 49 B2
Great Wakering Essex 20 C6
Great Waldingfield Suff 30 D6
Great Walsingham Norf 38 B5
Great Waltham Essex 30 G3
Great Warley Essex 20 B2
Great Washbourne Glos 26 E6
Great Weldon Northants 36 G5
Great Welnetham Suff 30 C5
Great Wenham Suff 31 E7
Great Whittington Northumb 62 F6
Great Wigborough Essex 30 G6
Great Wilbraham Cambs 30 C2
Great Wishford Wilts 17 H7
Great Witcombe Glos 26 G6
Great Witley Worcs 26 B4
Great Wolford Warks 27 E9
Great Wratting Suff 30 D3
Great Wymondley Herts 29 F9
Great Wyrley Staffs 34 E5
Great Wytheford Shrops 34 D1
Great Yarmouth Norf 39 E11
Great Yeldham Essex 30 E4
Greater Doward Hereford 26 G2
Greatford Lincs 37 D6
Greatgate Staffs 35 A6
Greatham Hants 11 A6
Greatham Hrtlpl 58 D5
Greatham W Sus 11 C9
Greatstone on Sea Kent 13 D9
Greatworth Northants 28 D2
Greave Lancs 50 G4
Greeba IoM 48 D3
Green Denb 42 F3
Green End Bedford 29 C8
Green Hammerton N Yorks 51 D10
Green Lane Powys 33 F7
Green Ore Som 16 F2
Green St Green London 19 E11
Green Street Herts 19 B8
Greenbank Shetland 96 C7
Greenburn W Loth 69 D8
Greendikes Northumb 71 H9
Greenfield C Beds 29 E7
Greenfield Flint 42 E4
Greenfield Gtr Man 44 B3
Greenfield Highld 80 C4
Greenfield Oxon 18 B4
Greenford London 19 C8
Greengairs N Lanark 68 C6
Greenham W Berks 17 E11
Greenhaugh Northumb 62 E3
Greenhead Northumb 62 G2
Greenhill Falk 69 C7
Greenhill Kent 21 E8
Greenhill Leics 35 D10
Greenhill London 19 C8
Greenhills N Ayrs 67 A6
Greenhithe Kent 20 D2
Greenholm E Ayrs 67 C8
Greenholme Cumb 57 F7
Greenhouse Borders 61 A11
Greenhow Hill N Yorks 51 C7
Greenigoe Orkney 95 H5
Greenland Highld 94 D4
Greenlands Bucks 18 C4
Greenlaw Aberds 89 C6
Greenlaw Borders 70 F6
Greenlea Dumfries 60 F6
Greenloaning Perth 75 G11
Greenmount Gtr Man 43 A10
Greenmow Shetland 96 L6
Greenock Involyd 73 F11
Greenock West Involyd 73 F11
Greenodd Cumb 49 A3
Greenrow Cumb 56 A3
Greens Norton Northants 28 D3
Greenside T&W 63 G7
Greensidehill Northumb 62 B5
Greenstead Green Essex 30 F5
Greensted Essex 20 A2
Greenwich London 19 D10
Greet Glos 27 E7
Greete Shrops 26 A2
Greetham Lincs 47 E7
Greetham Rutland 36 D5
Greetland W Yorks 51 G6
Gregg Hall Cumb 56 G6
Gregson Lane Lancs 50 G1
Greinetobht W Isles 84 A3
Greinton Som 15 H10
Gremista Shetland 96 J6
Grenaby IoM 48 E2
Grendon Northants 28 B5
Grendon Warks 35 E8
Grendon Common Warks 35 F8
Grendon Green Hereford 26 C2
Grendon Underwood Bucks 28 F3
Grenofen Devon 4 D5
Grenoside S Yorks 45 C7
Greosabhagh W Isles 90 H6
Gresford Wrex 42 G6
Gresham Norf 39 B7
Greshornish Highld 85 C8
Gressenhall Norf 38 D5
Gressingham Lancs 50 C1
Gresty Green Ches E 43 G10
Greta Bridge Durham 58 E1
Gretna Dumfries 61 G9
Gretna Green Dumfries 61 G9
Gretton Glos 27 E7
Gretton Northants 36 F4
Gretton Shrops 33 F11
Grewelthorpe N Yorks 51 B8
Grey Green N Lincs 45 B11
Greygarth N Yorks 51 B7
Greynor Carms 23 F10
Greysouthen Cumb 56 D2
Greystoke Cumb 56 C6
Greystone Angus 77 C8
Greystone Dumfries 60 F5
Greywell Hants 18 F4
Griais W Isles 91 C9
Grianan W Isles 91 D9
Gribthorpe E Yorks 52 F3
Gridley Corner Devon 6 G2
Griff Warks 35 G9
Griffithstown Torf 15 B8
Grimbister Orkney 95 G4
Grimblethorpe Lincs 46 D6
Grimeford Village Lancs 43 A9
Grimethorpe S Yorks 45 B8
Griminis W Isles 84 C2
Grimister Shetland 96 D6
Grimley Worcs 26 B5
Grimness Orkney 95 J5
Grimoldby Lincs 47 D7
Grimpo Shrops 33 C9
Grimsargh Lancs 50 F1
Grimsbury Oxon 27 D11
Grimsby NE Lincs 46 A6
Grimscote Northants 28 C3
Grimscott Corn 6 F1
Grimsthorpe Lincs 36 C6
Grimston E Yorks 53 F8
Grimston Leics 36 C2
Grimston Norf 38 C3
Grimston York 52 D2
Grimstone Dorset 8 E4
Grinacombe Moor Devon 6 G3
Grindale E Yorks 53 B7
Grindigar Orkney 95 H6
Grindiscol Shetland 96 K6
Grindle Shrops 34 E3
Grindleford Derbys 44 E6
Grindleton Lancs 50 E3
Grindley Staffs 34 C6
Grindley Brook Shrops 33 A11
Grindlow Derbys 44 E5
Grindon Northumb 71 F8
Grindon Staffs 44 G4
Grindonmoor Gate Staffs 44 G4
Gringley on the Hill Notts 45 C11
Grinsdale Cumb 61 H9
Grinshill Shrops 33 C11
Grinton N Yorks 58 G1
Griomsidar W Isles 91 E8
Grishipoll Argyll 78 F4
Grisling Common E Sus 12 D3
Gristhorpe N Yorks 53 A6
Griston Norf 38 F5
Gritley Orkney 95 H6
Grittenham Wilts 17 C7
Grittleton Wilts 16 C5
Grizebeck Cumb 49 A2
Grizedale Cumb 56 G5
Grobister Orkney 95 F7
Groby Leics 35 E11
Groes Conwy 42 F3
Groes Neath 14 C3
Groes-faen Rhondda 14 C6
Groes-lwyd Powys 33 D8
Groesffordd Marli Denb 42 E3
Groeslon Gwyn 40 E6
Groeslon Gwyn 41 D7
Grogport Argyll 65 D9
Gromford Suff 31 C10
Gronant Flint 42 D3
Groombridge E Sus 12 C4
Grosmont Mon 25 F11
Grosmont N Yorks 59 F9
Groton Suff 30 D6
Grougfoot Falk 69 C9
Grouville Jersey 11
Grove Dorset 8 G6
Grove Kent 21 E9
Grove Notts 45 E11
Grove Oxon 17 B11
Grove Park London 19 D11
Grove Vale W Mid 34 F6
Grovesend Swansea 23 F10
Grudie Highld 86 E6
Gruids Highld 93 J8
Gruinard House Highld 86 B2
Grula Highld 85 F8
Gruline Argyll 79 G8
Grunasound Shetland 96 K5
Grundisburgh Suff 31 C9
Grunsagill Lancs 50 D3
Gruting Shetland 96 J4
Grutness Shetland 96 N6
Gualachulain Highld 74 C4
Gualin Ho. Highld 92 D6
Guardbridge Fife 77 F7
Guarlford Worcs 26 D5
Guay Perth 76 C3
Guestling Green E Sus 13 E7
Guestling Thorn E Sus 13 E7
Guestwick Norf 39 C6
Guestwick Green Norf 39 C6
Guide Blackburn 50 G3
Guide Post Northumb 63 E8
Guilden Morden Cambs 29 D9
Guilden Sutton Ches W 43 F7
Guildford Sur 18 G6
Guildtown Perth 76 D4
Guilsborough Northants 28 A3
Guilsfield Powys 33 D8
Guilton Kent 21 F9
Guineaford Devon 6 C4
Guisborough Redcar 59 E7
Guiseley W Yorks 51 E7
Guist Norf 38 C5
Guith Orkney 95 E6
Guiting Power Glos 27 F7
Gulberwick Shetland 96 K6
Gullane E Loth 70 B3
Gulval Corn 2 F3
Gulworthy Devon 4 D5
Gumfreston Pembs 22 F6
Gumley Leics 36 F2
Gummow's Shop Corn 3 D7
Gun Hill E Sus 12 E4
Gunby E Yorks 52 F3
Gunby Lincs 36 C5
Gundleton Hants 10 A5
Gunn Devon 6 C5
Gunnerside N Yorks 57 G11
Gunnerton Northumb 62 F5
Gunness N Lincs 46 A2
Gunnislake Corn 4 D5
Gunnista Shetland 96 J7
Gunthorpe Norf 38 B6
Gunthorpe Notts 36 A2
Gunthorpe Pboro 37 E7
Gunville IoW 10 F3
Gunwalloe Corn 2 G5
Gurnard IoW 10 E3
Gurnett Ches E 44 E3
Gurney Slade Som 16 G3
Gurnos Powys 24 H4
Gussage All Saints Dorset 9 C9
Gussage St Michael Dorset 9 C8
Guston Kent 21 G10
Gutcher Shetland 96 D7
Guthrie Angus 77 B8
Guyhirn Cambs 37 E9
Guyhirn Gull Cambs 37 E9
Guy's Head Lincs 37 C10
Guy's Marsh Dorset 9 B7
Guyzance Northumb 63 C8
Gwaenysgor Flint 42 D3
Gwalchmai Anglesey 40 C5
Gwaun-Cae-Gurwen Neath 24 G4
Gwaun-Leision Neath 24 G4
Gwbert Ceredig 22 B6
Gweek Corn 2 G6
Gwehelog Mon 15 A9
Gwenddwr Powys 25 D7
Gwennap Corn 2 F6
Gwenter Corn 2 H6
Gwernaffield Flint 42 F5
Gwernesney Mon 15 A10
Gwernogle Carms 23 C10
Gwernymynydd Flint 42 F5
Gwersyllt Wrex 42 G6
Gwespyr Flint 42 D4
Gwithian Corn 2 E5
Gwredog Anglesey 40 B6
Gwyddelwern Denb 42 H3
Gwyddgrug Carms 23 C9
Gwydyr Uchaf Conwy 41 D9
Gwynfryn Wrex 42 G5
Gwystre Powys 25 B7
Gwytherin Conwy 41 D10
Gyfelia Wrex 42 H6
Gyffin Conwy 41 C9
Gyre Orkney 95 H4
Gyrn-goch Gwyn 40 F6

H

Habberley Shrops 33 E9
Habergham Lancs 50 F4
Habrough NE Lincs 46 A5
Haceby Lincs 36 B6
Hacheston Suff 31 C10
Hackbridge London 19 E9
Hackenthorpe S Yorks 45 D8
Hackford Norf 39 E6
Hackforth N Yorks 58 G3
Hackland Orkney 95 F4
Hackleton Northants 28 C5
Hackness N Yorks 59 G10
Hackness Orkney 95 J4
Hackney London 19 C10
Hackthorn Lincs 46 D3
Hackthorpe Cumb 57 D7
Haconby Lincs 37 C7
Hacton London 20 C2
Hadden Borders 70 G6
Haddenham Bucks 28 H4
Haddenham Cambs 37 H10
Haddington E Loth 70 C4
Haddington Lincs 46 F3
Haddiscoe Norf 39 F10
Haddon Cambs 37 F7
Haddon Ches E 44 F3
Hade Edge W Yorks 44 B5
Hademore Staffs 35 E7
Hadfield Derbys 44 C4
Hadham Cross Herts 29 G11
Hadham Ford Herts 29 F11
Hadleigh Essex 20 C5
Hadleigh Suff 31 D7
Hadley Telford 34 D2
Hadley End Staffs 35 C7
Hadlow Kent 20 G3
Hadlow Down E Sus 12 D4
Hadnall Shrops 33 D11
Hadstock Essex 30 D2
Hady Derbys 45 E7
Hadzor Worcs 26 B6
Haffenden Quarter Kent 13 B7
Hafod-Dinbych Conwy 41 E10
Hafod-Iom Conwy 41 C10
Haggate Lancs 50 F4
Haggbeck Cumb 61 F10
Haggerston Northumb 71 F9
Haggrister Shetland 96 F5
Hagley Hereford 26 D2
Hagley Worcs 34 G5
Hagworthingham Lincs 47 F7
Haigh Gtr Man 43 B9
Haigh S Yorks 44 A6
Haigh Moor W Yorks 51 G8
Haighton Green Lancs 50 F1
Hail Weston Cambs 29 B8
Haile Cumb 56 F2
Hailes Glos 27 E7
Hailey Herts 29 G10
Hailey Oxon 27 G10
Hailsham E Sus 12 F4
Haimer Highld 94 D3
Hainault London 19 B11
Hainford Norf 39 D8
Hainton Lincs 46 D5
Hairmyres S Lanark 68 E5
Haisthorpe E Yorks 53 C7
Hakin Pembs 22 F3
Halam Notts 45 G10
Halbeath Fife 69 B10
Halberton Devon 7 E9
Halcro Highld 94 D4
Hale Gtr Man 43 D10
Hale Halton 43 D7
Hale Hants 9 C10
Hale Bank Halton 43 D7
Hale Street Kent 20 G3
Halebarns Gtr Man 43 D10
Hales Norf 39 F9
Hales Staffs 34 B3
Hales Place Kent 21 F8
Halesfield Telford 34 E3
Halesgate Lincs 37 C9
Halesowen W Mid 34 G5
Halesworth Suff 39 H9
Halewood Mers 43 D7
Halford Shrops 33 G10
Halford Warks 27 D9
Halfpenny Furze Carms 23 E7
Halfpenny Green Staffs 34 F4
Halfway Carms 24 E3
Halfway Carms 24 E5
Halfway W Berks 17 E11
Halfway Bridge W Sus 11 B8
Halfway House Shrops 33 D9
Halfway Houses Kent 20 D6
Halifax W Yorks 51 G6
Halket E Ayrs 67 A7
Halkirk Highld 94 E3
Halkyn Flint 42 E5
Hall Dunnerdale Cumb 56 G4
Hall Green W Mid 35 G7
Hall Green W Yorks 51 H9
Hall Grove Herts 29 G9
Hall of Tankerness Orkney 95 H6
Hall of the Forest Shrops 33 G8
Halland E Sus 12 E3
Hallaton Leics 36 F3
Hallatrow Bath 16 F3
Hallbankgate Cumb 61 H11
Hallen S Glos 15 C11
Halliburton Borders 70 F5
Hallin Highld 84 C7
Halling Medway 20 E4
Hallington Lincs 47 D7
Hallington Northumb 62 F5
Halliwell Gtr Man 43 A10
Halloughton Notts 45 G10
Hallow Worcs 26 C5
Hallrule Borders 61 B11
Halls E Loth 70 C5
Hall's Green Herts 29 F9
Hallsands Devon 5 H9
Hallthwaites Cumb 56 H3
Hallworthy Corn 4 C2
Hallyburton House Perth 76 D5
Hallyne Borders 69 F10
Halmer End Staffs 43 H10
Halmore Glos 16 A3
Halmyre Mains Borders 69 F10
Halnaker W Sus 11 D8
Halsall Lancs 42 A6
Halse Northants 28 D2
Halse Som 7 D10
Halsetown Corn 2 F4
Halsham E Yorks 53 G8
Halsinger Devon 6 C4
Halstead Essex 30 E5
Halstead Kent 19 E11
Halstead Leics 36 E3
Halstock Dorset 8 D4
Haltham Lincs 46 F6
Haltoft End Lincs 47 H7
Halton Bucks 28 G5
Halton Halton 43 D8
Halton Lancs 49 C5
Halton Northumb 62 G5
Halton W Yorks 51 F9
Halton Wrex 33 B9
Halton East N Yorks 50 D6
Halton Gill N Yorks 50 B4
Halton Holegate Lincs 47 F8
Halton Lea Gate Northumb 62 H2
Halton West N Yorks 50 D4
Haltwhistle Northumb 62 G3
Halvergate Norf 39 E10
Halwell Devon 5 F8
Halwill Devon 6 G3
Halwill Junction Devon 6 F3
Ham Devon 7 F11
Ham Glos 16 B3
Ham Highld 94 C4
Ham Kent 21 F10
Ham London 19 D8
Ham Shetland 96 K1
Ham Wilts 17 E10
Ham Common Dorset 9 B7
Ham Green Hereford 26 D4
Ham Green Kent 13 D7
Ham Green Kent 20 E5
Ham Green N Som 15 D11
Ham Green Worcs 27 B7
Ham Street Som 8 A4
Hamble-le-Rice Hants 10 D3
Hambleden Bucks 18 C4
Hambledon Hants 10 C5
Hambledon Sur 18 H6
Hambleton Lancs 49 E3
Hambleton N Yorks 52 F1
Hambridge Som 8 B2
Hambrook S Glos 16 D3
Hambrook W Sus 11 D6
Hameringham Lincs 47 F7
Hamerton Cambs 37 H7
Hametoun Shetland 96 K1
Hamilton S Lanark 68 E6
Hammer W Sus 11 A7
Hammerpot W Sus 11 D9
Hammersmith London 19 D9
Hammerwich Staffs 35 E6
Hammerwood E Sus 12 C3
Hammond Street Herts 19 A10
Hammoon Dorset 9 C7
Hamnavoe Shetland 96 E4
Hamnavoe Shetland 96 E6
Hamnavoe Shetland 96 F6
Hamnavoe Shetland 96 K5
Hampden Park E Sus 12 F5
Hamperden End Essex 30 E2
Hampnett Glos 27 G7
Hampole S Yorks 45 A9
Hampreston Dorset 9 E9
Hampstead London 19 C9
Hampstead Norreys W Berks 18 D2
Hampsthwaite N Yorks 51 D8
Hampton London 19 E8
Hampton Shrops 34 G3
Hampton Worcs 27 D7
Hampton Bishop Hereford 26 E2
Hampton Heath Ches W 43 H7
Hampton in Arden W Mid 35 G8
Hampton Loade Shrops 34 G3
Hampton Lovett Worcs 26 B5
Hampton Lucy Warks 27 C9
Hampton on the Hill Warks 27 B9
Hampton Poyle Oxon 28 G2
Hamrow Norf 38 C5
Hamsey E Sus 12 E3
Hamsey Green London 19 F10
Hamstall Ridware Staffs 35 D7
Hamstead IoW 10 E3
Hamstead W Mid 34 F6
Hamstead Marshall W Berks 17 E11
Hamsterley Durham 58 C2
Hamsterley Durham 63 H7
Hamstreet Kent 13 C9
Hamworthy Poole 9 E8
Hanbury Staffs 35 C7
Hanbury Worcs 26 B6
Hanbury Woodend Staffs 35 C7
Hanby Lincs 36 B6
Hanchurch Staffs 34 A4
Handbridge Ches W 43 F7
Handcross W Sus 12 D1
Handforth Ches E 44 D2
Handley Ches W 43 G7
Handsacre Staffs 35 D6
Handsworth S Yorks 45 D8
Handsworth W Mid 34 F6
Handy Cross Devon 6 D3
Hanford Stoke 34 A4
Hanging Langford Wilts 17 H7
Hangleton W Sus 11 D9
Hanham S Glos 16 D3
Hankelow Ches E 43 H9
Hankerton Wilts 16 B6
Hankham E Sus 12 F5
Hanley Stoke 44 H2
Hanley Castle Worcs 26 D5
Hanley Child Worcs 26 B3
Hanley Swan Worcs 26 D5
Hanley William Worcs 26 B3
Hanlith N Yorks 50 C5
Hanmer Wrex 33 B10
Hannah Lincs 47 E9
Hannington Hants 18 F2
Hannington Northants 28 A5
Hannington Swindon 17 B8
Hannington Wick Swindon 17 B8
Hansel Village S Ayrs 67 C6
Hanslope M Keynes 28 D5
Hanthorpe Lincs 37 C6
Hanwell London 19 C8
Hanwell Oxon 27 D11
Hanwood Shrops 33 E10
Hanworth London 19 D8
Hanworth Norf 39 B7
Happendon S Lanark 69 G7
Happisburgh Norf 39 B9
Happisburgh Common Norf 39 C9
Hapsford Ches W 43 E7
Hapton Lancs 50 F3
Hapton Norf 39 F7
Harberton Devon 5 F8
Harbertonford Devon 5 F8
Harbledown Kent 21 F8
Harborne W Mid 34 G6
Harborough Magna Warks 35 H10
Harbottle Northumb 62 C5
Harbury Warks 27 C10
Harby Leics 36 B3
Harby Notts 46 E2
Harcombe Devon 7 G10
Harden W Mid 34 E6
Harden W Yorks 51 F6
Hardenhuish Wilts 16 D6
Hardgate Aberds 83 C9
Hardham W Sus 11 C9
Hardingham Norf 38 E6
Hardingstone Northants 28 C4
Hardington Som 16 F4
Hardington Mandeville Som 8 C4
Hardington Marsh Som 8 D4
Hardley Hants 10 D3
Hardley Street Norf 39 E9
Hardmead M Keynes 28 D6
Hardrow N Yorks 57 G10
Hardstoft Derbys 45 F8
Hardway Hants 10 D5
Hardway Som 8 A6
Hardwick Bucks 28 G5
Hardwick Cambs 29 C10
Hardwick Norf 38 D2
Hardwick Norf 39 G8
Hardwick Northants 28 B5
Hardwick Notts 45 E10
Hardwick Oxon 27 H10
Hardwick Oxon 28 F2
Hardwick W Mid 35 F6
Hardwicke Glos 26 F6
Hardwicke Glos 26 G4
Hardwicke Hereford 25 D9
Hardy's Green Essex 30 F6
Hare Green Essex 31 F7
Hare Hatch Wokingham 18 D5
Hare Street Herts 29 F10
Hareby Lincs 47 F7
Hareden Lancs 50 D2
Harefield London 19 B7
Harehills W Yorks 51 F9
Harehope Northumb 62 A6
Haresceugh Cumb 57 B8
Harescombe Glos 26 G5
Haresfield Glos 26 G5
Hareshaw N Lanark 69 D7
Hareshaw Head Northumb 62 E4
Harewood W Yorks 51 E9
Harewood End Hereford 26 F2
Harford Carms 24 D3
Harford Devon 5 F7
Hargate Norf 39 F7
Hargatewall Derbys 44 E5
Hargrave Ches W 43 F7
Hargrave Northants 29 A7
Hargrave Suff 30 C4
Harker Cumb 61 G9
Harkland Shetland 96 E6
Harkstead Suff 31 E8
Harlaston Staffs 35 D8
Harlaw Ho. Aberds 83 A9
Harlaxton Lincs 36 B4
Harle Syke Lancs 50 F4
Harlech Gwyn 41 G7
Harlequin Notts 36 B2
Harlescott Shrops 33 D11
Harlesden London 19 C9
Harleston Devon 5 G8
Harleston Norf 39 G8
Harleston Suff 31 C7
Harlestone Northants 28 B4
Harley S Yorks 45 C7
Harley Shrops 34 E1
Harleyholm S Lanark 69 G8
Harlington C Beds 29 E7
Harlington London 19 D7
Harlington S Yorks 45 B8
Harlosh Highld 85 D7
Harlow Essex 29 G11
Harlow Hill N Yorks 51 D8
Harlow Hill Northumb 62 G6
Harlthorpe E Yorks 52 F3
Harlton Cambs 29 C10
Harman's Cross Dorset 9 F8
Harmby N Yorks 58 H2
Harmer Green Herts 29 G9
Harmer Hill Shrops 33 C10
Harmondsworth London 19 D7
Harmston Lincs 46 F3
Harnham Northumb 62 F6
Harnhill Glos 17 A7
Harold Hill London 20 B2
Harold Wood London 20 B2
Haroldston West Pembs 22 E3
Haroldswick Shetland 96 B8
Harome N Yorks 52 A2
Harpenden Herts 29 G8
Harpford Devon 7 G9
Harpham E Yorks 53 C6
Harpley Norf 38 C3
Harpley Worcs 26 B3
Harpole Northants 28 B3
Harpsdale Highld 94 E3
Harpsden Oxon 18 C4
Harpswell Lincs 46 D3
Harpur Hill Derbys 44 E4
Harpurhey Gtr Man 44 B2
Harraby Cumb 56 A6
Harrapool Highld 85 F11
Harrier Shetland 96 J1
Harrietfield Perth 76 E2
Harrietsham Kent 20 F5
Harrington Cumb 56 D1
Harrington Lincs 47 E7
Harrington Northants 36 G3
Harringworth Northants 36 F5
Harris Highld 78 B6
Harrogate N Yorks 51 D9
Harrold Bedford 28 C6
Harrow London 19 C8
Harrow on the Hill London 19 C8
Harrow Street Suff 30 E6
Harrow Weald London 19 B8
Harrowbarrow Corn 4 E4
Harrowden Bedford 29 D7
Harrowgate Hill Darl 58 E3
Harston Cambs 29 C11
Harston Leics 36 B4
Harswell E Yorks 52 E4

Hart Hrtlpl 58 C5
Hart Common Gtr Man 43 B9
Hart Hill Luton 29 F8
Hart Station Hrtlpl 58 C5
Hartburn Northumb 62 E6
Hartburn Stockton 58 E5
Hartest Suff 30 C5
Hartfield E Sus 12 C3
Hartford Cambs 29 A9
Hartford Ches W 43 E9
Hartford End Essex 30 G3
Hartfordbridge Hants 18 F4
Hartforth N Yorks 58 F2
Harthill Ches W 43 G8
Harthill N Lanark 69 D8
Harthill S Yorks 45 D8
Hartington Derbys 44 F5
Hartland Devon 6 D1
Hartlebury Worcs 26 A5
Hartlepool Hrtlpl 58 C6
Hartley Cumb 57 F9
Hartley Kent 13 C6
Hartley Kent 20 E3
Hartley Northumb 63 F9
Hartley Westpall Hants 18 F3
Hartley Wintney Hants 18 F4
Hartlip Kent 20 E5
Hartoft End N Yorks 59 G8
Harton N Yorks 52 C3
Harton Shrops 33 G10
Harton T&W 63 G9
Hartpury Glos 26 F4
Hartshead W Yorks 51 G7
Hartshill Warks 35 F9
Hartshorne Derbys 35 C9
Hartsop Cumb 56 E6
Hartwell Northants 28 C4
Hartwood N Lanark 69 E7
Harvieston Stirling 68 B4
Harvington Worcs 27 D7
Harvington Cross Worcs 27 D7
Harwell Oxon 17 C11
Harwich Essex 31 E9
Harwood Durham 57 C10
Harwood Gtr Man 43 A10
Harwood Dale N Yorks 59 G10
Harworth Notts 45 C10
Hasbury W Mid 34 G5
Hascombe Sur 18 G6
Haselbech Northants 36 H3
Haselbury Plucknett Som 8 C3
Haseley Warks 27 B9
Haselor Warks 27 C8
Hasfield Glos 26 F5
Hasguard Pembs 22 F3
Haskayne Lancs 42 B6
Hasketon Suff 31 C9
Hasland Derbys 45 F7
Haslemere Sur 11 A8
Haslingden Lancs 50 G3
Haslingfield Cambs 29 C11
Haslington Ches E 43 G10
Hassall Ches E 43 G10
Hassall Green Ches E 43 G10
Hassell Street Kent 21 G7
Hassendean Borders 61 A11
Hassingham Norf 39 E9
Hassocks W Sus 12 E1
Hassop Derbys 44 E6
Hastigrow Highld 94 D4
Hastingleigh Kent 13 B9
Hastings E Sus 13 F7
Hastingwood Essex 29 H11
Hastoe Herts 28 H6
Haswell Durham 58 B4
Haswell Plough Durham 58 B4
Hatch C Beds 29 D8
Hatch Hants 18 F3
Hatch Wilts 9 B8
Hatch Beauchamp Som 8 B2
Hatch End London 19 B8
Hatch Green Som 8 C2
Hatchet Gate Hants 10 D2
Hatching Green Herts 29 G8
Hatchmere Ches W 43 E8
Hatcliffe NE Lincs 46 B6
Hatfield Hereford 26 C2
Hatfield Herts 29 H9
Hatfield S Yorks 45 B10
Hatfield Worcs 26 C5
Hatfield Broad Oak Essex 30 G2
Hatfield Garden Village Herts 29 H9
Hatfield Heath Essex 30 G2
Hatfield Hyde Herts 29 G9
Hatfield Peverel Essex 30 G4
Hatfield Woodhouse S Yorks 45 B10
Hatford Oxon 17 B10
Hatherden Hants 17 F10
Hatherleigh Devon 6 F4
Hathern Leics 35 C10
Hatherop Glos 27 H8
Hathersage Derbys 44 D6
Hathershaw Gtr Man 44 B3
Hatherton Ches E 43 H9
Hatherton Staffs 34 D5
Hatley St George Cambs 29 C9
Hatt Corn 4 E4
Hattingley Hants 18 H3
Hatton Aberds 89 E10
Hatton Derbys 35 C8
Hatton Lincs 46 E5
Hatton Shrops 33 F10
Hatton Warks 27 B9
Hatton Warr 43 D8
Hatton Castle Aberds 89 D7
Hatton Heath Ches W 43 F7
Hatton of Fintray Aberds 83 B10
Hattoncrook Aberds 89 F8
Haugh E Ayrs 67 D7
Haugh Gtr Man 44 A3
Haugh Lincs 47 E8
Haugh Head Northumb 71 H9
Haugh of Glass Moray 88 E4
Haugh of Urr Dumfries 55 C11
Haugham Lincs 47 D7
Haughley Suff 31 B7
Haughley Green Suff 31 B7
Haughs of Clinterty Aberdeen 83 B10
Haughton Notts 45 E10
Haughton Shrops 33 C9
Haughton Shrops 34 D1
Haughton Shrops 34 E3
Haughton Shrops 34 F2
Haughton Staffs 34 C4
Haughton Castle Northumb 62 F5
Haughton Green Gtr Man 44 C3
Haughton Moss Ches E 43 G8
Haultwick Herts 29 F10
Haunn Argyll 78 G6
Haunn W Isles 84 G2
Haunton Staffs 35 D8
Hauxley Northumb 63 C8
Hauxton Cambs 29 C11
Havant Hants 10 D6
Haven Hereford 25 C11
Haven Bank Lincs 46 G6
Haven Side E Yorks 53 G7
Havenstreet IoW 10 E4
Havercroft W Yorks 45 A7
Haverfordwest = Hwlffordd Pembs 22 E4
Haverhill Suff 30 D3
Haverigg Cumb 49 B1
Havering-atte-Bower London 20 B2
Haveringland Norf 39 C7
Haversham M Keynes 28 D5
Haverthwaite Cumb 49 A3
Haverton Hill Stockton 58 D5
Hawarden = Penarlâg Flint 42 F6
Hawcoat Cumb 49 B2
Hawen Ceredig 23 B8
Hawes N Yorks 57 H10
Hawes' Green Norf 39 F8
Hawes Side Blackpool 49 F3
Hawford Worcs 26 B5
Hawick Borders 61 B11
Hawk Green Gtr Man 44 D3
Hawkchurch Devon 8 D2
Hawkedon Suff 30 C4
Hawkenbury Kent 12 C4
Hawkenbury Kent 13 B7
Hawkeridge Wilts 16 F5
Hawkerland Devon 7 H9
Hawkes End W Mid 35 G9
Hawkesbury S Glos 16 C4
Hawkesbury Warks 35 G9
Hawkesbury Upton S Glos 16 C4
Hawkhill Northumb 63 B8
Hawkhurst Kent 13 C6
Hawkinge Kent 21 H9
Hawkley Hants 10 B6
Hawkridge Som 7 C7
Hawkshead Cumb 56 G5
Hawkshead Hill Cumb 56 G5
Hawksland S Lanark 69 G7
Hawkswick N Yorks 50 B5
Hawksworth Notts 36 A3
Hawksworth W Yorks 51 E7
Hawksworth W Yorks 51 F8
Hawkwell Essex 20 B5
Hawley Hants 18 F5
Hawley Kent 20 D2
Hawling Glos 27 F7
Hawnby N Yorks 59 H6
Haworth W Yorks 50 F6
Hawstead Suff 30 C5
Hawthorn Durham 58 B5
Hawthorn Rhondda 15 C7
Hawthorn Wilts 16 E5
Hawthorn Hill Brack 18 D5
Hawthorn Hill Lincs 46 G6
Hawthorpe Lincs 36 C6
Hawton Notts 45 G11
Haxby York 52 D2
Haxey N Lincs 45 C11
Hay Green Norf 37 D11
Hay-on-Wye = Y Gelli Gandryll Powys 25 D9
Hay Street Herts 29 F10
Haydock Mers 43 C8
Haydon Dorset 8 C5
Haydon Bridge Northumb 62 G4
Haydon Wick Swindon 17 C8
Haye Corn 4 E4
Hayes London 19 C8
Hayes London 19 E11
Hayfield Derbys 44 D4
Hayfield Fife 69 A11
Hayhill E Ayrs 67 E7
Hayhillock Angus 77 C8
Hayle Corn 2 F4
Haynes C Beds 29 D7
Haynes Church End C Beds 29 D7
Hayscastle Pembs 22 D3
Hayscastle Cross Pembs 22 D4
Hayshead Angus 77 C9
Hayton Aberdeen 83 C11
Hayton Cumb 56 B3
Hayton Cumb 61 H11
Hayton E Yorks 52 E4
Hayton Notts 45 D11
Hayton's Bent Shrops 33 G11
Haytor Vale Devon 5 D8
Haywards Heath W Sus 12 D2
Haywood S Yorks 45 A9
Haywood Oaks Notts 45 G10
Hazel Grove Gtr Man 44 D3
Hazel Street Kent 12 C5
Hazelbank S Lanark 69 F7
Hazelbury Bryan Dorset 8 D6
Hazeley Hants 18 F4
Hazelhurst Gtr Man 44 B3
Hazelslade Staffs 34 D6
Hazelton Glos 27 G7
Hazelton Walls Fife 76 E6
Hazelwood Derbys 45 H7
Hazlemere Bucks 18 B5
Hazlerigg T&W 63 F8
Hazlewood N Yorks 51 D6
Hazon Northumb 63 C7
Heacham Norf 38 B2
Head of Muir Falk 69 B7
Headbourne Worthy Hants 10 A3
Headbrook Hereford 25 C10
Headcorn Kent 13 B7
Headingley W Yorks 51 F8
Headington Oxon 28 H2
Headlam Durham 58 E2
Headless Cross Worcs 27 B7
Headley Hants 18 E2
Headley Hants 18 H5
Headley Sur 19 F9
Headon Notts 45 E11
Heads S Lanark 68 F6
Heads Nook Cumb 61 H10
Heage Derbys 45 G7
Healaugh N Yorks 51 E10
Healaugh N Yorks 58 G1
Heald Green Gtr Man 44 D2
Heale Devon 6 B5
Heale Som 16 G3
Healey Gtr Man 50 H4
Healey N Yorks 51 A7
Healey Northumb 62 H6
Healing NE Lincs 46 A6
Heamoor Corn 2 F3
Heanish Argyll 78 G3
Heanor Derbys 45 H8
Heanton Punchardon Devon 6 C4
Heapham Lincs 46 D2
Hearthstane Borders 69 H10
Heasley Mill Devon 7 C6
Heast Highld 85 G11
Heath Cardiff 15 D7
Heath Derbys 45 F8
Heath and Reach C Beds 28 F6
Heath End Hants 18 E2
Heath End Sur 18 G5
Heath End Warks 27 B9
Heath Hayes Staffs 34 D6
Heath Hill Shrops 34 D3
Heath House Som 15 G10
Heath Town W Mid 34 F5
Heathcote Derbys 44 F5
Heather Leics 35 D9
Heatherfield Highld 85 D9
Heathfield Devon 5 D9
Heathfield E Sus 12 D4
Heathfield Som 7 D10
Heathhall Dumfries 60 F5
Heathrow Airport London 19 D7
Heathstock Devon 8 D1
Heathton Shrops 34 F4
Heatley Warr 43 D10
Heaton Lancs 49 C4
Heaton Staffs 44 F3
Heaton T&W 63 G8
Heaton W Yorks 51 F7
Heaton Moor Gtr Man 44 C2
Heaverham Kent 20 F2
Heaviley Gtr Man 44 D3
Heavitree Devon 7 G8
Hebburn T&W 63 G9
Hebden N Yorks 50 C6
Hebden Bridge W Yorks 50 G5
Hebron Anglesey 40 B6
Hebron Carms 22 D6
Hebron Northumb 63 E7
Heck Dumfries 60 E6
Heckfield Hants 18 E4
Heckfield Green Suff 39 H7
Heckfordbridge Essex 30 F6
Heckington Lincs 37 A7
Heckmondwike W Yorks 51 G8
Heddington Wilts 16 E6
Heddle Orkney 95 G4
Heddon-on-the-Wall Northumb 63 G7
Hedenham Norf 39 F9
Hedge End Hants 10 C3
Hedgerley Bucks 18 C6
Hedging Som 8 B2
Hedley on the Hill Northumb 62 H6
Hednesford Staffs 34 D6
Hedon E Yorks 53 G7
Hedsor Bucks 18 C6
Hedworth T&W 63 G9
Hegdon Hill Hereford 26 C2
Heggerscales Cumb 57 E10
Heglibister Shetland 96 H5
Heighington Darl 58 D3
Heighington Lincs 46 F4
Heights of Brae Highld 87 E8
Heights of Kinlochewe Highld 86 E3
Heilam Highld 92 C7
Heiton Borders 70 G6
Hele Devon 6 B4
Hele Devon 7 F8
Helensburgh Argyll 73 E11
Helford Corn 3 G6
Helford Passage Corn 3 G6
Helhoughton Norf 38 C4
Helions Bumpstead Essex 30 D3
Hellaby S Yorks 45 C9
Helland Corn 4 D1
Hellesdon Norf 39 D8
Hellidon Northants 28 C2
Hellifield N Yorks 50 D4
Hellingly E Sus 12 E4
Hellington Norf 39 E9
Hellister Shetland 96 J5
Helm Northumb 63 D7
Helmdon Northants 28 D2
Helmingham Suff 31 C8
Helmington Row Durham 58 C2
Helmsdale Highld 93 H13
Helmshore Lancs 50 G3
Helmsley N Yorks 52 A2
Helperby N Yorks 51 C10
Helperthorpe N Yorks 52 B5
Helpringham Lincs 37 A7
Helpston Pboro 37 E7
Helsby Ches W 43 E7
Helsey Lincs 47 E9
Helston Corn 2 G5
Helstone Corn 4 C1
Helton Cumb 57 D7
Helwith Bridge N Yorks 50 C4
Hemblington Norf 39 D9
Hemel Hempstead Herts 29 H7
Hemingbrough N Yorks 52 F2
Hemingby Lincs 46 E6
Hemingford Abbots Cambs 29 A9
Hemingford Grey Cambs 29 A9
Hemingstone Suff 31 C8
Hemington Leics 35 C10
Hemington Northants 37 G6
Hemington Som 16 F4
Hemley Suff 31 D9
Hemlington Mbro 58 E6
Hemp Green Suff 31 B10
Hempholme E Yorks 53 D6
Hempnall Norf 39 F8
Hempnall Green Norf 39 F8
Hempriggs House Highld 94 F5
Hempstead Essex 30 E3
Hempstead Medway 20 E4
Hempstead Norf 39 B7
Hempstead Norf 39 C10
Hempsted Glos 26 G5
Hempton Norf 38 C5
Hempton Oxon 27 E11
Hemsby Norf 39 D10
Hemswell Lincs 46 C3
Hemswell Cliff Lincs 46 D3
Hemsworth W Yorks 45 A8
Hemyock Devon 7 E10
Hen-feddau fawr Pembs 23 C7
Henbury Bristol 16 D2
Henbury Ches E 44 E2
Hendon London 19 C9
Hendon T&W 63 H10
Hendre Flint 42 F4
Hendre-ddu Conwy 41 D10
Hendreforgan Rhondda 14 C5
Hendy Carms 23 F10
Heneglwys Anglesey 40 C6
Henfield W Sus 11 C11
Henford Devon 6 G2
Henghurst Kent 13 C8
Hengoed Caerph 15 B7
Hengoed Powys 25 C9
Hengoed Shrops 33 B8
Hengrave Suff 30 B5
Henham Essex 30 F2
Heniarth Powys 33 E7
Henlade Som 8 B1
Henley Shrops 33 H11
Henley Som 8 A3
Henley Suff 31 C8
Henley W Sus 11 B7
Henley-in-Arden Warks 27 B8
Henley-on-Thames Oxon 18 C4
Henley's Down E Sus 12 F6
Henllan Ceredig 23 B8
Henllan Denb 42 F3
Henllan Amgoed Carms 22 D6
Henllys Torf 15 B8
Henlow C Beds 29 E8
Hennock Devon 5 C9
Henny Street Essex 30 E5
Henryd Conwy 41 C9
Henry's Moat Pembs 22 D5
Hensall N Yorks 52 G1
Henshaw Northumb 62 G3
Hensingham Cumb 56 E1
Henstead Suff 39 G10
Henstridge Som 8 C6
Henstridge Ash Som 8 B6
Henstridge Marsh Som 8 B6
Henton Oxon 18 A4
Henton Som 15 G10
Henwood Corn 4 D3
Heogan Shetland 96 J6
Heol-las Swansea 14 B2
Heol Senni Powys 24 F6
Heol-y-Cyw Bridgend 14 C5
Hepburn Northumb 62 A6
Hepple Northumb 62 C5
Hepscott Northumb 63 E8
Heptonstall W Yorks 50 G5
Hepworth Suff 30 A6
Hepworth W Yorks 44 B5
Herbrandston Pembs 22 F3
Hereford Hereford 26 D2
Heriot Borders 70 E2
Hermiston Edin 69 C10
Hermitage Borders 61 D11
Hermitage Dorset 8 D5
Hermitage W Berks 18 D2
Hermitage W Sus 11 D6
Hermon Anglesey 40 D5
Hermon Carms 23 C8
Hermon Carms 24 F3
Hermon Pembs 23 C7
Herne Kent 21 E8
Herne Bay Kent 21 E8
Herner Devon 6 D4
Hernhill Kent 21 E7
Herodsfoot Corn 4 E3
Herongate Essex 20 B3
Heronsford S Ayrs 54 A4
Herriard Hants 18 G3
Herringfleet Suff 39 F10
Herringswell Suff 30 A4
Hersden Kent 21 E9
Hersham Corn 6 F1
Hersham Sur 19 E8
Herstmonceux E Sus 12 E5
Herston Orkney 95 J5
Hertford Herts 29 G10
Hertford Heath Herts 29 G10
Hertingfordbury Herts 29 G10
Hesket Newmarket Cumb 56 C5
Hesketh Bank Lancs 49 G4
Hesketh Lane Lancs 50 E2
Heskin Green Lancs 49 H5
Hesleden Durham 58 C5
Hesleyside Northumb 62 E4
Heslington York 52 D2
Hessay York 51 D11
Hessenford Corn 4 F4
Hessett Suff 30 B6
Hessle E Yorks 52 G6
Hest Bank Lancs 49 C4
Heston London 19 D8
Hestwall Orkney 95 G3
Heswall Mers 42 D5
Hethe Oxon 28 F2
Hethersett Norf 39 E7
Hethersgill Cumb 61 G10
Hethpool Northumb 71 H7
Hett Durham 58 C3
Hetton N Yorks 50 D5
Hetton-le-Hole T&W 58 B4
Hetton Steads Northumb 71 G9
Heugh Northumb 62 F6
Heugh-head Aberds 82 B5
Heveningham Suff 31 A10
Hever Kent 12 B3
Heversham Cumb 49 A4
Hevingham Norf 39 C7
Hewas Water Corn 3 E8
Hewelsfield Glos 16 A2
Hewish N Som 15 E10
Hewish Som 8 D3
Heworth York 52 D2
Hexham Northumb 62 G5
Hextable Kent 20 D2
Hexton Herts 29 E8
Hexworthy Devon 5 D7
Hey Lancs 50 E4
Heybridge Essex 20 B3
Heybridge Essex 30 H5
Heybridge Basin Essex 30 H5
Heybrook Bay Devon 4 G6
Heydon Cambs 29 D11
Heydon Norf 39 C7
Heydour Lincs 36 B6
Heylipol Argyll 78 G2
Heylor Shetland 96 E4
Heysham Lancs 49 C4
Heyshott W Sus 11 C7
Heyside Gtr Man 44 B3
Heytesbury Wilts 16 G6
Heythrop Oxon 27 F10
Heywood Gtr Man 44 A2
Heywood Wilts 16 F5
Hibaldstow N Lincs 46 B3
Hickleton S Yorks 45 B8
Hickling Norf 39 C10
Hickling Notts 36 C2
Hickling Green Norf 39 C10
Hickling Heath Norf 39 C10
Hickstead W Sus 12 D1
Hidcote Boyce Glos 27 D8
High Ackworth W Yorks 51 H10
High Angerton Northumb 62 E6
High Bankhill Cumb 57 B7
High Barnes T&W 63 H9
High Beach Essex 19 B11
High Bentham N Yorks 50 C2
High Bickington Devon 6 D5
High Birkwith N Yorks 50 B3
High Blantyre S Lanark 68 E5
High Bonnybridge Falk 69 C7
High Bradfield S Yorks 44 C6
High Bray Devon 6 C5
High Brooms Kent 12 B4
High Bullen Devon 6 D4
High Buston Northumb 63 C8
High Callerton Northumb 63 F7
High Catton E Yorks 52 D3
High Cogges Oxon 27 H10
High Coniscliffe Darl 58 E3
High Cross Hants 10 B6
High Cross Herts 29 G10
High Easter Essex 30 G3
High Eggborough N Yorks 52 G1
High Ellington N Yorks 51 A7
High Ercall Telford 34 D1
High Etherley Durham 58 D2
High Garrett Essex 30 F4
High Grange Durham 58 C2
High Green Norf 39 E7
High Green S Yorks 45 C7
High Green Worcs 26 D5
High Halden Kent 13 C7
High Halstow Medway 20 D4
High Ham Som 8 A3
High Harrington Cumb 56 D2
High Hatton Shrops 34 C2
High Hawsker N Yorks 59 F10
High Hesket Cumb 57 B6
High Hesleden Durham 58 C5
High Hoyland S Yorks 44 A6
High Hunsley E Yorks 52 F5
High Hurstwood E Sus 12 D3
High Hutton N Yorks 52 C3
High Ireby Cumb 56 C4
High Kelling Norf 39 A7
High Kilburn N Yorks 51 B11
High Lands Durham 58 D2
High Lane Gtr Man 44 D3
High Lane Worcs 26 B3
High Laver Essex 30 H2
High Legh Ches E 43 D10
High Leven Stockton 58 E5
High Littleton Bath 16 F3
High Lorton Cumb 56 D3
High Marishes N Yorks 52 B4
High Marnham Notts 46 E2
High Melton S Yorks 45 B9
High Mickley Northumb 62 G6
High Mindork Dumfries 54 D6
High Newton Cumb 49 A4
High Newton-by-the-Sea Northumb 71 H11
High Nibthwaite Cumb 56 H4
High Offley Staffs 34 C3
High Ongar Essex 20 A2
High Onn Staffs 34 D4
High Roding Essex 30 G3
High Row Cumb 56 C5
High Salvington W Sus 11 D10
High Sellafield Cumb 56 F2
High Shaw N Yorks 57 G10
High Spen T&W 63 H7
High Stoop Durham 58 B2
High Street Corn 3 D8
High Street Kent 12 C6
High Street Suff 30 D5
High Street Suff 31 A11
High Street Suff 31 C11
High Street Green Suff 31 C7
High Throston Hrtlpl 58 C5
High Toynton Lincs 46 F6
High Trewhitt Northumb 62 C6
High Valleyfield Fife 69 B9
High Westwood Durham 63 H7
High Wray Cumb 56 G5
High Wych Herts 29 G11
High Wycombe Bucks 18 B5
Higham Derbys 45 G7
Higham Kent 20 D4
Higham Lancs 50 F4
Higham Suff 30 B4
Higham Suff 31 E7
Higham Dykes Northumb 63 F7
Higham Ferrers Northants 28 B6
Higham Gobion C Beds 29 E8
Higham on the Hill Leics 35 F9
Higham Wood Kent 20 G2
Highampton Devon 6 F3
Highbridge Highld 80 E3
Highbridge Som 15 G9
Highbrook W Sus 12 C2
Highburton W Yorks 44 A5
Highbury Som 16 G3
Highclere Hants 17 E11
Highcliffe Dorset 9 E11
Higher Ansty Dorset 9 D6
Higher Ashton Devon 5 C9
Higher Ballam Lancs 49 F3
Higher Bartle Lancs 49 F5
Higher Boscaswell Corn 2 F2
Higher Burwardsley Ches W 43 G8
Higher Clovelly Devon 6 D2
Higher End Gtr Man 43 B8
Higher Kinnerton Flint 42 F6
Higher Penwortham Lancs 49 G5
Higher Town Scilly 2 C3
Higher Walreddon Devon 4 D5
Higher Walton Lancs 50 G1
Higher Walton Warr 43 D8
Higher Wheelton Lancs 50 G2
Higher Whitley Ches W 43 D9
Higher Wincham Ches W 43 E9
Higher Wych Ches W 33 A10
Highfield E Yorks 52 F3
Highfield Gtr Man 43 B10
Highfield N Ayrs 66 A6
Highfield Oxon 28 F2
Highfield S Yorks 45 D7
Highfield T&W 63 H7
Highfields Cambs 29 C10
Highfields Northumb 71 E8
Highgate London 19 C9
Highlane Ches E 44 F2
Highlane Derbys 45 D8
Highlaws Cumb 56 B3
Highleadon Glos 26 F4
Highleigh W Sus 11 E7
Highley Shrops 34 G3
Highmoor Cross Oxon 18 C4
Highmoor Hill Mon 15 C10
Highnam Glos 26 G4
Highnam Green Glos 26 F4
Highsted Kent 20 E6
Highstreet Green Essex 30 E4
Hightae Dumfries 60 F6
Hightown Ches E 44 F2
Hightown Mers 42 B6
Hightown Green Suff 30 C6
Highway Wilts 17 D7
Highweek Devon 5 D9
Highworth Swindon 17 B9
Hilborough Norf 38 E4
Hilcote Derbys 45 G8
Hilcott Wilts 17 F8
Hilden Park Kent 20 G2
Hildenborough Kent 20 G2
Hildersham Cambs 30 D2
Hilderstone Staffs 34 B5
Hilderthorpe E Yorks 53 C7
Hilfield Dorset 8 D5
Hilgay Norf 38 F2
Hill Pembs 22 F6
Hill S Glos 16 B3
Hill W Mid 35 F7
Hill Brow W Sus 11 B6
Hill Dale Lancs 43 A7
Hill Dyke Lincs 47 H7
Hill End Durham 58 C1
Hill End Fife 76 H3
Hill End N Yorks 51 D6
Hill Head Hants 10 D4
Hill Head Northumb 62 G5
Hill Mountain Pembs 22 F4
Hill of Beath Fife 69 A10
Hill of Fearn Highld 87 D11
Hill of Mountblairy Aberds 89 C6
Hill Ridware Staffs 35 D6
Hill Top Durham 57 D11
Hill Top Hants 10 D3
Hill Top W Mid 34 F5
Hill Top W Yorks 51 H9
Hill View Dorset 9 E8
Hillam N Yorks 51 G11
Hillbeck Cumb 57 E9
Hillborough Kent 21 E9
Hillbrae Aberds 83 A9
Hillbrae Aberds 88 D6
Hillbutts Dorset 9 D8
Hillclifflane Derbys 44 H6
Hillcommon Som 7 D10
Hillend Fife 69 B10
Hillerton Devon 7 G6
Hillesden Bucks 28 F3
Hillesley Glos 16 C4
Hillfarance Som 7 D10
Hillhead Aberds 88 E5
Hillhead Devon 5 F10
Hillhead S Ayrs 67 E7
Hillhead of Auchentumb Aberds 89 C9
Hillhead of Cocklaw Aberds 89 D10
Hillhouse Borders 70 E4
Hilliclay Highld 94 D3
Hillingdon London 19 C7
Hillington Glasgow 68 D4
Hillington Norf 38 C3
Hillmorton Warks 28 A2
Hillockhead Aberds 82 B6
Hillockhead Aberds 82 C5
Hillside Aberds 83 D11
Hillside Angus 77 A10
Hillside Mers 42 A6
Hillside Orkney 95 J5
Hillside Shetland 96 G6
Hillswick Shetland 96 F4
Hillway IoW 10 F5
Hillwell Shetland 96 M5
Hilmarton Wilts 17 D7
Hilperton Wilts 16 F5
Hilsea Ptsmth 10 D5
Hilston E Yorks 53 F8
Hilton Aberds 89 E9
Hilton Cambs 29 B9
Hilton Cumb 57 D9
Hilton Derbys 35 B8
Hilton Dorset 9 D6
Hilton Durham 58 D2
Hilton Highld 87 C10
Hilton Shrops 34 F3
Hilton Stockton 58 E5
Hilton of Cadboll Highld 87 D11
Himbleton Worcs 26 C6
Himley Staffs 34 F4
Hincaster Cumb 49 A5
Hinckley Leics 35 F10
Hinderclay Suff 38 H6
Hinderton Ches W 42 E6
Hinderwell N Yorks 59 E8
Hindford Shrops 33 B9
Hindhead Sur 18 H5
Hindley Gtr Man 43 B9
Hindley Green Gtr Man 43 B9
Hindlip Worcs 26 C5
Hindolveston Norf 38 C6
Hindon Wilts 9 A8
Hindringham Norf 38 B5
Hingham Norf 38 E6
Hinstock Shrops 34 C2
Hintlesham Suff 31 D7
Hinton Hants 9 E11
Hinton Hereford 25 E10
Hinton Northants 28 C2
Hinton S Glos 16 D4
Hinton Shrops 33 E10
Hinton Ampner Hants 10 B4
Hinton Blewett Bath 16 F2
Hinton Charterhouse Bath 16 F4
Hinton-in-the-Hedges Northants 28 E2
Hinton Martell Dorset 9 D9
Hinton on the Green Worcs 27 D7
Hinton Parva Swindon 17 C9
Hinton St George Som 8 C3
Hinton St Mary Dorset 9 C6
Hinton Waldrist Oxon 17 B10
Hints Shrops 26 A3
Hints Staffs 35 E7
Hinwick Bedford 28 B6
Hinxhill Kent 13 B9
Hinxton Cambs 29 D11
Hinxworth Herts 29 D9
Hipperholme W Yorks 51 G7
Hipswell N Yorks 58 G2
Hirael Gwyn 41 C7
Hiraeth Carms 22 D6
Hirn Aberds 83 C9
Hirnant Powys 33 C6
Hirst N Lanark 69 D7
Hirst Northumb 63 E8
Hirst Courtney N Yorks 52 G2
Hirwaen Denb 42 F4
Hirwaun Rhondda 24 H6
Hiscott Devon 6 D4
Histon Cambs 29 B11
Hitcham Suff 30 C6
Hitchin Herts 29 F8
Hither Green London 19 D10
Hittisleigh Devon 7 G6
Hive E Yorks 52 F4
Hixon Staffs 34 C6
Hoaden Kent 21 F9
Hoaldalbert Mon 25 F10
Hoar Cross Staffs 35 C7
Hoarwithy Hereford 26 F2
Hoath Kent 21 E9
Hobarris Shrops 33 H9
Hobbister Orkney 95 H4
Hobkirk Borders 61 B11
Hobson Durham 63 H7
Hoby Leics 36 D2
Hockering Norf 39 D6
Hockerton Notts 45 G11
Hockley Essex 20 B5
Hockley Heath W Mid 27 A8
Hockliffe C Beds 28 F6
Hockwold cum Wilton Norf 38 G3
Hockworthy Devon 7 E9
Hoddesdon Herts 29 H10
Hoddlesden Blackburn 50 G3
Hoddom Mains Dumfries 61 F7
Hoddomcross Dumfries 61 F7
Hodgeston Pembs 22 G5
Hodley Powys 33 F7
Hodnet Shrops 34 C2
Hodthorpe Derbys 45 E9
Hoe Hants 10 C4
Hoe Norf 38 D5
Hoe Gate Hants 10 C5
Hoff Cumb 57 E8
Hog Patch Sur 18 G5
Hoggard's Green Suff 30 C5
Hoggeston Bucks 28 F5
Hogha Gearraidh W Isles 84 A2
Hoghton Lancs 50 G2
Hognaston Derbys 44 G6
Hogsthorpe Lincs 47 E9
Holbeach Lincs 37 C9
Holbeach Bank Lincs 37 C9
Holbeach Clough Lincs 37 C9
Holbeach Drove Lincs 37 D9
Holbeach Hurn Lincs 37 C9
Holbeach St Johns Lincs 37 D9
Holbeach St Marks Lincs 37 B9
Holbeach St Matthew Lincs 37 B10
Holbeck Notts 45 E9
Holbeck W Yorks 51 F8
Holbeck Woodhouse Notts 45 E9
Holberrow Green Worcs 27 C7
Holbeton Devon 5 F7
Holborn London 19 C10
Holbrook Derbys 35 A9
Holbrook S Yorks 45 D8
Holbrook Suff 31 E8
Holburn Northumb 71 G9
Holbury Hants 10 D3
Holcombe Devon 5 D10
Holcombe Som 16 G3
Holcombe Rogus Devon 7 E9
Holcot Northants 28 B4
Holden Lancs 50 E3
Holdenby Northants 28 B3
Holdenhurst Bmouth 9 E10
Holdgate Shrops 34 G1
Holdingham Lincs 46 H4
Holditch Dorset 8 D2
Hole-in-the-Wall Hereford 26 F3
Holefield Borders 71 G7
Holehouses Ches E 43 E10
Holemoor Devon 6 F3
Holestane Dumfries 60 D4
Holford Som 7 B10
Holgate York 52 D1
Holker Cumb 49 B3
Holkham Norf 38 A4
Hollacombe Devon 6 F2
Holland Orkney 95 C5
Holland Orkney 95 F7
Holland Fen Lincs 46 H6
Holland-on-Sea Essex 31 G9
Hollandstoun Orkney 95 C8
Hollee Dumfries 61 G8
Hollesley Suff 31 D10
Hollicombe Torbay 5 E9
Hollingbourne Kent 20 F5
Hollington Derbys 35 B8
Hollington E Sus 13 E6
Hollington Staffs 35 B6
Hollington Grove Derbys 35 B8
Hollingworth Gtr Man 44 C4
Hollins Gtr Man 44 B2
Hollins Green Warr 43 C9
Hollins Lane Lancs 49 D4
Hollinsclough Staffs 44 F4
Hollinwood Gtr Man 44 B3
Hollinwood Shrops 33 B11
Hollocombe Devon 6 E5
Hollow Meadows S Yorks 44 D6
Holloway Derbys 45 G7
Hollowell Northants 28 A3
Holly End Norf 37 E10
Holly Green Worcs 26 D5
Hollybush Caerph 15 A7
Hollybush E Ayrs 67 E6
Hollybush Worcs 26 E4
Hollym E Yorks 53 G9
Hollywood Worcs 35 H6
Holmbridge W Yorks 44 B5
Holmbury St Mary Sur 19 G8
Holmbush Corn 3 D9
Holmcroft Staffs 34 C5
Holme Cambs 37 G7
Holme Cumb 49 B5
Holme N Yorks 51 A9
Holme Notts 46 G2
Holme W Yorks 44 B5
Holme Chapel Lancs 50 G4
Holme Green N Yorks 52 E1
Holme Hale Norf 38 E4
Holme Lacy Hereford 26 E2
Holme Marsh Hereford 25 C10
Holme next the Sea Norf 38 A3
Holme-on-Spalding-Moor E Yorks 52 F4
Holme on the Wolds E Yorks 52 E5
Holme Pierrepont Notts 36 B2
Holme St Cuthbert Cumb 56 B3
Holme Wood W Yorks 51 F7
Holmer Hereford 26 D2
Holmer Green Bucks 18 B6
Holmes Chapel Ches E 43 F10
Holmesfield Derbys 45 E7
Holmeswood Lancs 49 H4
Holmewood Derbys 45 F8
Holmfirth W Yorks 44 B5
Holmhead Dumfries 60 E3
Holmhead E Ayrs 67 D8
Holmisdale Highld 84 D6
Holmpton E Yorks 53 G9
Holmrook Cumb 56 G2
Holmsgarth Shetland 96 J6
Holmwrangle Cumb 57 B7
Holne Devon 5 E8
Holnest Dorset 8 D5
Holsworthy Devon 6 F2
Holsworthy Beacon Devon 6 F2
Holt Dorset 9 D9
Holt Norf 39 B6
Holt Wilts 16 E5
Holt Worcs 26 B5
Holt Wrex 43 G7
Holt End Hants 18 H3
Holt End Worcs 27 B7
Holt Fleet Worcs 26 B5
Holt Heath Worcs 26 B5
Holt Park W Yorks 51 E8
Holtby York 52 D2
Holton Oxon 28 H3
Holton Som 8 B5
Holton Suff 39 H9
Holton cum Beckering Lincs 46 D5
Holton Heath Dorset 9 E8
Holton le Clay Lincs 46 B6
Holton le Moor Lincs 46 C4
Holton St Mary Suff 31 E7
Holwell Dorset 8 C6
Holwell Herts 29 E8
Holwell Leics 36 C3
Holwell Oxon 27 H9
Holwick Durham 57 D11
Holworth Dorset 9 F6
Holy Cross Worcs 34 H5
Holy Island Northumb 71 F10
Holybourne Hants 18 G4
Holyhead = Caergybi Anglesey 40 B4
Holymoorside Derbys 45 F7
Holyport Windsor 18 D5
Holystone Northumb 62 C5
Holytown N Lanark 68 D6
Holywell Cambs 29 A10
Holywell Corn 3 D6
Holywell Dorset 8 D4
Holywell E Sus 12 G4
Holywell = Treffynnon Flint 42 E4
Holywell Northumb 63 F9
Holywell Green W Yorks 51 H6
Holywell Lake Som 7 D10
Holywell Row Suff 38 H3
Holywood Dumfries 60 E5
Hom Green Hereford 26 F2
Homer Shrops 34 E2
Homersfield Suff 39 G8
Homington Wilts 9 B10
Honey Hill Kent 21 E8
Honey Street Wilts 17 E8
Honey Tye Suff 30 E6
Honeyborough Pembs 22 F4
Honeybourne Worcs 27 D8
Honeychurch Devon 6 F5
Honiley Warks 27 A9
Honing Norf 39 C9
Honingham Norf 39 D7
Honington Lincs 36 A5
Honington Suff 30 A6
Honington Warks 27 D9
Honiton Devon 7 F10
Honley W Yorks 44 A5
Hoo Green Ches E 43 D10
Hoo St Werburgh Medway 20 D4
Hood Green S Yorks 45 B7
Hooe E Sus 12 F5
Hooe Plym 4 F6
Hooe Common E Sus 12 E5
Hook E Yorks 52 G3
Hook Hants 18 F4
Hook London 19 E8
Hook Pembs 22 E4
Hook Wilts 17 C7
Hook Green Kent 12 C5
Hook Green Kent 20 E3
Hook Norton Oxon 27 E10
Hooke Dorset 8 E4
Hookgate Staffs 34 B3
Hookway Devon 7 G7
Hookwood Sur 12 B1
Hoole Ches W 43 F7
Hooley Sur 19 F9
Hoop Mon 26 H2
Hooton Ches W 42 E6
Hooton Levitt S Yorks 45 C9
Hooton Pagnell S Yorks 45 B8
Hooton Roberts S Yorks 45 C8
Hop Pole Lincs 37 D7
Hope Derbys 44 D5
Hope Devon 5 H7
Hope = Yr Hôb Flint 42 G6
Hope Highld 92 C7
Hope Powys 33 E8
Hope Shrops 33 E9
Hope Staffs 44 G5
Hope Bagot Shrops 26 A2
Hope Bowdler Shrops 33 F10
Hope End Green Essex 30 F2
Hope Green Ches E 44 D3
Hope Mansell Hereford 26 G3
Hope under Dinmore Hereford 26 C2
Hopeman Moray 88 B1
Hope's Green Essex 20 C4
Hopesay Shrops 33 G9
Hopley's Green Hereford 25 C10
Hopperton N Yorks 51 D10
Hopstone Shrops 34 F3
Hopton Shrops 33 C9
Hopton Shrops 34 C1
Hopton Staffs 34 C5
Hopton Suff 38 H5
Hopton Cangeford Shrops 33 G11
Hopton Castle Shrops 33 H9
Hopton on Sea Norf 39 E11
Hopton Wafers Shrops 34 H2
Hoptonheath Shrops 33 H9
Hopwas Staffs 35 E7
Hopwood Gtr Man 44 B2
Hopwood Worcs 34 H6
Horam E Sus 12 E4
Horbling Lincs 37 B7
Horbury W Yorks 51 H8
Horcott Glos 17 A8
Horden Durham 58 B5
Horderley Shrops 33 G10
Hordle Hants 10 E1
Hordley Shrops 33 B9
Horeb Carms 23 D10
Horeb Carms 23 F9
Horeb Ceredig 23 B8
Horfield Bristol 16 D3
Horham Suff 31 A9
Horkesley Heath Essex 30 F6
Horkstow N Lincs 52 H5
Horley Oxon 27 D11
Horley Sur 12 B1
Hornblotton Green Som 8 A4
Hornby Lancs 50 C1
Hornby N Yorks 58 F4
Hornby N Yorks 58 G3
Horncastle Lincs 46 F6
Hornchurch London 20 C2
Horncliffe Northumb 71 F8
Horndean Borders 71 F7
Horndean Hants 10 C6
Horndon Devon 4 D6
Horndon on the Hill Thurrock 20 C3
Horne Sur 12 B2
Horniehaugh Angus 77 A7
Horning Norf 39 D9
Horninghold Leics 36 F4
Horninglow Staffs 35 C8
Horningsea Cambs 29 B11
Horningsham Wilts 16 G5
Horningtoft Norf 38 C5
Horns Corner Kent 12 D6
Horns Cross Devon 6 D2
Horns Cross E Sus 13 D7
Hornsby Cumb 57 A7
Hornsea E Yorks 53 E8
Hornsea Bridge E Yorks 53 E8
Hornsey London 19 C10
Hornton Oxon 27 D10
Horrabridge Devon 4 E6
Horringer Suff 30 B5
Horringford IoW 10 F4
Horse Bridge Staffs 44 G3
Horsebridge Devon 4 D5
Horsebridge Hants 10 A2
Horsebrook Staffs 34 D4
Horsehay Telford 34 E2
Horseheath Cambs 30 D3
Horsehouse N Yorks 50 A6
Horsell Sur 18 F6
Horseman's Green Wrex 33 A10
Horseway Cambs 37 G10
Horsey Norf 39 C10
Horsford Norf 39 D7
Horsforth W Yorks 51 F8
Horsham W Sus 11 A10
Horsham Worcs 26 C4
Horsham St Faith Norf 39 D8
Horsington Lincs 46 F5
Horsington Som 8 B6
Horsley Derbys 35 A9
Horsley Glos 16 B5
Horsley Northumb 62 D4
Horsley Northumb 62 G6
Horsley Cross Essex 31 F8
Horsley Woodhouse Derbys 35 A9
Horsleycross Street Essex 31 F8
Horsleyhill Borders 61 B11
Horsleyhope Durham 58 B1
Horsmonden Kent 12 B5
Horspath Oxon 28 H2
Horstead Norf 39 D8
Horsted Keynes W Sus 12 D2
Horton Bucks 28 G6
Horton Dorset 9 D9
Horton Lancs 50 D4
Horton Northants 28 C5
Horton S Glos 16 C4
Horton Shrops 33 C10
Horton Som 8 C2
Horton Staffs 44 G3
Horton Swansea 23 H9

Kirby Underdale E Yorks 52 D4
Kirby Wiske N Yorks 51 A9
Kirdford W Sus 11 B9
Kirk Highld 94 E4
Kirk Bramwith S Yorks 45 A10
Kirk Deighton N Yorks 51 D9
Kirk Ella E Yorks 52 G6
Kirk Hallam Derbys 35 A10
Kirk Hammerton N Yorks 51 D10
Kirk Ireton Derbys 44 G6
Kirk Langley Derbys 35 B8
Kirk Merrington Durham 58 C3
Kirk Michael IoM 48 C3
Kirk of Shotts N Lanark 69 D7
Kirk Sandall S Yorks 45 B10
Kirk Smeaton N Yorks 51 H11
Kirk Yetholm Borders 71 H7
Kirkabister Shetland 96 K6
Kirkandrews Dumfries 55 E9
Kirkandrews upon Eden Cumb 61 H9
Kirkbampton Cumb 61 H9
Kirkbean Dumfries 60 H5
Kirkbride Cumb 61 H8
Kirkbuddo Angus 77 C8
Kirkburn Borders 69 G11
Kirkburn E Yorks 52 D5
Kirkburton W Yorks 44 A5
Kirkby Lincs 46 C4
Kirkby Mers 43 C7
Kirkby N Yorks 59 F6
Kirkby Fleetham N Yorks 58 G3
Kirkby Green Lincs 46 G4
Kirkby In Ashfield Notts 45 G9
Kirkby-in-Furness Cumb 49 A2
Kirkby la Thorpe Lincs 46 H5
Kirkby Lonsdale Cumb 50 B2
Kirkby Malham N Yorks 50 C4
Kirkby Mallory Leics 35 E10
Kirkby Malzeard N Yorks 51 B8
Kirkby Mills N Yorks 59 H8
Kirkby on Bain Lincs 46 F6
Kirkby Overflow N Yorks 51 E9
Kirkby Stephen Cumb 57 F9
Kirkby Thore Cumb 57 D8
Kirkby Underwood Lincs 37 C6
Kirkby Wharfe N Yorks 51 E11
Kirkbymoorside N Yorks 59 H7
Kirkcaldy Fife 69 A11
Kirkcambeck Cumb 61 G11
Kirkcarswell Dumfries 55 E10
Kirkcolm Dumfries 54 C3
Kirkconnel Dumfries 60 B3
Kirkconnell Dumfries 60 G5
Kirkcowan Dumfries 54 C6
Kirkcudbright Dumfries 55 D9
Kirkdale Mers 42 C6
Kirkfieldbank S Lanark 69 F7
Kirkgunzeon Dumfries 55 C11
Kirkham Lancs 49 F4
Kirkham N Yorks 52 C3
Kirkhamgate W Yorks 51 G8
Kirkharle Northumb 62 E6
Kirkheaton Northumb 62 F6
Kirkheaton W Yorks 51 H7
Kirkhill Angus 77 A9
Kirkhill Highld 87 G8
Kirkhill Midloth 69 D11
Kirkhill Moray 88 E2
Kirkhope Borders 61 A9
Kirkhouse Borders 70 G2
Kirkiboll Highld 93 D8
Kirkibost Highld 85 G10
Kirkinch Angus 76 C6
Kirkinner Dumfries 55 D7
Kirkintilloch E Dunb 68 C5
Kirkland Cumb 56 E2
Kirkland Cumb 57 C8
Kirkland Dumfries 60 B3
Kirkland Dumfries 60 D4
Kirkleatham Redcar 59 D6
Kirklevington Stockton 58 F5
Kirkley Suff 39 F11
Kirklington N Yorks 51 A9
Kirklington Notts 45 G10
Kirklinton Cumb 61 G10
Kirkliston Edin 69 C10
Kirkmaiden Dumfries 54 F4
Kirkmichael Perth 76 B3
Kirkmichael S Ayrs 66 F6
Kirkmuirhill S Lanark 68 F6
Kirknewton Northumb 71 G8
Kirknewton W Loth 69 D10
Kirkney Aberds 88 E5
Kirkoswald Cumb 57 B7
Kirkoswald S Ayrs 66 F5
Kirkpatrick Durham Dumfries 60 F3
Kirkpatrick-Fleming Dumfries 61 F8
Kirksanton Cumb 49 A1
Kirkstall W Yorks 51 F8
Kirkstead Lincs 46 F5
Kirkstile Aberds 88 E5
Kirkstyle Highld 94 C5
Kirkton Aberds 83 A8
Kirkton Aberds 89 D6
Kirkton Angus 77 C7
Kirkton Angus 77 D7
Kirkton Borders 61 B11
Kirkton Dumfries 60 E5
Kirkton Fife 76 E6
Kirkton Highld 85 F13
Kirkton Highld 86 G2
Kirkton Highld 87 B10
Kirkton Highld 87 F10
Kirkton Perth 76 F2
Kirkton S Lanark 60 A5
Kirkton Stirling 75 G8
Kirkton Manor Borders 69 G11
Kirkton of Airlie Angus 76 B6
Kirkton of Auchterhouse Angus 76 D6
Kirkton of Auchterless Aberds 89 D7
Kirkton of Barevan Highld 87 G11
Kirkton of Bourtie Aberds 89 F8
Kirkton of Collace Perth 76 D4
Kirkton of Craig Angus 77 B10
Kirkton of Culsalmond Aberds 89 E6
Kirkton of Durris Aberds 83 D9
Kirkton of Glenbuchat Aberds 82 B5
Kirkton of Glenisla Angus 76 A5
Kirkton of Kingoldrum Angus 76 B6
Kirkton of Largo Fife 77 G7
Kirkton of Lethendy Perth 76 C4
Kirkton of Logie Buchan Aberds 89 F9
Kirkton of Maryculter Aberds 83 D10
Kirkton of Menmuir Angus 77 A8
Kirkton of Monikie Angus 77 D8
Kirkton of Oyne Aberds 83 A8
Kirkton of Rayne Aberds 83 A8
Kirkton of Skene Aberds 83 C10
Kirkton of Tough Aberds 83 B8
Kirktonhill Borders 70 E3
Kirktown Aberds 89 C10
Kirktown of Alvah Aberds 89 B6
Kirktown of Deskford Moray 88 B5
Kirktown of Fetteresso Aberds 83 E10
Kirktown of Mortlach Moray 88 E3
Kirktown of Slains Aberds 89 F10
Kirkurd Borders 69 F10
Kirkwall Orkney 95 G5
Kirkwhelpington Northumb 62 E5
Kirmington N Lincs 46 A5
Kirmond le Mire Lincs 46 C5
Kirn Argyll 73 F10
Kirriemuir Angus 76 B6
Kirstead Green Norf 39 F8
Kirtlebridge Dumfries 61 F8
Kirtleton Dumfries 61 E8
Kirtling Cambs 30 C3
Kirtling Green Cambs 30 C3
Kirtlington Oxon 27 G11
Kirtomy Highld 93 C10
Kirton Lincs 37 B9
Kirton Notts 45 F10
Kirton Suff 31 E9
Kirton End Lincs 37 A8
Kirton Holme Lincs 37 A8
Kirton in Lindsey N Lincs 46 C3
Kislingbury Northants 28 C3
Kites Hardwick Warks 27 B11
Kittisford Som 7 D9
Kittle Swansea 23 H10
Kitt's Green W Mid 35 G7
Kitt's Moss Gtr Man 44 D2
Kittybrewster Aberdeen 83 C11
Kitwood Hants 10 A5
Kivernoll Hereford 25 E11
Kiveton Park S Yorks 45 D8
Knaith Lincs 46 D2
Knaith Park Lincs 46 D2
Knap Corner Dorset 9 B7
Knaphill Sur 18 F6
Knapp Perth 76 D5
Knapp Som 8 B2
Knapthorpe Notts 45 G11
Knapton Norf 39 B9
Knapton York 52 D1
Knapton Green Hereford 25 C11
Knapwell Cambs 29 B10
Knaresborough N Yorks 51 D9
Knarsdale Northumb 57 A8
Knauchland Moray 88 C5
Knaven Aberds 89 D8
Knayton N Yorks 58 H5
Knebworth Herts 29 F9
Knedlington E Yorks 52 G3
Kneesall Notts 45 F11
Kneesworth Cambs 29 D10
Kneeton Notts 45 H11
Knelston Swansea 23 H9
Knenhall Staffs 34 B5
Knettishall Suff 38 G5
Knightacott Devon 6 C5
Knightcote Warks 27 C10
Knightley Dale Staffs 34 C4
Knighton Devon 4 G6
Knighton Leicester 36 E1
Knighton = Tref-y-Clawdd Powys 25 A9
Knighton Staffs 34 A3
Knighton Staffs 34 C3
Knightswood Glasgow 68 D4
Knightwick Worcs 26 C4
Knill Hereford 25 B9
Knipton Leics 36 B4
Knitsley Durham 58 B2
Kniveton Derbys 44 G6
Knock Argyll 79 H8
Knock Cumb 57 D8
Knock Moray 88 C5
Knockally Highld 94 H3
Knockan Highld 92 H5
Knockandhu Moray 82 A4
Knockando Moray 88 D1
Knockando Ho. Moray 88 D2
Knockbain Highld 87 F9
Knockbreck Highld 84 B7
Knockbrex Dumfries 55 E8
Knockdee Highld 94 D3
Knockdolian S Ayrs 66 H4
Knockenkelly N Ayrs 66 D3
Knockentiber E Ayrs 67 C6
Knockespock Ho. Aberds 83 A7
Knockfarrel Highld 87 F8
Knockglass Dumfries 54 D3
Knockholt Kent 19 F11
Knockholt Pound Kent 19 F11
Knockie Lodge Highld 80 B6
Knockin Shrops 33 C9
Knockinlaw E Ayrs 67 C7
Knocklearn Dumfries 60 F3
Knocknaha Argyll 65 G7
Knocknain Dumfries 54 C2
Knockrome Argyll 72 F4
Knocksharry IoM 48 D2
Knodishall Suff 31 B11
Knolls Green Ches E 44 E2
Knolton Wrex 33 B9
Knolton Bryn Wrex 33 B9
Knook Wilts 16 G6
Knossington Leics 36 E4
Knott End-on-Sea Lancs 49 E3
Knotting Bedford 29 B7
Knotting Green Bedford 29 B7
Knottingley W Yorks 51 G11
Knotts Cumb 56 D6
Knotts Lancs 50 D3
Knotty Ash Mers 43 C7
Knotty Green Bucks 18 B6
Knowbury Shrops 26 A2
Knowe Dumfries 54 B6
Knowehead Dumfries 67 G9
Knowes of Elrick Aberds 88 C6
Knowesgate Northumb 62 E5
Knoweton N Lanark 68 E6
Knowhead Aberds 89 C9
Knowl Hill Windsor 18 D5
Knowle Bristol 16 D3
Knowle Devon 6 C3
Knowle Devon 7 F6
Knowle Devon 7 H9
Knowle Shrops 26 A2
Knowle W Mid 35 H7
Knowle Green Lancs 50 F2
Knowle Park W Yorks 51 E6
Knowlton Dorset 9 C9
Knowlton Kent 21 F9
Knowsley Mers 43 C7
Knowstone Devon 7 D7
Knox Bridge Kent 13 B6
Knucklas Powys 25 A9
Knuston Northants 28 B6
Knutsford Ches E 43 E10
Knutton Staffs 44 H2
Knypersley Staffs 44 G2
Kuggar Corn 2 H6
Kyle of Lochalsh Highld 85 F12
Kyleakin Highld 85 F12
Kylerhea Highld 85 F12
Kylesknoydart Highld 79 B11
Kylesku Highld 92 F5
Kylesmorar Highld 79 B11
Kylestrome Highld 92 F5
Kyllachy House Highld 81 A9
Kynaston Shrops 33 C9
Kynnersley Telford 34 D2
Kyre Magna Worcs 26 B3

L

La Fontenelle Guern 11
La Planque Guern 11
Labost W Isles 91 C7
Lacasaidh W Isles 91 E8
Lacasdal W Isles 91 D9
Laceby NE Lincs 46 B6
Lacey Green Bucks 18 B5
Lach Dennis Ches W 43 E10
Lackford Suff 30 A4
Lacock Wilts 16 E6
Ladbroke Warks 27 C11
Laddingford Kent 20 G3
Lade Bank Lincs 47 G7
Ladock Corn 3 D7
Lady Orkney 95 D7
Ladybank Fife 76 F6
Ladykirk Borders 71 F7
Ladysford Aberds 89 B9
Laga Highld 79 E9
Lagalochan Argyll 73 B7
Lagavulin Argyll 64 D5
Lagg Argyll 72 F4
Lagg N Ayrs 66 D2
Laggan Argyll 64 C3
Laggan Highld 79 D10
Laggan Highld 80 D4
Laggan Highld 81 D8
Laggan S Ayrs 54 A5
Lagganulva Argyll 78 G7
Laide Highld 91 H13
Laigh Fenwick E Ayrs 67 B7
Laigh Glengall S Ayrs 66 E6
Laighmuir E Ayrs 67 B7
Laindon Essex 20 C3
Lair Highld 86 G3
Lairg Highld 93 J8
Lairg Lodge Highld 93 J8
Lairg Muir Highld 93 J8
Lairgmore Highld 87 H8
Laisterdyke W Yorks 51 F7
Laithes Cumb 56 C6
Lake IoW 10 F4
Lake Wilts 17 H8
Lakenham Norf 39 E8
Lakenheath Suff 38 G3
Lakesend Norf 37 F11
Lakeside Cumb 56 H5
Laleham Sur 19 E7
Laleston Bridgend 14 D4
Lamarsh Essex 30 E5
Lamas Norf 39 C8
Lambden Borders 70 F6
Lamberhurst Kent 12 C5
Lamberhurst Quarter Kent 12 C5
Lamberton Borders 71 E8
Lambeth London 19 D10
Lambhill Glasgow 68 D4
Lambley Northumb 62 H2
Lambley Notts 45 H10
Lamborough Hill Oxon 17 A11
Lambourn W Berks 17 D10
Lambourne End Essex 19 B11
Lambs Green W Sus 19 H9
Lambston Pembs 22 E4
Lambton T&W 58 A3
Lamerton Devon 4 D5
Lamesley T&W 63 H8
Laminess Orkney 95 E7
Lamington Highld 87 D10
Lamington S Lanark 69 G8
Lamlash N Ayrs 66 C3
Lamloch Dumfries 67 G8
Lamonby Cumb 56 C6
Lamorna Corn 2 G3
Lamorran Corn 3 E7
Lampardbrook Suff 31 B9
Lampeter = Llanbedr Pont Steffan Ceredig 23 B10
Lampeter Velfrey Pembs 22 E6
Lamphey Pembs 22 F5
Lamplugh Cumb 56 D2
Lamport Northants 28 A4
Lamyatt Som 16 H3
Lana Devon 6 G2
Lanark S Lanark 69 F7
Lancaster Lancs 49 C4
Lanchester Durham 58 B2
Lancing W Sus 11 D10
Landbeach Cambs 29 B11
Landcross Devon 6 D3
Landerberry Aberds 83 C9
Landford Wilts 10 C1
Landford Manor Wilts 10 B1
Landimore Swansea 23 G9
Landkey Devon 6 C4
Landore Swansea 14 B2
Landrake Corn 4 E4
Landscove Devon 5 E8
Landshipping Pembs 22 E5
Landshipping Quay Pembs 22 E5
Landulph Corn 4 E5
Landwade Suff 30 B3
Lane Corn 3 C7
Lane End Bucks 18 B5
Lane End Cumb 56 G3
Lane End Dorset 9 E7
Lane End Hants 10 B4
Lane End IoW 10 F5
Lane End Lancs 50 E4
Lane Ends Lancs 50 D3
Lane Ends Lancs 50 F3
Lane Ends N Yorks 50 E5
Lane Head Derbys 44 E5
Lane Head Durham 58 E2
Lane Head Gtr Man 43 C9
Lane Head W Yorks 44 B5
Lane Side Lancs 50 G3
Laneast Corn 4 C3
Laneham Notts 46 E2
Lanehead Durham 57 B10
Lanehead Northumb 62 E3
Lanercost Cumb 61 G11
Laneshaw Bridge Lancs 50 E5
Lanfach Caerph 15 B8
Langar Notts 36 B3
Langbank Renfs 68 C2
Langbar N Yorks 51 D6
Langburnshiels Borders 61 C11
Langcliffe N Yorks 50 C4
Langdale Highld 93 E9
Langdale End N Yorks 59 G10
Langdon Corn 4 C4
Langdon Beck Durham 57 C10
Langdon Hills Essex 20 C3
Langdyke Fife 76 G6
Langenhoe Essex 31 G7
Langford C Beds 29 D8
Langford Devon 7 F9
Langford Essex 30 H5
Langford Notts 46 G2
Langford Oxon 17 A9
Langford Budville Som 7 D10
Langham Essex 31 E7
Langham Norf 38 A6
Langham Rutland 36 D4
Langham Suff 30 B6
Langhaugh Borders 69 G11
Langho Lancs 50 F3
Langholm Dumfries 61 E9
Langleeford Northumb 62 A5
Langley Ches E 44 E3
Langley Hants 10 D3
Langley Herts 29 F9
Langley Kent 20 F5
Langley Northumb 62 G4
Langley Slough 19 D7
Langley W Sus 11 B7
Langley Warks 27 B8
Langley Burrell Wilts 16 D6
Langley Common Derbys 35 B8
Langley Heath Kent 20 F5
Langley Lower Green Essex 29 E11
Langley Marsh Som 7 D9
Langley Park Durham 58 B3
Langley Street Norf 39 E9
Langley Upper Green Essex 29 E11
Langney E Sus 12 F5
Langold Notts 45 D9
Langore Corn 4 C4
Langport Som 8 B3
Langrick Lincs 46 H6
Langridge Bath 16 E4
Langridge Ford Devon 6 D4
Langrigg Cumb 56 B3
Langrish Hants 10 B6
Langsett S Yorks 44 B6
Langshaw Borders 70 G4
Langside Perth 75 F10
Langskaill Orkney 95 D5
Langstone Hants 10 D6
Langstone Newport 15 B9
Langthorne N Yorks 58 G3
Langthorpe N Yorks 51 C9
Langthwaite N Yorks 58 F1
Langtoft E Yorks 52 C6
Langtoft Lincs 37 D7
Langton Durham 58 E2
Langton Lincs 46 F6
Langton Lincs 47 E7
Langton N Yorks 52 C3
Langton by Wragby Lincs 46 E5
Langton Green Kent 12 C4
Langton Green Suff 31 A8
Langton Herring Dorset 8 F5
Langton Matravers Dorset 9 G9
Langtree Devon 6 E3
Langwathby Cumb 57 C7
Langwell Ho. Highld 94 H3
Langwell Lodge Highld 92 J4
Langwith Derbys 45 F9
Langwith Junction Derbys 45 F9
Langworth Lincs 46 E4
Lanivet Corn 3 C9
Lanlivery Corn 4 F1
Lanner Corn 2 F6
Lanreath Corn 4 F2
Lansallos Corn 4 F2
Lansdown Glos 26 F6
Lanteglos Highway Corn 4 F2
Lanton Borders 62 A2
Lanton Northumb 71 G8
Lapford Devon 7 F6
Laphroaig Argyll 64 D4
Lapley Staffs 34 D4
Lapworth Warks 27 A8
Larachbeg Highld 79 G9
Larbert Falk 69 B7
Larden Green Ches E 43 G8
Largie Aberds 88 E6
Largiemore Argyll 73 E8
Largoward Fife 77 G7
Largs N Ayrs 73 H11
Largybeg N Ayrs 66 D3
Largymore N Ayrs 66 D3
Larkfield Invclyd 73 F11
Larkhall S Lanark 68 E6
Larkhill Wilts 17 G8
Larling Norf 38 G5
Larriston Borders 61 D11
Lartington Durham 58 E1
Lary Aberds 82 C5
Lasham Hants 18 G3
Lashenden Kent 13 B7
Lassington Glos 26 F4
Lassodie Fife 69 A10
Lastingham N Yorks 59 G8
Latcham Som 15 G10
Latchford Herts 29 F10
Latchford Warr 43 D9
Latchingdon Essex 20 A5
Latchley Corn 4 D5
Lately Common Warr 43 C9
Lathbury M Keynes 28 D5
Latheron Highld 94 G3
Latheronwheel Highld 94 G3
Latheronwheel Ho. Highld 94 G3
Lathones Fife 77 G7
Latimer Bucks 19 B7
Latteridge S Glos 16 C3
Lattiford Som 8 B5
Latton Wilts 17 B7
Latton Bush Essex 29 H11
Lauchintilly Aberds 83 B9
Lauder Borders 70 F4
Laugharne Carms 23 E8
Laughterton Lincs 46 E2
Laughton E Sus 12 E4
Laughton Leics 36 G2
Laughton Lincs 37 B6
Laughton Lincs 46 C2
Laughton Common S Yorks 45 D9
Laughton en le Morthen S Yorks 45 D9
Launcells Corn 6 F1
Launceston Corn 4 C4
Launton Oxon 28 F3
Laurencekirk Aberds 83 F9
Laurieston Dumfries 55 C9
Laurieston Falk 69 C8
Lavendon M Keynes 28 C6
Lavenham Suff 30 D6
Laverhay Dumfries 61 D7
Laversdale Cumb 61 G10
Laverstock Wilts 9 A10
Laverstoke Hants 17 G11
Laverton Glos 27 E7
Laverton N Yorks 51 B8
Laverton Som 16 F4
Lavister Wrex 42 G6
Law S Lanark 69 E7
Lawers Perth 75 D9
Lawers Perth 75 E10
Lawford Essex 31 E7
Lawhitton Corn 4 C4
Lawkland N Yorks 50 C3
Lawley Telford 34 E2
Lawnhead Staffs 34 C4
Lawrenny Pembs 22 F5
Lawshall Suff 30 C5
Lawton Hereford 25 C11
Laxey IoM 48 D4
Laxfield Suff 31 A9
Laxfirth Shetland 96 H6
Laxfirth Shetland 96 J6
Laxford Bridge Highld 92 E5
Laxo Shetland 96 G6
Laxobigging Shetland 96 F6
Laxton E Yorks 52 G3
Laxton Northants 36 F5
Laxton Notts 45 F11
Laycock W Yorks 50 E6
Layer Breton Essex 30 G6
Layer de la Haye Essex 30 F6
Layer Marney Essex 30 G6
Layham Suff 31 D7
Laylands Green W Berks 17 E10
Laytham E Yorks 52 F3
Layton Blackpool 49 F3
Lazenby Redcar 59 E6
Lazonby Cumb 57 C7
Le Planel Guern 11
Le Skerne Haughton Darl 58 E4
Le Villocq Guern 11
Lea Derbys 45 G7
Lea Hereford 26 F3
Lea Lincs 46 D2
Lea Shrops 33 E10
Lea Shrops 33 G9
Lea Wilts 16 C6
Lea Marston Warks 35 F8
Lea Town Lancs 49 F4
Leabrooks Derbys 45 G8
Leac a Li W Isles 90 H6
Leachkin Highld 87 G9
Leadburn Midloth 69 E11
Leaden Roding Essex 30 G2
Leadenham Lincs 46 G3
Leadgate Cumb 57 B9
Leadgate Durham 58 A2
Leadgate T&W 63 H7
Leadhills S Lanark 60 B4
Leafield Oxon 27 G10
Leagrave Luton 29 F7
Leake N Yorks 58 G5
Leake Commonside Lincs 47 G7
Lealholm N Yorks 59 F8
Lealt Argyll 72 D5
Lealt Highld 85 B10
Leamington Hastings Warks 27 B11
Leamonsley Staffs 35 E7
Leamside Durham 58 B4
Leanaig Highld 87 F8
Leargybreck Argyll 72 F4
Leasgill Cumb 49 A4
Leasingham Lincs 46 H4
Leasingthorne Durham 58 D3
Leasowe Mers 42 C5
Leatherhead Sur 19 F8
Leatherhead Common Sur 19 F8
Leathley N Yorks 51 E8
Leaton Shrops 33 D10
Leaveland Kent 21 F7
Leavening N Yorks 52 C3
Leaves Green London 19 E11
Leazes Durham 63 H7
Lebberston N Yorks 53 A6
Lechlade-on-Thames Glos 17 B9
Leck Lancs 50 B2
Leckford Hants 17 H10
Leckfurin Highld 93 D10
Leckgruinart Argyll 64 B3
Leckhampstead Bucks 28 E4
Leckhampstead W Berks 17 D11
Leckhampstead Thicket W Berks 17 D11
Leckhampton Glos 26 G6
Leckie Highld 86 E3
Leckmelm Highld 86 B4
Leckwith V Glam 15 D7
Leconfield E Yorks 52 E6
Ledaig Argyll 74 D2
Ledburn Bucks 28 F6
Ledbury Hereford 26 E4
Ledcharrie Stirling 75 E8
Ledgemoor Hereford 25 C11
Ledicot Hereford 25 B11
Ledmore Highld 92 H5
Lednagullin Highld 93 C10
Ledsham Ches W 42 E6
Ledsham W Yorks 51 G10
Ledston W Yorks 51 G10
Ledston Luck W Yorks 51 F10
Ledwell Oxon 27 F11
Lee Argyll 78 J7
Lee Devon 6 B3
Lee Hants 10 C2
Lee Lancs 50 D1
Lee Shrops 33 B10
Lee Brockhurst Shrops 33 C11
Lee Clump Bucks 18 A6
Lee Mill Devon 5 F7
Lee Moor Devon 5 E6
Lee-on-the-Solent Hants 10 D4
Leeans Shetland 96 J5
Leebotten Shetland 96 L6
Leebotwood Shrops 33 F10
Leece Cumb 49 C2
Leechpool Pembs 22 E4
Leeds Kent 20 F5
Leeds W Yorks 51 F8
Leedstown Corn 2 F5
Leek Staffs 44 G3
Leek Wootton Warks 27 B9
Leekbrook Staffs 44 G3
Leeming N Yorks 58 H3
Leeming Bar N Yorks 58 G3
Lees Derbys 35 B8
Lees Gtr Man 44 B3
Lees W Yorks 50 F6
Leeswood Flint 42 F5
Legbourne Lincs 47 D7
Legerwood Borders 70 F4
Legsby Lincs 46 D5
Leicester Leicester 36 E1
Leicester Forest East Leics 35 E11
Leigh Dorset 8 D5
Leigh Glos 26 F5
Leigh Gtr Man 43 B9
Leigh Kent 20 G2
Leigh Shrops 33 E9
Leigh Sur 19 G9
Leigh Wilts 17 B7
Leigh Worcs 26 C4
Leigh Beck Essex 20 C5
Leigh Common Som 8 B6
Leigh Delamere Wilts 16 D5
Leigh Green Kent 13 C8
Leigh on Sea Southend 20 C5
Leigh Park Hants 10 D6
Leigh Sinton Worcs 26 C4
Leigh upon Mendip Som 16 G3
Leigh Woods N Som 16 D2
Leighswood W Mid 35 E6
Leighterton Glos 16 B5
Leighton N Yorks 51 B7
Leighton Powys 33 E8
Leighton Shrops 34 E2
Leighton Som 16 G4
Leighton Bromswold Cambs 37 H7
Leighton Buzzard C Beds 28 F6
Leinthall Earls Hereford 25 B11
Leinthall Starkes Hereford 25 B11
Leintwardine Hereford 25 A11
Leire Leics 35 F11
Leirinmore Highld 92 C7
Leiston Suff 31 B11
Leitfie Perth 76 C5
Leith Edin 69 C11
Leitholm Borders 70 F6
Lelant Corn 2 F4
Lelley E Yorks 53 F8
Lem Hill Worcs 26 A4
Lemmington Hall Northumb 63 B7
Lempitlaw Borders 70 G6
Lenchwick Worcs 27 D7
Lendalfoot S Ayrs 66 H4
Lendrick Lodge Stirling 75 G8
Lenham Kent 20 F5
Lenham Heath Kent 20 G6
Lennel Borders 71 F7
Lennoxtown E Dunb 68 C5
Lenton Lincs 36 B6
Lenton Nottingham 36 B1
Lentran Highld 87 G8
Lenwade Norf 39 D6
Leny Ho. Stirling 75 G9
Lenzie E Dunb 68 C5
Leoch Angus 76 D6
Leochel-Cushnie Aberds 83 B7
Leominster Hereford 25 C11
Leonard Stanley Glos 16 A5
Leorin Argyll 64 D4
Lepe Hants 10 E3
Lephin Highld 84 D6
Lephinchapel Argyll 73 D8
Lephinmore Argyll 73 D8
Leppington N Yorks 52 C3
Lepton W Yorks 51 H8
Lerryn Corn 4 F2
Lerwick Shetland 96 J6
Lesbury Northumb 63 B8
Leslie Aberds 83 A7
Leslie Fife 76 G5
Lesmahagow S Lanark 69 G7
Lesnewth Corn 4 B2
Lessendrum Aberds 88 D5
Lessingham Norf 39 C9
Lessonhall Cumb 56 A4
Leswalt Dumfries 54 C3
Letchmore Heath Herts 19 B8
Letchworth Herts 29 E9
Letcombe Bassett Oxon 17 C10
Letcombe Regis Oxon 17 C10
Letham Angus 77 C8
Letham Falk 69 B7
Letham Fife 76 F6
Letham Perth 76 E3
Letham Grange Angus 77 C9
Lethenty Aberds 89 D8
Letheringham Suff 31 C9
Letheringsett Norf 39 B6
Lettaford Devon 5 C8
Lettan Orkney 95 D8
Letterewe Highld 86 D2
Letterfearn Highld 85 F13
Letterfinlay Highld 80 D4
Lettermorar Highld 79 C10
Lettermore Argyll 78 G7
Letters Highld 86 C4
Letterston Pembs 22 D4
Lettoch Highld 82 B2
Lettoch Highld 87 H13
Letton Hereford 25 A10
Letton Hereford 25 D10
Letton Green Norf 38 E5
Letty Green Herts 29 G9
Letwell S Yorks 45 D9
Leuchars Fife 77 E7
Leuchars Ho. Moray 88 B2
Leumrabhagh W Isles 91 F8
Levan Invclyd 73 F11
Levaneap Shetland 96 G6
Levedale Staffs 34 D4
Leven E Yorks 53 E7
Leven Fife 76 G6
Levencorroch N Ayrs 66 D3
Levens Cumb 57 H6
Levens Green Herts 29 F10
Levenshulme Gtr Man 44 C2
Levenwick Shetland 96 L6
Leverburgh = An t-Ob W Isles 90 J5
Leverington Cambs 37 D10
Leverton Lincs 47 H8
Leverton Highgate Lincs 47 H8
Leverton Lucasgate Lincs 47 H8
Leverton Outgate Lincs 47 H8
Levington Suff 31 E9
Levisham N Yorks 59 G9
Levishie Highld 80 B6
Lew Oxon 27 H10
Lewannick Corn 4 C3
Lewdown Devon 4 C5
Lewes E Sus 12 E3
Leweston Pembs 22 D4
Lewisham London 19 D10
Lewiston Highld 81 A7
Lewistown Bridgend 14 C5
Lewknor Oxon 18 B4
Leworthy Devon 6 C5
Leworthy Devon 6 F2
Lewtrenchard Devon 4 C5
Lexden Essex 30 F6
Ley Aberds 83 B7
Ley Corn 4 E2
Leybourne Kent 20 F3
Leyburn N Yorks 58 G2
Leyfields Staffs 35 E8
Leyhill Bucks 18 A6
Leyland Lancs 49 G5
Leylodge Aberds 83 B9
Leymoor W Yorks 51 H7
Leys Aberds 89 C10
Leys Perth 76 D5
Leys Castle Highld 87 G9
Leys of Cossans Angus 76 C6
Leysdown-on-Sea Kent 21 D7
Leysmill Angus 77 C9
Leysters Pole Hereford 26 B2
Leyton London 19 C10
Leytonstone London 19 C10
Lezant Corn 4 D4
Leziate Norf 38 D2
Lhanbryde Moray 88 B2
Liatrie Highld 86 H5
Libanus Powys 24 F6
Libberton S Lanark 69 F8
Liberton Edin 69 D11
Liceasto W Isles 90 H6
Lichfield Staffs 35 E7
Lickey Worcs 34 H5
Lickey End Worcs 26 A6
Lickfold W Sus 11 B8
Liddel Orkney 95 K5
Liddesdale Highld 79 F10
Liddington Swindon 17 C9
Lidgate Suff 30 C4
Lidget S Yorks 45 B10
Lidget Green W Yorks 51 F7
Lidgett Notts 45 F10
Lidlington C Beds 28 E6
Lidstone Oxon 27 F10
Lieurary Highld 94 D2
Liff Angus 76 D6
Lifton Devon 4 C4
Liftondown Devon 4 C4
Lighthorne Warks 27 C10
Lightwater Sur 18 E6
Lightwood Stoke 34 A5
Lightwood Green Ches E 34 A2
Lightwood Green Wrex 33 A9
Lilbourne Northants 36 H1
Lilburn Tower Northumb 62 A6
Lilleshall Telford 34 D3
Lilley Herts 29 F8
Lilley W Berks 17 D11
Lilliesleaf Borders 61 A11
Lillingstone Dayrell Bucks 28 E4
Lillingstone Lovell Bucks 28 D4
Lillington Dorset 8 C5
Lillington Warks 27 B10
Lilliput Poole 9 E9
Lilstock Som 7 B10
Lilyhurst Shrops 34 D3
Limbury Luton 29 F7
Limebrook Hereford 25 B10
Limefield Gtr Man 44 A2
Limekilnburn S Lanark 68 E6
Limekilns Fife 69 B9
Limerigg Falk 69 C7
Limerstone IoW 10 F3
Limington Som 8 B4
Limpenhoe Norf 39 E9
Limpley Stoke Wilts 16 E4
Limpsfield Sur 19 F11
Limpsfield Chart Sur 19 F11
Linby Notts 45 G9
Linchmere W Sus 11 A7
Lincluden Dumfries 60 F5
Lincoln Lincs 46 E3
Lincomb Worcs 26 B5
Lincombe Devon 5 F8
Lindal in Furness Cumb 49 B2
Lindale Cumb 49 A4
Lindean Borders 70 G3
Lindfield W Sus 12 D2
Lindford Hants 18 H5
Lindifferon Fife 76 F6
Lindley W Yorks 51 H7
Lindley Green N Yorks 51 E8
Lindores Fife 76 F5
Lindridge Worcs 26 B3
Lindsell Essex 30 F3
Lindsey Suff 30 D6
Linford Hants 9 D10
Linford Thurrock 20 D3
Lingague IoM 48 E2
Lingards Wood W Yorks 44 A4
Lingbob W Yorks 51 F6
Lingdale Redcar 59 E7
Lingen Hereford 25 B10
Lingfield Sur 12 B2
Lingreabhagh W Isles 90 J5
Lingwood Norf 39 E9
Linicro Highld 85 B8
Linkenholt Hants 17 F10
Linkhill Kent 13 D7
Linkinhorne Corn 4 D4
Linklater Orkney 95 K5
Linksness Orkney 95 H3
Linktown Fife 69 A11
Linley Shrops 33 F9
Linley Green Hereford 26 C3
Linlithgow W Loth 69 C9
Linlithgow Bridge W Loth 69 C8
Linshiels Northumb 62 C4
Linsiadar W Isles 90 D7
Linsidemore Highld 87 B8
Linslade C Beds 28 F6
Linstead Parva Suff 39 H9
Linstock Cumb 61 H10
Linthwaite W Yorks 44 A5
Lintlaw Borders 71 E7
Lintmill Moray 88 B5
Linton Borders 70 H6
Linton Cambs 30 D2
Linton Derbys 35 D8
Linton Hereford 26 F3
Linton Kent 20 G4
Linton N Yorks 50 C5
Linton Northumb 63 D8
Linton W Yorks 51 E9
Linton-on-Ouse N Yorks 51 C10
Linwood Hants 9 D10
Linwood Lincs 46 D5
Linwood Renfs 68 D3
Lionacleit W Isles 84 D2
Lional W Isles 91 A10
Liphook Hants 11 A7
Liscard Mers 42 C6
Liscombe Som 7 C7
Liskeard Corn 4 E3
L'Islet Guern 11
Liss Hants 11 B6
Liss Forest Hants 11 B6
Lissett E Yorks 53 D7
Lissington Lincs 46 D5
Lisvane Cardiff 15 C7
Liswerry Newport 15 C9
Litcham Norf 38 D4
Litchborough Northants 28 C3
Litchfield Hants 17 F11
Litherland Mers 42 C6
Litlington Cambs 29 D10
Litlington E Sus 12 F4
Little Abington Cambs 30 D2
Little Addington Northants 28 A6
Little Alne Warks 27 B8
Little Altcar Mers 42 B6
Little Asby Cumb 57 F8
Little Assynt Highld 92 G4
Little Aston Staffs 35 E6
Little Atherfield IoW 10 F3
Little Ayre Orkney 95 J4
Little-ayre Shetland 96 G5
Little Ayton N Yorks 59 E6
Little Baddow Essex 30 H4
Little Badminton S Glos 16 C5
Little Ballinluig Perth 76 B2
Little Bampton Cumb 61 H8
Little Bardfield Essex 30 E3
Little Barford Bedford 29 C8
Little Barningham Norf 39 B7
Little Barrington Glos 27 G9
Little Barrow Ches W 43 E7
Little Barugh N Yorks 52 B3
Little Bavington Northumb 62 F5
Little Bealings Suff 31 D9
Little Bedwyn Wilts 17 E9
Little Bentley Essex 31 F8
Little Berkhamsted Herts 29 H9
Little Billing Northants 28 B5
Little Birch Hereford 26 E2
Little Blakenham Suff 31 D8
Little Blencow Cumb 56 C6
Little Bollington Ches E 43 D10
Little Bookham Sur 19 F8
Little Bowden Leics 36 G3
Little Bradley Suff 30 C3
Little Brampton Shrops 33 G9
Little Brechin Angus 77 A8
Little Brickhill M Keynes 28 E6
Little Brington Northants 28 B3
Little Bromley Essex 31 F7
Little Broughton Cumb 56 C2
Little Budworth Ches W 43 F8
Little Burstead Essex 20 B3
Little Bytham Lincs 36 D6
Little Carlton Lincs 47 D7
Little Carlton Notts 45 G11
Little Casterton Rutland 36 E6
Little Cawthorpe Lincs 47 D7
Little Chalfont Bucks 18 B6
Little Chart Kent 20 G6
Little Chesterford Essex 30 D2
Little Cheverell Wilts 16 F6
Little Chishill Cambs 29 E11
Little Clacton Essex 31 G8
Little Clifton Cumb 56 D2
Little Colp Aberds 89 D7
Little Comberton Worcs 26 D6
Little Common E Sus 12 F6
Little Compton Warks 27 E9
Little Cornard Suff 30 E5
Little Cowarne Hereford 26 C3
Little Coxwell Oxon 17 B9
Little Crakehall N Yorks 58 G3
Little Cressingham Norf 38 F4
Little Crosby Mers 42 B6
Little Dalby Leics 36 D3
Little Dawley Telford 34 E2
Little Dens Aberds 89 D10
Little Dewchurch Hereford 26 E2
Little Downham Cambs 37 G11
Little Driffield E Yorks 52 D6
Little Dunham Norf 38 D4
Little Dunkeld Perth 76 C3
Little Dunmow Essex 30 F3
Little Easton Essex 30 F3
Little Eaton Derbys 35 A9
Little Eccleston Lancs 49 E4
Little Ellingham Norf 38 F6
Little End Essex 20 A2
Little Eversden Cambs 29 C10
Little Faringdon Oxon 17 A9
Little Fencote N Yorks 58 G3
Little Fenton N Yorks 51 F11
Little Finborough Suff 31 C7
Little Fransham Norf 38 D5
Little Gaddesden Herts 28 G6
Little Gidding Cambs 37 G7
Little Glemham Suff 31 C10
Little Glenshee Perth 76 D2
Little Gransden Cambs 29 C9
Little Green Som 16 G4
Little Grimsby Lincs 47 C7
Little Gruinard Highld 86 C2
Little Habton N Yorks 52 B3
Little Hadham Herts 29 F11
Little Hale Lincs 37 A7
Little Hallingbury Essex 29 G11
Little Hampden Bucks 18 A5
Little Harrowden Northants 28 A5
Little Haseley Oxon 18 A3
Little Hatfield E Yorks 53 E7
Little Hautbois Norf 39 C8
Little Haven Pembs 22 E3
Little Hay Staffs 35 E7
Little Hayfield Derbys 44 D4
Little Haywood Staffs 34 C6
Little Heath W Mid 35 G9
Little Hereford Hereford 26 B2
Little Horkesley Essex 30 E6
Little Horsted E Sus 12 E3
Little Horton W Yorks 51 F7
Little Horwood Bucks 28 E4
Little Houghton Northants 28 C5
Little Houghton S Yorks 45 B8
Little Hucklow Derbys 44 E5
Little Hulton Gtr Man 43 B10
Little Humber E Yorks 53 G7
Little Hungerford W Berks 18 D2
Little Irchester Northants 28 B6
Little Kimble Bucks 28 H5
Little Kineton Warks 27 C10
Little Kingshill Bucks 18 B5
Little Langdale Cumb 56 F5
Little Langford Wilts 17 H7
Little Laver Essex 30 H2
Little Leigh Ches W 43 E9
Little Leighs Essex 30 G4
Little Lever Gtr Man 43 B10
Little London Bucks 28 G3
Little London E Sus 12 E4
Little London Hants 17 G10
Little London Hants 18 F3
Little London Lincs 37 C10
Little London Lincs 37 C8
Little London Norf 39 C7
Little London Powys 32 G6
Little Longstone Derbys 44 E5
Little Lynturk Aberds 83 B7
Little Malvern Worcs 26 D4
Little Maplestead Essex 30 E5
Little Marcle Hereford 26 E3
Little Marlow Bucks 18 C5
Little Marsden Lancs 50 F4
Little Massingham Norf 38 C3
Little Melton Norf 39 E7
Little Mill Mon 15 A9
Little Milton Oxon 18 A3
Little Missenden Bucks 18 B6
Little Musgrave Cumb 57 E9
Little Ness Shrops 33 D10
Little Neston Ches W 42 E5
Little Newcastle Pembs 22 D4
Little Newsham Durham 58 E2
Little Oakley Essex 31 F9
Little Oakley Northants 36 G4
Little Orton Cumb 61 H9

128 Mon–Nor

Monmouth Cap Mon 25 F10
Monnington on Wye Hereford 25 D10
Monreith Dumfries 54 E6
Monreith Mains Dumfries 54 E6
Mont Saint Guern 11
Montacute Som 8 C3
Montcoffer Ho. Aberds 89 B6
Montford Argyll 73 G10
Montford Shrops 33 D10
Montford Bridge Shrops 33 D10
Montgarrie Aberds 83 B7
Montgomery = Trefaldwyn Powys 33 F8
Montrave Fife 76 G6
Montrose Angus 77 B10
Montsale Essex 21 B7
Monxton Hants 17 G10
Monyash Derbys 44 F5
Monymusk Aberds 83 B8
Monzie Perth 75 E11
Monzie Castle Perth 75 E11
Moodiesburn N Lanark 68 C5
Moonzie Fife 76 F6
Moor Allerton W Yorks 51 F8
Moor Crichel Dorset 9 D8
Moor End E Yorks 52 F4
Moor End York 52 D2
Moor Monkton N Yorks 51 D11
Moor of Granary Moray 87 F13
Moor of Ravenstone Dumfries 54 E6
Moor Row Cumb 56 E2
Moor Street Kent 20 E5
Moorby Lincs 46 F6
Moordown Bmouth 9 E9
Moore Halton 43 D8
Moorend Glos 16 A4
Moorends S Yorks 52 H2
Moorgate S Yorks 45 C8
Moorgreen Notts 45 H8
Moorhall Derbys 45 E7
Moorhampton Hereford 25 D10
Moorhead W Yorks 51 F7
Moorhouse Cumb 61 H9
Moorhouse Notts 45 F11
Moorlinch Som 15 H9
Moorsholm Redcar 59 E7
Moorside Gtr Man 44 B3
Moorthorpe W Yorks 45 A8
Moortown Hants 9 D10
Moortown IoW 10 F3
Moortown Lincs 46 C4
Morangie Highld 87 C10
Morar Highld 79 B9
Morborne Cambs 37 F7
Morchard Bishop Devon 7 F6
Morcombelake Dorset 8 E3
Morcott Rutland 36 E5
Morda Shrops 33 C8
Morden Dorset 9 E8
Morden London 19 E9
Mordiford Hereford 26 E2
Mordon Durham 58 D4
More Shrops 33 F9
Morebath Devon 7 D8
Morebattle Borders 62 A3
Morecambe Lancs 49 C4
Morefield Highld 86 B4
Moreleigh Devon 5 F8
Morenish Perth 75 D8
Moresby Cumb 56 D1
Moresby Parks Cumb 56 E1
Morestead Hants 10 B4
Moreton Dorset 9 F7
Moreton Essex 30 H2
Moreton Mers 42 C5
Moreton Oxon 18 A3
Moreton Staffs 34 D3
Moreton Corbet Shrops 34 C1
Moreton-in-Marsh Glos 27 E9
Moreton Jeffries Hereford 26 D3
Moreton Morrell Warks 27 C10
Moreton on Lugg Hereford 26 D2
Moreton Pinkney Northants 28 D2
Moreton Say Shrops 34 B2
Moreton Valence Glos 26 H4
Moretonhampstead Devon 5 C8
Morfa Carms 23 E10
Morfa Carms 23 G10
Morfa Bach Carms 23 E8
Morfa Bychan Gwyn 41 G7
Morfa Dinlle Gwyn 40 E6
Morfa Glas Neath 24 H5
Morfa Nefyn Gwyn 40 F4
Morfydd Denb 42 H4
Morgan's Vale Wilts 9 B10
Moriah Ceredig 32 H2
Morland Cumb 57 D7
Morley Derbys 35 A9
Morley Durham 58 D2
Morley W Yorks 51 G8
Morley Green Ches E 44 D2
Morley St Botolph Norf 39 F6
Morningside Edin 69 C11
Morningside N Lanark 69 E7
Morningthorpe Norf 39 F8
Morpeth Northumb 63 E8
Morphie Aberds 77 A10
Morrey Staffs 35 D7
Morris Green Essex 30 E4
Morriston Swansea 14 B2
Morston Norf 38 A6
Mortehoe Devon 6 B3
Mortimer W Berks 18 E3
Mortimer West End Hants 18 E3
Mortimer's Cross Hereford 25 B11
Mortlake London 19 D9
Morton Cumb 56 A5
Morton Derbys 45 F8
Morton Lincs 37 C6
Morton Lincs 46 C2
Morton Lincs 46 F2
Morton Norf 39 D7
Morton Notts 45 G11
Morton S Glos 16 B3
Morton Shrops 33 C8
Morton Bagot Warks 27 B8
Morton-on-Swale N Yorks 58 G4
Morvah Corn 2 F3
Morval Corn 4 F3
Morvich Highld 80 A1
Morvich Highld 93 J10
Morville Shrops 34 F2
Morville Heath Shrops 34 F2
Morwenstow Corn 6 E1
Mosborough S Yorks 45 D8
Moscow E Ayrs 67 B7
Mosedale Cumb 56 C5
Moseley W Mid 34 F5
Moseley W Mid 35 G6
Moseley Worcs 26 C5
Moss Argyll 78 G2
Moss Highld 79 E9
Moss S Yorks 45 A9
Moss Wrex 42 G6
Moss Bank Mers 43 C8
Moss Edge Lancs 49 E4
Moss End Brack 18 D5
Moss of Barmuckity Moray 88 B2
Moss Pit Staffs 34 C5
Moss-side Highld 87 F11
Moss Side Lancs 49 F3
Mossat Aberds 82 B6
Mossbank Shetland 96 F6
Mossbay Cumb 56 D1
Mossblown S Ayrs 67 D7
Mossbrow Gtr Man 43 D10
Mossburnford Borders 62 B2
Mossdale Dumfries 55 B9
Mossend N Lanark 68 D6
Mosser Cumb 56 D3
Mossfield Highld 87 D9
Mossgiel E Ayrs 67 D7
Mosside Angus 77 B7
Mossley Ches E 44 F2
Mossley Gtr Man 44 B3
Mossley Hill Mers 43 D6
Mosstodloch Moray 88 C3
Mosston Angus 77 C8
Mossy Lea Lancs 43 A8
Mosterton Dorset 8 D3
Moston Gtr Man 44 B2
Moston Shrops 34 C1
Moston Green Ches E 43 F10
Mostyn Flint 42 D4
Mostyn Quay Flint 42 D4
Motcombe Dorset 9 B7
Mothecombe Devon 5 G7
Motherby Cumb 56 D6
Motherwell N Lanark 68 E6
Mottingham London 19 D11
Mottisfont Hants 10 B2
Mottistone IoW 10 F3
Mottram in Longdendale Gtr Man 44 C3
Mottram St Andrew Ches E 44 E2
Mouilpied Guern 11
Mouldsworth Ches W 43 E8
Moulin Perth 76 B2
Moulsecoomb Brighton 12 F2
Moulsford Oxon 18 C2
Moulsoe M Keynes 28 D6
Moulton Ches W 43 F9
Moulton Lincs 37 C9
Moulton N Yorks 58 F3
Moulton Northants 28 B4
Moulton Suff 30 B3
Moulton V Glam 14 D6
Moulton Chapel Lincs 37 D8
Moulton Eaugate Lincs 37 D9
Moulton St Mary Norf 39 E9
Moulton Seas End Lincs 37 C9
Mounie Castle Aberds 83 A9
Mount Corn 3 D6
Mount Corn 4 E2
Mount Highld 87 G12
Mount Bures Essex 30 E6
Mount Canisp Highld 87 D10
Mount Hawke Corn 2 E6
Mount Pleasant Ches E 44 G2
Mount Pleasant Derbys 35 D8
Mount Pleasant Derbys 45 H7
Mount Pleasant Flint 42 E5
Mount Pleasant Hants 10 E1
Mount Pleasant W Yorks 51 G8
Mount Sorrel Wilts 9 B9
Mount Tabor W Yorks 51 F6
Mountain W Yorks 51 F6
Mountain Ash = Aberpennar Rhondda 14 B6
Mountain Cross Borders 69 F10
Mountain Water Pembs 22 D4
Mountbenger Borders 70 H2
Mountfield E Sus 12 D6
Mountgerald Highld 87 E8
Mountjoy Corn 3 C7
Mountnessing Essex 20 B3
Mounton Mon 15 B11
Mountsorrel Leics 36 D1
Mousehole Corn 2 G3
Mousen Northumb 71 G10
Mouswald Dumfries 60 F6
Mow Cop Ches E 44 G2
Mowhaugh Borders 62 A4
Mowsley Leics 36 G2
Moxley W Mid 34 F5
Moy Highld 80 E6
Moy Highld 87 H10
Moy Hall Highld 87 H10
Moy Ho. Moray 87 E13
Moy Lodge Highld 80 E6
Moyles Court Hants 9 D10
Moylgrove Pembs 22 B6
Muasdale Argyll 65 D7
Much Birch Hereford 26 E2
Much Cowarne Hereford 26 D3
Much Dewchurch Hereford 25 E11
Much Hadham Herts 29 G11
Much Hoole Lancs 49 G4
Much Marcle Hereford 26 E3
Much Wenlock Shrops 34 E2
Muchalls Aberds 83 D11
Muchelney Som 8 B3
Muchlarnick Corn 4 F3
Muchrachd Highld 86 H5
Muckernich Highld 87 F8
Mucking Thurrock 20 C3
Muckleford Dorset 8 E5
Mucklestone Staffs 34 B3
Muckleton Shrops 34 C1
Muckletown Aberds 83 A7
Muckley Corner Staffs 35 E6
Muckton Lincs 47 D7
Mudale Highld 93 F8
Muddiford Devon 6 C4
Mudeford Dorset 9 E10
Mudford Som 8 C4
Mudgley Som 15 G10
Mugdock Stirling 68 C4
Mugeary Highld 85 E9
Mugginton Derbys 35 A8
Muggleswick Durham 58 B1
Muie Highld 93 J9
Muir Aberds 82 E2
Muir of Fairburn Highld 86 F7
Muir of Fowlis Aberds 83 B7
Muir of Ord Highld 87 F8
Muir of Pert Angus 77 D7
Muirden Aberds 89 C7
Muirdrum Angus 77 D8
Muirhead Angus 76 D6
Muirhead Fife 76 G5
Muirhead N Lanark 68 D5
Muirhead S Ayrs 66 C6
Muirhouselaw Borders 70 H5
Muirhouses Falk 69 B9
Muirkirk E Ayrs 68 H5
Muirmill Stirling 68 B6
Muirshearlich Highld 80 E3
Muirskie Aberds 83 D10
Muirtack Aberds 89 E9
Muirton Highld 87 E10
Muirton Perth 76 E4
Muirton Perth 76 F2
Muirton Mains Highld 86 F7
Muirton of Ardblair Perth 76 C4
Muirton of Ballochy Angus 77 A9
Muiryfold Aberds 89 C7
Muker N Yorks 57 G11
Mulbarton Norf 39 E7
Mulben Moray 88 C3
Mulindry Argyll 64 C4
Mullardoch House Highld 86 H5
Mullion Corn 2 H5
Mullion Cove Corn 2 H5
Mumby Lincs 47 E9
Munderfield Row Hereford 26 C3
Munderfield Stocks Hereford 26 C3
Mundesley Norf 39 B9
Mundford Norf 38 F4
Mundham Norf 39 F9
Mundon Essex 20 A5
Mundurno Aberdeen 83 B11
Munerigie Highld 80 C4
Muness Shetland 96 C8
Mungasdale Highld 86 B2
Mungrisdale Cumb 56 C5
Munlochy Highld 87 F9
Munsley Hereford 26 D3
Munslow Shrops 33 G11
Murchington Devon 5 C7
Murcott Oxon 28 G2
Murkle Highld 94 D3
Murlaggan Highld 80 D2
Murlaggan Highld 80 E5
Murra Orkney 95 H3
Murrayfield Edin 69 C11
Murrow Cambs 37 E9
Mursley Bucks 28 F5
Murthill Angus 77 B7
Murthly Perth 76 D3
Murton Cumb 57 D9
Murton Durham 58 B4
Murton Northumb 71 F8
Murton York 52 D2
Musbury Devon 8 E1
Muscoates N Yorks 52 A2
Musdale Argyll 74 E2
Musselburgh E Loth 70 C2
Muston Leics 36 B4
Muston N Yorks 53 B6
Mustow Green Worcs 26 A5
Mutehill Dumfries 55 E9
Mutford Suff 39 G10
Muthill Perth 75 F11
Mutterton Devon 7 F9
Muxton Telford 34 D3
Mybster Highld 94 E3
Myddfai Carms 24 F4
Myddle Shrops 33 C10
Mydroilyn Ceredig 23 A9
Myerscough Lancs 49 F4
Mylor Bridge Corn 3 F7
Mynachlog-ddu Pembs 22 C6
Myndtown Shrops 33 G9
Mynydd Bach Ceredig 32 H3
Mynydd-bach Mon 15 B10
Mynydd Bodafon Anglesey 40 B6
Mynydd-isa Flint 42 F5
Mynyddygarreg Carms 23 F9
Mynytho Gwyn 40 G5
Myrebird Aberds 83 D9
Myrelandhorn Highld 94 E4
Myreside Perth 76 E5
Myrtle Hill Carms 24 E4
Mytchett Sur 18 F5
Mytholm W Yorks 50 G5
Mytholmroyd W Yorks 50 G6
Myton-on-Swale N Yorks 51 C10
Mytton Shrops 33 D10
N
Na Gearrannan W Isles 90 C6
Naast Highld 91 J13
Naburn York 52 E1
Nackington Kent 21 F8
Nacton Suff 31 D9
Nafferton E Yorks 53 D6
Nailbridge Glos 26 G3
Nailsbourne Som 7 D11
Nailsea N Som 15 D10
Nailstone Leics 35 E10
Nailsworth Glos 16 B5
Nairn Highld 87 F11
Nalderswood Sur 19 G9
Nancegollan Corn 2 F5
Nancledra Corn 2 F3
Nanhoron Gwyn 40 G4
Nannau Gwyn 32 C3
Nannerch Flint 42 F4
Nanpantan Leics 35 D11
Nanpean Corn 3 D8
Nanstallon Corn 3 C9
Nant-ddu Powys 25 G7
Nant-glas Powys 24 B6
Nant Peris Gwyn 41 E8
Nant Uchaf Denb 42 G3
Nant-y-Bai Carms 24 D4
Nant-y-cafn Neath 24 H5
Nant-y-derry Mon 25 H10
Nant-y-ffin Carms 23 C10
Nant-y-moel Bridgend 14 B5
Nant-y-pandy Conwy 41 C8
Nanternis Ceredig 23 A8
Nantgaredig Carms 23 D9
Nantgarw Rhondda 15 C7
Nantglyn Denb 42 F3
Nantgwyn Powys 32 H5
Nantlle Gwyn 41 E7
Nantmawr Shrops 33 C8
Nantmel Powys 25 B7
Nantmor Gwyn 41 F8
Nantwich Ches E 43 G9
Nantycaws Carms 23 E9
Nantyffyllon Bridgend 14 B4
Nantyglo Bl Gwent 25 G8
Naphill Bucks 18 B5
Nappa N Yorks 50 D4
Napton on the Hill Warks 27 B11
Narberth = Arberth Pembs 22 E6
Narborough Leics 35 F11
Narborough Norf 38 D3
Nasareth Gwyn 40 E6
Naseby Northants 36 H2
Nash Bucks 28 E4
Nash Hereford 25 B10
Nash Newport 15 C9
Nash Shrops 26 A3
Nash Lee Bucks 28 H5
Nassington Northants 37 F6
Nasty Herts 29 F10
Nateby Cumb 57 F9
Nateby Lancs 49 E4
Natland Cumb 57 H7
Naughton Suff 31 D7
Naunton Glos 27 F8
Naunton Worcs 26 E5
Naunton Beauchamp Worcs 26 C6
Navenby Lincs 46 G3
Navestock Heath Essex 20 B2
Navestock Side Essex 20 B2
Navidale Highld 93 H13
Nawton N Yorks 52 A2
Nayland Suff 30 E6
Nazeing Essex 29 H11
Neacroft Hants 9 E10
Neal's Green Warks 35 G9
Neap Shetland 96 H7
Near Sawrey Cumb 56 G5
Neasham Darl 58 E4
Neath = Castell-Nedd Neath 14 B3
Neath Abbey Neath 14 B3
Neatishead Norf 39 C9
Nebo Anglesey 40 A6
Nebo Ceredig 24 B2
Nebo Conwy 41 E10
Nebo Gwyn 40 E6
Necton Norf 38 E4
Nedd Highld 92 F4
Nedderton Northumb 63 E8
Nedging Tye Suff 31 D7
Needham Norf 39 G8
Needham Market Suff 31 C7
Needingworth Cambs 29 A10
Needwood Staffs 35 C7
Neen Savage Shrops 34 H2
Neen Sollars Shrops 26 A3
Neenton Shrops 34 G2
Nefyn Gwyn 40 F5
Neilston E Renf 68 E3
Neinthirion Powys 32 E5
Neithrop Oxon 27 D11
Nelly Andrews Green Powys 33 E8
Nelson Caerph 15 B7
Nelson Lancs 50 F4
Nelson Village Northumb 63 F8
Nemphlar S Lanark 69 F7
Nempnett Thrubwell N Som 15 E11
Nene Terrace Lincs 37 E8
Nenthall Cumb 57 B9
Nenthead Cumb 57 B9
Nenthorn Borders 70 G5
Nerabus Argyll 64 C3
Nercwys Flint 42 F5
Nerston S Lanark 68 E5
Nesbit Northumb 71 G8
Ness Ches W 42 E6
Nesscliffe Shrops 33 D9
Neston Ches W 42 E5
Neston Wilts 16 E5
Nether Alderley Ches E 44 E2
Nether Blainslie Borders 70 F4
Nether Booth Derbys 44 D5
Nether Broughton Leics 36 C2
Nether Burrow Lancs 50 B2
Nether Cerne Dorset 8 E5
Nether Compton Dorset 8 C4
Nether Crimond Aberds 89 F8
Nether Dalgliesh Borders 61 C8
Nether Dallachy Moray 88 B3
Nether Exe Devon 7 F8
Nether Glasslaw Aberds 89 C8
Nether Handwick Angus 76 C6
Nether Haugh S Yorks 45 C8
Nether Heage Derbys 45 G7
Nether Heyford Northants 28 C3
Nether Hindhope Borders 62 B3
Nether Howecleuch S Lanark 60 B6
Nether Kellet Lancs 49 C5
Nether Kinmundy Aberds 89 D10
Nether Langwith Notts 45 E9
Nether Leask Aberds 89 E10
Nether Lenshie Aberds 89 D6
Nether Monynut Borders 70 D6
Nether Padley Derbys 44 E6
Nether Park Aberds 89 C10
Nether Poppleton York 52 D1
Nether Silton N Yorks 58 G5
Nether Stowey Som 7 C10
Nether Urquhart Fife 76 G4
Nether Wallop Hants 17 H10
Nether Wasdale Cumb 56 F3
Nether Whitacre Warks 35 F8
Nether Worton Oxon 27 E11
Netheravon Wilts 17 G8
Netherbrae Aberds 89 C7
Netherbrough Orkney 95 G4
Netherburn S Lanark 69 F7
Netherbury Dorset 8 E3
Netherby Cumb 61 F9
Netherby N Yorks 51 E9
Nethercote Warks 28 B2
Nethercott Devon 6 C3
Netherend Glos 16 A2
Netherfield E Sus 12 E6
Netherhampton Wilts 9 B10
Netherlaw Dumfries 55 E10
Netherley Aberds 83 D10
Netherley Mers 43 D7
Nethermill Dumfries 60 E6
Nethermuir Aberds 89 D9
Netherplace E Renf 68 E4
Netherseal Derbys 35 D8
Netherthird E Ayrs 67 E8
Netherthong W Yorks 44 B5
Netherthorpe S Yorks 45 D9
Netherton Angus 77 B8
Netherton Devon 5 D9
Netherton Hants 17 F10
Netherton Mers 42 B6
Netherton Northumb 62 C5
Netherton Oxon 17 B11
Netherton Perth 76 B4
Netherton Stirling 68 C4
Netherton W Mid 34 G5
Netherton W Yorks 44 A5
Netherton W Yorks 51 H8
Netherton Worcs 26 D6
Nethertown Cumb 56 F1
Nethertown Highld 94 C5
Netherwitton Northumb 63 D7
Netherwood E Ayrs 68 H5
Nethy Bridge Highld 82 A2
Netley Hants 10 D3
Netley Marsh Hants 10 C2
Netteswell Essex 29 G11
Nettlebed Oxon 18 C4
Nettlebridge Som 16 G3
Nettlecombe Dorset 8 E4
Nettleden Herts 29 G7
Nettleham Lincs 46 E4
Nettlestead Kent 20 F3
Nettlestead Green Kent 20 F3
Nettlestone IoW 10 E5
Nettlesworth Durham 58 B3
Nettleton Lincs 46 B5
Nettleton Wilts 16 D5
Neuadd Carms 24 F3
Nevendon Essex 20 B4
Nevern Pembs 22 B5
New Abbey Dumfries 60 G5
New Aberdour Aberds 89 B8
New Addington London 19 E10
New Alresford Hants 10 A4
New Alyth Perth 76 C5
New Arley Warks 35 G8
New Ash Green Kent 20 E3
New Barn Kent 20 E3
New Barnetby N Lincs 46 A4
New Barton Northants 28 B5
New Bewick Northumb 62 A6
New-bigging Angus 76 D6
New Bilton Warks 35 H10
New Bolingbroke Lincs 47 G7
New Boultham Lincs 46 E3
New Bradwell M Keynes 28 D5
New Brancepeth Durham 58 B3
New Bridge Wrex 33 A8
New Brighton Flint 42 F5
New Brighton Mers 42 C6
New Brinsley Notts 45 G8
New Broughton Wrex 42 G6
New Buckenham Norf 39 F6
New Byth Aberds 89 C8
New Catton Norf 39 D8
New Cheriton Hants 10 B4
New Costessey Norf 39 D7
New Cowper Cumb 56 B3
New Cross Ceredig 32 H2
New Cross London 19 D10
New Cumnock E Ayrs 67 E9
New Deer Aberds 89 D8
New Delaval Northumb 63 F8
New Duston Northants 28 B4
New Earswick York 52 D2
New Edlington S Yorks 45 C9
New Elgin Moray 88 B2
New Ellerby E Yorks 53 F7
New Eltham London 19 D11
New End Worcs 27 C7
New Farnley W Yorks 51 F8
New Ferry Mers 42 D6
New Fryston W Yorks 51 G10
New Galloway Dumfries 55 B9
New Gilston Fife 77 G7
New Grimsby Scilly 2 C2
New Hainford Norf 39 D8
New Hartley Northumb 63 F9
New Haw Sur 19 E7
New Hedges Pembs 22 F6
New Herrington T&W 58 A4
New Hinksey Oxon 18 A2
New Holkham Norf 38 B4
New Holland N Lincs 53 G6
New Houghton Derbys 45 F8
New Houghton Norf 38 C3
New Houses N Yorks 50 B4
New Humberstone Leicester 36 E2
New Hutton Cumb 57 G7
New Hythe Kent 20 F4
New Inn Carms 23 C9
New Inn Mon 15 A10
New Inn Pembs 22 C5
New Inn Torf 15 B9
New Invention Shrops 33 H8
New Invention W Mid 34 E5
New Kelso Highld 86 G2
New Kingston Notts 35 C11
New Lanark S Lanark 69 F7
New Lane Lancs 43 A7
New Lane End Warr 43 C9
New Leake Lincs 47 G8
New Leeds Aberds 89 C9
New Longton Lancs 49 G5
New Luce Dumfries 54 C4
New Malden London 19 E9
New Marske Redcar 59 D7
New Marton Shrops 33 B9
New Micklefield W Yorks 51 F10
New Mill Aberds 83 E9
New Mill Herts 28 G6
New Mill W Yorks 44 B5
New Mill Wilts 17 E8
New Mills Ches E 43 D10
New Mills Corn 3 D7
New Mills Derbys 44 D3
New Mills Powys 33 E6
New Milton Hants 9 E11
New Moat Pembs 22 D5
New Ollerton Notts 45 F10
New Oscott W Mid 35 F6
New Park N Yorks 51 D8
New Pitsligo Aberds 89 C8
New Polzeath Corn 3 B8
New Quay = Ceinewydd Ceredig 23 A8
New Rackheath Norf 39 D8
New Radnor Powys 25 B9
New Rent Cumb 56 C6
New Ridley Northumb 62 H6
New Road Side N Yorks 50 E5
New Romney Kent 13 D9
New Rossington S Yorks 45 C10
New Row Ceredig 24 A4
New Row Lancs 50 F2
New Row N Yorks 59 E7
New Sarum Wilts 9 A10
New Silksworth T&W 58 A4
New Stevenston N Lanark 68 E6
New Street Staffs 44 G4
New Street Lane Shrops 34 B2
New Swanage Dorset 9 F9
New Totley S Yorks 45 E7
New Town E Loth 70 C3
New Tredegar = Tredegar Newydd Caerph 15 A7
New Trows S Lanark 69 G7
New Ulva Argyll 72 E6
New Walsoken Cambs 37 E10
New Waltham NE Lincs 46 B6
New Whittington Derbys 45 E7
New Wimpole Cambs 29 D10
New Winton E Loth 70 C3
New Yatt Oxon 27 G10
New York Lincs 46 G6
New York N Yorks 51 C7
Newall W Yorks 51 E7
Newark Orkney 95 D8
Newark Pboro 37 E8
Newark-on-Trent Notts 45 G11
Newarthill N Lanark 68 E6
Newbarns Cumb 49 B2
Newbattle Midloth 70 D2
Newbiggin Cumb 49 C2
Newbiggin Cumb 56 D6
Newbiggin Cumb 56 G2
Newbiggin Cumb 57 B7
Newbiggin Cumb 57 D8
Newbiggin Durham 57 D11
Newbiggin N Yorks 57 G11
Newbiggin N Yorks 57 H11
Newbiggin-by-the-Sea Northumb 63 E9
Newbiggin-on-Lune Cumb 57 F9
Newbigging Angus 77 D7
Newbigging Angus 77 D7
Newbigging S Lanark 69 F9
Newbold Derbys 45 E7
Newbold Leics 35 D10
Newbold on Avon Warks 35 H10
Newbold on Stour Warks 27 D9
Newbold Pacey Warks 27 C9
Newbold Verdon Leics 35 E10
Newborough Anglesey 40 D6
Newborough Pboro 37 E8
Newborough Staffs 35 C7
Newbottle Northants 28 E2
Newbottle T&W 58 A4
Newbourne Suff 31 D9
Newbridge Caerph 15 B8
Newbridge Ceredig 23 A10
Newbridge Corn 2 F3
Newbridge Corn 4 E4
Newbridge Dumfries 60 F5
Newbridge Edin 69 C10
Newbridge Hants 10 C1
Newbridge IoW 10 F3
Newbridge Pembs 22 C4
Newbridge Green Worcs 26 E5
Newbridge-on-Usk Mon 15 B9
Newbridge on Wye Powys 25 C7
Newbrough Northumb 62 G4
Newbuildings Devon 7 F6
Newburgh Aberds 89 C9
Newburgh Aberds 89 F9
Newburgh Borders 61 B9
Newburgh Fife 76 F5
Newburgh Lancs 43 A7
Newburn T&W 63 G7
Newbury W Berks 17 E11
Newbury Park London 19 C11
Newby Cumb 57 D7
Newby Lancs 50 E4
Newby N Yorks 50 B3
Newby N Yorks 58 E6
Newby N Yorks 59 G11
Newby Bridge Cumb 56 H5
Newby East Cumb 61 H10
Newby West Cumb 56 A5
Newby Wiske N Yorks 58 H4
Newcastle Mon 25 G11
Newcastle Shrops 33 G8
Newcastle Emlyn = Castell Newydd Emlyn Carms 23 B8
Newcastle-under-Lyme Staffs 44 H2
Newcastle Upon Tyne T&W 63 G8
Newcastleton or Copshaw Holm Borders 61 E10
Newchapel Pembs 23 C7
Newchapel Powys 32 G5
Newchapel Staffs 44 G2
Newchapel Sur 12 B2
Newchurch Carms 23 D8
Newchurch IoW 10 F4
Newchurch Kent 13 C9
Newchurch Lancs 50 F4
Newchurch Mon 15 B10
Newchurch Powys 25 C9
Newchurch Staffs 35 C7
Newcott Devon 7 F11
Newcraighall Edin 70 C2
Newdigate Sur 19 G8
Newell Green Brack 18 D5
Newenden Kent 13 D7
Newent Glos 26 F4
Newerne Glos 16 A3
Newfield Durham 58 C3
Newfield Highld 87 D10
Newford Scilly 2 C3
Newfound Hants 18 F2
Newgale Pembs 22 D3
Newgate Norf 39 A6
Newgate Street Herts 19 A10
Newhall Ches E 43 H9
Newhall Derbys 35 C8
Newhall House Highld 87 E9
Newhall Point Highld 87 E10
Newham Northumb 71 H10
Newham Hall Northumb 71 H10
Newhaven Derbys 44 G5
Newhaven E Sus 12 F3
Newhaven Edin 69 C11
Newhey Gtr Man 44 A3
Newholm N Yorks 59 E9
Newhouse N Lanark 68 D6
Newick E Sus 12 D3
Newingreen Kent 13 C10
Newington Kent 20 E5
Newington Kent 21 E10
Newington Kent 21 H8
Newington Notts 45 C10
Newington Oxon 18 B3
Newington Shrops 33 G10
Newland Glos 26 H2
Newland Hull 53 F6
Newland N Yorks 52 G2
Newland Worcs 26 D4
Newlandrig Midloth 70 D2
Newlands Borders 61 D11
Newlands Highld 87 G10
Newlands Moray 88 C3
Newlands Northumb 62 H6
Newland's Corner Sur 19 G7
Newlands of Geise Highld 94 D2
Newlands of Tynet Moray 88 B3
Newlands Park Anglesey 40 B4
Newlandsmuir S Lanark 68 E5
Newlot Orkney 95 G6
Newlyn Corn 2 G3
Newmachar Aberds 83 B10
Newmains N Lanark 69 E7
Newmarket Suff 30 B3
Newmarket W Isles 91 D9
Newmill Borders 61 B10
Newmill Corn 2 F3
Newmill Moray 88 C4
Newmill of Inshewan Angus 77 A7
Newmills of Boyne Aberds 88 C5
Newmiln Perth 76 D4
Newmilns E Ayrs 67 C8
Newnham Cambs 29 C11
Newnham Glos 26 G3
Newnham Hants 18 F4
Newnham Herts 29 E9
Newnham Kent 20 F6
Newnham Northants 28 C2
Newnham Bridge Worcs 26 B3
Newpark Fife 77 F7
Newport Devon 6 C4
Newport E Yorks 52 F4
Newport Essex 30 E2
Newport Highld 94 H3
Newport IoW 10 F4
Newport = Casnewydd Newport 15 C9
Newport Norf 39 D11
Newport = Trefdraeth Pembs 22 C5
Newport Telford 34 D3
Newport-on-Tay Fife 77 E7
Newport Pagnell M Keynes 28 D5
Newpound Common W Sus 11 B9
Newquay Corn 3 C7
Newsbank Ches E 44 F2
Newseat Aberds 89 D10
Newseat Aberds 89 E7
Newsham N Yorks 51 A9
Newsham N Yorks 58 E2
Newsham Northumb 63 F9
Newsholme E Yorks 52 G3
Newsholme Lancs 50 D4
Newsome W Yorks 44 A5
Newstead Borders 70 G4
Newstead Northumb 71 H10
Newstead Notts 45 G9
Newthorpe N Yorks 51 F10
Newton Argyll 73 D9
Newton Borders 62 A2
Newton Bridgend 14 D4
Newton Cambs 29 D11
Newton Cambs 37 D10
Newton Cardiff 15 D8
Newton Ches W 43 E8
Newton Ches W 43 F7
Newton Ches W 43 G8
Newton Cumb 49 B2
Newton Derbys 45 G8
Newton Dorset 9 C6
Newton Dumfries 61 D7
Newton Dumfries 61 F7
Newton Gtr Man 44 C3
Newton Hereford 25 E10
Newton Hereford 26 C2
Newton Highld 87 E10
Newton Highld 87 G10
Newton Highld 92 F5
Newton Highld 94 F5
Newton Lancs 49 F4
Newton Lancs 50 B1
Newton Lancs 50 D2
Newton Lincs 36 B6
Newton Moray 88 B1
Newton Norf 38 D4
Newton Northants 36 G4
Newton Northumb 62 G6
Newton Notts 36 A2
Newton Perth 75 D11
Newton S Lanark 68 D5
Newton S Lanark 69 G8
Newton S Yorks 45 B9
Newton Staffs 34 C6
Newton Suff 30 D6
Newton Swansea 14 C2
Newton W Loth 69 C9
Newton Warks 35 H11
Newton Wilts 9 B11
Newton Abbot Devon 5 D9
Newton Arlosh Cumb 61 H7
Newton Aycliffe Durham 58 D3
Newton Bewley Hrtlpl 58 D5
Newton Blossomville M Keynes 28 C6
Newton Bromswold Northants 28 B6
Newton Burgoland Leics 35 E9
Newton by Toft Lincs 46 D4
Newton Ferrers Devon 4 G6
Newton Flotman Norf 39 F8
Newton Hall Northumb 62 G6
Newton Harcourt Leics 36 F2
Newton Heath Gtr Man 44 B2
Newton Ho. Aberds 83 A8
Newton Kyme N Yorks 51 E10
Newton-le-Willows Mers 43 C8
Newton-le-Willows N Yorks 58 H3
Newton Longville Bucks 28 E5
Newton Mearns E Renf 68 E4
Newton Morrell N Yorks 58 F3
Newton Mulgrave N Yorks 59 E8
Newton of Ardtoe Highld 79 D9
Newton of Balcanquhal Perth 76 F4
Newton of Falkland Fife 76 G5
Newton on Ayr S Ayrs 66 D6
Newton on Ouse N Yorks 51 D11
Newton-on-Rawcliffe N Yorks 59 G9
Newton-on-the-Moor Northumb 63 C7
Newton on Trent Lincs 46 E2
Newton Park Argyll 73 G10
Newton Poppleford Devon 7 H9
Newton Purcell Oxon 28 E3
Newton Regis Warks 35 E8
Newton Reigny Cumb 57 C6
Newton St Cyres Devon 7 G7
Newton St Faith Norf 39 D8
Newton St Loe Bath 16 E4
Newton St Petrock Devon 6 E3
Newton Solney Derbys 35 C8
Newton Stacey Hants 17 G11
Newton Stewart Dumfries 55 C7
Newton Tony Wilts 17 G9
Newton Tracey Devon 6 D4
Newton under Roseberry Redcar 59 E6
Newton upon Derwent E Yorks 52 E3
Newton Valence Hants 10 A6
Newtonairds Dumfries 60 E4
Newtongrange Midloth 70 D2
Newtonhill Aberds 83 D11
Newtonhill Highld 87 G8
Newtonmill Angus 77 A9
Newtonmore Highld 81 D9
Newtown Argyll 73 C9
Newtown Ches W 43 E8
Newtown Corn 2 G6
Newtown Cumb 56 B2
Newtown Cumb 61 G11
Newtown Derbys 44 D3
Newtown Devon 7 D6
Newtown Glos 16 A3
Newtown Glos 26 E6
Newtown Hants 10 B2
Newtown Hants 10 C4
Newtown Hants 10 C1
Newtown Hants 10 C5
Newtown Hants 10 D5
Newtown Hants 17 E11
Newtown Hereford 26 D3
Newtown Highld 80 C5
Newtown IoM 48 E3
Newtown IoW 10 E3
Newtown Northumb 62 C6
Newtown Northumb 71 G8
Newtown Northumb 71 H9
Newtown Poole 9 E9
Newtown = Y Drenewydd Powys 33 F7
Newtown Shrops 33 B10
Newtown Staffs 44 F4
Newtown Staffs 44 F3
Newtown Wilts 9 B8
Newtown Linford Leics 35 E11
Newtown St Boswells Borders 70 G4
Newtown Unthank Leics 35 E10
Newtyle Angus 76 C5
Neyland Pembs 22 F4
Niarbyl IoM 48 E2
Nibley S Glos 16 C3
Nibley Green Glos 16 B4
Nibon Shetland 96 F5
Nicholashayne Devon 7 E10
Nicholaston Swansea 23 H10
Nidd N Yorks 51 C9
Nigg Aberdeen 83 C11
Nigg Highld 87 D11
Nigg Ferry Highld 87 E10
Nightcott Som 7 D7
Nilig Denb 42 G3
Nine Ashes Essex 20 A2
Nine Mile Burn Midloth 69 E10
Nine Wells Pembs 22 D2
Ninebanks Northumb 57 A9
Ninfield E Sus 12 E6
Ningwood IoW 10 F2
Nisbet Borders 70 H5
Nisthouse Orkney 95 G4
Nisthouse Shetland 96 G7
Niton IoW 10 G4
Nitshill Glasgow 68 D4
No Man's Heath Ches W 43 H8
No Man's Heath Warks 35 E8
Noak Hill London 20 B2
Noblethorpe S Yorks 44 B6
Nobottle Northants 28 B3
Nocton Lincs 46 F4
Noke Oxon 28 G2
Nolton Pembs 22 E3
Nolton Haven Pembs 22 E3
Nomansland Devon 7 E7
Nomansland Wilts 10 C1
Noneley Shrops 33 C10
Nonikiln Highld 87 D9
Nonington Kent 21 F9
Noonsbrough Shetland 96 H4
Norbreck Blackpool 49 E3
Norbridge Hereford 26 D4
Norbury Ches E 43 H8
Norbury Derbys 35 A7
Norbury Shrops 33 F9
Norbury Staffs 34 C3
Nordelph Norf 38 E1
Norden Gtr Man 44 A2
Norden Heath Dorset 9 F8
Nordley Shrops 34 F2
Norham Northumb 71 F8
Norley Ches W 43 E8
Norleywood Hants 10 E2
Norman Cross Cambs 37 F7
Normanby N Lincs 52 H4
Normanby N Yorks 52 A3
Normanby Redcar 59 E6
Normanby-by-Spital Lincs 46 D4
Normanby by Stow Lincs 46 D2
Normanby le Wold Lincs 46 C5
Normandy Sur 18 F6
Norman's Bay E Sus 12 F5
Norman's Green Devon 7 F9
Normanstone Suff 39 F11
Normanton Derby 35 B9
Normanton Leics 36 A4
Normanton Lincs 46 H3
Normanton Notts 45 G11
Normanton Rutland 36 E5
Normanton W Yorks 51 G9
Normanton le Heath Leics 35 D9
Normanton on Soar Notts 35 C11
Normanton-on-the-Wolds Notts 36 B2
Normanton on Trent Notts 45 F11
Normoss Lancs 49 F3
Norney Sur 18 G6
Norrington Common Wilts 16 E5
Norris Green Mers 43 C6
Norris Hill Leics 35 D9
North Anston S Yorks 45 D9
North Aston Oxon 27 F11
North Baddesley Hants 10 C2
North Ballachulish Highld 74 A3
North Barrow Som 8 B5
North Barsham Norf 38 B5
North Benfleet Essex 20 C4
North Bersted W Sus 11 D8
North Berwick E Loth 70 B4
North Boarhunt Hants 10 C5
North Bovey Devon 5 C8
North Bradley Wilts 16 F5
North Brentor Devon 4 C5
North Brewham Som 16 H4
North Buckland Devon 6 B3
North Burlingham Norf 39 D9
North Cadbury Som 8 B5
North Cairn Dumfries 54 B2
North Carlton Lincs 46 E3
North Carrine Argyll 65 H7
North Cave E Yorks 52 F4
North Cerney Glos 27 H7
North Charford Wilts 9 C10
North Charlton Northumb 63 A7
North Cheriton Som 8 B5
North Cliff E Yorks 53 E8
North Cliffe E Yorks 52 F4
North Clifton Notts 46 E2
North Cockerington Lincs 47 C7
North Coker Som 8 C4
North Collafirth Shetland 96 E5
North Common E Sus 12 D2
North Connel Argyll 74 D2
North Cornelly Bridgend 14 C4
North Cotes Lincs 47 B7
North Cove Suff 39 G10
North Cowton N Yorks 58 F3
North Crawley M Keynes 28 D6
North Cray London 19 D11
North Creake Norf 38 B4
North Curry Som 8 B2
North Dalton E Yorks 52 D5
North Dawn Orkney 95 H5
North Deighton N Yorks 51 D9
North Duffield N Yorks 52 F2
North Elkington Lincs 46 C5
North Elmham Norf 38 C5

Nor–Pen 129

North Elmshall W Yorks 45 A8
North End Bucks 28 F5
North End E Yorks 53 F8
North End Essex 30 G3
North End Hants 17 E11
North End Lincs 37 A8
North End N Som 15 E10
North End Ptsmth 10 D5
North End Som 8 B1
North End W Sus 11 D10
North Erradale Highld 91 J12
North Fambridge Essex 20 B5
North Fearns Highld 85 E10
North Featherstone W Yorks 51 G10
North Ferriby E Yorks 52 G5
North Frodingham E Yorks 53 D7
North Gluss Shetland 96 F5
North Gorley Hants 9 C10
North Green Norf 39 G8
North Green Suff 31 B10
North Greetwell Lincs 46 E4
North Grimston N Yorks 52 C4
North Halley Orkney 95 H6
North Halling Medway 20 E4
North Hayling Hants 10 D6
North Hazelrigg Northumb 71 G9
North Heasley Devon 7 C6
North Heath W Sus 11 B9
North Hill Cambs 37 H10
North Hill Corn 4 D3
North Hinksey Oxon 27 H11
North Holmwood Sur 19 G8
North Howden E Yorks 52 F3
North Huish Devon 5 F8
North Hykeham Lincs 46 F3
North Johnston Pembs 22 E4
North Kelsey Lincs 46 B4
North Kelsey Moor Lincs 46 B4
North Kessock Highld 87 G9
North Killingholme N Lincs 53 H7
North Kilvington N Yorks 58 H5
North Kilworth Leics 36 G2
North Kirkton Aberds 89 C11
North Kiscadale N Ayrs 66 D3
North Kyme Lincs 46 G5
North Lancing W Sus 11 D10
North Lee Bucks 28 H5
North Leigh Oxon 27 G10
North Leverton with Habblesthorpe Notts 45 D11
North Littleton Worcs 27 D7
North Lopham Norf 38 G6
North Luffenham Rutland 36 E5
North Marden W Sus 11 C7
North Marston Bucks 28 F4
North Middleton Midloth 70 E2
North Middleton Northumb 62 A6
North Molton Devon 7 D6
North Moreton Oxon 18 C2
North Mundham W Sus 11 D7
North Muskham Notts 45 G11
North Newbald E Yorks 52 F5
North Newington Oxon 27 E11
North Newnton Wilts 17 F8
North Newton Som 8 A1
North Nibley Glos 16 B4
North Oakley Hants 18 F2
North Ockendon London 20 C2
North Ormesby Mbro 58 D6
North Ormsby Lincs 46 C6
North Otterington N Yorks 58 H4
North Owersby Lincs 46 C4
North Perrott Som 8 D3
North Petherton Som 8 A1
North Petherwin Corn 4 C3
North Pickenham Norf 38 E4
North Piddle Worcs 26 C6
North Poorton Dorset 8 E4
North Port Argyll 74 E3
North Queensferry Fife 69 B10
North Radworthy Devon 7 C6
North Rauceby Lincs 46 H4
North Reston Lincs 47 D7
North Rigton N Yorks 51 E8
North Rode Ches E 44 F2
North Roe Shetland 96 E5
North Runcton Norf 38 D2
North Sandwick Shetland 96 D7
North Scale Cumb 49 C1
North Scarle Lincs 46 F2
North Seaton Northumb 63 E8
North Shian Argyll 74 C2
North Shields T&W 63 G9
North Shoebury Southend 20 C6
North Shore Blackpool 49 F3
North Side Cumb 56 D2
North Side Pboro 37 F8
North Skelton Redcar 59 E7
North Somercotes Lincs 47 C8
North Stainley N Yorks 51 B8
North Stainmore Cumb 57 E10
North Stifford Thurrock 20 C3
North Stoke Bath 16 E4
North Stoke Oxon 18 C3
North Stoke W Sus 11 C9
North Street Hants 10 A5
North Street Kent 21 F7
North Street Medway 20 D5
North Street W Berks 18 D3
North Sunderland Northumb 71 G11
North Tamerton Corn 6 G2
North Tawton Devon 6 F5
North Thoresby Lincs 46 C6
North Tidworth Wilts 17 G9
North Togston Northumb 63 C8
North Tuddenham Norf 38 D6
North Walbottle T&W 63 G7
North Walsham Norf 39 B8
North Waltham Hants 18 G2
North Warnborough Hants 18 F4
North Water Bridge Angus 83 G8
North Watten Highld 94 E4
North Weald Bassett Essex 19 A11
North Wheatley Notts 45 D11
North Whilborough Devon 5 E9
North Wick Bath 16 E2
North Willingham Lincs 46 D5
North Wingfield Derbys 45 F8
North Witham Lincs 36 C5
North Woolwich London 19 D11
North Wootton Dorset 8 C5
North Wootton Norf 38 C2
North Wootton Som 16 G2
North Wraxall Wilts 16 D5
North Wroughton Swindon 17 C8
Northacre Norf 38 F5
Northallerton N Yorks 58 G4
Northam Devon 6 D3
Northam Soton 10 C3
Northampton Northants 28 B4
Northaw Herts 19 A9
Northbeck Lincs 37 A6
Northborough Pboro 37 E7
Northbourne Kent 21 F10
Northbridge Street E Sus 12 D6
Northchapel W Sus 11 B8
Northchurch Herts 28 H6
Northcott Devon 6 G2
Northdown Kent 21 D10
Northdyke Orkney 95 F3
Northend Bath 16 E4
Northend Bucks 18 B4
Northend Warks 27 C10
Northenden Gtr Man 44 C2
Northfield Aberdeen 83 C11
Northfield Borders 71 D8
Northfield E Yorks 52 G6
Northfield W Mid 34 H6
Northfields Lincs 36 E6
Northfleet Kent 20 D3
Northgate Lincs 37 C7
Northhouse Borders 61 C10
Northiam E Sus 13 D7
Northill C Beds 29 D8
Northington Hants 18 H2
Northlands Lincs 47 G7
Northlea Durham 58 A5
Northleach Glos 27 G8
Northleigh Devon 7 G10
Northlew Devon 6 G4
Northmoor Oxon 17 A11
Northmoor Green or Moorland Som 8 A2
Northmuir Angus 76 B6
Northney Hants 10 D6
Northolt London 19 C8
Northop Flint 42 F5
Northop Hall Flint 42 F5
Northorpe Lincs 37 B8
Northorpe Lincs 37 D6
Northorpe Lincs 46 C2
Northover Som 8 B4
Northover Som 15 H10
Northowram W Yorks 51 G7
Northport Dorset 9 F8
Northpunds Shetland 96 L6
Northrepps Norf 39 B8
Northtown Orkney 95 J5
Northway Glos 26 E6
Northwich Ches W 43 E9
Northwick S Glos 16 C2
Northwold Norf 38 F3
Northwood Derbys 44 F6
Northwood IoW 10 E3
Northwood Kent 21 E10
Northwood London 19 B7
Northwood Shrops 33 B10
Northwood Green Glos 26 G4
Norton E Sus 12 F3
Norton Glos 26 F5
Norton Halton 43 D8
Norton Herts 29 E9
Norton IoW 10 F2
Norton Mon 25 G11
Norton Northants 28 B3
Norton Notts 45 E9
Norton Powys 25 B10
Norton S Yorks 51 H11
Norton Shrops 33 G10
Norton Shrops 34 E1
Norton Shrops 34 E3
Norton Stockton 58 D5
Norton Suff 30 B6
Norton W Sus 11 D8
Norton W Sus 11 E7
Norton Wilts 16 C5
Norton Worcs 26 C5
Norton Worcs 27 D7
Norton Bavant Wilts 16 G6
Norton Bridge Staffs 34 B4
Norton Canes Staffs 34 E6
Norton Canon Hereford 25 D10
Norton Corner Norf 39 C6
Norton Disney Lincs 46 G2
Norton East Staffs 34 E6
Norton Ferris Wilts 16 H4
Norton Fitzwarren Som 7 D10
Norton Green IoW 10 F2
Norton Hawkfield Bath 16 E2
Norton Heath Essex 20 A3
Norton in Hales Shrops 34 B3
Norton-in-the-Moors Stoke 44 G2
Norton-Juxta-Twycross Leics 35 E9
Norton-le-Clay N Yorks 51 B10
Norton Lindsey Warks 27 B9
Norton Malreward Bath 16 E3
Norton Mandeville Essex 20 A2
Norton-on-Derwent N Yorks 52 B3
Norton St Philip Som 16 F4
Norton sub Hamdon Som 8 C3
Norton Woodseats S Yorks 45 D7
Norwell Notts 45 F11
Norwell Woodhouse Notts 45 F11
Norwich Norf 39 E8
Norwick Shetland 96 B8
Norwood Derbys 45 D8
Norwood Hill Sur 19 G9
Norwoodside Cambs 37 F10
Noseley Leics 36 F3
Noss Shetland 96 M5
Noss Mayo Devon 4 G6
Nosterfield N Yorks 51 A8
Nostie Highld 85 F13
Notgrove Glos 27 F8
Nottage Bridgend 14 D4
Nottingham Nottingham 36 B1
Nottington Dorset 8 F5
Notton W Yorks 45 A7
Notton Wilts 16 E6
Nounsley Essex 30 G4
Noutard's Green Worcs 26 B4
Novar House Highld 87 E9
Nox Shrops 33 D10
Nuffield Oxon 18 C3
Nun Hills Lancs 50 G4
Nun Monkton N Yorks 51 D11
Nunburnholme E Yorks 52 E4
Nuncargate Notts 45 G9
Nuneaton Warks 35 F9
Nuneham Courtenay Oxon 18 B2
Nunney Som 16 G4
Nunnington N Yorks 52 B2
Nunnykirk Northumb 62 D6
Nunsthorpe NE Lincs 46 B6
Nunthorpe Mbro 59 E6
Nunthorpe York 52 D2
Nunton Wilts 9 B10
Nunwick N Yorks 51 B9
Nupend Glos 26 H4
Nursling Hants 10 C2
Nursted Hants 11 B6
Nutbourne W Sus 11 C9
Nutbourne W Sus 11 D6
Nutfield Sur 19 F10
Nuthall Notts 35 A11
Nuthampstead Herts 29 E11
Nuthurst W Sus 11 B10
Nutley E Sus 12 D3
Nutley Hants 18 G3
Nutwell S Yorks 45 B10
Nybster Highld 94 D5
Nyetimber W Sus 11 E7
Nyewood W Sus 11 B7
Nymet Rowland Devon 6 F6
Nymet Tracey Devon 7 F6
Nympsfield Glos 16 A5
Nynehead Som 7 D10
Nyton W Sus 11 D8

O

Oad Street Kent 20 E5
Oadby Leics 36 E2
Oak Cross Devon 6 G4
Oakamoor Staffs 35 A6
Oakbank W Loth 69 D9
Oakdale Caerph 15 B7
Oake Som 7 D10
Oaken Staffs 34 E4
Oakenclough Lancs 49 E5
Oakengates Telford 34 D3
Oakenholt Flint 42 E5
Oakenshaw Durham 58 C3
Oakenshaw W Yorks 51 G7
Oakerthorpe Derbys 45 G7
Oakes W Yorks 51 H7
Oakfield Torf 15 B9
Oakford Ceredig 23 A9
Oakford Devon 7 D8
Oakfordbridge Devon 7 D8
Oakgrove Ches E 44 F3
Oakham Rutland 36 E4
Oakhanger Hants 18 H4
Oakhill Som 16 G3
Oakhurst Kent 20 F2
Oakington Cambs 29 B11
Oaklands Herts 29 G9
Oaklands Powys 25 C7
Oakle Street Glos 26 G4
Oakley Bedford 29 C7
Oakley Bucks 28 G3
Oakley Fife 69 B9
Oakley Hants 18 F2
Oakley Oxon 18 A4
Oakley Poole 9 E9
Oakley Suff 39 H7
Oakley Green Windsor 18 D6
Oakley Park Powys 32 G5
Oakmere Ches W 43 F8
Oakridge Glos 16 A6
Oakridge Hants 10 F3
Oaks Shrops 33 E10
Oaks Green Derbys 35 B7
Oaksey Wilts 16 B6
Oakthorpe Leics 35 D9
Oakwoodhill Sur 19 H8
Oakworth W Yorks 50 F6
Oape Highld 92 J7
Oare Kent 21 E7
Oare Som 7 B7
Oare W Berks 18 D2
Oare Wilts 17 E8
Oasby Lincs 36 B6
Oathlaw Angus 77 B7
Oatlands N Yorks 51 D9
Oban Argyll 79 J11
Oban Highld 79 C11
Oborne Dorset 8 C5
Obthorpe Lincs 37 D6
Occlestone Green Ches W 43 F9
Occold Suff 31 A8
Ochiltree E Ayrs 67 D8
Ochtermuthill Perth 75 F11
Ochtertyre Perth 75 E11
Ockbrook Derbys 35 B10
Ockham Sur 19 F7
Ockle Highld 79 D8
Ockley Sur 19 H8
Ocle Pychard Hereford 26 D2
Octon E Yorks 52 C6
Octon Cross Roads E Yorks 52 C6
Odcombe Som 8 C4
Odd Down Bath 16 E4
Oddendale Cumb 57 E7
Odder Lincs 46 E3
Oddingley Worcs 26 C6
Oddington Glos 27 F9
Oddington Oxon 28 G2
Odell Bedford 28 C6
Odie Orkney 95 F7
Odiham Hants 18 F4
Odstock Wilts 9 B10
Odstone Leics 35 E9
Offchurch Warks 27 B10
Offenham Worcs 27 D7
Offham E Sus 12 E2
Offham Kent 20 F3
Offham W Sus 11 D9
Offord Cluny Cambs 29 B9
Offord Darcy Cambs 29 B9
Offton Suff 31 D7
Offwell Devon 7 G10
Ogbourne Maizey Wilts 17 D8
Ogbourne St Andrew Wilts 17 D8
Ogbourne St George Wilts 17 D9
Ogil Angus 77 A7
Ogle Northumb 63 F7
Ogmore V Glam 14 D4
Ogmore-by-Sea V Glam 14 D4
Ogmore Vale Bridgend 14 B5
Okeford Fitzpaine Dorset 9 C7
Okehampton Devon 6 G4
Okehampton Camp Devon 6 G4
Okraquoy Shetland 96 K6
Old Northants 28 A4
Old Aberdeen Aberdeen 83 C11
Old Alresford Hants 10 A4
Old Arley Warks 35 F8
Old Basford Nottingham 35 A11
Old Basing Hants 18 F3
Old Bewick Northumb 62 A6
Old Bolingbroke Lincs 47 F7
Old Bramhope W Yorks 51 E8
Old Brampton Derbys 45 E7
Old Bridge of Tilt Perth 81 G10
Old Bridge of Urr Dumfries 55 C10
Old Buckenham Norf 39 F6
Old Burghclere Hants 17 F11
Old Byland N Yorks 59 H6
Old Cassop Durham 58 C4
Old Castleton Borders 61 D11
Old Catton Norf 39 D8
Old Clee NE Lincs 46 B6
Old Cleeve Som 7 B9
Old Clipstone Notts 45 F10
Old Colwyn Conwy 41 C10
Old Coulsdon London 19 F10
Old Crombie Aberds 88 C5
Old Dailly S Ayrs 66 G5
Old Dalby Leics 36 C2
Old Deer Aberds 89 D9
Old Denaby S Yorks 45 C8
Old Edlington S Yorks 45 C9
Old Eldon Durham 58 D3
Old Ellerby E Yorks 53 F7
Old Felixstowe Suff 31 E10
Old Fletton Pboro 37 F7
Old Glossop Derbys 44 C4
Old Goole E Yorks 52 G3
Old Hall Powys 32 G5
Old Heath Essex 31 F7
Old Heathfield E Sus 12 D4
Old Hill W Mid 34 G5
Old Hunstanton Norf 38 A2
Old Hurst Cambs 37 H8
Old Hutton Cumb 57 H7
Old Kea Corn 3 E7
Old Kilpatrick W Dunb 68 C3
Old Kinnernie Aberds 83 C9
Old Knebworth Herts 29 F9
Old Langho Lancs 50 F3
Old Laxey IoM 48 D4
Old Leake Lincs 47 G8
Old Malton N Yorks 52 B3
Old Micklefield W Yorks 51 F10
Old Milton Hants 9 E11
Old Milverton Warks 27 B9
Old Monkland N Lanark 68 D6
Old Netley Hants 10 D3
Old Philpstoun W Loth 69 C9
Old Quarrington Durham 58 C4
Old Radnor Powys 25 C9
Old Rattray Aberds 89 C10
Old Rayne Aberds 83 A8
Old Romney Kent 13 D9
Old Sodbury S Glos 16 C4
Old Somerby Lincs 36 B5
Old Stratford Northants 28 D4
Old Thirsk N Yorks 51 A10
Old Town Cumb 50 A1
Old Town Cumb 57 B6
Old Town Northumb 62 D4
Old Town Scilly 2 C3
Old Trafford Gtr Man 44 C2
Old Tupton Derbys 45 F7
Old Warden C Beds 29 D8
Old Weston Cambs 37 H6
Old Whittington Derbys 45 E7
Old Wick Highld 94 E5
Old Windsor Windsor 18 D6
Old Wives Lees Kent 21 F7
Old Woking Sur 19 F7
Old Woodhall Lincs 46 F6
Oldany Highld 92 F4
Oldberrow Warks 27 B8
Oldborough Devon 7 F6
Oldbury Shrops 34 F3
Oldbury W Mid 34 G5
Oldbury Warks 35 F9
Oldbury-on-Severn S Glos 16 B3
Oldbury on the Hill Glos 16 C5
Oldcastle Bridgend 14 D5
Oldcastle Mon 25 F10
Oldcotes Notts 45 D9
Oldfallow Staffs 34 D5
Oldfield Worcs 26 B5
Oldford Som 16 F4
Oldham Gtr Man 44 B3
Oldhamstocks E Loth 70 C6
Oldland S Glos 16 D3
Oldmeldrum Aberds 89 F8
Oldshore Beg Highld 92 D4
Oldshoremore Highld 92 D5
Oldstead N Yorks 51 A11
Oldtown Aberds 83 A7
Oldtown of Ord Aberds 88 C6
Oldway Swansea 23 H10
Oldways End Devon 7 D7
Oldwhat Aberds 89 C8
Olgrinmore Highld 94 E2
Oliver's Battery Hants 10 B3
Ollaberry Shetland 96 E5
Ollerton Ches E 43 E10
Ollerton Notts 45 F10
Ollerton Shrops 34 C2
Olmarch Ceredig 24 C3
Olney M Keynes 28 C5
Olrig Ho. Highld 94 D3
Olton W Mid 35 G7
Olveston S Glos 16 C3
Olwen Ceredig 23 B10
Ombersley Worcs 26 B5
Ompton Notts 45 F10
Onchan IoM 48 E3
Onecote Staffs 44 G4
Onen Mon 25 G11
Ongar Hill Norf 38 C1
Ongar Street Hereford 25 B10
Onibury Shrops 33 H10
Onich Highld 74 A3
Onllwyn Neath 24 G5
Onneley Staffs 34 A3
Onslow Village Sur 18 G6
Onthank E Ayrs 67 B7
Openwoodgate Derbys 45 H7
Opinan Highld 85 A12
Opinan Highld 91 H13
Orange Lane Borders 70 F6
Orange Row Norf 37 C11
Orasaigh W Isles 91 F8
Orbliston Moray 88 C3
Orbost Highld 84 D7
Orby Lincs 47 F8
Orchard Hill Devon 6 D3
Orchard Portman Som 8 B1
Orcheston Wilts 17 G7
Orcop Hereford 25 F11
Orcop Hill Hereford 25 F11
Ord Highld 85 G11
Ordhead Aberds 83 B8
Ordie Aberds 82 C6
Ordiequish Moray 88 C3
Ordsall Notts 45 D10
Ore E Sus 13 E7
Oreton Shrops 34 G2
Orford Suff 31 D11
Orford Warr 43 C9
Orgreave Staffs 35 D7
Orlestone Kent 13 C8
Orleton Hereford 25 B11
Orleton Worcs 26 B3
Orlingbury Northants 28 A5
Ormesby Redcar 59 E6
Ormesby St Margaret Norf 39 D10
Ormesby St Michael Norf 39 D10
Ormiclate Castle W Isles 84 E2
Ormiscaig Highld 91 H13
Ormiston E Loth 70 D3
Ormsaigbeg Highld 78 E7
Ormsaigmore Highld 78 E7
Ormsary Argyll 72 F6
Ormsgill Cumb 49 B1
Ormskirk Lancs 43 B7
Orpington London 19 E11
Orrell Gtr Man 43 B8
Orrell Mers 42 C6
Orrisdale IoM 48 C3
Orroland Dumfries 55 E10
Orsett Thurrock 20 C3
Orslow Staffs 34 D4
Orston Notts 36 A3
Orthwaite Cumb 56 C4
Ortner Lancs 49 D5
Orton Cumb 57 F8
Orton Northants 36 H4
Orton Longueville Pboro 37 F7
Orton-on-the-Hill Leics 35 E9
Orton Waterville Pboro 37 F7
Orwell Cambs 29 C10
Osbaldeston Lancs 50 F2
Osbaldwick York 52 D2
Osbaston Shrops 33 C9
Osbournby Lincs 37 B6
Oscroft Ches W 43 F8
Ose Highld 85 D8
Osgathorpe Leics 35 D10
Osgodby Lincs 46 C4
Osgodby N Yorks 52 F2
Osgodby N Yorks 53 A6
Oskaig Highld 85 E10
Oskamull Argyll 78 G7
Osmaston Derby 35 B9
Osmaston Derbys 35 A8
Osmington Dorset 8 F6
Osmington Mills Dorset 8 F6
Osmotherley N Yorks 58 G5
Ospisdale Highld 87 C10
Ospringe Kent 21 E7
Ossett W Yorks 51 G8
Ossington Notts 45 F11
Ostend Essex 20 B6
Oswaldkirk N Yorks 52 B2
Oswaldtwistle Lancs 50 G3
Oswestry Shrops 33 C8
Otford Kent 20 F2
Otham Kent 20 F4
Othery Som 8 A2
Otley Suff 31 C9
Otley W Yorks 51 E8
Otter Ferry Argyll 73 E8
Otterbourne Hants 10 B3
Otterburn N Yorks 50 D4
Otterburn Northumb 62 D4
Otterburn Camp Northumb 62 D4
Otterham Corn 4 B2
Otterhampton Som 15 G8
Ottershaw Sur 19 E7
Otterswick Shetland 96 E7
Otterton Devon 7 H9
Ottery St Mary Devon 7 G10
Ottinge Kent 21 G8
Ottringham E Yorks 53 G8
Oughterby Cumb 61 H8
Oughtershaw N Yorks 50 A4
Oughterside Cumb 56 B3
Oughtibridge S Yorks 45 C7
Oughtrington Warr 43 D9
Oulston N Yorks 51 B11
Oulton Cumb 56 A4
Oulton Norf 39 C7
Oulton Staffs 34 B5
Oulton Suff 39 F11
Oulton W Yorks 51 G9
Oulton Broad Suff 39 F11
Oulton Street Norf 39 C7
Oundle Northants 36 G6
Ousby Cumb 57 C8
Ousdale Highld 94 H2
Ousden Suff 30 C4
Ousefleet E Yorks 52 G4
Ouston Durham 58 A3
Ouston Northumb 62 F6
Out Newton E Yorks 53 G9
Out Rawcliffe Lancs 49 E4
Outertown Orkney 95 G3
Outgate Cumb 56 G5
Outhgill Cumb 57 F9
Outlane W Yorks 51 H6
Outwell Norf 37 E11
Outwick Hants 9 C10
Outwood Sur 19 G10
Outwood W Yorks 51 G9
Outwoods Staffs 34 D3
Ovenden W Yorks 51 G6
Ovenscloss Borders 70 G3
Over Cambs 29 A10
Over Ches W 43 F9
Over S Glos 16 C2
Over Compton Dorset 8 C4
Over Green W Mid 35 F7
Over Haddon Derbys 44 F6
Over Hulton Gtr Man 43 B9
Over Kellet Lancs 49 B5
Over Kiddington Oxon 27 F11
Over Knutsford Ches E 43 E10
Over Monnow Mon 26 G2
Over Norton Oxon 27 F10
Over Peover Ches E 43 E10
Over Silton N Yorks 58 G5
Over Stowey Som 7 C10
Over Stratton Som 8 C3
Over Tabley Ches E 43 D10
Over Wallop Hants 17 H9
Over Whitacre Warks 35 F8
Over Worton Oxon 27 F11
Overbister Orkney 95 D7
Overbury Worcs 26 E6
Overcombe Dorset 8 F5
Overgreen Derbys 45 E7
Overleigh Som 15 H10
Overley Green Warks 27 C7
Overpool Ches W 43 E6
Overscaig Hotel Highld 92 G7
Overseal Derbys 35 D8
Oversland Kent 21 F7
Overstone Northants 28 B5
Overstrand Norf 39 A8
Overthorpe Northants 27 D11
Overton Aberdeen 83 B10
Overton Ches W 43 E8
Overton Dumfries 60 G5
Overton Hants 18 G2
Overton Lancs 49 D4
Overton N Yorks 52 D1
Overton Shrops 26 A2
Overton Swansea 23 H9
Overton W Yorks 51 H8
Overton = Owrtyn Wrex 33 A9
Overton Bridge Wrex 33 A9
Overtown N Lanark 69 E7
Oving Bucks 28 F4
Oving W Sus 11 D8
Ovingdean Brighton 12 F2
Ovingham Northumb 62 G6
Ovington Durham 58 E2
Ovington Essex 30 D4
Ovington Hants 10 A4
Ovington Norf 38 E5
Ovington Northumb 62 G6
Ower Hants 10 C2
Owermoigne Dorset 9 F6
Owlbury Shrops 33 F9
Owler Bar Derbys 44 E6
Owlerton S Yorks 45 D7
Owl's Green Suff 31 B9
Owlswick Bucks 28 H4
Owmby Lincs 46 B4
Owmby-by-Spital Lincs 46 D4
Owrtyn = Overton Wrex 33 A9
Owslebury Hants 10 B4
Owston Leics 36 E3
Owston S Yorks 45 A9
Owston Ferry N Lincs 46 B2
Owstwick E Yorks 53 F8
Owthorne E Yorks 53 G9
Owthorpe Notts 36 B2
Oxborough Norf 38 E3
Oxcombe Lincs 47 E7
Oxen Park Cumb 56 H5
Oxenholme Cumb 57 H7
Oxenhope W Yorks 50 F6
Oxenton Glos 26 E6
Oxenwood Wilts 17 F10
Oxford Oxon 28 H2
Oxhey Herts 19 B8
Oxhill Warks 27 D10
Oxley W Mid 34 E5
Oxley Green Essex 30 G6
Oxley's Green E Sus 12 D5
Oxnam Borders 62 B3
Oxshott Sur 19 E8
Oxspring S Yorks 44 B6
Oxted Sur 19 F10
Oxton Borders 70 E3
Oxton Notts 45 G10
Oxwich Swansea 23 H9
Oxwick Norf 38 C5
Oykel Bridge Highld 92 J6
Oyne Aberds 83 A8

P

Pabail Iarach W Isles 91 D10
Pabail Uarach W Isles 91 D10
Pace Gate N Yorks 51 D7
Packington Leics 35 D9
Padanaram Angus 77 B7
Padbury Bucks 28 E4
Paddington London 19 C9
Paddlesworth Kent 21 H8
Paddock Wood Kent 12 B5
Paddockhaugh Moray 88 C2
Paddockhole Dumfries 61 E8
Padfield Derbys 44 C4
Padiham Lancs 50 F3
Padog Conwy 41 E10
Padside N Yorks 51 D7
Padstow Corn 3 B8
Padworth W Berks 18 E3
Page Bank Durham 58 C3
Pagham W Sus 11 E7
Paglesham Churchend Essex 20 B6
Paglesham Eastend Essex 20 B6
Paibeil W Isles 84 B2
Paible W Isles 90 H5
Paignton Torbay 5 E9
Pailton Warks 35 G10
Painscastle Powys 25 D8
Painshawfield Northumb 62 G6
Painsthorpe E Yorks 52 D4
Painswick Glos 26 H5
Pairc Shiaboist W Isles 90 C7
Paisley Renfs 68 D3
Pakefield Suff 39 F11
Pakenham Suff 30 B6
Pale Gwyn 32 B5
Palestine Hants 17 G9
Paley Street Windsor 18 D5
Palfrey W Mid 34 F6
Palgowan Dumfries 54 A6
Palgrave Suff 39 H7
Pallion T&W 63 H9
Palmarsh Kent 13 C10
Palnackie Dumfries 55 D11
Palnure Dumfries 55 C7
Palterton Derbys 45 F8
Pamber End Hants 18 F3
Pamber Green Hants 18 F3
Pamber Heath Hants 18 E3
Pamphill Dorset 9 D8
Pampisford Cambs 29 D11
Pan Orkney 95 J4
Panbride Angus 77 D8
Pancrasweek Devon 6 F1
Pandy Gwyn 32 E2
Pandy Mon 25 F10
Pandy Powys 32 E5
Pandy Wrex 33 B7
Pandy Tudur Conwy 41 D10
Panfield Essex 30 F4
Pangbourne W Berks 18 D3
Pannal N Yorks 51 D9
Panshanger Herts 29 G9
Pant Shrops 33 C8
Pant-glâs Powys 32 F3
Pant-glas Carms 23 D10
Pant-glas Gwyn 40 F6
Pant-glas Shrops 33 B8
Pant-lasau Swansea 14 B2
Pant Mawr Powys 32 G4
Pant-teg Carms 23 D9
Pant-y-Caws Carms 22 D6
Pant-y-dwr Powys 32 H5
Pant-y-ffridd Powys 33 E7
Pant-y-Wacco Flint 42 E4
Pant-yr-awel Bridgend 14 C5
Pantgwyn Carms 23 D10
Pantgwyn Ceredig 23 B7
Panton Lincs 46 E5
Pantperthog Gwyn 32 E3
Pantyffynnon Carms 24 G3
Pantymwyn Flint 42 F4
Panxworth Norf 39 D9
Papcastle Cumb 56 C3
Papigoe Highld 94 E5
Papil Shetland 96 K5
Papley Orkney 95 J5
Papple E Loth 70 C4
Papplewick Notts 45 G9
Papworth Everard Cambs 29 B9
Papworth St Agnes Cambs 29 B9
Par Corn 4 F1
Parbold Lancs 43 A7
Parbrook Som 16 H2
Parbrook W Sus 11 B9
Parc Gwyn 41 G10
Parc-Seymour Newport 15 B10
Parc-y-rhôs Carms 23 B10
Parcllyn Ceredig 23 A7
Pardshaw Cumb 56 D2
Parham Suff 31 B10
Park Dumfries 60 D5
Park Corner Oxon 18 C3
Park Corner Windsor 18 C5
Park End Mbro 58 E6
Park End Northumb 62 F4
Park Gate Hants 10 D4
Park Hill N Yorks 51 C9
Park Hill Notts 45 G10
Park Street W Sus 11 A10
Parkend Glos 26 H3
Parkeston Essex 31 E9
Parkgate Ches W 42 E5
Parkgate Dumfries 60 E6
Parkgate Kent 13 C7
Parkgate Sur 19 G9
Parkham Devon 6 D2
Parkham Ash Devon 6 D2
Parkhill Ho. Aberds 83 B10
Parkhouse Mon 15 A10
Parkhouse Green Derbys 45 F8
Parkhurst IoW 10 E3
Parkmill Swansea 23 H10
Parkneuk Aberds 83 F9
Parkstone Poole 9 E9
Parley Cross Dorset 9 E9
Parracombe Devon 6 B5
Parrog Pembs 22 C5
Parsley Hay Derbys 44 F5
Parson Cross S Yorks 45 C7
Parson Drove Cambs 37 E9
Parsonage Green Essex 30 H4
Parsonby Cumb 56 C3
Parson's Heath Essex 31 F7
Partick Glasgow 68 D4
Partington Gtr Man 43 C10
Partney Lincs 47 F8
Parton Cumb 56 D1
Parton Dumfries 55 B9
Parton Glos 26 F5
Partridge Green W Sus 11 C10
Parwich Derbys 44 G5
Passenham Northants 28 E4
Paston Norf 39 B9
Patchacott Devon 6 G3
Patcham Brighton 12 F2
Patching W Sus 11 D9
Patchole Devon 6 B5
Pateley Bridge N Yorks 51 C7
Paternoster Heath Essex 30 G6
Path of Condie Perth 76 F3
Pathe Som 8 B2
Pathhead Aberds 77 A10
Pathhead E Ayrs 67 E9
Pathhead Fife 69 A11
Pathhead Midloth 70 D2
Pathstruie Perth 76 F3
Patna E Ayrs 67 E7
Patney Wilts 17 F7
Patrick IoM 48 D2
Patrick Brompton N Yorks 58 G3
Patrington E Yorks 53 G9
Patrixbourne Kent 21 F8
Patterdale Cumb 56 E5
Pattingham Staffs 34 F4
Pattishall Northants 28 C3
Pattiswick Green Essex 30 F5
Patton Bridge Cumb 57 G7
Paul Corn 2 G3
Paulerspury Northants 28 D4
Paull E Yorks 53 G7
Paulton Bath 16 F3
Pavenham Bedford 28 C6
Pawlett Som 15 G9
Pawston Northumb 71 G7
Paxford Glos 27 E8
Paxton Borders 71 E8
Payhembury Devon 7 F9
Paythorne Lancs 50 D4
Peacehaven E Sus 12 F3
Peak Dale Derbys 44 E4
Peak Forest Derbys 44 E5
Peakirk Pboro 37 E7
Pearsie Angus 76 B6
Pease Pottage W Sus 12 C1
Peasedown St John Bath 16 F4
Peasemore W Berks 17 D11
Peasenhall Suff 31 B10
Peaslake Sur 19 G7
Peasley Cross Mers 43 C8
Peasmarsh E Sus 13 D7
Peaston E Loth 70 D3
Peastonbank E Loth 70 D3
Peat Inn Fife 77 G7
Peathill Aberds 89 B9
Peatling Magna Leics 36 F1
Peatling Parva Leics 36 G1
Peaton Shrops 33 G11
Peats Corner Suff 31 B8
Pebmarsh Essex 30 E5
Pebworth Worcs 27 D8
Pecket Well W Yorks 50 G5
Peckforton Ches E 43 G8
Peckham London 19 D10
Peckleton Leics 35 E10
Pedlinge Kent 13 C10
Pedmore W Mid 34 G5
Pedwell Som 15 H10
Peebles Borders 69 F11
Peel IoM 48 D2
Peel Common Hants 10 D4
Peel Park S Lanark 68 E5
Peening Quarter Kent 13 D7
Pegsdon C Beds 29 E8
Pegswood Northumb 63 E8
Pegwell Kent 21 E10
Peinchorran Highld 85 E10
Peinlich Highld 85 C9
Pelaw T&W 63 G8
Pelcomb Bridge Pembs 22 E4
Pelcomb Cross Pembs 22 E4
Peldon Essex 30 G6
Pellon W Yorks 51 G6
Pelsall W Mid 34 E6
Pelton Durham 58 A3
Pelutho Cumb 56 B3
Pelynt Corn 4 F3
Pemberton Gtr Man 43 B8
Pembrey Carms 23 F9
Pembridge Hereford 25 C10
Pembroke = Penfro Pembs 22 F4
Pembroke Dock = Doc Penfro Pembs 22 F4
Pembury Kent 12 B5
Pen-bont Rhydybeddau Ceredig 32 G2
Pen-clawdd Swansea 23 G10
Pen-ffordd Pembs 22 D5
Pen-groes-oped Mon 25 H10
Pen-llyn Anglesey 40 B5
Pen-lon Anglesey 40 D6
Pen-sarn Gwyn 32 C1
Pen-sarn Gwyn 40 F6
Pen-twyn Mon 26 H2
Pen-y-banc Carms 24 F3
Pen-y-bont Carms 23 D8
Pen-y-bont Gwyn 32 C2
Pen-y-bont Gwyn 32 E3
Pen-y-bont Powys 33 C8
Pen-y-bont ar Ogwr = Bridgend Bridgend 14 D5
Pen-y-bryn Gwyn 32 D2
Pen-y-bryn Pembs 22 B6
Pen-y-cae Powys 24 G5
Pen-y-cae-mawr Mon 15 B10
Pen-y-cefn Flint 42 E4
Pen-y-clawdd Mon 25 H11
Pen-y-coedcae Rhondda 14 C6
Pen-y-fai Bridgend 14 C4
Pen-y-garn Carms 23 C10
Pen-y-garn Ceredig 32 G2
Pen-y-garnedd Anglesey 41 C7
Pen-y-gop Conwy 32 A5
Pen-y-graig Gwyn 40 G3
Pen-y-groes Carms 23 E10
Pen-y-groeslon Gwyn 40 G4
Pen-y-Gwryd Hotel Gwyn 41 E8
Pen-y-stryt Denb 42 G4
Pen-yr-heol Mon 25 G11
Pen-yr-Heolgerrig M Tydf 25 H7
Penallt Mon 26 G2
Penally Pembs 22 G6
Penalt Hereford 26 F2
Penare Corn 3 E8
Penarlâg = Hawarden Flint 42 F6
Penarth V Glam 15 D7
Penbryn Ceredig 23 A7
Pencader Carms 23 C9
Pencaenewydd Gwyn 40 F6
Pencaitland E Loth 70 D3
Pencarnisiog Anglesey 40 C5
Pencarreg Carms 23 B10
Pencelli Powys 25 F7
Pencoed Bridgend 14 C5
Pencombe Hereford 26 C2
Pencoyd Hereford 26 F2
Pencraig Hereford 26 F2
Pencraig Powys 32 C6
Pendeen Corn 2 F2
Penderyn Rhondda 24 H6
Pendine Carms 23 F7
Pendlebury Gtr Man 43 B10
Pendleton Lancs 43 F3
Pendock Worcs 26 E4
Pendoggett Corn 3 B9
Pendomer Som 8 C4
Pendoylan V Glam 14 D6
Pendre Bridgend 14 C5
Penegoes Powys 32 E3
Penfro = Pembroke Pembs 22 F4
Pengam Caerph 15 B7
Penge London 19 D10
Pengenffordd Powys 25 E8
Pengorffwysfa Anglesey 40 A6
Pengover Green Corn 4 E3
Penhale Corn 2 H5
Penhale Corn 3 D8
Penhalvaen Corn 2 F6
Penhill Swindon 17 C8
Penhow Newport 15 B10
Penhurst E Sus 12 E5
Peniarth Gwyn 32 E2
Penicuik Midloth 69 D11
Peniel Carms 23 D9
Peniel Denb 42 F3
Penifiler Highld 85 D9
Peninver Argyll 65 F8
Penisarwaun Gwyn 41 D7
Penistone S Yorks 44 B6
Penjerrick Corn 3 F6
Penketh Warr 43 D8
Penkill S Ayrs 66 G5
Penkridge Staffs 34 D5
Penley Wrex 33 B10
Penllergaer Swansea 14 B2
Penllyn V Glam 14 D5
Penmachno Conwy 41 E9
Penmaen Swansea 23 H10
Penmaenan Conwy 41 C9
Penmaenmawr Conwy 41 C9
Penmaenpool Gwyn 32 D2
Penmark V Glam 14 E6
Penmarth Corn 2 F6
Penmon Anglesey 41 B8
Penmore Mill Argyll 78 F7
Penmorfa Ceredig 23 A8
Penmorfa Gwyn 41 F7
Penmynydd Anglesey 41 C7
Penn Bucks 18 B6
Penn W Mid 34 F4
Penn Street Bucks 18 B6
Pennal Gwyn 32 E3
Pennan Aberds 89 B8
Pennant Ceredig 24 B2
Pennant Denb 32 B6
Pennant Denb 42 G3
Pennant Powys 32 F4
Pennant Melangell Powys 32 C6
Pennar Pembs 22 F4
Pennard Swansea 23 H10
Pennerley Shrops 33 F9
Pennington Cumb 49 B2
Pennington Gtr Man 43 C9
Pennington Hants 10 E2
Penny Bridge Cumb 49 A3
Pennycross Argyll 79 J8
Pennygate Norf 39 C9
Pennygown Argyll 79 G8
Pennymoor Devon 7 E7
Pennywell T&W 63 H9
Penparc Ceredig 23 B7
Penparc Pembs 22 C3
Penparcau Ceredig 32 G1
Penperlleni Mon 15 A9
Penpillick Corn 4 F1
Penpol Corn 3 F7
Penpoll Corn 4 F2
Penpont Dumfries 60 D4
Penpont Powys 24 F6
Penrhôs Mon 25 G11
Penrherber Carms 23 C7
Penrhiw goch Carms 23 E10
Penrhiw-llan Ceredig 23 B8
Penrhiw-pâl Ceredig 23 B8
Penrhiwceiber Rhondda 14 B6
Penrhos Gwyn 40 G5
Penrhos Powys 24 G4
Penrhosfeilw Anglesey 40 B4
Penrhyn Bay Conwy 41 B10
Penrhyn-coch Ceredig 32 G2
Penrhyndeudraeth Gwyn 41 G8
Penrhynside Conwy 41 B10
Penrice Swansea 23 H9
Penrith Cumb 57 C7
Penrose Corn 3 B7
Penruddock Cumb 56 D6
Penryn Corn 3 F6
Pensarn Carms 23 E9
Pensarn Conwy 42 E2
Pensax Worcs 26 B4
Pensby Mers 42 D5
Penselwood Som 9 A6
Pensford Bath 16 E3
Penshaw T&W 58 A4
Penshurst Kent 12 B4
Pensilva Corn 4 E3
Penston E Loth 70 C3
Pentewan Corn 3 E9
Pentir Gwyn 41 D7
Pentire Corn 3 C6
Pentlow Essex 30 D5
Pentney Norf 38 D3
Penton Mewsey Hants 17 G10
Pentraeth Anglesey 41 C7
Pentre Carms 23 E10
Pentre Powys 33 F8
Pentre Powys 33 G6
Pentre Rhondda 14 B5
Pentre Shrops 33 D9
Pentre Wrex 33 A8
Pentre Wrex 33 B7
Pentre-bâch Ceredig 23 B10
Pentre-bach Powys 24 E6
Pentre Berw Anglesey 40 C6
Pentre-bont Conwy 41 E9
Pentre-celyn Denb 42 G4
Pentre-Celyn Powys 32 E4
Pentre-chwyth Swansea 14 B2
Pentre-cwrt Carms 23 C8
Pentre Dolau-Honddu Powys 24 D6
Pentre-dwr Swansea 14 B2
Pentre-galar Pembs 22 C6
Pentre-Gwenlais Carms 24 G3
Pentre Gwynfryn Gwyn 32 C1
Pentre Halkyn Flint 42 E5
Pentre-Isaf Conwy 41 D10
Pentre Llanrhaeadr Denb 42 F3
Pentre-llwyn-llŵyd Powys 24 C6
Pentre-llyn Ceredig 24 A3

Pentre-llyn cymmer Conwy 42 G2
Pentre Meyrick V Glam 14 D5
Pentre-poeth Newport 15 C8
Pentre-rhew Ceredig 24 C3
Pentre-tafarn-y-fedw Conwy 41 D10
Pentre-ty-gwyn Carms 24 E5
Pentrebach M Tydf 14 A6
Pentrebach Swansea 24 H3
Pentrebeirdd Powys 33 D7
Pentrecagal Carms 23 B8
Pentredwr Denb 42 H4
Pentrefelin Carms 23 D10
Pentrefelin Ceredig 24 D3
Pentrefelin Conwy 41 C10
Pentrefelin Gwyn 41 G7
Pentrefoelas Conwy 41 E10
Pentregat Ceredig 23 A8
Pentreheyling Shrops 33 F8
Pentre'r Felin Conwy 41 D10
Pentre'r-felin Powys 24 E6
Pentrich Derbys 45 G7
Pentridge Dorset 9 C9
Pentyrch Cardiff 15 C7
Penuchadre V Glam 14 D4
Penuwch Ceredig 24 B2
Penwithick Corn 3 D9
Penwyllt Powys 24 G5
Penybanc Carms 24 G3
Penybont Powys 25 B8
Penybontfawr Powys 33 C6
Penycae Wrex 42 H5
Penycwm Pembs 22 D3
Penyffordd Flint 42 F6
Penyffridd Gwyn 41 E7
Penygarnedd Powys 33 C7
Penygraig Rhondda 14 B5
Penygroes Gwyn 40 E6
Penygroes Pembs 22 C6
Penyrheol Caerph 15 C7
Penysarn Anglesey 40 A6
Penywaun Rhondda 14 A5
Penzance Corn 2 F3
Peopleton Worcs 26 C6
Peover Heath Ches E 43 E10
Peper Harow Sur 18 G6
Perceton N Ayrs 67 B6
Percie Aberds 83 D7
Percyhorner Aberds 89 B9
Periton Som 7 B8
Perivale London 19 C8
Perkinsville Durham 58 A3
Perlethorpe Notts 45 E10
Perranarworthal Corn 3 F6
Perranporth Corn 3 D6
Perranuthnoe Corn 2 G4
Perranzabuloe Corn 3 D6
Perry Barr W Mid 35 F6
Perry Green Herts 29 G11
Perry Green Wilts 16 C6
Perry Street Kent 20 D3
Perryfoot Derbys 44 D5
Pershall Staffs 34 B4
Pershore Worcs 26 D6
Pert Angus 83 G8
Pertenhall Bedford 29 B7
Perth Perth 76 E4
Perthy Shrops 33 B9
Perton Staffs 34 F4
Pertwood Wilts 16 H5
Peter Tavy Devon 4 D6
Peterborough Pboro 37 F7
Peterburn Highld 91 J12
Peterchurch Hereford 25 E10
Peterculter Aberdeen 83 C10
Peterhead Aberds 89 D11
Peterlee Durham 58 B5
Peter's Green Herts 29 G8
Peters Marland Devon 6 E3
Petersfield Hants 10 B6
Peterston super-Ely V Glam 14 D6
Peterstone Wentlooge Newport 15 C8
Peterstow Hereford 26 F2
Petertown Orkney 95 H4
Petham Kent 21 F8
Petrockstow Devon 6 F4
Pett E Sus 13 E7
Pettaugh Suff 31 C8
Petteridge Kent 12 B5
Pettinain S Lanark 69 F8
Pettistree Suff 31 C9
Petton Devon 7 D9
Petton Shrops 33 C10
Petts Wood London 19 E11
Petty Aberds 89 E7
Pettycur Fife 69 B11
Pettymuick Aberds 89 F9
Petworth W Sus 11 B8
Pevensey E Sus 12 F5
Pevensey Bay E Sus 12 F5
Pewsey Wilts 17 E8
Philham Devon 6 D1
Philiphaugh Borders 70 H3
Phillack Corn 2 F4
Philleigh Corn 3 F7
Philpstoun W Loth 69 C9
Phocle Green Hereford 26 F3
Phoenix Green Hants 18 F4
Pica Cumb 56 D2
Piccotts End Herts 29 H7
Pickering N Yorks 52 A3
Picket Piece Hants 17 G10
Picket Post Hants 9 D10
Pickhill N Yorks 51 A9
Picklescott Shrops 33 F10
Pickletillem Fife 77 E7
Pickmere Ches E 43 E9
Pickney Som 7 D10
Pickstock Telford 34 C3
Pickwell Devon 6 B3
Pickwell Leics 36 D3
Pickworth Lincs 36 B6
Pickworth Rutland 36 D5
Picton Ches W 43 E7
Picton Flint 42 D4
Picton N Yorks 58 F5
Piddinghoe E Sus 12 F3
Piddington Northants 28 C5
Piddington Oxon 28 G3
Piddlehinton Dorset 8 E6
Piddletrenthide Dorset 8 E6
Pidley Cambs 37 H9
Piercebridge Darl 58 E3
Pierowall Orkney 95 D5
Pigdon Northumb 63 E7
Pikehall Derbys 44 G5
Pilgrims Hatch Essex 20 B2
Pilham Lincs 46 C2
Pill N Som 15 D11
Pillaton Corn 4 E4
Pillerton Hersey Warks 27 D10
Pillerton Priors Warks 27 D9
Pilleth Powys 25 B9
Pilley Hants 10 E2
Pilley S Yorks 45 B7
Pilling Lancs 49 E4
Pilling Lane Lancs 49 E3
Pillowell Glos 26 H3
Pillwell Dorset 9 C6
Pilning S Glos 16 C2
Pilsbury Derbys 44 F5
Pilsdon Dorset 8 E3
Pilsgate Pboro 37 E6
Pilsley Derbys 44 E6
Pilsley Derbys 45 F8
Pilton Devon 6 C4
Pilton Northants 36 G6
Pilton Rutland 36 E5
Pilton Som 16 G2
Pilton Green Swansea 23 H9
Pimperne Dorset 9 D8
Pin Mill Suff 31 E9
Pinchbeck Lincs 37 C8
Pinchbeck Bars Lincs 37 C7
Pinchbeck West Lincs 37 C8
Pincheon Green S Yorks 52 H2
Pinehurst Swindon 17 C8
Pinfold Lancs 43 A6
Pinged Carms 23 F9
Pinhoe Devon 7 G8
Pinkneys Green Windsor 18 C5
Pinley W Mid 35 H9
Pinminnoch S Ayrs 66 G4
Pinmore S Ayrs 66 G5
Pinmore Mains S Ayrs 66 G5
Pinner London 19 C8
Pinvin Worcs 26 D6
Pinwherry S Ayrs 66 H4
Pinxton Derbys 45 G8
Pipe and Lyde Hereford 26 D2
Pipe Gate Shrops 34 A3
Piperhill Highld 87 F11
Piper's Pool Corn 4 C3
Pipewell Northants 36 G4
Pippacott Devon 6 C4
Pipton Powys 25 E8
Pirbright Sur 18 F6
Pirnmill N Ayrs 66 B1
Pirton Herts 29 E8
Pirton Worcs 26 D5
Pisgah Ceredig 32 H2
Pisgah Stirling 75 G10
Pishill Oxon 18 C4
Pistyll Gwyn 40 F5
Pitagowan Perth 81 G10
Pitblae Aberds 89 B9
Pitcairngreen Perth 76 E3
Pitcalnie Highld 87 D11
Pitcaple Aberds 83 A9
Pitch Green Bucks 18 A4
Pitch Place Sur 18 F6
Pitchcombe Glos 26 H5
Pitchcott Bucks 28 F4
Pitchford Shrops 33 E11
Pitcombe Som 8 A5
Pitcorthie Fife 77 G8
Pitcox E Loth 70 C5
Pitcur Perth 76 D5
Pitfichie Aberds 83 B8
Pitforthie Aberds 83 F10
Pitgrudy Highld 87 B10
Pitkennedy Angus 77 B8
Pitkevy Fife 76 G5
Pitkierie Fife 77 G8
Pitlessie Fife 76 G6
Pitlochry Perth 76 B2
Pitmachie Aberds 83 A8
Pitmain Highld 81 C9
Pitmedden Aberds 89 F8
Pitminster Som 7 E11
Pitmuies Angus 77 C8
Pitmunie Aberds 83 B8
Pitney Som 8 B3
Pitscottie Fife 77 F7
Pitsea Essex 20 C4
Pitsford Northants 28 B4
Pitsmoor S Yorks 45 D7
Pitstone Bucks 28 G6
Pitstone Green Bucks 28 G6
Pittendreich Moray 88 B1
Pittentrail Highld 93 J10
Pittenweem Fife 77 G8
Pittington Durham 58 B4
Pittodrie Aberds 83 A8
Pitton Wilts 9 A11
Pittswood Kent 20 G3
Pittulie Aberds 89 B9
Pity Me Durham 58 B3
Pityme Corn 3 B8
Pityoulish Highld 81 B11
Pixey Green Suff 39 H8
Pixham Sur 19 F8
Pixley Hereford 26 E3
Place Newton N Yorks 52 B4
Plaidy Aberds 89 C7
Plains N Lanark 68 D6
Plaish Shrops 33 F11
Plaistow W Sus 11 A9
Plaitford Wilts 10 C1
Plank Lane Gtr Man 43 C9
Plas-canol Gwyn 32 D1
Plas Gogerddan Ceredig 32 G2
Plas Llwyngwern Powys 32 E3
Plas Nantyr Wrex 33 B7
Plas-yn-Cefn Denb 42 E3
Plastow Green Hants 18 E2
Platt Kent 20 F3
Platt Bridge Gtr Man 43 B9
Platts Common S Yorks 45 B7
Plawsworth Durham 58 B3
Plaxtol Kent 20 F3
Play Hatch Oxon 18 D4
Playden E Sus 13 D7
Playford Suff 31 D9
Playing Place Corn 3 E7
Playley Green Glos 26 E4
Plealey Shrops 33 E10
Plean Stirling 69 B7
Pleasington Blackburn 50 G2
Pleasley Derbys 45 F9
Pleckgate Blackburn 50 F2
Plenmeller Northumb 62 G3
Pleshey Essex 30 G3
Plockton Highld 85 E13
Plocrapol W Isles 90 H6
Ploughfield Hereford 25 D10
Plowden Shrops 33 G9
Ploxgreen Shrops 33 E9
Pluckley Kent 20 G6
Pluckley Thorne Kent 13 B8
Plumbland Cumb 56 C3
Plumley Ches E 43 E10
Plumpton Cumb 57 C6
Plumpton E Sus 12 E2
Plumpton Green E Sus 12 E2
Plumpton Head Cumb 57 C7
Plumstead London 19 D11
Plumstead Norf 39 B7
Plumtree Notts 36 B2
Plungar Leics 36 B3
Plush Dorset 8 D6
Plwmp Ceredig 23 A8
Plymouth Plym 4 F5
Plympton Plym 4 F6
Plymstock Plym 4 F6
Plymtree Devon 7 F9
Pockley N Yorks 59 H7
Pocklington E Yorks 52 E4
Pode Hole Lincs 37 C8
Podimore Som 8 B4
Podington Bedford 28 B6
Podmore Staffs 34 B3
Point Clear Essex 31 G7
Pointon Lincs 37 B7
Pokesdown Bmouth 9 E10
Pol a Charra W Isles 84 G2
Polbae Dumfries 54 B5
Polbain Highld 92 H2
Polbathic Corn 4 F4
Polbeth W Loth 69 D9
Polchar Highld 81 C10
Pole Elm Worcs 26 D5
Polebrook Northants 37 G6
Polegate E Sus 12 F4
Poles Highld 87 B10
Polesworth Warks 35 E8
Polgigga Corn 2 G2
Polglass Highld 92 J3
Polgooth Corn 3 D8
Poling W Sus 11 D9
Polkerris Corn 4 F1
Polla Highld 92 D6
Pollington E Yorks 52 H2
Polloch Highld 79 E10
Pollok Glasgow 68 D4
Pollokshields Glasgow 68 D4
Polmassick Corn 3 E8
Polmont Falk 69 C8
Polnessan E Ayrs 67 E7
Polnish Highld 79 C10
Polperro Corn 4 F3
Polruan Corn 4 F2
Polsham Som 15 G11
Polstead Suff 30 E6
Poltalloch Argyll 73 D7
Poltimore Devon 7 G8
Polton Midloth 69 D11
Polwarth Borders 70 E6
Polyphant Corn 4 C3
Polzeath Corn 3 B8
Ponders End London 19 B10
Pondersbridge Cambs 37 F8
Pondtail Hants 18 F5
Ponsanooth Corn 3 F6
Ponsworthy Devon 5 D8
Pont Aber Carms 24 F4
Pont Aber-Geirw Gwyn 32 C3
Pont-ar-gothi Carms 23 D10
Pont ar Hydfer Powys 24 F5
Pont-ar-llechau Carms 24 F4
Pont Cwm Pydew Denb 32 B6
Pont Cyfyng Conwy 41 E9
Pont Cysyllte Wrex 33 A8
Pont Dolydd Prysor Gwyn 41 G9
Pont-faen Powys 24 E6
Pont Fronwydd Gwyn 32 C4
Pont-gareg Pembs 22 B6
Pont-Henri Carms 23 F9
Pont-Llogel Powys 32 D6
Pont Pen-y-benglog Gwyn 41 D8
Pont Rhyd-goch Conwy 41 D8
Pont-Rhyd-sarn Gwyn 32 C4
Pont Rhyd-y-cyff Bridgend 14 C4
Pont-rhyd-y-groes Ceredig 24 A4
Pont-rug Gwyn 41 D7
Pont Senni = Sennybridge Powys 24 F6
Pont-siân Ceredig 23 B9
Pont-y-gwaith Rhondda 14 B6
Pont-y-Pŵl = Pontypool Torf 15 A8
Pont-y-pant Conwy 41 E9
Pont y Pennant Gwyn 32 C5
Pont yr Afon-Gam Gwyn 41 F9
Pont-yr-hafod Pembs 22 D4
Pontamman Carms 24 G3
Pontantwn Carms 23 E9
Pontardawe Neath 14 A3
Pontarddulais Swansea 23 F10
Pontarsais Carms 23 D9
Pontblyddyn Flint 42 F5
Pontbren Araeth Carms 24 F3
Pontbren Llwyd Rhondda 24 H6
Pontefract W Yorks 51 G10
Ponteland Northumb 63 F7
Ponterwyd Ceredig 32 G3
Pontesbury Shrops 33 E9
Pontfadog Wrex 33 B8
Pontfaen Pembs 22 C5
Pontgarreg Ceredig 23 A8
Ponthir Torf 15 B9
Ponthirwaun Ceredig 23 B7
Pontllanfraith Caerph 15 B7
Pontlliw Swansea 14 A2
Pontllyfni Gwyn 40 E6
Pontlottyn Caerph 25 H8
Pontneddfechan Powys 24 H6
Pontnewydd Torf 15 B8
Pontrhydfendigaid Ceredig 24 B4
Pontrhydyfen Neath 14 B3
Pontrilas Hereford 25 F10
Pontrobert Powys 33 D7
Ponts Green E Sus 12 E5
Pontshill Hereford 26 F3
Pontsticill M Tydf 25 G7
Pontwgan Conwy 41 C9
Pontyates Carms 23 F9
Pontyberem Carms 23 E10
Pontyclun Rhondda 14 C6
Pontycymer Bridgend 14 B5
Pontyglasier Pembs 22 C6
Pontypool = Pont-y-Pŵl Torf 15 A8
Pontypridd Rhondda 14 C6
Pontywaun Caerph 15 B8
Pooksgreen Hants 10 C2
Pool Corn 2 E5
Pool W Yorks 51 E8
Pool o' Muckhart Clack 76 G3
Pool Quay Powys 33 D8
Poole Poole 9 E9
Poole Keynes Glos 16 B6
Poolend Staffs 44 G3
Poolewe Highld 91 J13
Pooley Bridge Cumb 56 D6
Poolfold Staffs 44 G2
Poolhill Glos 26 F4
Poolsbrook Derbys 45 E8
Pootings Kent 19 G11
Pope Hill Pembs 22 E4
Popeswood Brack 18 E5
Popham Hants 18 G2
Poplar London 19 C10
Popley Hants 18 F3
Porchester Nottingham 36 A1
Porchfield IoW 10 E3
Porin Highld 86 F6
Poringland Norf 39 E8
Porkellis Corn 2 F5
Porlock Som 7 B7
Porlock Weir Som 7 B7
Port Ann Argyll 73 E8
Port Appin Argyll 74 C2
Port Arthur Shetland 96 K5
Port Askaig Argyll 64 B5
Port Bannatyne Argyll 73 G9
Port Carlisle Cumb 61 G8
Port Charlotte Argyll 64 C3
Port Clarence Stockton 58 D5
Port Driseach Argyll 73 F8
Port e Vullen IoM 48 C4
Port Ellen Argyll 64 D4
Port Elphinstone Aberds 83 B9
Port Erin IoM 48 F1
Port Erroll Aberds 89 E10
Port-Eynon Swansea 23 H9
Port Gaverne Corn 3 A9
Port Glasgow Invclyd 68 C2
Port Henderson Highld 85 A12
Port Isaac Corn 3 A8
Port Lamont Argyll 73 F9
Port Lion Pembs 22 F4
Port Logan Dumfries 54 E3
Port Mholair W Isles 91 D10
Port Mor Highld 78 D7
Port Mulgrave N Yorks 59 E8
Port Nan Giùran W Isles 91 D10
Port nan Long W Isles 84 A3
Port Nis W Isles 91 A10
Port of Menteith Stirling 75 G8
Port Quin Corn 3 A8
Port Ramsay Argyll 79 G11
Port St Mary IoM 48 F2
Port Sunlight Mers 42 D6
Port Talbot Neath 14 B3
Port Tennant Swansea 14 B2
Port Wemyss Argyll 64 C2
Port William Dumfries 54 E6
Portachoillan Argyll 72 H6
Portavadie Argyll 73 G8
Portbury N Som 15 D11
Portchester Hants 10 D5
Portclair Highld 80 B6
Portencalzie Dumfries 54 B3
Portencross N Ayrs 66 B4
Portesham Dorset 8 F5
Portessie Moray 88 B4
Portfield Gate Pembs 22 E4
Portgate Devon 4 C5
Portgordon Moray 88 B3
Portgower Highld 93 H13
Porth Corn 3 C7
Porth Rhondda 14 B6
Porth Navas Corn 3 G6
Porth Tywyn = Burry Port Carms 23 F9
Porth-y-waen Shrops 33 C8
Porthaethwy = Menai Bridge Anglesey 41 C7
Porthallow Corn 3 G6
Porthallow Corn 4 F3
Porthcawl Bridgend 14 D4
Porthcothan Corn 3 B7
Porthcurno Corn 2 G2
Porthgain Pembs 22 C3
Porthill Shrops 33 D10
Porthkerry V Glam 14 E6
Porthleven Corn 2 G5
Porthllechog Anglesey 40 A6
Porthmadog Gwyn 41 G7
Porthmeor Corn 2 F3
Portholland Corn 3 E8
Porthoustock Corn 3 G7
Porthpean Corn 3 D9
Porthtowan Corn 2 E5
Porthyrhyd Carms 23 E10
Porthyrhyd Carms 24 E4
Portincaple Argyll 73 D11
Portington E Yorks 52 F3
Portinnisherrich Argyll 73 B8
Portinscale Cumb 56 D4
Portishead N Som 15 D10
Portkil Argyll 73 E11
Portknockie Moray 88 B4
Portlethen Aberds 83 D11
Portling Dumfries 55 D11
Portloe Corn 3 F8
Portmahomack Highld 87 C12
Portmeirion Gwyn 41 G7
Portmellon Corn 3 E9
Portmore Hants 10 E2
Portnacroish Argyll 74 C2
Portnahaven Argyll 64 C2
Portnalong Highld 85 E8
Portnaluchaig Highld 79 C9
Portnancon Highld 92 C7
Portnellan Stirling 75 E7
Portobello Edin 70 C2
Porton Wilts 17 H8
Portpatrick Dumfries 54 D3
Portreath Corn 2 E5
Portree Highld 85 D9
Portscatho Corn 3 F7
Portsea Ptsmth 10 D5
Portskerra Highld 93 C11
Portskewett Mon 15 C11
Portslade Brighton 12 F1
Portslade-by-Sea Brighton 12 F1
Portsmouth Ptsmth 10 D5
Portsmouth W Yorks 50 G5
Portsonachan Argyll 74 E3
Portsoy Aberds 88 B5
Portswood Soton 10 C3
Porttanachy Moray 88 B3
Portuairk Highld 78 E7
Portway Hereford 25 E11
Portway Worcs 27 A7
Portwrinkle Corn 4 F4
Poslingford Suff 30 D4
Postbridge Devon 5 D7
Postcombe Oxon 18 B4
Postling Kent 13 C10
Postwick Norf 39 E8
Potholm Dumfries 61 E9
Potsgrove C Beds 28 F6
Pott Row Norf 38 C3
Pott Shrigley Ches E 44 E3
Potten End Herts 29 H7
Potter Brompton N Yorks 52 B5
Potter Heigham Norf 39 D10
Potter Street Essex 29 H11
Potterhanworth Lincs 46 F4
Potterhanworth Booths Lincs 46 F4
Potterne Wilts 16 F6
Potterne Wick Wilts 17 F7
Potternewton W Yorks 51 F9
Potters Bar Herts 19 A9
Potter's Cross Staffs 34 G4
Potterspury Northants 28 D4
Potterton Aberds 83 B11
Potterton W Yorks 51 F10
Potto N Yorks 58 F5
Potton C Beds 29 D9
Poughill Corn 6 F1
Poughill Devon 7 F7
Poulshot Wilts 16 F6
Poulton Glos 17 A8
Poulton Mers 42 C6
Poulton-le-Fylde Lancs 49 F3
Pound Bank Worcs 26 A4
Pound Green E Sus 12 D4
Pound Green IoW 10 F2
Pound Green Worcs 34 H3
Pound Hill W Sus 12 C1
Poundfield E Sus 12 C4
Poundland S Ayrs 66 H4
Poundon Bucks 28 F3
Poundsgate Devon 5 E8
Poundstock Corn 4 B3
Powburn Northumb 62 B6
Powderham Devon 5 C10
Powerstock Dorset 8 E4
Powfoot Dumfries 61 G7
Powick Worcs 26 C5
Powmill Perth 76 H3
Poxwell Dorset 8 F6
Poyle Slough 19 D7
Poynings W Sus 12 E1
Poyntington Dorset 8 C5
Poynton Ches E 44 D3
Poynton Green Telford 34 D1
Poystreet Green Suff 30 C6
Praa Sands Corn 2 G4
Pratt's Bottom London 19 E11
Praze Corn 2 F4
Praze-an-Beeble Corn 2 F5
Predannack Wollas Corn 2 H5
Prees Shrops 34 B1
Prees Green Shrops 34 B1
Prees Heath Shrops 34 B1
Prees Higher Heath Shrops 34 B1
Prees Lower Heath Shrops 34 B1
Preesall Lancs 49 E3
Preesgweene Shrops 33 B8
Prenderguest Borders 71 E8
Prendwick Northumb 62 B6
Prengwyn Ceredig 23 B9
Prenteg Gwyn 41 F7
Prenton Mers 42 D6
Prescot Mers 43 C7
Prescott Shrops 33 C10
Pressen Northumb 71 G7
Prestatyn Denb 42 D3
Prestbury Ches E 44 E3
Prestbury Glos 26 F6
Presteigne = Llanandras Powys 25 B10
Presthope Shrops 34 F1
Prestleigh Som 16 G3
Preston Borders 70 E6
Preston Brighton 12 F2
Preston Devon 5 D9
Preston Dorset 8 F6
Preston E Loth 70 C4
Preston E Yorks 53 F7
Preston Glos 17 A7
Preston Glos 26 E3
Preston Herts 29 F8
Preston Kent 21 E9
Preston Kent 21 E7
Preston Lancs 49 G5
Preston Northumb 71 H10
Preston Rutland 36 E4
Preston Shrops 33 D11
Preston Wilts 17 D7
Preston Wilts 17 D9
Preston Bagot Warks 27 B8
Preston Bissett Bucks 28 F3
Preston Bowyer Som 7 D10
Preston Brockhurst Shrops 33 C11
Preston Brook Halton 43 D8
Preston Candover Hants 18 G3
Preston Capes Northants 28 C2
Preston Crowmarsh Oxon 18 B3
Preston Gubbals Shrops 33 D10
Preston on Stour Warks 27 C9
Preston on the Hill Halton 43 D8
Preston on Wye Hereford 25 D10
Preston Plucknett Som 8 C4
Preston St Mary Suff 30 C6
Preston-under-Scar N Yorks 58 G1
Preston upon the Weald Moors Telford 34 D2
Preston Wynne Hereford 26 D2
Prestonmill Dumfries 60 H5
Prestonpans E Loth 70 C2
Prestwich Gtr Man 44 B2
Prestwick Northumb 63 F7
Prestwick S Ayrs 67 D6
Prestwood Bucks 18 A5
Price Town Bridgend 14 B5
Prickwillow Cambs 38 G1
Priddy Som 15 F11
Priest Hutton Lancs 49 B5
Priest Weston Shrops 33 F8
Priesthaugh Borders 61 C10
Primethorpe Leics 35 F11
Primrose Green Norf 39 D6
Primrose Valley N Yorks 53 B7
Primrosehill Herts 19 A7
Princes Gate Pembs 22 E6
Princes Risborough Bucks 18 A5
Princethorpe Warks 27 A11
Princetown Caerph 25 G8
Princetown Devon 5 D6
Prion Denb 42 F3
Prior Muir Fife 77 F8
Prior Park Northumb 71 E8
Priors Frome Hereford 26 E2
Priors Hardwick Warks 27 C11
Priors Marston Warks 27 C11
Priorslee Telford 34 D3
Priory Wood Hereford 25 D9
Priston Bath 16 E3
Pristow Green Norf 39 G7
Prittlewell Southend 20 C5
Privett Hants 10 B5
Prixford Devon 6 C4
Probus Corn 3 E7
Proncy Highld 87 B10
Prospect Cumb 56 B3
Prudhoe Northumb 62 G6
Ptarmigan Lodge Stirling 74 G6
Pubil Perth 75 C7
Puckeridge Herts 29 F10
Puckington Som 8 C2
Pucklechurch S Glos 16 D3
Pucknall Hants 10 B2
Puckrup Glos 26 E5
Puddinglake Ches W 43 F10
Puddington Ches W 42 E6
Puddington Devon 7 E7
Puddledock Norf 39 F6
Puddletown Dorset 9 E6
Pudleston Hereford 26 C2
Pudsey W Yorks 51 F8
Pulborough W Sus 11 C9
Puleston Telford 34 C3
Pulford Ches W 43 G6
Pulham Dorset 8 D6
Pulham Market Norf 39 G7
Pulham St Mary Norf 39 G8
Pulloxhill C Beds 29 E7
Pumpherston W Loth 69 D9
Pumsaint Carms 24 D3
Puncheston Pembs 22 D5
Puncknowle Dorset 8 F4
Punnett's Town E Sus 12 D5
Purbrook Hants 10 D5
Purewell Dorset 9 E10
Purfleet Thurrock 20 D2
Puriton Som 15 G9
Purleigh Essex 20 A5
Purley London 19 E10
Purley W Berks 18 D3
Purlogue Shrops 33 H8
Purls Bridge Cambs 37 G10
Purse Caundle Dorset 8 C5
Purslow Shrops 33 G9
Purston Jaglin W Yorks 51 H10
Purton Glos 16 A3
Purton Glos 16 A3
Purton Wilts 17 C7
Purton Stoke Wilts 17 B7
Pury End Northants 28 D4
Pusey Oxon 17 B10
Putley Hereford 26 E3
Putney London 19 D9
Putsborough Devon 6 B3
Puttenham Herts 28 G5
Puttenham Sur 18 G6
Puxton N Som 15 E10
Pwll Carms 23 F9
Pwll-glas Denb 42 G4
Pwll-trap Carms 23 E7
Pwll-y-glaw Neath 14 B3
Pwllcrochan Pembs 22 F4
Pwllgloyw Powys 25 E7
Pwllheli Gwyn 40 G5
Pwllmeyric Mon 15 B11
Pye Corner Newport 15 C9
Pye Green Staffs 34 D5
Pyecombe W Sus 12 E1
Pyewipe NE Lincs 46 A6
Pyle = Y Pîl Bridgend 14 C4
Pyle IoW 10 G3
Pylle Som 16 H3
Pymoor Cambs 37 G10
Pyrford Sur 19 F7
Pyrton Oxon 18 B3
Pytchley Northants 28 A5
Pyworthy Devon 6 F2

Q

Quabbs Shrops 33 G8
Quadring Lincs 37 B8
Quainton Bucks 28 G4
Quarley Hants 17 G9
Quarndon Derbys 35 A9
Quarrier's Homes Invclyd 68 D2
Quarrington Lincs 37 A6
Quarrington Hill Durham 58 C4
Quarry Bank W Mid 34 G5
Quarryford E Loth 70 D4
Quarryhill Highld 87 C10
Quarrywood Moray 88 B1
Quarter S Lanark 68 E6
Quatford Shrops 34 F3
Quatt Shrops 34 G3
Quebec Durham 58 B2
Quedgeley Glos 26 G5
Queen Adelaide Cambs 38 G1
Queen Camel Som 8 B4
Queen Charlton Bath 16 E3
Queen Dart Devon 7 E7
Queen Oak Dorset 9 A6
Queen Street Kent 20 G3
Queen Street Wilts 17 C7
Queenborough Kent 20 D6
Queenhill Worcs 26 E5
Queen's Head Shrops 33 C9
Queen's Park Bedford 29 D7
Queen's Park Northants 28 B4
Queensbury W Yorks 51 F7
Queensferry Edin 69 C10
Queensferry Flint 42 F6
Queenstown Blackpool 49 F3
Queenzieburn N Lanark 68 C5
Quemerford Wilts 17 E7
Quendale Shetland 96 M5
Quendon Essex 30 E2
Queniborough Leics 36 D2
Quenington Glos 17 A8
Quernmore Lancs 49 D5
Quethiock Corn 4 E4
Quholm Orkney 95 G3
Quicks Green W Berks 18 D2
Quidenham Norf 38 G6
Quidhampton Hants 18 F2
Quidhampton Wilts 9 A10
Quilquox Aberds 89 E9
Quina Brook Shrops 33 B11
Quindry Orkney 95 J5
Quinton Northants 28 C4
Quinton W Mid 34 G5
Quintrell Downs Corn 3 C7
Quixhill Staffs 35 A7
Quoditch Devon 6 G3
Quoig Perth 75 E11
Quorndon Leics 36 D1
Quothquan S Lanark 69 G8
Quoyloo Orkney 95 F3
Quoyness Orkney 95 H3
Quoys Shetland 96 B8
Quoys Shetland 96 G6

R

Raasay Ho. Highld 85 E10
Rabbit's Cross Kent 20 G4
Raby Mers 42 E6
Rachan Mill Borders 69 G10
Rachub Gwyn 41 D8
Rackenford Devon 7 E7
Rackham W Sus 11 C9
Rackheath Norf 39 D8
Racks Dumfries 60 F6
Rackwick Orkney 95 D5
Rackwick Orkney 95 J3
Radbourne Derbys 35 B8
Radcliffe Gtr Man 43 B10
Radcliffe Northumb 63 C8
Radcliffe on Trent Notts 36 B2
Radclive Bucks 28 E3
Radcot Oxon 17 B9
Raddery Highld 87 F10
Radernie Fife 77 G7
Radford Semele Warks 27 B10
Radipole Dorset 8 F5
Radlett Herts 19 B8
Radley Oxon 18 B2
Radmanthwaite Notts 45 F9
Radmoor Shrops 34 C2
Radmore Green Ches E 43 G8
Radnage Bucks 18 B4
Radstock Bath 16 F3
Radstone Northants 28 D2
Radway Warks 27 D10
Radway Green Ches E 43 G10
Radwell Bedford 29 C7
Radwell Herts 29 E9
Radwinter Essex 30 E3
Radyr Cardiff 15 C7
Rafford Moray 87 F13
Ragdale Leics 36 D2
Raglan Mon 25 H11
Ragnall Notts 46 E2
Rahane Argyll 73 E11
Rainford Mers 43 B7
Rainford Junction Mers 43 B7
Rainham London 20 C2
Rainham Medway 20 E5
Rainhill Mers 43 C7
Rainhill Stoops Mers 43 C8
Rainow Ches E 44 E3
Rainton N Yorks 51 B9
Rainworth Notts 45 G9
Raisbeck Cumb 57 F8
Raise Cumb 57 B9
Rait Perth 76 E5
Raithby Lincs 47 D7
Raithby Lincs 47 F7
Rake W Sus 11 B7
Rakewood Gtr Man 44 A3
Ram Carms 23 B10
Ram Lane Kent 20 G6
Ramasaig Highld 84 D6
Rame Corn 2 F6
Rame Corn 4 G5
Rameldry Mill Bank Fife 76 G6
Ramnageo Shetland 96 C8
Rampisham Dorset 8 D4
Rampside Cumb 49 C2
Rampton Cambs 29 B11
Rampton Notts 45 E11
Ramsbottom Gtr Man 50 H3
Ramsbury Wilts 17 D9
Ramscraigs Highld 94 H3
Ramsdean Hants 10 B6
Ramsdell Hants 18 F2
Ramsden Oxon 27 G10
Ramsden Bellhouse Essex 20 B4
Ramsden Heath Essex 20 B4
Ramsey Cambs 37 G8
Ramsey Essex 31 E9
Ramsey IoM 48 C4
Ramsey Forty Foot Cambs 37 G9
Ramsey Heights Cambs 37 G8
Ramsey Island Essex 30 H6
Ramsey Mereside Cambs 37 G8
Ramsey St Mary's Cambs 37 G8
Ramseycleuch Borders 61 B8
Ramsgate Kent 21 E10
Ramsgill N Yorks 51 B7
Ramshorn Staffs 44 H4
Ramsnest Common Sur 11 A8
Ranais W Isles 91 E9
Ranby Lincs 46 E6
Ranby Notts 45 D10
Rand Lincs 46 E5
Randwick Glos 26 H5
Ranfurly Renfs 68 D2
Rangag Highld 94 F3
Rangemore Staffs 35 C7
Rangeworthy S Glos 16 C3
Rankinston E Ayrs 67 E7
Ranmoor S Yorks 45 D7
Ranmore Common Sur 19 F8
Rannerdale Cumb 56 E3
Rannoch Station Perth 75 B7
Ranochan Highld 79 C11
Ranskill Notts 45 D10
Ranton Staffs 34 C4
Ranworth Norf 39 D9
Raploch Stirling 68 A6
Rapness Orkney 95 D6
Rascal Moor E Yorks 52 F4
Rascarrel Dumfries 55 E10
Rashiereive Aberds 89 F9
Raskelf N Yorks 51 B10
Rassau Bl Gwent 25 G8
Rastrick W Yorks 51 G7
Ratagan Highld 85 G14
Ratby Leics 35 E11
Ratcliffe Culey Leics 35 F9
Ratcliffe on Soar Leics 35 C10
Ratcliffe on the Wreake Leics 36 D2
Rathen Aberds 89 B10
Rathillet Fife 76 E6
Rathmell N Yorks 50 D4
Ratho Edin 69 C10
Ratho Station Edin 69 C10
Rathven Moray 88 B4
Ratley Warks 27 D10
Ratlinghope Shrops 33 F10
Rattar Highld 94 C4
Ratten Row Lancs 49 E4
Rattery Devon 5 E8
Rattlesden Suff 30 C6
Rattray Perth 76 C4
Raughton Head Cumb 56 B5
Raunds Northants 28 A6
Ravenfield S Yorks 45 C8
Ravenglass Cumb 56 G2
Raveningham Norf 39 F9
Ravenscar N Yorks 59 F10
Ravenscraig Invclyd 73 F11
Ravensdale IoM 48 C3
Ravensden Bedford 29 C7
Ravenseat N Yorks 57 F10
Ravenshead Notts 45 G9
Ravensmoor Ches E 43 G9
Ravensthorpe Northants 28 A3
Ravensthorpe W Yorks 51 G8
Ravenstone Leics 35 D10
Ravenstone M Keynes 28 C5
Ravenstonedale Cumb 57 F9
Ravenstown Cumb 49 B3
Ravenstruther S Lanark 69 F8
Ravensworth N Yorks 58 F2
Raw N Yorks 59 F10
Rawcliffe E Yorks 52 G2
Rawcliffe York 52 D1
Rawcliffe Bridge E Yorks 52 G2
Rawdon W Yorks 51 F8
Rawmarsh S Yorks 45 C8
Rawreth Essex 20 B4
Rawridge Devon 7 F11
Rawtenstall Lancs 50 G4
Raxton Aberds 89 E8
Raydon Suff 31 E7
Raylees Northumb 62 D5
Rayleigh Essex 20 B5
Rayne Essex 30 F4
Rayners Lane London 19 C8
Raynes Park London 19 E9
Reach Cambs 30 B2
Read Lancs 50 F3
Reading Reading 18 D4
Reading Street Kent 13 C8
Reagill Cumb 57 E8
Rearquhar Highld 87 B10
Rearsby Leics 36 D2
Reaster Highld 94 D4
Reawick Shetland 96 J5
Reay Highld 93 C12
Rechullin Highld 85 C13
Reculver Kent 21 E9
Red Dial Cumb 56 B4
Red Hill Worcs 26 C5
Red Houses Jersey 11
Red Lodge Suff 30 A3
Red Rail Hereford 26 F2
Red Rock Gtr Man 43 B8
Red Roses Carms 23 E7
Red Row Northumb 63 D8
Red Street Staffs 44 G2
Red Wharf Bay Anglesey 41 B7
Redberth Pembs 22 F5
Redbourn Herts 29 G8
Redbourne N Lincs 46 C3
Redbrook Mon 26 G2
Redbrook Wrex 33 A11
Redburn Highld 87 E8
Redburn Highld 87 G12
Redburn Northumb 62 G3
Redcar Redcar 59 D7
Redcastle Angus 77 B9
Redcastle Highld 87 G8
Redcliff Bay N Som 15 D10
Redding Falk 69 C8
Reddingmuirhead Falk 69 C8
Reddish Gtr Man 44 C2
Redditch Worcs 27 B7
Rede Suff 30 C5
Redenhall Norf 39 G8
Redesdale Camp Northumb 62 D4
Redesmouth Northumb 62 E4
Redford Aberds 83 F9
Redford Angus 77 C8
Redford Durham 58 C1
Redfordgreen Borders 61 B9
Redgorton Perth 76 E3
Redgrave Suff 38 H6
Redhill Aberds 83 C9
Redhill Aberds 89 E6
Redhill N Som 15 E11
Redhill Sur 19 F9
Redhouse Argyll 73 G7
Redhouses Argyll 64 B4
Redisham Suff 39 G10
Redland Bristol 16 D2
Redland Orkney 95 F4
Redlingfield Suff 31 A8
Redlynch Som 8 A6
Redlynch Wilts 9 B11
Redmarley D'Abitot Glos 26 E4
Redmarshall Stockton 58 D4
Redmile Leics 36 B3
Redmire N Yorks 58 G1
Redmoor Corn 4 E1
Rednal Shrops 33 C9
Redpath Borders 70 G4
Redpoint Highld 85 B12
Redruth Corn 2 E5
Redvales Gtr Man 44 B2
Redwick Newport 15 C10
Redwick S Glos 15 C11
Redworth Darl 58 D3
Reed Herts 29 E10
Reedham Norf 39 E10
Reedness E Yorks 52 G3
Reeds Beck Lincs 46 F6
Reepham Lincs 46 E4
Reepham Norf 39 C6
Reeth N Yorks 58 G1
Regaby IoM 48 C4
Regoul Highld 87 F11
Reiff Highld 92 H2
Reigate Sur 19 F9
Reighton N Yorks 53 B7
Reighton Gap N Yorks 53 B7
Reinigeadal W Isles 90 G7
Reiss Highld 94 E5
Rejerrah Corn 3 D6
Releath Corn 2 F5
Relubbus Corn 2 F4
Relugas Moray 87 G12
Remenham Wokingham 18 C4
Remenham Hill Wokingham 18 C4
Remony Perth 75 C10
Rempstone Notts 36 C1
Rendcomb Glos 27 H7
Rendham Suff 31 B10
Rendlesham Suff 31 C10
Renfrew Renfs 68 D4
Renhold Bedford 29 C7
Renishaw Derbys 45 E8
Rennington Northumb 63 B8
Renton W Dunb 68 C2
Renwick Cumb 57 B7
Repps Norf 39 D10
Repton Derbys 35 C9
Reraig Highld 85 F13
Rescobie Angus 77 B8
Resipole Highld 79 F10
Resolis Highld 87 E9
Resolven Neath 14 A4
Reston Borders 71 D7
Reswallie Angus 77 B8
Retew Corn 3 D8
Retford Notts 45 D11
Rettendon Essex 20 B4
Rettendon Place Essex 20 B4
Revesby Lincs 46 F6
Revesby Bridge Lincs 47 F7
Rew Street IoW 10 E3
Rewe Devon 7 G8
Reydon Suff 39 H10
Reydon Smear Suff 39 H10
Reymerston Norf 38 E6
Reynalton Pembs 22 F5
Reynoldston Swansea 23 G9
Rezare Corn 4 D4
Rhôs Carms 23 C8
Rhôs Neath 14 A3
Rhŷd-y-foel Conwy 42 E2
Rhaeadr Gwy = Rhayader Powys 24 B6
Rhandirmwyn Carms 24 D4
Rhayader = Rhaeadr Gwy Powys 24 B6
Rhedyn Gwyn 40 G4
Rhemore Highld 79 F8
Rhencullen IoM 48 C3
Rhes-y-cae Flint 42 E4
Rhewl Denb 42 F4
Rhewl Denb 42 H4
Rhian Highld 93 H8
Rhicarn Highld 92 G3
Rhiconich Highld 92 D5
Rhicullen Highld 87 D9
Rhidorroch Ho. Highld 86 B4
Rhifail Highld 93 E10
Rhigos Rhondda 24 H6
Rhilochan Highld 93 J10
Rhiroy Highld 86 C4
Rhisga = Risca Caerph 15 B8
Rhiw Gwyn 40 H4
Rhiwabon = Ruabon Wrex 33 A9
Rhiwbina Cardiff 15 C7
Rhiwbryfdir Gwyn 41 F8
Rhiwderin Newport 15 C8
Rhiwlas Gwyn 32 B5
Rhiwlas Gwyn 41 D7
Rhiwlas Powys 33 B7
Rhodes Gtr Man 44 B2
Rhodes Minnis Kent 21 G8
Rhodesia Notts 45 E9
Rhodiad Pembs 22 D2
Rhondda Rhondda 14 B5
Rhonehouse or Kelton Hill Dumfries 55 D10
Rhoose = Y Rhws V Glam 14 E6
Rhos-fawr Gwyn 40 G5
Rhos-goch Powys 25 D8
Rhos-hill Pembs 22 B6
Rhos-on-Sea Conwy 41 B10
Rhos-y-brithdir Powys 33 C7
Rhos-y-garth Ceredig 24 A3
Rhos-y-gwaliau Gwyn 32 B5
Rhos-y-llan Gwyn 40 G4
Rhos-y-Madoc Wrex 33 A9
Rhos-y-meirch Powys 25 B9
Rhosaman Carms 24 G4
Rhosbeirio Anglesey 40 A5
Rhoscefnhir Anglesey 41 C7
Rhoscolyn Anglesey 40 C4
Rhoscrowther Pembs 22 F4
Rhosesmor Flint 42 F5
Rhosgadfan Gwyn 41 E7
Rhosgoch Anglesey 40 B6
Rhoshirwaun Gwyn 40 H3
Rhoslan Gwyn 40 F6
Rhoslefain Gwyn 32 E1
Rhosllanerchrugog Wrex 42 H5
Rhosmaen Carms 24 F3
Rhosmeirch Anglesey 40 C6
Rhosneigr Anglesey 40 C5
Rhosnesni Wrex 42 G6
Rhosrobin Wrex 42 G6
Rhossili Swansea 23 H9
Rhosson Pembs 22 D2
Rhostryfan Gwyn 40 E6
Rhostyllen Wrex 42 H6
Rhosybol Anglesey 40 B6
Rhu Argyll 73 E11
Rhu Argyll 73 G7
Rhuallt Denb 42 E3

Rhuddall Heath Ches W 43 F8
Rhuddlan Ceredig 23 B9
Rhuddlan Denb 42 E3
Rhue Highld 86 B3
Rhulen Powys 25 D8
Rhunahaorine Argyll 65 D8
Rhuthun = Ruthin Denb 42 G4
Rhyd Gwyn 41 F8
Rhyd Powys 32 E5
Rhyd-Ddu Gwyn 41 E7
Rhyd-moel-ddu Powys 33 H6
Rhyd-Rosser Ceredig 24 B2
Rhyd-uchaf Gwyn 32 B5
Rhyd-wen Gwyn 32 D3
Rhyd-y-clafdy Gwyn 40 G5
Rhyd-y-fro Neath 24 H4
Rhyd-y-gwin Swansea 14 A2
Rhyd-y-meirch Mon 25 H10
Rhyd-y-meudwy Denb 42 G4
Rhyd-y-pandy Swansea 14 A2
Rhyd-y-sarn Gwyn 41 F8
Rhyd-yr-onen Gwyn 32 E2
Rhydaman = Ammanford Carms 24 G3
Rhydargaeau Carms 23 D9
Rhydcymerau Carms 23 C10
Rhydd Worcs 26 D5
Rhydding Neath 14 B3
Rhydfudr Ceredig 24 B2
Rhydlewis Ceredig 23 B8
Rhydlios Gwyn 40 G3
Rhydlydan Conwy 41 E10
Rhydness Powys 25 D8
Rhydowen Ceredig 23 B9
Rhydspence Hereford 25 D9
Rhydtalog Flint 42 G5
Rhydwyn Anglesey 40 B5
Rhydycroesau Powys 33 B8
Rhydyfelin Ceredig 32 H1
Rhydyfelin Rhondda 14 C6
Rhydymain Gwyn 32 C4
Rhydymwyn Flint 42 F5
Rhyl = Y Rhyl Denb 42 D3
Rhymney = Rhymni Caerph 25 H8
Rhymni = Rhymney Caerph 25 H8
Rhynd Fife 77 E7
Rhynd Perth 76 E4
Rhynie Aberds 82 A6
Rhynie Highld 87 D11
Ribbesford Worcs 26 A4
Ribblehead N Yorks 50 B3
Ribbleton Lancs 50 F1
Ribchester Lancs 50 F2
Ribigill Highld 93 D8
Riby Lincs 46 B5
Riby Cross Roads Lincs 46 B5
Riccall N Yorks 52 F2
Riccarton E Ayrs 67 C7
Richards Castle Hereford 25 B11
Richings Park Bucks 19 D7
Richmond London 19 D8
Richmond N Yorks 58 F2
Rickarton Aberds 83 E10
Rickinghall Suff 38 H6
Rickleton T&W 58 A3
Rickling Essex 29 E11
Rickmansworth Herts 19 B7
Riddings Cumb 61 F10
Riddings Derbys 45 G8
Riddlecombe Devon 6 E5
Riddlesden W Yorks 51 E6
Riddrie Glasgow 68 D5
Ridge Dorset 9 F8
Ridge Hants 10 C2
Ridge Wilts 9 A8
Ridge Green Sur 19 G10
Ridge Lane Warks 35 F8
Ridgebourne Powys 25 B7
Ridgehill N Som 15 E11
Ridgeway Cross Hereford 26 D4
Ridgewell Essex 30 D4
Ridgewood E Sus 12 E3
Ridgmont C Beds 28 E6
Riding Mill Northumb 62 G6
Ridleywood Wrex 43 G7
Ridlington Norf 39 B9
Ridlington Rutland 36 E4
Ridsdale Northumb 62 E5
Riechip Perth 76 C3
Riemore Perth 76 C3
Rienachait Highld 92 F3
Rievaulx N Yorks 59 H6
Rift House Hrtlpl 58 C5
Rigg Dumfries 61 G8
Riggend N Lanark 68 C6
Rigsby Lincs 47 E8
Rigside S Lanark 69 G7
Riley Green Lancs 50 G2
Rileyhill Staffs 35 D7
Rilla Mill Corn 4 D3
Rillington N Yorks 52 B4
Rimington Lancs 50 E4
Rimpton Som 8 B5
Rimswell E Yorks 53 G9
Rinaston Pembs 22 D4
Ringasta Shetland 96 M5
Ringford Dumfries 55 D9
Ringinglow S Yorks 44 D6
Ringland Norf 39 D7
Ringles Cross E Sus 12 D3
Ringmer E Sus 12 E3
Ringmore Devon 5 G7
Ringorm Moray 88 D2
Ring's End Cambs 37 E9
Ringsfield Suff 39 G10
Ringsfield Corner Suff 39 G10
Ringshall Herts 28 G6
Ringshall Suff 31 C7
Ringshall Stocks Suff 31 C7
Ringstead Norf 38 A3
Ringstead Northants 36 H5
Ringwood Hants 9 D10
Ringwould Kent 21 G10
Rinmore Aberds 82 B6
Rinnigill Orkney 95 J4
Rinsey Corn 2 G4
Riof W Isles 90 D6
Ripe E Sus 12 E4
Ripley Derbys 45 G7
Ripley Hants 9 E10
Ripley N Yorks 51 C8
Ripley Sur 19 F7
Riplingham E Yorks 52 F5
Ripon N Yorks 51 B9
Rippingale Lincs 37 C6
Ripple Kent 21 G10
Ripple Worcs 26 E5
Ripponden W Yorks 50 H6
Rireavach Highld 86 B3
Risabus Argyll 64 D4
Risbury Hereford 26 C2
Risby Suff 30 B4
Risca = Rhisga Caerph 15 B8
Rise E Yorks 53 E7
Riseden E Sus 12 C5
Risegate Lincs 37 C8
Riseholme Lincs 46 E3
Riseley Bedford 29 B7
Riseley Wokingham 18 E4
Rishangles Suff 31 B8
Rishton Lancs 50 F3
Rishworth W Yorks 50 H6
Rising Bridge Lancs 50 G3
Risley Derbys 35 B10
Risley Warr 43 C9
Risplith N Yorks 51 C8
Rispond Highld 92 C7
Rivar Wilts 17 E10
Rivenhall End Essex 30 G5
River Bank Cambs 30 B2
Riverhead Kent 20 F2
Rivington Lancs 43 A9
Roa Island Cumb 49 C2
Roachill Devon 7 D7
Road Green Norf 39 F8
Roade Northants 28 C4
Roadhead Cumb 61 F11
Roadmeetings S Lanark 69 F7
Roadside Highld 94 D3
Roadside of Catterline Aberds 83 F10
Roadside of Kinneff Aberds 83 F10
Roadwater Som 7 C9
Roag Highld 85 D7
Roath Cardiff 15 D7
Roberton Borders 61 B10
Roberton S Lanark 69 H8
Robertsbridge E Sus 12 D6
Roberttown W Yorks 51 G7
Robeston Cross Pembs 22 F3
Robeston Wathen Pembs 22 E5
Robin Hood W Yorks 51 G9
Robin Hood's Bay N Yorks 59 F10
Roborough Devon 4 E6
Roborough Devon 6 E4
Roby Mers 43 C7
Roby Mill Lancs 43 B8
Rocester Staffs 35 B7
Roch Pembs 22 D3
Roch Gate Pembs 22 D3
Rochdale Gtr Man 44 A2
Roche Corn 3 C8
Rochester Medway 20 E4
Rochester Northumb 62 D4
Rochford Essex 20 B5
Rock Corn 3 B8
Rock Northumb 63 A8
Rock W Sus 11 C10
Rock Worcs 26 A4
Rock Ferry Mers 42 D6
Rockbeare Devon 7 G9
Rockbourne Hants 9 C10
Rockcliffe Cumb 61 G9
Rockcliffe Dumfries 55 D11
Rockfield Highld 87 C12
Rockfield Mon 25 G11
Rockford Hants 9 D10
Rockhampton S Glos 16 B3
Rockingham Northants 36 F4
Rockland All Saints Norf 38 F5
Rockland St Mary Norf 39 E9
Rockland St Peter Norf 38 F5
Rockley Wilts 17 D8
Rockwell End Bucks 18 C4
Rockwell Green Som 7 D10
Rodborough Glos 16 A5
Rodbourne Swindon 17 C8
Rodbourne Wilts 16 C6
Rodbourne Cheney Swindon 17 C8
Rodd Hereford 25 B10
Roddam Northumb 62 A6
Rodden Dorset 8 F5
Rode Som 16 F5
Rode Heath Ches E 44 G2
Rodeheath Ches E 44 F2
Roden Telford 34 D1
Rodhuish Som 7 C9
Rodington Telford 34 D1
Rodley Glos 26 G4
Rodley W Yorks 51 F8
Rodmarton Glos 16 B6
Rodmell E Sus 12 F3
Rodmersham Kent 20 E6
Rodney Stoke Som 15 F10
Rodsley Derbys 35 A8
Rodway Som 15 H8
Rodwell Dorset 8 G5
Roe Green Herts 29 E10
Roecliffe N Yorks 51 C9
Roehampton London 19 D9
Roesound Shetland 96 G5
Roffey W Sus 11 A10
Rogart Highld 93 J10
Rogart Station Highld 93 J10
Rogate W Sus 11 B7
Rogerstone Newport 15 C8
Roghadal W Isles 90 J5
Rogiet Mon 15 C10
Rogue's Alley Cambs 37 E9
Roke Oxon 18 B3
Roker T&W 63 H10
Rollesby Norf 39 D10
Rolleston Leics 36 E3
Rolleston Notts 45 G11
Rolleston-on-Dove Staffs 35 C8
Rolston E Yorks 53 E8
Rolvenden Kent 13 C7
Rolvenden Layne Kent 13 C7
Romaldkirk Durham 57 D11
Romanby N Yorks 58 G4
Romannobridge Borders 69 F10
Romansleigh Devon 7 D6
Romford London 20 C2
Romiley Gtr Man 44 C3
Romsey Hants 10 B2
Romsey Town Cambs 29 C11
Romsley Shrops 34 G3
Romsley Worcs 34 H5
Ronague IoM 48 E2
Rookhope Durham 57 B11
Rookley IoW 10 F4
Rooks Bridge Som 15 F9
Roos E Yorks 53 F8
Roosebeck Cumb 49 C2
Rootham's Green Bedford 29 C8
Rootpark S Lanark 69 E8
Ropley Hants 10 A5
Ropley Dean Hants 10 A5
Ropsley Lincs 36 B5
Rora Aberds 89 C10
Rorandle Aberds 83 B8
Rorrington Shrops 33 E9
Roscroggan Corn 2 E5
Rose Corn 3 D6
Rose Ash Devon 7 D6
Rose Green W Sus 11 E8
Rose Grove Lancs 50 F4
Rose Hill E Sus 12 E3
Rose Hill Lancs 50 F4
Rose Hill Suff 31 D8
Roseacre Kent 20 F4
Roseacre Lancs 49 F4
Rosebank S Lanark 69 F7
Rosebrough Northumb 71 H10
Rosebush Pembs 22 D5
Rosecare Corn 4 B2
Rosedale Abbey N Yorks 59 G8
Roseden Northumb 62 A6
Rosefield Highld 87 F11
Rosehall Highld 92 J7
Rosehaugh Mains Highld 87 F9
Rosehearty Aberds 89 B9
Rosehill Shrops 34 B2
Roseisle Moray 88 B1
Roselands E Sus 12 F5
Rosemarket Pembs 22 F4
Rosemarkie Highld 87 F10
Rosemary Lane Devon 7 E10
Rosemount Perth 76 C4
Rosenannon Corn 3 C8
Rosewell Midloth 69 D11
Roseworth Stockton 58 D5
Roseworthy Corn 2 F5
Rosgill Cumb 57 E7
Roshven Highld 79 D10
Roskhill Highld 85 D7
Roskill House Highld 87 F9
Rosley Cumb 56 B5
Roslin Midloth 69 D11
Rosliston Derbys 35 D8
Rosneath Argyll 73 E11
Ross Dumfries 55 E9
Ross Northumb 71 G10
Ross Perth 75 E10
Ross-on-Wye Hereford 26 F3
Rossett Wrex 42 G6
Rossett Green N Yorks 51 D9
Rossie Ochill Perth 76 F3
Rossie Priory Perth 76 D5
Rossington S Yorks 45 C10
Rosskeen Highld 87 E9
Rossland Renfs 68 C3
Roster Highld 94 G4
Rostherne Ches E 43 D10
Rosthwaite Cumb 56 E4
Roston Derbys 35 A7
Rosyth Fife 69 B10
Rothbury Northumb 62 C6
Rotherby Leics 36 D2
Rotherfield E Sus 12 D4
Rotherfield Greys Oxon 18 C4
Rotherfield Peppard Oxon 18 C4
Rotherham S Yorks 45 C8
Rothersthorpe Northants 28 C4
Rotherwick Hants 18 F4
Rothes Moray 88 D2
Rothesay Argyll 73 G9
Rothiebrisbane Aberds 89 E7
Rothienorman Aberds 89 E7
Rothiesholm Orkney 95 F7
Rothley Leics 36 D1
Rothley Northumb 62 E6
Rothley Shield East Northumb 62 D6
Rothmaise Aberds 89 E6
Rothwell Lincs 46 C5
Rothwell Northants 36 G4
Rothwell W Yorks 51 G9
Rothwell Haigh W Yorks 51 G9
Rotsea E Yorks 53 D6
Rottal Angus 82 G5
Rotten End Suff 31 B10
Rottingdean Brighton 12 F2
Rottington Cumb 56 E1
Roud IoW 10 F4
Rough Close Staffs 34 B5
Rough Common Kent 21 F8
Rougham Norf 38 C4
Rougham Suff 30 B6
Rougham Green Suff 30 B6
Roughburn Highld 80 E5
Roughlee Lancs 50 E4
Roughley W Mid 35 F7
Roughsike Cumb 61 F11
Roughton Lincs 46 F6
Roughton Norf 39 B8
Roughton Shrops 34 F3
Roughton Moor Lincs 46 F6
Roundhay W Yorks 51 F9
Roundstonefoot Dumfries 61 C7
Roundstreet Common W Sus 11 B9
Roundway Wilts 17 E7
Rous Lench Worcs 27 C7
Rousdon Devon 8 E1
Routenburn N Ayrs 73 G10
Routh E Yorks 53 E6
Row Corn 4 D1
Row Cumb 56 H6
Row Heath Essex 31 G8
Rowanburn Dumfries 61 F10
Rowardennan Stirling 74 H6
Rowde Wilts 16 E6
Rowen Conwy 41 C9
Rowfoot Northumb 62 G2
Rowhedge Essex 31 F7
Rowhook W Sus 11 A10
Rowington Warks 27 B9
Rowland Derbys 44 E6
Rowlands Castle Hants 10 C6
Rowlands Gill T&W 63 H7
Rowledge Sur 18 G5
Rowlestone Hereford 25 F10
Rowley E Yorks 52 F5
Rowley Shrops 33 E9
Rowley Hill W Yorks 44 A5
Rowley Regis W Mid 34 G5
Rowly Sur 19 G7
Rowney Green Worcs 27 A7
Rownhams Hants 10 C2
Rowrah Cumb 56 E2
Rowsham Bucks 28 G5
Rowsley Derbys 44 F6
Rowstock Oxon 17 C11
Rowston Lincs 46 G4
Rowton Ches W 43 F7
Rowton Shrops 33 D9
Rowton Telford 34 D2
Roxburgh Borders 70 G6
Roxby N Lincs 52 H5
Roxby N Yorks 59 E8
Roxton Bedford 29 C8
Roxwell Essex 30 H3
Royal Leamington Spa Warks 27 B10
Royal Oak Darl 58 D3
Royal Oak Lancs 43 B7
Royal Tunbridge Wells Kent 12 C4
Royal Wootton Bassett Wilts 17 C7
Roybridge Highld 80 E4
Roydhouse W Yorks 44 A6
Roydon Essex 29 H11
Roydon Norf 38 C3
Roydon Norf 39 G6
Roydon Hamlet Essex 29 H11
Royston Herts 29 D10
Royston S Yorks 45 A7
Royton Gtr Man 44 B3
Rozel Jersey 11
Ruabon = Rhiwabon Wrex 33 A9
Ruaig Argyll 78 G3
Ruan Lanihorne Corn 3 E7
Ruan Minor Corn 2 H6
Ruarach Highld 80 A1
Ruardean Glos 26 G3
Ruardean Woodside Glos 26 G3
Rubery Worcs 34 H5
Ruckcroft Cumb 57 B7
Ruckhall Hereford 25 E11
Ruckinge Kent 13 C9
Ruckland Lincs 47 E7
Ruckley Shrops 33 E11
Rudbaxton Pembs 22 D4
Rudby N Yorks 58 F5
Ruddington Notts 36 B1
Rudford Glos 26 F4
Rudge Shrops 34 F4
Rudge Som 16 F5
Rudgeway S Glos 16 C3
Rudgwick W Sus 11 A9
Rudhall Hereford 26 F3
Rudheath Ches W 43 E9
Rudley Green Essex 20 A5
Rudry Caerph 15 C7
Rudston E Yorks 53 C6
Rudyard Staffs 44 G3
Rufford Lancs 49 H4
Rufforth York 51 D11
Rugby Warks 35 H11
Rugeley Staffs 34 D6
Ruglen S Ayrs 66 F5
Ruilick Highld 87 G8
Ruishton Som 8 B1
Ruisigearraidh W Isles 90 J4
Ruislip London 19 C7
Ruislip Common London 19 C7
Rumbling Bridge Perth 76 H3
Rumburgh Suff 39 G9
Rumford Corn 3 B7
Rumney Cardiff 15 D8
Runcorn Halton 43 D8
Runcton W Sus 11 D7
Runcton Holme Norf 38 E2
Rundlestone Devon 5 D6
Runfold Sur 18 G5
Runhall Norf 39 E6
Runham Norf 39 D10
Runham Norf 39 E11
Runnington Som 7 D10
Runsell Green Essex 30 H4
Runswick Bay N Yorks 59 E9
Runwell Essex 20 B4
Ruscombe Wokingham 18 D4
Rush Green London 20 C2
Rush-head Aberds 89 D8
Rushall Hereford 26 E3
Rushall Norf 39 G7
Rushall Wilts 17 F8
Rushall W Mid 34 E6
Rushbrooke Suff 30 B5
Rushbury Shrops 33 F11
Rushden Herts 29 E10
Rushden Northants 28 B6
Rushenden Kent 20 D6
Rushford Norf 38 G5
Rushlake Green E Sus 12 E5
Rushmere Suff 39 G10
Rushmere St Andrew Suff 31 D9
Rushmoor Sur 18 G5
Rushock Worcs 26 A5
Rusholme Gtr Man 44 C2
Rushton Ches W 43 F8
Rushton Northants 36 G4
Rushton Shrops 34 E2
Rushton Spencer Staffs 44 F3
Rushwick Worcs 26 C5
Rushyford Durham 58 D3
Ruskie Stirling 75 G9
Ruskington Lincs 46 G4
Rusland Cumb 56 H5
Rusper W Sus 19 H9
Ruspidge Glos 26 G3
Russell's Water Oxon 18 C4
Russel's Green Suff 31 A9
Rusthall Kent 12 C4
Rustington W Sus 11 D9
Ruston N Yorks 52 A5
Ruston Parva E Yorks 53 C6
Ruswarp N Yorks 59 F9
Rutherford Borders 70 G5
Rutherglen S Lanark 68 D5
Ruthernbridge Corn 3 C9
Ruthin = Rhuthun Denb 42 G4
Ruthrieston Aberdeen 83 C11
Ruthven Aberds 88 D5
Ruthven Angus 76 C5
Ruthven Highld 81 D9
Ruthven Highld 87 H11
Ruthven House Angus 76 C6
Ruthvoes Corn 3 C8
Ruthwell Dumfries 60 G6
Ruyton-XI-Towns Shrops 33 C9
Ryal Northumb 62 F6
Ryal Fold Blackburn 50 G2
Ryall Dorset 8 E3
Ryarsh Kent 20 F3
Rydal Cumb 56 F5
Ryde IoW 10 E4
Rye E Sus 13 D7
Rye Foreign E Sus 13 D7
Rye Harbour E Sus 13 E8
Rye Park Herts 29 G10
Rye Street Worcs 26 E4
Ryecroft Gate Staffs 44 F3
Ryehill E Yorks 53 G8
Ryhall Rutland 36 D6
Ryhill W Yorks 45 A7
Ryhope T&W 58 A5
Rylstone N Yorks 50 D5
Ryme Intrinseca Dorset 8 C4
Ryther N Yorks 52 F1
Ryton Glos 26 E4
Ryton N Yorks 52 B3
Ryton Shrops 34 E3
Ryton T&W 63 G7
Ryton-on-Dunsmore Warks 27 A10

S

Sabden Lancs 50 F3
Sacombe Herts 29 G10
Sacriston Durham 58 B3
Sadberge Darl 58 E4
Saddell Argyll 65 E8
Saddington Leics 36 F2
Saddle Bow Norf 38 D2
Saddlescombe W Sus 12 E1
Sadgill Cumb 57 F6
Saffron Walden Essex 30 E2
Sageston Pembs 22 F5
Saham Hills Norf 38 E5
Saham Toney Norf 38 E5
Saighdinis W Isles 84 B3
Saighton Ches W 43 F7
St Abbs Borders 71 D8
St Abb's Haven Borders 71 D8
St Agnes Corn 2 D6
St Agnes Scilly 2 D2
St Albans Herts 29 H8
St Allen Corn 3 D7
St Andrews Fife 77 F8
St Andrew's Major V Glam 15 D7
St Anne Ald 11
St Annes Lancs 49 G3
St Ann's Dumfries 60 D6
St Ann's Chapel Corn 4 D5
St Ann's Chapel Devon 5 G7
St Anthony-in-Meneage Corn 3 G6
St Anthony's Hill E Sus 12 F5
St Arvans Mon 15 B11
St Asaph = Llanelwy Denb 42 E3
St Athan V Glam 14 E6
St Aubin Jersey 11
St Austell Corn 3 D9
St Bees Cumb 56 E1
St Blazey Corn 4 F1
St. Boswells Borders 70 G4
St Brelade Jersey 11
St Breock Corn 3 B8
St Breward Corn 4 D1
St Briavels Glos 16 A2
St Bride's Pembs 22 E3
St Brides Major V Glam 14 D4
St Bride's Netherwent Mon 15 C10
St Brides super Ely V Glam 14 D6
St Brides Wentlooge Newport 15 C8
St Budeaux Plym 4 F5
St Buryan Corn 2 G3
St Catherine Bath 16 D4
St Catherine's Argyll 73 C10
St Clears = Sanclêr Carms 23 E7
St Cleer Corn 4 E3
St Clement Corn 3 E7
St Clements Jersey 11
St Clether Corn 4 C3
St Colmac Argyll 73 G9
St Columb Major Corn 3 C8
St Columb Minor Corn 3 C7
St Columb Road Corn 3 D8
St Combs Aberds 89 B10
St Cross South Elmham Suff 39 G8
St Cyrus Aberds 77 A10
St David's = Tyddewi Pembs 22 D2
St David's Perth 76 E2
St Day Corn 2 E6
St Dennis Corn 3 D8
St Devereux Hereford 25 E11
St Dogmaels Pembs 22 B6
St Dogwells Pembs 22 D4
St Dominick Corn 4 E5
St Donat's V Glam 14 E5
St Edith's Wilts 16 E6
St Endellion Corn 3 B8
St Enoder Corn 3 D7
St Erme Corn 3 D7
St Erney Corn 4 F4
St Erth Corn 2 F4
St Ervan Corn 3 B7
St Eval Corn 3 C7
St Ewe Corn 3 E8
St Fagans Cardiff 15 D7
St Fergus Aberds 89 C10
St Fillans Perth 75 E9
St Florence Pembs 22 F5
St Genny's Corn 4 B2
St George Conwy 42 E2
St George's V Glam 14 D6
St Germans Corn 4 F4
St Giles Lincs 46 E3
St Giles in the Wood Devon 6 E4
St Giles on the Heath Devon 6 G2
St Harmon Powys 24 A6
St Helen Auckland Durham 58 D2
St Helena Warks 35 E8
St Helen's E Sus 13 E7
St Helens IoW 10 F5
St Helens Mers 43 C8
St Helier Jersey 11
St Helier London 19 E9
St Hilary Corn 2 F4
St Hilary V Glam 14 D6
Saint Hill W Sus 12 C2
St Illtyd Bl Gwent 15 A8
St Ippollytts Herts 29 F8
St Ishmael's Pembs 22 F3
St Issey Corn 3 B8
St Ive Corn 4 E4
St Ives Cambs 29 A10
St Ives Corn 2 E4
St Ives Dorset 9 D10
St James South Elmham Suff 39 G9
St Jidgey Corn 3 C8
St John Corn 4 F5
St John's IoM 48 D2
St John's Jersey 11
St John's Sur 18 F6
St John's Worcs 26 C5
St John's Chapel Durham 57 C10
St John's Fen End Norf 37 D11
St John's Highway Norf 37 D11
St John's Town of Dalry Dumfries 55 A9
St Judes IoM 48 C3
St Just Corn 2 F2
St Just in Roseland Corn 3 F7
St Katherine's Aberds 89 E7
St Keverne Corn 3 G6
St Kew Corn 3 B9
St Kew Highway Corn 3 B9
St Keyne Corn 4 E3
St Lawrence Corn 3 C9
St Lawrence Essex 20 A6
St Lawrence IoW 10 G4
St Leonard's Bucks 28 H6
St Leonards Dorset 9 D10
St Leonards E Sus 13 F6
Saint Leonards S Lanark 68 E5
St Levan Corn 2 G2
St Lythans V Glam 15 D7
St Mabyn Corn 3 B9
St Madoes Perth 76 E4
St Margaret South Elmham Suff 39 G9
St Margaret's Hereford 25 E10
St Margarets Herts 29 G10
St Margaret's at Cliffe Kent 21 G10
St Margaret's Hope Orkney 95 J5
St Mark's IoM 48 E2
St Martin Corn 3 G6
St Martin Corn 4 F3
St Martins Corn 2 G6
St Martin's Jersey 11
St Martins Perth 76 D4
St Martin's Shrops 33 B9
St Mary Bourne Hants 17 F11
St Mary Church V Glam 14 D6
St Mary Cray London 19 E11
St Mary Hill V Glam 14 D5
St Mary Hoo Medway 20 D5
St Mary in the Marsh Kent 13 D9
St Mary's Jersey 11
St Mary's Orkney 95 H5
St Mary's Bay Kent 13 D9
St Maughans Mon 25 G11
St Mawes Corn 3 F7
St Mawgan Corn 3 C7
St Mellion Corn 4 E4
St Mellons Cardiff 15 C8
St Merryn Corn 3 B7
St Mewan Corn 3 D8
St Michael Caerhays Corn 3 E8
St Michael Penkevil Corn 3 E7
St Michael South Elmham Suff 39 G9
St Michael's Kent 13 C7
St Michaels Worcs 26 B2
St Michael's on Wyre Lancs 49 E4
St Minver Corn 3 B8
St Monans Fife 77 G8
St Neot Corn 4 E2
St Neots Cambs 29 B8
St Newlyn East Corn 3 D7
St Nicholas Pembs 22 C3
St Nicholas V Glam 14 D6
St Nicholas at Wade Kent 21 E9
St Ninians Stirling 68 A6
St Osyth Essex 31 G8
St Osyth Heath Essex 31 G8
St Ouens Jersey 11
St Owens Cross Hereford 26 F2
St Paul's Cray London 19 E11
St Paul's Walden Herts 29 F8
St Peter Port Guern 11
St Peter's Jersey 11
St Peter's Kent 21 E10
St Petrox Pembs 22 G4
St Pinnock Corn 4 E3
St Quivox S Ayrs 67 D6
St Ruan Corn 2 H6
St Sampson Guern 11
St Stephen Corn 3 D8
St Stephen's Corn 4 C4
St Stephens Corn 4 F5
St Stephens Herts 29 H8
St Teath Corn 4 C1
St Thomas Devon 7 G8
St Tudy Corn 4 D1
St Twynnells Pembs 22 G4
St Veep Corn 4 F2
St Vigeans Angus 77 C9
St Wenn Corn 3 C8
St Weonards Hereford 25 F11
Saintbury Glos 27 E8
Salcombe Devon 5 H8
Salcombe Regis Devon 7 H10
Salcott Essex 30 G6
Sale Gtr Man 43 C10
Sale Green Worcs 26 C6
Saleby Lincs 47 E8
Salehurst E Sus 12 D6
Salem Carms 24 F3
Salem Ceredig 32 G2
Salen Argyll 79 G8
Salen Highld 79 E9
Salesbury Lancs 50 F2
Salford C Beds 28 E6
Salford Gtr Man 44 C2
Salford Oxon 27 F9
Salford Priors Warks 27 C7
Salfords Sur 19 G9
Salhouse Norf 39 D9
Saline Fife 69 A9
Salisbury Wilts 9 B10
Sallachan Highld 74 A2
Sallachy Highld 86 H2
Sallachy Highld 93 J8
Salle Norf 39 C7
Salmonby Lincs 47 E7
Salmond's Muir Angus 77 D8
Salperton Glos 27 F7
Salph End Bedford 29 C7
Salsburgh N Lanark 69 D7
Salt Staffs 34 C5
Salt End E Yorks 53 G7
Saltaire W Yorks 51 F7
Saltash Corn 4 F5
Saltburn Highld 87 E10
Saltburn-by-the-Sea Redcar 59 D7
Saltby Leics 36 C4
Saltcoats Cumb 56 G2
Saltcoats N Ayrs 66 B5
Saltdean Brighton 12 F2
Salter Lancs 50 C2
Salterforth Lancs 50 E4
Salterswall Ches W 43 F9
Saltfleet Lincs 47 C8
Saltfleetby All Saints Lincs 47 C8
Saltfleetby St Clements Lincs 47 C8
Saltfleetby St Peter Lincs 47 D8
Saltford Bath 16 E3
Salthouse Norf 39 A6
Saltmarshe E Yorks 52 G3
Saltney Flint 43 F6
Salton N Yorks 52 B3
Saltwick Northumb 63 F7
Saltwood Kent 21 H8
Salum Argyll 78 G3
Salvington W Sus 11 D10
Salwarpe Worcs 26 B5
Salwayash Dorset 8 E3
Sambourne Warks 27 B7
Sambrook Telford 34 C3
Samhla W Isles 84 B2
Samlesbury Lancs 50 F1
Samlesbury Bottoms Lancs 50 G2
Sampford Arundel Som 7 E10
Sampford Brett Som 7 B9
Sampford Courtenay Devon 6 F5
Sampford Peverell Devon 7 E9
Sampford Spiney Devon 4 D6
Sampool Bridge Cumb 56 H6
Samuelston E Loth 70 C3
Sanachan Highld 85 D13
Sanaigmore Argyll 64 A3
Sanclêr = St Clears Carms 23 E7
Sancreed Corn 2 G3
Sancton E Yorks 52 F5
Sand Highld 86 B2
Sand Shetland 96 J5
Sand Hole E Yorks 52 F4
Sand Hutton N Yorks 52 D2
Sandaig Highld 85 H12
Sandal Magna W Yorks 51 H9
Sandale Cumb 56 B4
Sandbach Ches E 43 F10
Sandbank Argyll 73 E10
Sandbanks Poole 9 F9
Sandend Aberds 88 B5
Sanderstead London 19 E10
Sandfields Glos 26 F6
Sandford Cumb 57 E9
Sandford Devon 7 F7
Sandford Dorset 9 F8
Sandford IoW 10 F4
Sandford N Som 15 F10
Sandford S Lanark 68 F6
Sandford Shrops 34 B1
Sandford on Thames Oxon 18 A2
Sandford Orcas Dorset 8 B5
Sandford St Martin Oxon 27 F11
Sandfordhill Aberds 89 D11
Sandgate Kent 21 H8
Sandgreen Dumfries 55 D8
Sandhaven Aberds 89 B9
Sandhead Dumfries 54 E3
Sandhills Sur 18 H6
Sandhoe Northumb 62 G5
Sandholme E Yorks 52 F4
Sandholme Lincs 37 B9
Sandhurst Brack 18 E5
Sandhurst Glos 26 F5
Sandhurst Kent 13 D6
Sandhurst Cross Kent 13 D6
Sandhutton N Yorks 51 A9
Sandiacre Derbys 35 B10
Sandilands Lincs 47 D9
Sandilands S Lanark 69 G7
Sandiway Ches W 43 E9
Sandleheath Hants 9 C10
Sandling Kent 20 F4
Sandlow Green Ches E 43 F10
Sandness Shetland 96 H3
Sandon Essex 20 A4
Sandon Herts 29 E10
Sandon Staffs 34 B5
Sandown IoW 10 F4
Sandplace Corn 4 F3
Sandridge Herts 29 G8
Sandridge Wilts 16 E6
Sandringham Norf 38 C2
Sandsend N Yorks 59 E9
Sandside Ho. Highld 93 C12
Sandsound Shetland 96 J5
Sandtoft N Lincs 45 B11
Sandway Kent 20 F5
Sandwell W Mid 34 G6
Sandwich Kent 21 F10
Sandwick Cumb 56 E6
Sandwick Orkney 95 K5
Sandwick Shetland 96 L6
Sandwith Cumb 56 E1
Sandy C Beds 29 D8
Sandy Carms 23 F9
Sandy Bank Lincs 46 G6
Sandy Haven Pembs 22 F3
Sandy Lane Wilts 16 E6
Sandy Lane Wrex 33 A9
Sandycroft Flint 42 F6
Sandyford Dumfries 61 D8
Sandyford Stoke 44 G2
Sandygate IoM 48 C3
Sandyhills Dumfries 55 D11
Sandylands Lancs 49 C4
Sandypark Devon 5 C8
Sandysike Cumb 61 G9
Sangobeg Highld 92 C7
Sangomore Highld 92 C7
Sanna Highld 78 E7
Sanndabhaig W Isles 84 D3
Sanndabhaig W Isles 91 D9
Sannox N Ayrs 66 B3
Sanquhar Dumfries 60 C3
Santon N Lincs 46 A3
Santon Bridge Cumb 56 F3
Santon Downham Suff 38 G4
Sapcote Leics 35 F10
Sapey Common Hereford 26 B4
Sapiston Suff 38 H5
Sapley Cambs 29 A9
Sapperton Glos 16 A6
Sapperton Lincs 36 B6
Saracen's Head Lincs 37 C9
Sarclet Highld 94 F5
Sardis Carms 23 F10
Sarn Bridgend 14 C5
Sarn Powys 33 F8
Sarn Bach Gwyn 40 H5
Sarn Meyllteyrn Gwyn 40 G4
Sarnau Carms 23 E8
Sarnau Ceredig 23 A8
Sarnau Gwyn 32 B5
Sarnau Powys 25 E7
Sarnau Powys 33 D8
Sarnesfield Hereford 25 C10
Saron Carms 23 C8
Saron Carms 24 G3
Saron Denb 42 F3
Saron Gwyn 40 E6
Saron Gwyn 41 D7
Sarratt Herts 19 B7
Sarre Kent 21 E9
Sarsden Oxon 27 F9
Sarsgrum Highld 92 C6
Satley Durham 58 B2
Satron N Yorks 57 G11
Satterleigh Devon 6 D5
Satterthwaite Cumb 56 G5
Satwell Oxon 18 C4
Sauchen Aberds 83 B8
Saucher Perth 76 D4
Sauchie Clack 69 A7
Sauchieburn Aberds 83 G8
Saughall Ches W 42 E6
Saughtree Borders 61 D11
Saul Glos 26 H4
Saundby Notts 45 D11
Saundersfoot Pembs 22 F6
Saunderton Bucks 18 A4
Saunton Devon 6 C3
Sausthorpe Lincs 47 F7
Saval Highld 93 J8
Savary Highld 79 G9
Savile Park W Yorks 51 G6
Sawbridge Warks 28 B2
Sawbridgeworth Herts 29 G11
Sawdon N Yorks 59 H10
Sawley Derbys 35 B10
Sawley Lancs 50 E3
Sawley N Yorks 51 C8
Sawston Cambs 29 D11
Sawtry Cambs 37 G7
Saxby Leics 36 D4
Saxby Lincs 46 D4
Saxby All Saints N Lincs 52 H5
Saxelbye Leics 36 C3
Saxham Street Suff 31 B7
Saxilby Lincs 46 E2
Saxlingham Norf 38 B6
Saxlingham Green Norf 39 F8
Saxlingham Nethergate Norf 39 F8
Saxlingham Thorpe Norf 39 F8
Saxmundham Suff 31 B10
Saxon Street Cambs 30 C3
Saxondale Notts 36 B2
Saxtead Suff 31 B9
Saxtead Green Suff 31 B9
Saxthorpe Norf 39 B7
Saxton N Yorks 51 F10
Sayers Common W Sus 12 E1
Scackleton N Yorks 52 B2
Scadabhagh W Isles 90 H6
Scaftworth Notts 45 C10
Scagglethorpe N Yorks 52 B4
Scaitcliffe Lancs 50 G3
Scalasaig Argyll 72 D2
Scalby E Yorks 52 G4
Scalby N Yorks 59 G11
Scaldwell Northants 28 A4
Scale Houses Cumb 57 B7
Scaleby Cumb 61 G10
Scaleby Hill Cumb 61 G10
Scales Cumb 49 B2
Scales Cumb 56 D5
Scales Lancs 49 F4
Scalford Leics 36 C3
Scaling Redcar 59 E8
Scallastle Argyll 79 H9
Scalloway Shetland 96 K6
Scalpay W Isles 90 H7
Scalpay Ho. Highld 85 F11
Scalpsie Argyll 73 H9
Scamadale Highld 79 B10
Scamblesby Lincs 46 E6
Scamodale Highld 79 D11
Scampston N Yorks 52 B4
Scampton Lincs 46 E3
Scapa Orkney 95 H5
Scapegoat Hill W Yorks 51 H6
Scar Orkney 95 D7
Scarborough N Yorks 59 H11
Scarcliffe Derbys 45 F8
Scarcroft W Yorks 51 E9
Scarcroft Hill W Yorks 51 E9
Scardroy Highld 86 F5
Scarff Shetland 96 E4
Scarfskerry Highld 94 C4
Scargill Durham 58 E1
Scarinish Argyll 78 G3
Scarisbrick Lancs 43 A6
Scarning Norf 38 D5
Scarrington Notts 36 A3
Scartho NE Lincs 46 B6
Scarwell Orkney 95 F3
Scatness Shetland 96 M5
Scatraig Highld 87 H10
Scawby N Lincs 46 B3
Scawsby S Yorks 45 B9
Scawton N Yorks 51 A11
Scayne's Hill W Sus 12 D2
Scethrog Powys 25 F8
Scholar Green Ches E 44 G2
Scholes W Yorks 44 B5
Scholes W Yorks 51 F9
Scholes W Yorks 51 G7
School Green Ches W 43 F9
Scleddau Pembs 22 C4
Sco Ruston Norf 39 C8
Scofton Notts 45 D10
Scole Norf 39 H7
Scolpaig W Isles 84 A2
Scone Perth 76 E4
Sconser Highld 85 E10
Scoonie Fife 76 G6
Scoor Argyll 78 K7
Scopwick Lincs 46 G4
Scoraig Highld 86 B3
Scorborough E Yorks 52 E6
Scorrier Corn 2 E6
Scorton Lancs 49 E5
Scorton N Yorks 58 F3
Scotbheinn W Isles 84 C3
Scotby Cumb 61 H10
Scotch Corner N Yorks 58 F3
Scotforth Lancs 49 D4
Scothern Lincs 46 E4
Scotland Gate Northumb 63 E8
Scotlandwell Perth 76 G4
Scots' Gap Northumb 62 E6
Scotsburn Highld 87 D10
Scotscalder Station Highld 94 E2
Scotscraig Fife 77 E7
Scotston Aberds 83 F9
Scotston Perth 76 C2
Scotstoun Glasgow 68 D4
Scotstown Highld 79 E11
Scotswood T&W 63 G7
Scottas Highld 85 H12
Scotter Lincs 46 B2
Scotterthorpe Lincs 46 B2
Scottlethorpe Lincs 37 C6
Scotton Lincs 46 C2
Scotton N Yorks 51 D9
Scotton N Yorks 58 G2
Scottow Norf 39 C8
Scoughall E Loth 70 B5
Scoulag Argyll 73 H10
Scoulton Norf 38 E5
Scourie Highld 92 E4
Scourie More Highld 92 E4
Scousburgh Shetland 96 M5
Scrabster Highld 94 C2
Scrafield Lincs 47 F7
Scrainwood Northumb 62 C5
Scrane End Lincs 37 A9
Scraptoft Leics 36 E2
Scratby Norf 39 D11
Scrayingham N Yorks 52 C3
Scredington Lincs 37 A6
Scremby Lincs 47 F8
Scremerston Northumb 71 F9
Screveton Notts 36 A3
Scrivelsby Lincs 46 F6
Scriven N Yorks 51 D9
Scrooby Notts 45 C10
Scropton Derbys 35 B7
Scrub Hill Lincs 46 G6
Scruton N Yorks 58 G3
Sculcoates Hull 53 F6
Sculthorpe Norf 38 B4
Scunthorpe N Lincs 46 A2
Scurlage Swansea 23 H9
Sea Palling Norf 39 C10
Seaborough Dorset 8 D3
Seacombe Mers 42 C6
Seacroft Lincs 47 F9
Seacroft W Yorks 51 F9
Seadyke Lincs 37 B9
Seafield S Ayrs 66 D6
Seafield W Loth 69 D9
Seaford E Sus 12 G3
Seaforth Mers 42 C6
Seagrave Leics 36 D2
Seaham Durham 58 B5
Seahouses Northumb 71 G11
Seal Kent 20 F2
Sealand Flint 42 F6
Seale Sur 18 G5
Seamer N Yorks 52 A6
Seamer N Yorks 58 E5
Seamill N Ayrs 66 B5
Searby Lincs 46 B4
Seasalter Kent 21 E7
Seascale Cumb 56 F2
Seathorne Lincs 47 F9
Seathwaite Cumb 56 E4
Seathwaite Cumb 56 G4
Seatoller Cumb 56 E4
Seaton Corn 4 F4
Seaton Cumb 56 C2
Seaton Devon 8 F1
Seaton Durham 58 A4
Seaton E Yorks 53 E7
Seaton Northumb 63 F9
Seaton Rutland 36 F5
Seaton Burn T&W 63 F8
Seaton Carew Hrtlpl 58 D6
Seaton Delaval Northumb 63 F9
Seaton Ross E Yorks 52 E3
Seaton Sluice Northumb 63 F9
Seatown Aberds 88 B5
Seatown Dorset 8 E3
Seave Green N Yorks 59 F6
Seaview IoW 10 E5
Seaville Cumb 56 A3
Seavington St Mary Som 8 C3
Seavington St Michael Som 8 C3
Sebergham Cumb 56 B5
Seckington Warks 35 E8
Second Coast Highld 86 B2
Sedbergh Cumb 57 G8
Sedbury Glos 15 B11
Sedbusk N Yorks 57 G10
Sedgeberrow Worcs 27 E7
Sedgebrook Lincs 36 B4
Sedgefield Durham 58 D4
Sedgeford Norf 38 B3
Sedgehill Wilts 9 B7
Sedgley W Mid 34 F5
Sedgwick Cumb 57 H7
Sedlescombe E Sus 13 E6
Sedlescombe Street E Sus 13 E6
Seend Wilts 16 E6
Seend Cleeve Wilts 16 E6
Seer Green Bucks 18 B6
Seething Norf 39 F9
Sefton Mers 42 B6
Seghill Northumb 63 F8
Seifton Shrops 33 G10
Seighford Staffs 34 C4
Seilebost W Isles 90 H5
Seion Gwyn 41 D7
Seisdon Staffs 34 F4
Seisiadar W Isles 91 D10
Selattyn Shrops 33 B8
Selborne Hants 10 A6
Selby N Yorks 52 F2
Selham W Sus 11 B8
Selhurst London 19 E10
Selkirk Borders 70 H3
Sellack Hereford 26 F2
Sellafirth Shetland 96 D7
Sellibister Orkney 95 D8
Sellindge Kent 13 C10
Sellindge Lees Kent 13 C10
Selling Kent 21 F7
Sells Green Wilts 16 E6
Selly Oak W Mid 34 G6
Selmeston E Sus 12 F4
Selsdon London 19 E10
Selsey W Sus 11 E7
Selsfield Common W Sus 12 C2
Selsted Kent 21 G9
Selston Notts 45 G8
Selworthy Som 7 B8
Semblister Shetland 96 H5
Semer Suff 30 D6
Semington Wilts 16 E5
Semley Wilts 9 B7
Send Sur 19 F7
Send Marsh Sur 19 F7
Senghenydd Caerph 15 B7
Sennen Corn 2 G2
Sennen Cove Corn 2 G2
Sennybridge = Pont Senni Powys 24 F6
Serlby Notts 45 D10
Sessay N Yorks 51 B10
Setchey Norf 38 D2

Setley Hants 10 D2
Setter Shetland 96 E6
Setter Shetland 96 H5
Setter Shetland 96 J7
Settiscarth Orkney 95 G4
Settle N Yorks 50 C4
Settrington N Yorks 52 B4
Seven Kings London 19 C11
Seven Sisters Neath 24 H5
Sevenhampton Glos 27 F7
Sevenoaks Kent 20 F2
Sevenoaks Weald Kent 20 F2
Severn Beach S Glos 15 C11
Severn Stoke Worcs 26 D5
Severnhampton Swindon 17 B9
Sevington Kent 13 B9
Sewards End Essex 30 E2
Sewardstone Essex 19 B10
Sewardstonebury Essex 19 B10
Sewerby E Yorks 53 C7
Seworgan Corn 2 F6
Sewstern Leics 36 C4
Sezincote Glos 27 E8
Sgarasta Mhor W Isles 90 H5
Sgiogarstaigh W Isles 91 A10
Shabbington Bucks 28 H3
Shackerstone Leics 35 E9
Shackleford Sur 18 G6
Shade W Yorks 50 G5
Shadforth Durham 58 B4
Shadingfield Suff 39 G10
Shadoxhurst Kent 13 C8
Shadsworth Blackburn 50 G3
Shadwell Norf 38 G5
Shadwell W Yorks 51 F9
Shaftesbury Dorset 9 B7
Shafton S Yorks 45 A7
Shalbourne Wilts 17 E10
Shalcombe IoW 10 F2
Shalden Hants 18 G3
Shaldon Devon 5 D10
Shalfleet IoW 10 F3
Shalford Essex 30 F4
Shalford Sur 19 G7
Shalford Green Essex 30 F4
Shallowford Devon 6 B6
Shalmsford Street Kent 21 F7
Shalstone Bucks 28 E3
Shamley Green Sur 19 G7
Shandon Argyll 73 E11
Shandwick Highld 87 D11
Shangton Leics 36 F3
Shankhouse Northumb 63 F8
Shanklin IoW 10 F4
Shanquhar Aberds 88 E5
Shanzie Perth 76 B5
Shap Cumb 57 E7
Shapwick Dorset 9 D8
Shapwick Som 15 H10
Shardlow Derbys 35 B10
Shareshill Staffs 34 E5
Sharlston W Yorks 51 H9
Sharlston Common W Yorks 51 H9
Sharnbrook Bedford 28 C6
Sharnford Leics 35 F10
Sharoe Green Lancs 49 F5
Sharow N Yorks 51 B9
Sharp Street Norf 39 C9
Sharpenhoe C Beds 29 E7
Sharperton Northumb 62 C5
Sharpness Glos 16 A3
Sharpthorne W Sus 12 C2
Sharrington Norf 38 B6
Shatterford Worcs 34 G3
Shaugh Prior Devon 4 E6
Shavington Ches E 43 G10
Shaw Gtr Man 44 B3
Shaw W Berks 17 E11
Shaw Wilts 16 E5
Shaw Green Lancs 49 H5
Shaw Mills N Yorks 51 C8
Shawbury Shrops 34 C1
Shawdon Hall Northumb 62 B6
Shawell Leics 35 G11
Shawford Hants 10 B3
Shawforth Lancs 50 G4
Shawhead Dumfries 60 F4
Shawhill Dumfries 61 G8
Shawton S Lanark 68 F5
Shawtonhill S Lanark 68 F5
Shear Cross Wilts 16 G5
Shearington Dumfries 60 G6
Shearsby Leics 36 F2
Shebbear Devon 6 F3
Shebdon Staffs 34 C3
Shebster Highld 93 C13
Sheddens E Renf 68 E4
Shedfield Hants 10 C4
Sheen Staffs 44 F5
Sheepscar W Yorks 51 F9
Sheepscombe Glos 26 G5
Sheepstor Devon 5 E6
Sheepwash Devon 6 F3
Sheepway N Som 15 D10
Sheepy Magna Leics 35 E9
Sheepy Parva Leics 35 E9
Sheering Essex 30 G2
Sheerness Kent 20 D6
Sheet Hants 11 B6
Sheffield S Yorks 45 D7
Sheffield Bottom W Berks 18 E3
Sheffield Green E Sus 12 D3
Shefford C Beds 29 E8
Shefford Woodlands W Berks 17 D10
Sheigra Highld 92 C4
Sheinton Shrops 34 E2
Shelderton Shrops 33 H10
Sheldon Derbys 44 F5
Sheldon Devon 7 F10
Sheldon W Mid 35 G7
Sheldwich Kent 21 F7
Shelf W Yorks 51 G7
Shelfanger Norf 39 G7
Shelfield W Mid 34 E6
Shelfield Warks 27 B8
Shelford Notts 36 A2
Shellacres Northumb 71 F7
Shelley Essex 20 A2
Shelley Suff 31 E7
Shelley W Yorks 44 A6
Shellingford Oxon 17 B10
Shellow Bowells Essex 30 H3
Shelsley Beauchamp Worcs 26 B4
Shelsley Walsh Worcs 26 B4
Shelthorpe Leics 35 D11
Shelton Bedford 29 B7
Shelton Norf 39 F8
Shelton Notts 36 A3
Shelton Shrops 33 D10
Shelton Green Norf 39 F8
Shelve Shrops 33 F9
Shelwick Hereford 26 D2
Shenfield Essex 20 B3
Shenington Oxon 27 D10
Shenley Herts 19 A8
Shenley Brook End M Keynes 28 E5
Shenley Church End M Keynes 28 E5
Shenleybury Herts 19 A8
Shenmore Hereford 25 E10
Shennanton Dumfries 54 C6
Shenstone Staffs 35 E7
Shenstone Worcs 26 A5
Shenton Leics 35 E9
Shenval Highld 80 A6
Shenval Moray 82 A4
Shepeau Stow Lincs 37 D9
Shephall Herts 29 F9
Shepherd's Green Oxon 18 C4
Shepherd's Port Norf 38 B2
Shepherdswell Kent 21 G9
Shepley W Yorks 44 B5
Shepperdine S Glos 16 B3
Shepperton Sur 19 E7
Shepreth Cambs 29 D10
Shepshed Leics 35 D10
Shepton Beauchamp Som 8 C3
Shepton Mallet Som 16 G3
Shepton Montague Som 8 A5
Shepway Kent 20 F4
Sheraton Durham 58 C5
Sherborne Dorset 8 C5
Sherborne Glos 27 G8
Sherborne St John Hants 18 F3
Sherbourne Warks 27 B9
Sherburn Durham 58 B4
Sherburn N Yorks 52 B5
Sherburn Hill Durham 58 B4
Sherburn in Elmet N Yorks 51 F10
Shere Sur 19 G7
Shereford Norf 38 C4
Sherfield English Hants 10 B1
Sherfield on Loddon Hants 18 F3
Sherford Devon 5 G8
Sheriff Hutton N Yorks 52 C2
Sheriffhales Shrops 34 D3
Sheringham Norf 39 A7
Sherington M Keynes 28 D5
Shernal Green Worcs 26 B6
Shernborne Norf 38 B3
Sherrington Wilts 16 H6
Sherston Wilts 16 C5
Sherwood Green Devon 6 D4
Shettleston Glasgow 68 D5
Shevington Gtr Man 43 B8
Shevington Moor Gtr Man 43 A8
Shevington Vale Gtr Man 43 B8
Sheviock Corn 4 F4
Shide IoW 10 F3
Shiel Bridge Highld 80 B1
Shieldaig Highld 85 A13
Shieldaig Highld 85 C13
Shieldhill Dumfries 60 E6
Shieldhill Falk 69 C7
Shieldhill S Lanark 69 F9
Shielfoot Highld 79 E9
Shielhill Angus 77 B7
Shielhill Invclyd 73 F11
Shifford Oxon 17 A10
Shifnal Shrops 34 E3
Shilbottle Northumb 63 C7
Shildon Durham 58 D3
Shillingford Devon 7 D8
Shillingford Oxon 18 B2
Shillingford St George Devon 5 C10
Shillingstone Dorset 9 C7
Shillington C Beds 29 E8
Shillmoor Northumb 62 C4
Shilton Oxon 27 H9
Shilton Warks 35 G10
Shilvington Northumb 63 E7
Shimpling Norf 39 G7
Shimpling Suff 30 C5
Shimpling Street Suff 30 C5
Shincliffe Durham 58 B3
Shiney Row T&W 58 A4
Shinfield Wokingham 18 E4
Shingham Norf 38 E3
Shingle Street Suff 31 D10
Shinner's Bridge Devon 5 E8
Shinness Highld 93 H8
Shipbourne Kent 20 F2
Shipdham Norf 38 E5
Shipham Som 15 F10
Shiphay Torbay 5 E9
Shiplake Oxon 18 D4
Shipley Derbys 35 A10
Shipley Northumb 63 B7
Shipley Shrops 34 F4
Shipley W Sus 11 B10
Shipley W Yorks 51 F7
Shipley Shiels Northumb 62 D3
Shipmeadow Suff 39 G9
Shippea Hill Sta. Cambs 38 G2
Shippon Oxon 17 B11
Shipston-on-Stour Warks 27 D9
Shipton Glos 27 G7
Shipton N Yorks 52 D1
Shipton Shrops 34 F1
Shipton Bellinger Hants 17 G9
Shipton Gorge Dorset 8 E3
Shipton Green W Sus 11 D7
Shipton Moyne Glos 16 C5
Shipton on Cherwell Oxon 27 G11
Shipton Solers Glos 27 G7
Shipton-under-Wychwood Oxon 27 G9
Shiptonthorpe E Yorks 52 E4
Shirburn Oxon 18 B3
Shirdley Hill Lancs 42 A6
Shirebrook Derbys 45 F9
Shiregreen S Yorks 45 C7
Shirehampton Bristol 15 D11
Shiremoor T&W 63 F9
Shirenewton Mon 15 B10
Shireoaks Notts 45 D9
Shirkoak Kent 13 C8
Shirl Heath Hereford 25 C11
Shirland Derbys 45 G7
Shirley Derbys 35 A8
Shirley London 19 E10
Shirley Soton 10 C3
Shirley W Mid 35 H7
Shirrell Heath Hants 10 C4
Shirwell Devon 6 C4
Shirwell Cross Devon 6 C4
Shiskine N Ayrs 66 D2
Shobdon Hereford 25 B11
Shobnall Staffs 35 C8
Shobrooke Devon 7 F7
Shoby Leics 36 D2
Shocklach Ches W 43 H7
Shoeburyness Southend 20 C6
Sholden Kent 21 F10
Sholing Soton 10 C3
Shoot Hill Shrops 33 D10
Shop Corn 3 B7
Shop Corn 6 E1
Shop Corner Suff 31 E9
Shore Mill Highld 87 E10
Shoreditch London 19 C10
Shoreham Kent 20 E2
Shoreham-By-Sea W Sus 11 D11
Shoresdean Northumb 71 F8
Shoreswood Northumb 71 F8
Shoreton Highld 87 E9
Shorncote Glos 17 B7
Shorne Kent 20 D3
Short Heath W Mid 34 E5
Shortacombe Devon 4 C6
Shortgate E Sus 12 E3
Shortlanesend Corn 3 E7
Shortlees E Ayrs 67 C7
Shortstown Bedford 29 D7
Shorwell IoW 10 F3
Shoscombe Bath 16 F4
Shotatton Shrops 33 C9
Shotesham Norf 39 F8
Shotgate Essex 20 B4
Shotley Suff 31 E9
Shotley Bridge Durham 58 A1
Shotley Gate Suff 31 E9
Shotleyfield Northumb 58 A1
Shottenden Kent 21 F7
Shottermill Sur 11 A7
Shottery Warks 27 C8
Shotteswell Warks 27 D11
Shottisham Suff 31 D10
Shottle Derbys 45 H7
Shottlegate Derbys 45 H7
Shotton Durham 58 C5
Shotton Flint 42 F6
Shotton Northumb 71 G7
Shotton Colliery Durham 58 B4
Shotts N Lanark 69 D7
Shotwick Ches W 42 E6
Shouldham Norf 38 E2
Shouldham Thorpe Norf 38 E2
Shoulton Worcs 26 C5
Shover's Green E Sus 12 C5
Shrawardine Shrops 33 D10
Shrawley Worcs 26 B5
Shrewley Common Warks 27 B9
Shrewsbury Shrops 33 D10
Shrewton Wilts 17 G7
Shripney W Sus 11 D8
Shrivenham Oxon 17 C9
Shropham Norf 38 F5
Shrub End Essex 30 F6
Shucknall Hereford 26 D2
Shudy Camps Cambs 30 D3
Shulishadermor Highld 85 D9
Shurdington Glos 26 G6
Shurlock Row Windsor 18 D5
Shurrery Highld 93 D13
Shurrery Lodge Highld 93 D13
Shurton Som 7 B11
Shustoke Warks 35 F8
Shute Devon 7 F7
Shute Devon 8 E1
Shutford Oxon 27 D10
Shuthonger Glos 26 E5
Shutlanger Northants 28 C4
Shuttington Warks 35 E8
Shuttlewood Derbys 45 E8
Siabost bho Dheas W Isles 90 C7
Siabost bho Thuath W Isles 90 C7
Siadar W Isles 91 B8
Siadar Iarach W Isles 91 B8
Siadar Uarach W Isles 91 B8
Sibbaldbie Dumfries 61 E7
Sibbertoft Northants 36 G2
Sibdon Carwood Shrops 33 G10
Sibford Ferris Oxon 27 E10
Sibford Gower Oxon 27 E10
Sible Hedingham Essex 30 E4
Sibsey Lincs 47 G7
Sibson Cambs 37 F6
Sibson Leics 35 E9
Sibthorpe Notts 45 H11
Sibton Suff 31 B10
Sibton Green Suff 31 A10
Sicklesmere Suff 30 B5
Sicklinghall N Yorks 51 E9
Sid Devon 7 H10
Sidbury Devon 7 G10
Sidbury Shrops 34 G2
Sidcot N Som 15 F10
Sidcup London 19 D11
Siddick Cumb 56 C2
Siddington Ches E 44 E2
Siddington Glos 17 B7
Sidemoor Worcs 26 A6
Sidestrand Norf 39 B8
Sidford Devon 7 G10
Sidlesham W Sus 11 E7
Sidley E Sus 12 F6
Sidlow Sur 19 G9
Sidmouth Devon 7 H10
Sigford Devon 5 D8
Sigglesthorne E Yorks 53 E7
Sighthill Edin 69 C10
Sigingstone V Glam 14 D5
Signet Oxon 27 G9
Silchester Hants 18 E3
Sildinis W Isles 91 F7
Sileby Leics 36 D1
Silecroft Cumb 49 A1
Silfield Norf 39 F7
Silian Ceredig 23 A10
Silk Willoughby Lincs 37 A6
Silkstone S Yorks 44 B6
Silkstone Common S Yorks 44 B6
Silloth Cumb 56 A3
Sills Northumb 62 C4
Sillyearn Moray 88 C5
Siloh Carms 24 E4
Silpho N Yorks 59 G10
Silsden W Yorks 50 E6
Silsoe C Beds 29 E7
Silver End Essex 30 G5
Silverburn Midloth 69 D11
Silverdale Lancs 49 B4
Silverdale Staffs 44 H2
Silvergate Norf 39 C7
Silverhill E Sus 13 E6
Silverley's Green Suff 39 H8
Silverstone Northants 28 D3
Silverton Devon 7 F8
Silvington Shrops 34 H2
Silwick Shetland 96 J4
Simmondley Derbys 44 C4
Simonburn Northumb 62 F4
Simonsbath Som 7 C6
Simonstone Lancs 50 F3
Simprim Borders 71 F7
Simpson M Keynes 28 E5
Simpson Cross Pembs 22 E3
Sinclair's Hill Borders 71 E7
Sinclairston E Ayrs 67 E7
Sinderby N Yorks 51 A9
Sinderhope Northumb 57 A10
Sindlesham Wokingham 18 E4
Singdean Borders 61 C11
Singleborough Bucks 28 E4
Singleton Lancs 49 F3
Singleton W Sus 11 C7
Singlewell Kent 20 D3
Sinkhurst Green Kent 13 B7
Sinnahard Aberds 82 B6
Sinnington N Yorks 59 H8
Sinton Green Worcs 26 B5
Sipson London 19 D7
Sirhowy Bl Gwent 25 G8
Sisland Norf 39 F9
Sissinghurst Kent 13 C6
Sisterpath Borders 70 F6
Siston S Glos 16 D3
Sithney Corn 2 G5
Sittingbourne Kent 20 E5
Six Ashes Staffs 34 G3
Six Hills Leics 36 C2
Six Mile Bottom Cambs 30 C2
Sixhills Lincs 46 D5
Sixpenny Handley Dorset 9 C8
Sizewell Suff 31 B11
Skail Highld 93 E10
Skaill Orkney 95 E5
Skaill Orkney 95 G3
Skaill Orkney 95 H6
Skares E Ayrs 67 E8
Skateraw E Loth 70 C6
Skaw Shetland 96 G7
Skeabost Highld 85 D9
Skeabrae Orkney 95 F3
Skeeby N Yorks 58 F3
Skeffington Leics 36 E3
Skeffling E Yorks 53 H9
Skegby Notts 45 F8
Skegness Lincs 47 F9
Skelberry Shetland 96 M5
Skelbo Highld 87 B10
Skelbrooke S Yorks 45 A9
Skeldyke Lincs 37 B9
Skellingthorpe Lincs 46 E3
Skellister Shetland 96 H6
Skellow S Yorks 45 A9
Skelmanthorpe W Yorks 44 A6
Skelmersdale Lancs 43 B7
Skelmonae Aberds 89 E8
Skelmorlie N Ayrs 73 G10
Skelmuir Aberds 89 D9
Skelpick Highld 93 D10
Skelton Cumb 56 C6
Skelton E Yorks 52 G3
Skelton N Yorks 58 F1
Skelton Redcar 59 E7
Skelton York 52 D1
Skelton-on-Ure N Yorks 51 C9
Skelwick Orkney 95 D5
Skelwith Bridge Cumb 56 F5
Skendleby Lincs 47 F8
Skene Ho. Aberds 83 C9
Skenfrith Mon 25 F11
Skerne E Yorks 52 D6
Skeroblingarry Argyll 65 F8
Skerray Highld 93 C9
Skerton Lancs 49 C4
Sketchley Leics 35 F10
Sketty Swansea 14 B2
Skewen Neath 14 B3
Skewsby N Yorks 52 B2
Skeyton Norf 39 C8
Skiag Bridge Highld 92 G5
Skibo Castle Highld 87 C10
Skidbrooke Lincs 47 C8
Skidbrooke North End Lincs 47 C8
Skidby E Yorks 52 F6
Skilgate Som 7 D8
Skillington Lincs 36 C4
Skinburness Cumb 61 H7
Skinflats Falk 69 B8
Skinidin Highld 84 D7
Skinnet Highld 93 C8
Skinningrove Redcar 59 D8
Skipness Argyll 73 H7
Skippool Lancs 49 E3
Skipsea E Yorks 53 D7
Skipsea Brough E Yorks 53 D7
Skipton N Yorks 50 D5
Skipton-on-Swale N Yorks 51 B9
Skipwith N Yorks 52 F2
Skirbeck Lincs 37 A9
Skirbeck Quarter Lincs 37 A9
Skirlaugh E Yorks 53 F7
Skirling Borders 69 G9
Skirmett Bucks 18 C4
Skirpenbeck E Yorks 52 D3
Skirwith Cumb 57 C8
Skirza Highld 94 D5
Skulamus Highld 85 F11
Skullomie Highld 93 C9
Skyborry Green Shrops 25 A9
Skye of Curr Highld 82 A1
Skyreholme N Yorks 51 C6
Slackhall Derbys 44 D4
Slackhead Moray 88 B4
Slad Glos 26 H5
Slade Devon 6 B4
Slade Pembs 22 E4
Slade Green London 20 D2
Slaggyford Northumb 57 A8
Slaidburn Lancs 50 D3
Slaithwaite W Yorks 44 A4
Slaley Northumb 62 H5
Slamannan Falk 69 C7
Slapton Bucks 28 F6
Slapton Devon 5 G9
Slapton Northants 28 D3
Slatepit Dale Derbys 45 F7
Slattocks Gtr Man 44 B2
Slaugham W Sus 12 D1
Slaughterford Wilts 16 D5
Slawston Leics 36 F3
Sleaford Hants 18 H5
Sleaford Lincs 46 H4
Sleagill Cumb 57 E7
Sleapford Telford 34 D2
Sledge Green Worcs 26 E5
Sledmere E Yorks 52 C5
Sleightholme Durham 57 E11
Sleights N Yorks 59 F9
Slepe Dorset 9 E8
Slickly Highld 94 D4
Sliddery N Ayrs 66 D2
Sligachan Hotel Highld 85 F9
Slimbridge Glos 16 A4
Slindon Staffs 34 B4
Slindon W Sus 11 D8
Slinfold W Sus 11 A10
Sling Gwyn 41 D8
Slingsby N Yorks 52 B2
Slioch Aberds 88 E5
Slip End C Beds 29 G7
Slip End Herts 29 E9
Slipton Northants 36 H5
Slitting Mill Staffs 34 D6
Slochd Highld 81 A10
Slockavullin Argyll 73 D7
Sloley Norf 39 C8
Sloothby Lincs 47 E8
Slough Slough 18 D6
Slough Green W Sus 12 D1
Sluggan Highld 81 A10
Slumbay Highld 85 E13
Slyfield Sur 18 F6
Slyne Lancs 49 C4
Smailholm Borders 70 G5
Small Dole W Sus 11 C11
Small Hythe Kent 13 C7
Smallbridge Gtr Man 50 H5
Smallburgh Norf 39 C9
Smallburn Aberds 89 D10
Smallburn E Ayrs 68 H5
Smalley Derbys 35 A10
Smallfield Sur 12 B2
Smallridge Devon 8 D2
Smannell Hants 17 G10
Smardale Cumb 57 F9
Smarden Kent 13 B7
Smarden Bell Kent 13 B7
Smeatharpe Devon 7 E10
Smeeth Kent 13 C9
Smeeton Westerby Leics 36 F2
Smercleit W Isles 84 G2
Smerral Highld 94 G3
Smethwick W Mid 34 G6
Smirisary Highld 79 D9
Smisby Derbys 35 D9
Smith Green Lancs 49 D4
Smithfield Cumb 61 G10
Smithincott Devon 7 E9
Smith's Green Essex 30 F2
Smithstown Highld 85 A12
Smithton Highld 87 G10
Smithy Green Ches E 43 E10
Smockington Leics 35 G10
Smoogro Orkney 95 H4
Smythe's Green Essex 30 G6
Snaigow House Perth 76 C3
Snailbeach Shrops 33 E9
Snailwell Cambs 30 B3
Snainton N Yorks 52 A5
Snaith E Yorks 52 G2
Snape N Yorks 51 A8
Snape Suff 31 C10
Snape Green Lancs 43 A6
Snarestone Leics 35 E9
Snarford Lincs 46 D4
Snargate Kent 13 D8
Snave Kent 13 D9
Snead Powys 33 F9
Sneath Common Norf 39 G7
Sneaton N Yorks 59 F9
Sneatonthorpe N Yorks 59 F10
Snelland Lincs 46 D4
Snelston Derbys 35 A7
Snettisham Norf 38 B2
Sniseabhal W Isles 84 E2
Snitter Northumb 62 C6
Snitterby Lincs 46 C3
Snitterfield Warks 27 C9
Snitton Shrops 34 H1
Snodhill Hereford 25 D10
Snodland Kent 20 E3
Snowden Hill S Yorks 44 B6
Snowdown Kent 21 F9
Snowshill Glos 27 E7
Snydale W Yorks 51 H10
Soar Anglesey 40 C5
Soar Carms 24 F3
Soar Devon 5 H8
Soar-y-Mynydd Ceredig 24 C4
Soberton Hants 10 C5
Soberton Heath Hants 10 C5
Sockbridge Cumb 57 D7
Sockburn Darl 58 F4
Soham Cambs 30 A2
Soham Cotes Cambs 38 H1
Solas W Isles 84 A3
Soldon Cross Devon 6 E2
Soldridge Hants 10 A5
Sole Street Kent 20 E3
Sole Street Kent 21 G7
Solihull W Mid 35 H7
Sollers Dilwyn Hereford 25 C11
Sollers Hope Hereford 26 E3
Sollom Lancs 49 H4
Solva Pembs 22 D2
Somerby Leics 36 D3
Somerby Lincs 46 B4
Somercotes Derbys 45 G8
Somerford Dorset 9 E10
Somerford Keynes Glos 17 B7
Somerley W Sus 11 E7
Somerleyton Suff 39 F10
Somersal Herbert Derbys 35 B7
Somersby Lincs 47 E7
Somersham Cambs 37 H9
Somersham Suff 31 D7
Somerton Oxon 27 F11
Somerton Som 8 B3
Sompting W Sus 11 D10
Sonning Wokingham 18 D4
Sonning Common Oxon 18 C4
Sonning Eye Oxon 18 D4
Sontley Wrex 42 H6
Sopley Hants 9 E10
Sopwell Herts 29 H8
Sopworth Wilts 16 C5
Sorbie Dumfries 55 E7
Sordale Highld 94 D3
Sorisdale Argyll 78 E5
Sorn E Ayrs 68 H4
Sornhill E Ayrs 67 C8
Sortat Highld 94 D4
Sotby Lincs 46 E6
Sots Hole Lincs 46 F5
Sotterley Suff 39 G10
Soudley Shrops 34 C3
Soughton Flint 42 F5
Soulbury Bucks 28 F5
Soulby Cumb 57 E9
Souldern Oxon 28 E2
Souldrop Bedford 28 B6
Sound Ches E 43 H9
Sound Shetland 96 H5
Sound Shetland 96 J6
Sound Heath Ches E 43 H9
Soundwell S Glos 16 D3
Sourhope Borders 62 A4
Sourin Orkney 95 E5
Sourton Devon 6 G4
Soutergate Cumb 49 A2
South Acre Norf 38 D4
South Allington Devon 5 H8
South Alloa Falk 69 A7
South Ambersham W Sus 11 B8
South Anston S Yorks 45 D9
South Ascot Windsor 18 E6
South Ballachulish Highld 74 B3
South Balloch S Ayrs 66 G6
South Bank Redcar 59 D6
South Barrow Som 8 B5
South Beach Gwyn 40 G5
South Benfleet Essex 20 C4
South Bersted W Sus 11 D8
South Brent Devon 5 E7
South Brewham Som 16 H4
South Broomhill Northumb 63 D8
South Burlingham Norf 39 E9
South Cadbury Som 8 B5
South Cairn Dumfries 54 C2
South Carlton Lincs 46 E3
South Cave E Yorks 52 F5
South Cerney Glos 17 B7
South Chard Som 8 D2
South Charlton Northumb 63 A7
South Cheriton Som 8 B5
South Cliffe E Yorks 52 F4
South Clifton Notts 46 E2
South Cockerington Lincs 47 D7
South Cornelly Bridgend 14 C4
South Cove Suff 39 G10
South Creagan Argyll 74 C2
South Creake Norf 38 B4
South Croxton Leics 36 D2
South Croydon London 19 E10
South Dalton E Yorks 52 E5
South Darenth Kent 20 E2
South Duffield N Yorks 52 F2
South Elkington Lincs 46 D6
South Elmsall W Yorks 45 A8
South End Bucks 28 F5
South End Cumb 49 C2
South End N Lincs 53 G7
South Erradale Highld 85 A12
South Fambridge Essex 20 B5
South Fawley W Berks 17 C10
South Ferriby N Lincs 52 G5
South Garth Shetland 96 D7
South Garvan Highld 80 F1
South Glendale W Isles 84 G2
South Godstone Sur 19 G10
South Gorley Hants 9 C10
South Green Essex 20 B3
South Green Kent 20 E5
South-haa Shetland 96 E5
South Ham Hants 18 F3
South Hanningfield Essex 20 B4
South Harting W Sus 11 C6
South Hatfield Herts 29 H9
South Hayling Hants 10 E6
South Hazelrigg Northumb 71 G9
South Heath Bucks 18 A6
South Heighton E Sus 12 F3
South Hetton Durham 58 B4
South Hiendley W Yorks 45 A7
South Hill Corn 4 D4
South Hinksey Oxon 18 A2
South Hole Devon 6 D1
South Holme N Yorks 52 B2
South Holmwood Sur 19 G8
South Hornchurch London 20 C2
South Hykeham Lincs 46 F3
South Hylton T&W 63 H9
South Kelsey Lincs 46 C4
South Kessock Highld 87 G9
South Killingholme N Lincs 53 H7
South Kilvington N Yorks 51 A10
South Kilworth Leics 36 G2
South Kirkby W Yorks 45 A8
South Kirkton Aberds 83 C9
South Kiscadale N Ayrs 66 D3
South Kyme Lincs 46 H5
South Lancing W Sus 11 D10
South Leigh Oxon 27 H10
South Leverton Notts 45 D11
South Littleton Worcs 27 D7
South Lopham Norf 38 G6
South Luffenham Rutland 36 E5
South Malling E Sus 12 E3
South Marston Swindon 17 C8
South Middleton Northumb 62 A5
South Milford N Yorks 51 F10
South Millbrex Aberds 89 D8
South Milton Devon 5 G8
South Mimms Herts 19 A9
South Molton Devon 6 D6
South Moreton Oxon 18 C2
South Mundham W Sus 11 D7
South Muskham Notts 45 G11
South Newbald E Yorks 52 F5
South Newington Oxon 27 E11
South Newton Wilts 9 A9
South Normanton Derbys 45 G8
South Norwood London 19 E10
South Nutfield Sur 19 G10
South Ockendon Thurrock 20 C2
South Ormsby Lincs 47 E7
South Otterington N Yorks 58 H4
South Owersby Lincs 46 C4
South Oxhey Herts 19 B8
South Perrott Dorset 8 D3
South Petherton Som 8 C3
South Petherwin Corn 4 C4
South Pickenham Norf 38 E4
South Pool Devon 5 G8
South Port Argyll 74 E3
South Radworthy Devon 7 C6
South Rauceby Lincs 46 H4
South Raynham Norf 38 C4
South Reston Lincs 47 D8
South Runcton Norf 38 E2
South Scarle Notts 46 F2
South Shian Argyll 74 C2
South Shields T&W 63 G9
South Shore Blackpool 49 F3
South Somercotes Lincs 47 C8
South Stainley N Yorks 51 C9
South Stainmore Cumb 57 E10
South Stifford Thurrock 20 D3
South Stoke Oxon 18 C2
South Stoke W Sus 11 D9
South Street E Sus 12 E2
South Street Kent 21 E8
South Street Kent 21 F7
South Street London 19 F11
South Tawton Devon 6 G5
South Thoresby Lincs 47 E8
South Tidworth Wilts 17 G9
South Town Hants 18 H3
South View Hants 18 F3
South Walsham Norf 39 D9
South Warnborough Hants 18 G4
South Weald Essex 20 B2
South Weston Oxon 18 B4
South Wheatley Corn 4 B3
South Wheatley Notts 45 D11
South Whiteness Shetland 96 J5
South Widcombe Bath 16 F2
South Wigston Leics 36 F1
South Willingham Lincs 46 D5
South Wingfield Derbys 45 G7
South Witham Lincs 36 D5
South Wonston Hants 17 H11
South Woodham Ferrers Essex 20 B5
South Wootton Norf 38 C2
South Wraxall Wilts 16 E5
South Zeal Devon 6 G5
Southall London 19 C8
Southam Glos 26 F6
Southam Warks 27 B11
Southampton Soton 10 C3
Southborough Kent 12 B4
Southbourne Bmouth 9 E10
Southbourne W Sus 11 D6
Southburgh Norf 38 E5
Southburn E Yorks 52 D5
Southchurch Southend 20 C6
Southcott Wilts 17 F8
Southcourt Bucks 28 G5
Southdean Borders 62 C2
Southdene Mers 43 C7
Southease E Sus 12 F3
Southend Argyll 65 H7
Southend W Berks 18 D2
Southend Wilts 17 D8
Southend-on-Sea Southend 20 C5
Southernden Kent 20 G5
Southerndown V Glam 14 D4
Southerness Dumfries 60 H5
Southery Norf 38 F2
Southfield Northumb 63 F8
Southfleet Kent 20 D3
Southgate Ceredig 32 H1
Southgate London 19 B9
Southgate Norf 39 C7
Southgate Swansea 23 H10
Southill C Beds 29 D8
Southleigh Devon 7 G11
Southminster Essex 20 B6
Southmoor Oxon 17 B10
Southoe Cambs 29 B8
Southolt Suff 31 B8
Southorpe Pboro 37 E6
Southowram W Yorks 51 G7
Southport Mers 49 H3
Southpunds Shetland 96 L6
Southrepps Norf 39 B8
Southrey Lincs 46 F5
Southrop Glos 17 A8
Southrope Hants 18 G3
Southsea Ptsmth 10 E5
Southstoke Bath 16 E4
Southtown Norf 39 E11
Southtown Orkney 95 J5
Southwaite Cumb 56 B6
Southwark London 19 D10
Southwater W Sus 11 B10
Southwater Street W Sus 11 B10
Southway Som 15 G11
Southwell Dorset 8 G5
Southwell Notts 45 G10
Southwick Hants 10 D5
Southwick Northants 36 F6
Southwick T&W 63 H9
Southwick W Sus 11 D11
Southwick Wilts 16 F5
Southwold Suff 39 H11
Southwood Norf 39 E9
Southwood Som 8 A4
Soval Lodge W Isles 91 E8
Sowber Gate N Yorks 58 H4
Sowerby N Yorks 51 A10
Sowerby W Yorks 50 G6
Sowerby Bridge W Yorks 51 G6
Sowerby Row Cumb 56 C5
Sowood W Yorks 51 H6
Sowton Devon 7 G8
Soyal Highld 87 B8
Spa Common Norf 39 B8
Spacey Houses N Yorks 51 D9
Spadeadam Farm Cumb 61 F11
Spalding Lincs 37 C8
Spaldington E Yorks 52 F3
Spaldwick Cambs 29 A8
Spalford Notts 46 F2
Spanby Lincs 37 B6
Sparham Norf 39 D6
Spark Bridge Cumb 49 A3
Sparkford Som 8 B5
Sparkhill W Mid 35 G6
Sparkwell Devon 5 F6
Sparrow Green Norf 38 D5
Sparrowpit Derbys 44 D4
Sparsholt Hants 10 A3
Sparsholt Oxon 17 C10
Spartylea Northumb 57 B10
Spaunton N Yorks 59 H8
Spaxton Som 7 C11
Spean Bridge Highld 80 E4
Spear Hill W Sus 11 C10
Speen Bucks 18 B5
Speen W Berks 17 E11
Speeton N Yorks 53 B7
Speke Mers 43 D7
Speldhurst Kent 12 B4
Spellbrook Herts 29 G11
Spelsbury Oxon 27 F10
Spelter Bridgend 14 B4
Spencers Wood Wokingham 18 E4
Spennithorne N Yorks 58 H2
Spennymoor Durham 58 C3
Spetchley Worcs 26 C5
Spetisbury Dorset 9 D8
Spexhall Suff 39 G9
Spey Bay Moray 88 B3
Speybridge Highld 82 A2
Speyview Moray 88 D2
Spilsby Lincs 47 F8
Spindlestone Northumb 71 G10
Spinkhill Derbys 45 E8
Spinningdale Highld 87 C9
Spirthill Wilts 16 D6
Spital Hill S Yorks 45 C10
Spital in the Street Lincs 46 D3
Spithurst E Sus 12 E3
Spittal Dumfries 54 D6
Spittal E Loth 70 C3
Spittal Highld 94 E3
Spittal Northumb 71 E9
Spittal Pembs 22 D4
Spittal Stirling 68 B4
Spittal of Glenmuick Aberds 82 E5
Spittal of Glenshee Perth 82 F3
Spittalfield Perth 76 C4
Spixworth Norf 39 D8
Splayne's Green E Sus 12 D3
Spofforth N Yorks 51 D9
Spon End W Mid 35 H9
Spon Green Flint 42 F5
Spondon Derby 35 B10
Spooner Row Norf 39 F6
Sporle Norf 38 D4
Spott E Loth 70 C5
Spratton Northants 28 A4
Spreakley Sur 18 G5
Spreyton Devon 6 G5
Spridlington Lincs 46 D4
Spring Vale S Yorks 44 B6
Spring Valley IoM 48 E3
Springburn Glasgow 68 D5
Springfield Dumfries 61 G9
Springfield Essex 30 H4
Springfield Fife 76 F6
Springfield Moray 87 F13
Springfield W Mid 35 G6
Springhill Staffs 34 E5
Springholm Dumfries 55 C11
Springkell Dumfries 61 F8
Springside N Ayrs 67 C6
Springthorpe Lincs 46 D2
Springwell T&W 63 H8
Sproatley E Yorks 53 F7
Sproston Green Ches W 43 F10
Sprotbrough S Yorks 45 B9
Sproughton Suff 31 D8
Sprouston Borders 70 G6
Sprowston Norf 39 D8
Sproxton Leics 36 C4
Sproxton N Yorks 52 A2
Spurstow Ches E 43 G8
Spynie Moray 88 B2
Squires Gate Blackpool 49 F3
Srannda W Isles 90 J5
Sronphadruig Lodge Perth 81 F9
Stableford Shrops 34 F3
Stableford Staffs 34 B4
Stacey Bank S Yorks 44 C6
Stackhouse N Yorks 50 C4
Stackpole Pembs 22 G4
Staddiscombe Plym 4 F6
Staddlethorpe E Yorks 52 G4
Stadhampton Oxon 18 B3
Stadhlaigearraidh W Isles 84 E2
Staffield Cumb 57 B7
Staffin Highld 85 B9
Stafford Staffs 34 C5
Stagsden Bedford 28 D6
Stainburn Cumb 56 D2
Stainburn N Yorks 51 E8
Stainby Lincs 36 C5
Staincross S Yorks 45 A7
Staindrop Durham 58 D2
Staines-upon-Thames Sur 19 D7
Stainfield Lincs 37 C6
Stainfield Lincs 46 E5
Stainforth N Yorks 50 C4
Stainforth S Yorks 45 A10
Staining Lancs 49 F3
Stainland W Yorks 51 H6
Stainsacre N Yorks 59 F10
Stainsby Derbys 45 F8
Stainton Cumb 57 D6
Stainton Cumb 57 H7
Stainton Durham 58 E1
Stainton Mbro 58 E5
Stainton N Yorks 58 G2
Stainton S Yorks 45 C9
Stainton by Langworth Lincs 46 E4
Stainton le Vale Lincs 46 C5
Stainton with Adgarley Cumb 49 B2
Staintondale N Yorks 59 G10
Stair Cumb 56 D4
Stair E Ayrs 67 D7
Stairhaven Dumfries 54 D5
Staithes N Yorks 59 E8
Stake Pool Lancs 49 E4
Stakeford Northumb 63 E8
Stalbridge Dorset 8 C6
Stalbridge Weston Dorset 8 C6
Stalham Norf 39 C9
Stalham Green Norf 39 C9
Stalisfield Green Kent 20 F6
Stalling Busk N Yorks 57 H11
Stallingborough NE Lincs 46 A5
Stalmine Lancs 49 E3
Stalybridge Gtr Man 44 C3
Stambourne Essex 30 E4
Stambourne Green Essex 30 E4
Stamford Lincs 36 E6
Stamford Bridge Ches W 43 F7
Stamford Bridge E Yorks 52 D3
Stamfordham Northumb 62 F6
Stanah Cumb 56 E5
Stanborough Herts 29 G9
Stanbridge C Beds 28 F6
Stanbridge Dorset 9 D9
Stanbrook Worcs 26 D5
Stanbury W Yorks 50 F6
Stand Gtr Man 43 B10
Stand N Lanark 68 D6
Standburn Falk 69 C8
Standeford Staffs 34 E5
Standen Kent 13 B7
Standford Hants 11 A7
Standingstone Cumb 56 C2
Standish Gtr Man 43 A8
Standlake Oxon 17 A10
Standon Hants 10 B3
Standon Herts 29 F10
Standon Staffs 34 B4
Stane N Lanark 69 E7
Stanfield Norf 38 C5
Stanford C Beds 29 D8
Stanford Kent 13 C10
Stanford Bishop Hereford 26 C3
Stanford Bridge Worcs 26 B4
Stanford Dingley W Berks 18 D2
Stanford in the Vale Oxon 17 B10
Stanford-le-Hope Thurrock 20 C3
Stanford on Avon Northants 36 H1
Stanford on Soar Notts 35 C11
Stanford on Teme Worcs 26 B4
Stanford Rivers Essex 20 A2
Stanfree Derbys 45 E8
Stanghow Redcar 59 E7
Stanground Pboro 37 F8
Stanhoe Norf 38 B4
Stanhope Borders 69 H10
Stanhope Durham 57 C11
Stanion Northants 36 G5
Stanley Derbys 35 A10
Stanley Durham 58 A2
Stanley Lancs 43 B7
Stanley Perth 76 D4
Stanley Staffs 44 G3
Stanley W Yorks 51 G9
Stanley Common Derbys 35 A10
Stanley Gate Lancs 43 B7
Stanley Hill Hereford 26 D3
Stanlow Ches W 43 E7
Stanmer Brighton 12 F2
Stanmore Hants 10 B3
Stanmore London 19 B8
Stanmore W Berks 17 D11
Stannergate Dundee 77 D7
Stanningley W Yorks 51 F8
Stannington Northumb 63 F8
Stannington S Yorks 45 D7
Stansbatch Hereford 25 B10
Stansfield Suff 30 C4
Stanstead Suff 30 D5
Stanstead Abbotts Herts 29 G10
Stansted Kent 20 E3
Stansted Airport Essex 30 F2
Stansted Mountfitchet Essex 30 F2
Stanton Glos 27 E7
Stanton Mon 25 F10
Stanton Northumb 63 E7
Stanton Staffs 44 H5
Stanton Suff 30 A6
Stanton by Bridge Derbys 35 C9
Stanton-by-Dale Derbys 35 B10
Stanton Drew Bath 16 E2
Stanton Fitzwarren Swindon 17 B8

Sta–Thi 133

Stanton Harcourt Oxon 27 H11
Stanton Hill Notts 45 F8
Stanton in Peak Derbys 44 F6
Stanton Lacy Shrops 33 H10
Stanton Long Shrops 34 F1
Stanton-on-the-Wolds Notts 36 B2
Stanton Prior Bath 16 E3
Stanton St Bernard Wilts 17 E7
Stanton St John Oxon 28 H2
Stanton St Quintin Wilts 16 D6
Stanton Street Suff 30 B6
Stanton under Bardon Leics 35 D10
Stanton upon Hine Heath Shrops 34 C1
Stanton Wick Bath 16 E3
Stanwardine in the Fields Shrops 33 C10
Stanwardine in the Wood Shrops 33 C10
Stanway Essex 30 F6
Stanway Glos 27 E7
Stanway Green Suff 31 A9
Stanwell Sur 19 D7
Stanwell Moor Sur 19 D7
Stanwick Northants 28 A6
Stanwick-St-John N Yorks 58 E2
Stanwix Cumb 61 H10
Stanydale Shetland 96 H4
Staoinebrig W Isles 84 E2
Stape N Yorks 59 G8
Stapehill Dorset 9 D9
Stapeley Ches E 43 H9
Stapenhill Staffs 35 C8
Staple Kent 21 F9
Staple Som 7 B10
Staple Cross E Sus 13 D6
Staple Fitzpaine Som 8 C1
Staplefield W Sus 12 D1
Stapleford Cambs 29 C11
Stapleford Herts 29 G10
Stapleford Leics 36 D4
Stapleford Lincs 46 G2
Stapleford Notts 35 B10
Stapleford Wilts 17 H7
Stapleford Abbotts Essex 20 B2
Stapleford Tawney Essex 20 B2
Staplegrove Som 7 D11
Staplehay Som 7 D11
Staplehurst Kent 13 B6
Staplers IoW 10 F4
Stapleton Bristol 16 D3
Stapleton Cumb 61 F11
Stapleton Hereford 25 B10
Stapleton Leics 35 F10
Stapleton N Yorks 58 E3
Stapleton Shrops 33 E10
Stapleton Som 8 B3
Stapley Som 7 E10
Staploe Bedford 29 B8
Staplow Hereford 26 D3
Star Fife 76 G6
Star Pembs 23 C7
Star Som 15 F10
Stara Orkney 95 F3
Starbeck N Yorks 51 D9
Starbotton N Yorks 50 B5
Starcross Devon 5 C10
Stareton Warks 27 A10
Starkholmes Derbys 45 G7
Starlings Green Essex 29 E11
Starston Norf 39 G8
Startforth Durham 58 E1
Startley Wilts 16 C6
Stathe Som 8 B2
Stathern Leics 36 B3
Station Town Durham 58 C5
Staughton Green Cambs 29 B8
Staughton Highway Cambs 29 B8
Staunton Glos 26 F4
Staunton Glos 26 G2
Staunton in the Vale Notts 36 A4
Staunton on Arrow Hereford 25 B10
Staunton on Wye Hereford 25 D10
Staveley Cumb 56 G6
Staveley Cumb 56 H5
Staveley Derbys 45 E8
Staveley N Yorks 51 C9
Staverton Devon 5 E8
Staverton Glos 26 F5
Staverton Northants 28 B2
Staverton Wilts 16 E5
Staverton Bridge Glos 26 F5
Stawell Som 15 H9
Staxigoe Highld 94 E5
Staxton N Yorks 52 B6
Staylittle Powys 32 F4
Staynall Lancs 49 E3
Staythorpe Notts 45 G11
Stean N Yorks 51 B6
Stearsby N Yorks 52 B2
Steart Som 15 G8
Stebbing Essex 30 F3
Stebbing Green Essex 30 F3
Stedham W Sus 11 B7
Steele Road Borders 61 D11
Steen's Bridge Hereford 26 C2
Steep Hants 10 B6
Steep Marsh Hants 11 B6
Steeple Dorset 9 F8
Steeple Essex 20 A6
Steeple Ashton Wilts 16 F6
Steeple Aston Oxon 27 F11
Steeple Barton Oxon 27 F11
Steeple Bumpstead Essex 30 D3
Steeple Claydon Bucks 28 F3
Steeple Gidding Cambs 37 G7
Steeple Langford Wilts 17 H7
Steeple Morden Cambs 29 D9
Steeton W Yorks 50 E6
Stein Highld 84 C7
Steinmanhill Aberds 89 D7
Stelling Minnis Kent 21 G8
Stemster Highld 94 D3
Stemster Ho. Highld 94 D3
Stenalees Corn 3 D9
Stenhousemuir Falk 69 B7
Stenigot Lincs 46 D6
Stenness Shetland 96 F4
Stenscholl Highld 85 B9
Stenso Orkney 95 F4
Stenson Derbys 35 C9
Stenton E Loth 70 C5
Stenton Fife 76 H5
Stenwith Lincs 36 B4
Stepaside Pembs 22 F6
Stepping Hill Gtr Man 44 D3
Steppingley C Beds 29 E7
Stepps N Lanark 68 D5
Sterndale Moor Derbys 44 F5
Sternfield Suff 31 B10
Sterridge Devon 6 B4
Stert Wilts 17 F7
Stetchworth Cambs 30 C3
Stevenage Herts 29 F9
Stevenston N Ayrs 66 B5
Steventon Hants 18 G2
Steventon Oxon 17 B11
Stevington Bedford 28 C6
Stewartby Bedford 29 D7
Stewarton Argyll 65 G7
Stewarton E Ayrs 67 B7
Stewkley Bucks 28 F5
Stewton Lincs 47 D7
Steyne Cross IoW 10 F5
Steyning W Sus 11 C10
Steynton Pembs 22 F4
Stibb Corn 6 E1
Stibb Cross Devon 6 E3
Stibb Green Wilts 17 E9
Stibbard Norf 38 C5
Stibbington Cambs 37 F6
Stichill Borders 70 G6
Sticker Corn 3 D8
Stickford Lincs 47 G7
Sticklepath Devon 6 G5
Stickney Lincs 47 G7
Stiffkey Norf 38 A5
Stifford's Bridge Hereford 26 D4
Stillingfleet N Yorks 52 E1
Stillington N Yorks 52 C1
Stillington Stockton 58 D4
Stilton Cambs 37 G7
Stinchcombe Glos 16 B4
Stinsford Dorset 8 E6
Stirchley Telford 34 E3
Stirkoke Ho. Highld 94 E5
Stirling Aberds 89 D11
Stirling Stirling 68 A6
Stisted Essex 30 F4
Stithians Corn 2 F6
Stittenham Highld 87 D9
Stivichall W Mid 35 H9
Stixwould Lincs 46 F5
Stoak Ches W 43 E7
Stobieside S Lanark 68 G5
Stobo Borders 69 G10
Stoborough Dorset 9 F8
Stoborough Green Dorset 9 F8
Stobshiel E Loth 70 D3
Stobswood Northumb 63 D8
Stock Essex 20 B3
Stock Green Worcs 26 C6
Stock Wood Worcs 27 C7
Stockbridge Hants 10 A2
Stockbury Kent 20 E5
Stockcross W Berks 17 E11
Stockdalewath Cumb 56 B5
Stockerston Leics 36 F4
Stockheath Hants 10 D6
Stockiemuir Stirling 68 B4
Stocking Pelham Herts 29 F11
Stockingford Warks 35 F9
Stockland Devon 8 D1
Stockland Bristol Som 15 G8
Stockleigh English Devon 7 F7
Stockleigh Pomeroy Devon 7 F7
Stockley Wilts 17 E7
Stocklinch Som 8 C2
Stockport Gtr Man 44 C2
Stocksbridge S Yorks 44 C6
Stocksfield Northumb 62 G6
Stockton Hereford 26 B2
Stockton Norf 39 F9
Stockton Shrops 33 E8
Stockton Shrops 34 F3
Stockton Warks 27 B11
Stockton Wilts 16 H6
Stockton Heath Warr 43 D9
Stockton-on-Tees Stockton 58 E5
Stockton on Teme Worcs 26 B4
Stockton on the Forest York 52 D2
Stodmarsh Kent 21 E9
Stody Norf 39 B6
Stoer Highld 92 G3
Stoford Som 8 C4
Stoford Wilts 17 H7
Stogumber Som 7 C9
Stogursey Som 7 B11
Stoke Devon 6 D1
Stoke Hants 10 D6
Stoke Hants 17 F11
Stoke Medway 20 D5
Stoke Suff 31 D8
Stoke Abbott Dorset 8 D3
Stoke Albany Northants 36 G4
Stoke Ash Suff 31 A8
Stoke Bardolph Notts 36 A2
Stoke Bliss Worcs 26 B3
Stoke Bruerne Northants 28 D4
Stoke by Clare Suff 30 D4
Stoke-by-Nayland Suff 30 E6
Stoke Canon Devon 7 G8
Stoke Charity Hants 17 H11
Stoke Climsland Corn 4 D4
Stoke D'Abernon Sur 19 F8
Stoke Doyle Northants 36 G6
Stoke Dry Rutland 36 F4
Stoke Farthing Wilts 9 B9
Stoke Ferry Norf 38 F3
Stoke Fleming Devon 5 G9
Stoke Gabriel Devon 5 F9
Stoke Gifford S Glos 16 D3
Stoke Golding Leics 35 F9
Stoke Goldington M Keynes 28 D5
Stoke Green Bucks 18 C6
Stoke Hammond Bucks 28 F5
Stoke Heath Shrops 34 C2
Stoke Holy Cross Norf 39 E8
Stoke Lacy Hereford 26 D3
Stoke Lyne Oxon 28 F2
Stoke Mandeville Bucks 28 G5
Stoke Newington London 19 C10
Stoke on Tern Shrops 34 C2
Stoke-on-Trent Stoke 44 H2
Stoke Orchard Glos 26 F6
Stoke Poges Bucks 18 C6
Stoke Prior Hereford 26 C2
Stoke Prior Worcs 26 B6
Stoke Rivers Devon 6 C5
Stoke Rochford Lincs 36 C5
Stoke Row Oxon 18 C3
Stoke St Gregory Som 8 B2
Stoke St Mary Som 8 B1
Stoke St Michael Som 16 G3
Stoke St Milborough Shrops 34 G1
Stoke sub Hamdon Som 8 C3
Stoke Talmage Oxon 18 B3
Stoke Trister Som 8 B6
Stoke Wake Dorset 9 D6
Stokeford Dorset 9 F7
Stokeham Notts 45 E11
Stokeinteignhead Devon 5 D10
Stokenchurch Bucks 18 B4
Stokenham Devon 5 G9
Stokesay Shrops 33 G10
Stokesby Norf 39 D10
Stokesley N Yorks 59 F6
Stolford Som 7 B11
Ston Easton Som 16 F3
Stondon Massey Essex 20 A2
Stone Bucks 28 G4
Stone Glos 16 B3
Stone Kent 13 D8
Stone Kent 20 D2
Stone S Yorks 45 D9
Stone Staffs 34 B5
Stone Worcs 34 H4
Stone Allerton Som 15 F10
Stone Bridge Corner Pboro 37 E8
Stone Chair W Yorks 51 G7
Stone Cross E Sus 12 F5
Stone Cross Kent 21 F10
Stone-edge Batch N Som 15 D10
Stone House Cumb 57 H9
Stone Street Kent 20 F2
Stone Street Suff 30 E6
Stone Street Suff 39 G9
Stonebroom Derbys 45 G8
Stoneferry Hull 53 F7
Stonefield S Lanark 68 E5
Stonegate E Sus 12 D5
Stonegate N Yorks 59 F8
Stonegrave N Yorks 52 B2
Stonehaugh Northumb 62 F3
Stonehaven Aberds 83 E10
Stonehouse Glos 26 H5
Stonehouse Northumb 62 H2
Stonehouse S Lanark 68 F6
Stoneleigh Warks 27 A10
Stonely Cambs 29 B8
Stoner Hill Hants 10 B6
Stone's Green Essex 31 F8
Stonesby Leics 36 C4
Stonesfield Oxon 27 G10
Stonethwaite Cumb 56 E4
Stoney Cross Hants 10 C1
Stoney Middleton Derbys 44 E6
Stoney Stanton Leics 35 F10
Stoney Stoke Som 8 A6
Stoney Stratton Som 16 H3
Stoney Stretton Shrops 33 E9
Stoneybreck Shetland 96 N8
Stoneyburn W Loth 69 D8
Stoneygate Aberds 89 E10
Stoneygate Leicester 36 E2
Stoneyhills Essex 20 B6
Stoneykirk Dumfries 54 D3
Stoneywood Aberdeen 83 B10
Stoneywood Falk 68 B6
Stonganess Shetland 96 C7
Stonham Aspal Suff 31 C8
Stonnall Staffs 35 E6
Stonor Oxon 18 C4
Stonton Wyville Leics 36 F3
Stony Cross Hereford 26 D4
Stony Stratford M Keynes 28 D4
Stonyfield Highld 87 D9
Stoodleigh Devon 7 E8
Stopes S Yorks 44 D6
Stopham W Sus 11 C9
Stopsley Luton 29 F8
Stores Corner Suff 31 D10
Storeton Mers 42 D6
Stornoway W Isles 91 D9
Storridge Hereford 26 D4
Storrington W Sus 11 C9
Storrs Cumb 56 G5
Storth Cumb 49 A4
Storwood E Yorks 52 E3
Stotfield Moray 88 A2
Stotfold C Beds 29 E9
Stottesdon Shrops 34 G2
Stoughton Leics 36 E2
Stoughton Sur 18 F6
Stoughton W Sus 11 C7
Stoul Highld 79 B10
Stoulton Worcs 26 D6
Stour Provost Dorset 9 B6
Stour Row Dorset 9 B7
Stourbridge W Mid 34 G5
Stourpaine Dorset 9 D7
Stourport on Severn Worcs 26 A5
Stourton Staffs 34 G4
Stourton Warks 27 E9
Stourton Wilts 9 A6
Stourton Caundle Dorset 8 C6
Stove Orkney 95 E7
Stove Shetland 96 L6
Stoven Suff 39 G10
Stow Borders 70 F3
Stow Lincs 37 B6
Stow Lincs 46 D2
Stow Bardolph Norf 38 E2
Stow Bedon Norf 38 F5
Stow cum Quy Cambs 30 B2
Stow Longa Cambs 29 A8
Stow Maries Essex 20 B5
Stow-on-the-Wold Glos 27 F8
Stowbridge Norf 38 E2
Stowe Shrops 25 A10
Stowe-by-Chartley Staffs 34 C6
Stowe Green Glos 26 H2
Stowell Som 8 B5
Stowford Devon 4 C5
Stowlangtoft Suff 30 B6
Stowmarket Suff 31 C7
Stowting Kent 13 B10
Stowupland Suff 31 C7
Straad Argyll 73 G9
Strachan Aberds 83 D8
Stradbroke Suff 31 A9
Stradishall Suff 30 C4
Stradsett Norf 38 E2
Stragglethorpe Lincs 46 G3
Straid S Ayrs 66 G4
Straith Dumfries 60 E4
Straiton Edin 69 D11
Straiton S Ayrs 67 F6
Straloch Aberds 89 F8
Straloch Perth 76 A3
Stramshall Staffs 35 B6
Strang IoM 48 E3
Stranraer Dumfries 54 C3
Stratfield Mortimer W Berks 18 E3
Stratfield Saye Hants 18 E3
Stratfield Turgis Hants 18 F3
Stratford London 19 C10
Stratford St Andrew Suff 31 B10
Stratford St Mary Suff 31 E7
Stratford Sub Castle Wilts 9 A10
Stratford Tony Wilts 9 B9
Stratford-upon-Avon Warks 27 C8
Strath Highld 85 A12
Strath Highld 94 E4
Strathan Highld 80 D1
Strathan Highld 92 G3
Strathan Highld 93 C8
Strathaven S Lanark 68 F6
Strathblane Stirling 68 C4
Strathcanaird Highld 92 J4
Strathcarron Highld 86 G2
Strathcoil Argyll 79 H9
Strathdon Aberds 82 B5
Strathellie Aberds 89 B10
Strathkinness Fife 77 F7
Strathmashie House Highld 81 D7
Strathmiglo Fife 76 F5
Strathmore Lodge Highld 94 F3
Strathpeffer Highld 86 F7
Strathrannoch Highld 86 D6
Strathtay Perth 76 B2
Strathvaich Lodge Highld 86 D6
Strathwhillan N Ayrs 66 C3
Strathy Highld 93 C11
Strathyre Stirling 75 F8
Stratton Corn 6 F1
Stratton Dorset 8 E5
Stratton Glos 17 A7
Stratton Audley Oxon 28 F3
Stratton on the Fosse Som 16 F3
Stratton St Margaret Swindon 17 C8
Stratton St Michael Norf 39 F8
Stratton Strawless Norf 39 C8
Stravithie Fife 77 F8
Streat E Sus 12 E2
Streatham London 19 D10
Streatley C Beds 29 F7
Streatley W Berks 18 C2
Street Lancs 49 D5
Street N Yorks 59 F8
Street Som 15 H10
Street Dinas Shrops 33 B9
Street End Kent 21 F8
Street End W Sus 11 E7
Street Gate T&W 63 H8
Street Lydan Wrex 33 B10
Streethay Staffs 35 D7
Streetlam N Yorks 58 G4
Streetly W Mid 35 F6
Streetly End Cambs 30 D3
Strefford Shrops 33 G10
Strelley Notts 35 A11
Strensall York 52 C2
Stretcholt Som 15 G8
Strete Devon 5 G9
Stretford Gtr Man 44 C2
Strethall Essex 29 E11
Stretham Cambs 30 A2
Strettington W Sus 11 D7
Stretton Ches W 43 G7
Stretton Derbys 45 F7
Stretton Rutland 36 D5
Stretton Staffs 34 D4
Stretton Staffs 35 C8
Stretton Warr 43 D9
Stretton Grandison Hereford 26 D3
Stretton-on-Dunsmore Warks 27 A11
Stretton-on-Fosse Warks 27 E9
Stretton Sugwas Hereford 25 D11
Stretton under Fosse Warks 35 G10
Stretton Westwood Shrops 34 F1
Strichen Aberds 89 C9
Strines Gtr Man 44 D3
Stringston Som 7 B10
Strixton Northants 28 B6
Stroat Glos 16 B2
Stromeferry Highld 85 E13
Stromemore Highld 85 E13
Stromness Orkney 95 H3
Stronaba Highld 80 E4
Stronachlachar Stirling 75 F7
Stronchreggan Highld 80 F2
Stronchrubie Highld 92 H5
Strone Argyll 73 E10
Strone Highld 80 E3
Strone Highld 81 A7
Strone Invclyd 73 F11
Stronmilchan Argyll 74 E4
Strontian Highld 79 E11
Strood Medway 20 E4
Strood Green Sur 19 G9
Strood Green W Sus 11 A10
Strood Green W Sus 11 B9
Stroud Glos 26 H5
Stroud Hants 10 B6
Stroud Green Essex 20 B5
Stroxton Lincs 36 B5
Struan Highld 85 E8
Struan Perth 81 G10
Strubby Lincs 47 D8
Strumpshaw Norf 39 E9
Strutherhill S Lanark 68 F6
Struy Highld 86 H6
Stryt-issa Wrex 42 H5
Stuartfield Aberds 89 D9
Stub Place Cumb 56 G2
Stubbington Hants 10 D4
Stubbins Lancs 50 H3
Stubbs Cross Kent 13 C8
Stubbs Green Norf 39 F9
Stubb's Green Norf 39 F8
Stubhampton Dorset 9 C8
Stubton Lincs 46 H2
Stuckgowan Argyll 74 G6
Stuckton Hants 9 C10
Stud Green Windsor 18 D5
Studham C Beds 29 G7
Studland Dorset 9 F9
Studley Warks 27 B7
Studley Wilts 16 D6
Studley Roger N Yorks 51 B8
Stump Cross Essex 30 D2
Stuntney Cambs 38 H1
Sturbridge Staffs 34 B4
Sturmer Essex 30 D3
Sturminster Marshall Dorset 9 D8
Sturminster Newton Dorset 9 C6
Sturry Kent 21 E8
Sturton N Lincs 46 B3
Sturton by Stow Lincs 46 D2
Sturton le Steeple Notts 45 D11
Stuston Suff 39 H7
Stutton N Yorks 51 E10
Stutton Suff 31 E8
Styal Ches E 44 D2
Styrrup Notts 45 C10
Suainebost W Isles 91 A10
Suardail W Isles 91 D9
Succoth Aberds 88 E4
Succoth Argyll 74 G5
Suckley Worcs 26 C4
Suckquoy Orkney 95 K5
Sudborough Northants 36 G5
Sudbourne Suff 31 C11
Sudbrook Lincs 36 A5
Sudbrook Mon 15 C11
Sudbrooke Lincs 46 E4
Sudbury Derbys 35 B7
Sudbury London 19 C8
Sudbury Suff 30 D5
Suddie Highld 87 F9
Sudgrove Glos 26 H6
Suffield N Yorks 59 G10
Suffield Norf 39 B8
Sugnall Staffs 34 B3
Suladale Highld 85 C8
Sulaisiadar W Isles 91 D10
Sulby IoM 48 C3
Sulgrave Northants 28 D2
Sulham W Berks 18 D3
Sulhamstead W Berks 18 E3
Sulland Orkney 95 D6
Sullington W Sus 11 C9
Sullom Shetland 96 F5
Sullom Voe Oil Terminal Shetland 96 F5
Sully V Glam 15 E7
Sumburgh Shetland 96 N6
Summer Bridge N Yorks 51 C8
Summer-house Darl 58 E3
Summercourt Corn 3 D7
Summerfield Norf 38 B3
Summergangs Hull 53 F7
Summerleaze Mon 15 C10
Summersdale W Sus 11 D7
Summerseat Gtr Man 43 A10
Summertown Oxon 28 H2
Summit Gtr Man 44 B3
Sunbury-on-Thames Sur 19 E8
Sundaywell Dumfries 60 E4
Sunderland Argyll 64 B3
Sunderland Cumb 56 C3
Sunderland T&W 63 H9
Sunderland Bridge Durham 58 C3
Sundhope Borders 70 H2
Sundon Park Luton 29 F7
Sundridge Kent 19 F11
Sunipol Argyll 78 F6
Sunk Island E Yorks 53 H8
Sunningdale Windsor 18 E6
Sunninghill Windsor 18 E6
Sunningwell Oxon 17 A11
Sunniside Durham 58 C2
Sunniside T&W 63 H8
Sunnyhurst Blackburn 50 G2
Sunnylaw Stirling 75 H10
Sunnyside W Sus 12 C2
Sunton Wilts 17 F9
Surbiton London 19 E8
Surby IoM 48 E2
Surfleet Lincs 37 C8
Surfleet Seas End Lincs 37 C8
Surlingham Norf 39 E9
Sustead Norf 39 B7
Susworth Lincs 46 B2
Sutcombe Devon 6 E2
Suton Norf 39 F6
Sutors of Cromarty Highld 87 E11
Sutterby Lincs 47 E7
Sutterton Lincs 37 B8
Sutton C Beds 29 D9
Sutton Cambs 37 H10
Sutton Kent 21 G10
Sutton London 19 E9
Sutton Mers 43 C8
Sutton N Yorks 51 G10
Sutton Norf 39 C9
Sutton Notts 36 B3
Sutton Notts 45 D10
Sutton Oxon 27 H11
Sutton Pboro 37 F6
Sutton S Yorks 45 A9
Sutton Shrops 34 B2
Sutton Shrops 34 G3
Sutton Som 8 A5
Sutton Staffs 34 C3
Sutton Suff 31 D10
Sutton Sur 19 G7
Sutton W Sus 11 C8
Sutton at Hone Kent 20 D2
Sutton Bassett Northants 36 F3
Sutton Benger Wilts 16 D6
Sutton Bonington Notts 35 C11
Sutton Bridge Lincs 37 C10
Sutton Cheney Leics 35 E10
Sutton Coldfield W Mid 35 F7
Sutton Courtenay Oxon 18 B2
Sutton Crosses Lincs 37 C10
Sutton Grange N Yorks 51 B8
Sutton Green Sur 19 F7
Sutton Howgrave N Yorks 51 B9
Sutton In Ashfield Notts 45 G8
Sutton-in-Craven N Yorks 50 E6
Sutton in the Elms Leics 35 F11
Sutton Ings Hull 53 F7
Sutton Lane Ends Ches E 44 E3
Sutton Leach Mers 43 C8
Sutton Maddock Shrops 34 E3
Sutton Mallet Som 15 H9
Sutton Mandeville Wilts 9 B8
Sutton Manor Mers 43 C8
Sutton Montis Som 8 B5
Sutton on Hull Hull 53 F7
Sutton on Sea Lincs 47 D9
Sutton-on-the-Forest N Yorks 52 C1
Sutton on the Hill Derbys 35 B8
Sutton on Trent Notts 45 F11
Sutton St Edmund Lincs 37 D9
Sutton St James Lincs 37 D9
Sutton St Nicholas Hereford 26 D2
Sutton Scarsdale Derbys 45 F8
Sutton Scotney Hants 17 H11
Sutton under Brailes Warks 27 E10
Sutton-under-Whitestonecliffe N Yorks 51 A10
Sutton upon Derwent E Yorks 52 E3
Sutton Valence Kent 20 G5
Sutton Veny Wilts 16 G5
Sutton Waldron Dorset 9 C7
Sutton Weaver Ches W 43 E8
Sutton Wick Bath 16 F2
Swaby Lincs 47 E7
Swadlincote Derbys 35 D9
Swaffham Norf 38 E4
Swaffham Bulbeck Cambs 30 B2
Swaffham Prior Cambs 30 B2
Swafield Norf 39 B8
Swainby N Yorks 58 F5
Swainshill Hereford 25 D11
Swainsthorpe Norf 39 E8
Swainswick Bath 16 E4
Swalcliffe Oxon 27 E10
Swalecliffe Kent 21 E8
Swallow Lincs 46 B5
Swallowcliffe Wilts 9 B8
Swallowfield Wokingham 18 E4
Swallownest S Yorks 45 D8
Swallows Cross Essex 20 B3
Swan Green Ches W 43 E10
Swan Green Suff 31 A9
Swanage Dorset 9 G9
Swanbister Orkney 95 H4
Swanbourne Bucks 28 F5
Swanland E Yorks 52 G5
Swanley Kent 20 E2
Swanley Village Kent 20 E2
Swanmore Hants 10 C4
Swannington Leics 35 D10
Swannington Norf 39 D7
Swanscombe Kent 20 D3
Swansea = Abertawe Swansea 14 B2
Swanton Abbott Norf 39 C8
Swanton Morley Norf 38 D6
Swanton Novers Norf 38 B6
Swanton Street Kent 20 F5
Swanwick Derbys 45 G8
Swanwick Hants 10 D4
Swarby Lincs 36 A6
Swardeston Norf 39 E8
Swarister Shetland 96 E7
Swarkestone Derbys 35 C9
Swarland Northumb 63 C7
Swarland Estate Northumb 63 C7
Swarthmoor Cumb 49 B2
Swathwick Derbys 45 F7
Swaton Lincs 37 B7
Swavesey Cambs 29 B10
Sway Hants 10 E1
Swayfield Lincs 36 C5
Swaythling Soton 10 C3
Sweet Green Worcs 26 B3
Sweetham Devon 7 G7
Sweethouse Corn 4 E1
Sweffling Suff 31 B10
Swepstone Leics 35 D9
Swerford Oxon 27 E10
Swettenham Ches E 44 F2
Swetton N Yorks 51 B7
Swffryd Caerph 15 B8
Swiftsden E Sus 12 D6
Swilland Suff 31 C8
Swillington W Yorks 51 F9
Swimbridge Devon 6 D5
Swimbridge Newland Devon 6 C5
Swinbrook Oxon 27 G9
Swinderby Lincs 46 F2
Swindon Glos 26 F6
Swindon Staffs 34 F4
Swindon Swindon 17 C8
Swine E Yorks 53 F7
Swinefleet E Yorks 52 G3
Swineshead Bedford 29 B7
Swineshead Lincs 37 A8
Swineshead Bridge Lincs 37 A8
Swiney Highld 94 G4
Swinford Leics 36 H1
Swinford Oxon 27 H11
Swingate Notts 35 A11
Swingfield Minnis Kent 21 G9
Swingfield Street Kent 21 G9
Swinhoe Northumb 71 H11
Swinhope Lincs 46 C6
Swining Shetland 96 G6
Swinithwaite N Yorks 58 H1
Swinnow Moor W Yorks 51 F8
Swinscoe Staffs 44 H5
Swinside Hall Borders 62 B3
Swinstead Lincs 36 C6
Swinton Borders 71 F7
Swinton Gtr Man 43 B10
Swinton N Yorks 51 B8
Swinton N Yorks 52 B3
Swinton S Yorks 45 C8
Swintonmill Borders 71 F7
Swithland Leics 35 D11
Swordale Highld 87 E8
Swordland Highld 79 B10
Swordly Highld 93 C10
Sworton Heath Ches E 43 D9
Swydd-ffynnon Ceredig 24 B3
Swynnerton Staffs 34 B4
Swyre Dorset 8 F4
Sychtyn Powys 32 E5
Syde Glos 26 G6
Sydenham London 19 D10
Sydenham Oxon 18 A4
Sydenham Damerel Devon 4 D5
Syderstone Norf 38 B4
Sydling St Nicholas Dorset 8 E5
Sydmonton Hants 17 F11
Syerston Notts 45 H11
Syke Gtr Man 50 H4
Sykehouse S Yorks 52 H2
Sykes Lancs 50 D2
Syleham Suff 39 H8
Sylen Carms 23 F10
Symbister Shetland 96 G7
Symington S Ayrs 67 C6
Symington S Lanark 69 G8
Symonds Yat Hereford 26 G2
Symondsbury Dorset 8 E3
Synod Inn Ceredig 23 A9
Syre Highld 93 E9
Syreford Glos 27 F7
Syresham Northants 28 D3
Syston Leics 36 D2
Syston Lincs 36 A5
Sytchampton Worcs 26 B5
Sywell Northants 28 B5

T

Taagan Highld 86 E3
Tabost W Isles 91 F8
Tàbost W Isles 91 A10
Tackley Oxon 27 F11
Tacleit W Isles 90 D6
Tacolneston Norf 39 F7
Tadcaster N Yorks 51 E10
Taddington Derbys 44 E5
Taddiport Devon 6 E3
Tadley Hants 18 E3
Tadlow C Beds 29 D9
Tadmarton Oxon 27 E10
Tadworth Sur 19 F9
Tafarn-y-gelyn Denb 42 F4
Tafarnau-bach Bl Gwent 25 G8
Taff's Well Rhondda 15 C7
Tafolwern Powys 32 E4
Tai Conwy 41 D9
Tai-bach Powys 33 C7
Tai-mawr Conwy 32 A5
Tai-Ucha Denb 42 G3
Taibach Neath 14 C3
Taigh a Ghearraidh W Isles 84 A2
Tain Highld 87 C10
Tain Highld 94 D4
Tainant Wrex 42 H5
Tainlon Gwyn 40 E6
Tai'r-Bull Powys 24 F6
Tairbeart = Tarbert W Isles 90 G6
Tairgwaith Neath 24 G4
Takeley Essex 30 F2
Takeley Street Essex 30 F2
Tal-sarn Ceredig 23 A10
Tal-y-bont Ceredig 32 G2
Tal-y-Bont Conwy 41 D9
Tal-y-bont Gwyn 32 C1
Tal-y-bont Gwyn 41 C8
Tal-y-cafn Conwy 41 C9
Tal-y-llyn Gwyn 32 E3
Tal-y-wern Powys 32 E4
Talachddu Powys 25 E7
Talacre Flint 42 D4
Talardd Gwyn 32 C4
Talaton Devon 7 G9
Talbenny Pembs 22 E3
Talbot Green Rhondda 14 C6
Talbot Village Poole 9 E9
Tale Devon 7 F9
Talerddig Powys 32 E5
Talgarreg Ceredig 23 A9
Talgarth Powys 25 E8
Talisker Highld 85 E8
Talke Staffs 44 G2
Talkin Cumb 61 H11
Talla Linnfoots Borders 61 A7
Talladale Highld 86 D2
Tallarn Green Wrex 33 A10
Tallentire Cumb 56 C3
Talley Carms 24 E3
Tallington Lincs 37 E6
Talmine Highld 93 C8
Talog Carms 23 D8
Talsarn Carms 24 F4
Talsarnau Gwyn 41 G8
Talskiddy Corn 3 C8
Talwrn Anglesey 40 C6
Talwrn Wrex 42 H5
Talybont-on-Usk Powys 25 F8
Talygarn Rhondda 14 C6
Talyllyn Powys 25 F8
Talysarn Gwyn 40 E6
Talywain Torf 15 A8
Tame Bridge N Yorks 58 F6
Tamerton Foliot Plym 4 E5
Tamworth Staffs 35 E8
Tan Hinon Powys 32 G4
Tan-lan Conwy 41 D9
Tan-lan Gwyn 41 F8
Tan-y-bwlch Gwyn 41 F8
Tan-y-fron Conwy 42 F2
Tan-y-graig Anglesey 41 C7
Tan-y-graig Gwyn 40 G5
Tan-y-groes Ceredig 23 B7
Tan-y-pistyll Powys 33 C6
Tan-yr-allt Gwyn 40 E6
Tandem W Yorks 51 H7
Tanden Kent 13 C8
Tandridge Sur 19 F10
Tanerdy Carms 23 D9
Tanfield Durham 63 H7
Tanfield Lea Durham 58 A2
Tangasdal W Isles 84 J1
Tangiers Pembs 22 E4
Tangley Hants 17 F10
Tanglwst Carms 23 C8
Tangmere W Sus 11 D8
Tangwick Shetland 96 F4
Tankersley S Yorks 45 B7
Tankerton Kent 21 E8
Tannach Highld 94 F5
Tannachie Aberds 83 E9
Tannadice Angus 77 B7
Tannington Suff 31 B9
Tansley Derbys 45 G7
Tansley Knoll Derbys 45 F7
Tansor Northants 37 F6
Tantobie Durham 58 A2
Tanton N Yorks 58 E6
Tanworth-in-Arden Warks 27 A8
Tanygrisiau Gwyn 41 F8
Tanyrhydiau Ceredig 24 B4
Taobh a Chaolais W Isles 84 G2
Taobh a' Ghlinne W Isles 91 F8
Taobh a Thuath Loch Aineort W Isles 84 F2
Taobh a Tuath Loch Baghasdail W Isles 84 F2
Taobh Tuath W Isles 90 J4
Taplow Bucks 18 C6
Tapton Derbys 45 E7
Tarbat Ho. Highld 87 D10
Tarbert Argyll 65 C7
Tarbert Argyll 72 E5
Tarbert Argyll 73 G7
Tarbert = Tairbeart W Isles 90 G6
Tarbet Argyll 74 G6
Tarbet Highld 79 B10
Tarbet Highld 92 E4
Tarbock Green Mers 43 D7
Tarbolton S Ayrs 67 D7
Tarbrax S Lanark 69 E9
Tardebigge Worcs 27 B7
Tarfside Angus 82 F6
Tarland Aberds 82 C6
Tarleton Lancs 49 G4
Tarlogie Highld 87 C10
Tarlscough Lancs 43 A7
Tarlton Glos 16 B6
Tarnbrook Lancs 50 D1
Tarporley Ches W 43 F8
Tarr Som 7 C10
Tarrant Crawford Dorset 9 D8
Tarrant Gunville Dorset 9 C8
Tarrant Hinton Dorset 9 C8
Tarrant Keyneston Dorset 9 D8
Tarrant Launceston Dorset 9 D8
Tarrant Monkton Dorset 9 D8
Tarrant Rawston Dorset 9 D8
Tarrant Rushton Dorset 9 D8
Tarrel Highld 87 C11
Tarring Neville E Sus 12 F3
Tarrington Hereford 26 D3
Tarsappie Perth 76 E4
Tarskavaig Highld 85 H10
Tarves Aberds 89 E8
Tarvie Highld 86 F7
Tarvie Perth 76 A3
Tarvin Ches W 43 F7
Tasburgh Norf 39 F8
Tasley Shrops 34 F2
Taston Oxon 27 F10
Tatenhill Staffs 35 C8
Tathall End M Keynes 28 D5
Tatham Lancs 50 C2
Tathwell Lincs 47 D7
Tatling End Bucks 19 C7
Tatsfield Sur 19 F11
Tattenhall Ches W 43 G7
Tattenhoe M Keynes 28 E5
Tatterford Norf 38 C4
Tattersett Norf 38 B4
Tattershall Lincs 46 G6
Tattershall Bridge Lincs 46 G5
Tattershall Thorpe Lincs 46 G6
Tattingstone Suff 31 E8
Tatworth Som 8 D2
Taunton Som 7 D11
Taverham Norf 39 D7
Tavernspite Pembs 22 E6
Tavistock Devon 4 D5
Taw Green Devon 6 G5
Tawstock Devon 6 D4
Taxal Derbys 44 E4
Tay Bridge Dundee 77 E7
Tayinloan Argyll 65 D7
Taymouth Castle Perth 75 C10
Taynish Argyll 72 E6
Taynton Glos 26 F4
Taynton Oxon 27 G9
Taynuilt Argyll 74 D3
Tayport Fife 77 E7
Tayvallich Argyll 72 E6
Tealby Lincs 46 C5
Tealing Angus 77 D7
Teangue Highld 85 H11
Teanna Mhachair W Isles 84 B2
Tebay Cumb 57 F8
Tebworth C Beds 28 F6
Tedburn St Mary Devon 7 G7
Teddington Glos 26 E6
Teddington London 19 D8
Tedstone Delamere Hereford 26 C3
Tedstone Wafre Hereford 26 C3
Teeton Northants 28 A3
Teffont Evias Wilts 9 A8
Teffont Magna Wilts 9 A8
Tegryn Pembs 23 C7
Teigh Rutland 36 D4
Teigncombe Devon 5 C7
Teigngrace Devon 5 D9
Teignmouth Devon 5 D10
Telford Telford 34 E2
Telham E Sus 13 E6
Tellisford Som 16 F5
Telscombe E Sus 12 F3
Telscombe Cliffs E Sus 12 F2
Templand Dumfries 60 E6
Temple Corn 4 D2
Temple Glasgow 68 D4
Temple Midloth 70 E2
Temple Balsall W Mid 35 H8
Temple Bar Carms 23 E10
Temple Bar Ceredig 23 A10
Temple Cloud Bath 16 F3
Temple Combe Som 8 B6
Temple Ewell Kent 21 G9
Temple Grafton Warks 27 C8
Temple Guiting Glos 27 F7
Temple Herdewyke Warks 27 C10
Temple Hirst N Yorks 52 G2
Temple Normanton Derbys 45 F8
Temple Sowerby Cumb 57 D8
Templehall Fife 69 A11
Templeton Devon 7 E7
Templeton Pembs 22 E6
Templeton Bridge Devon 7 E7
Templetown Durham 58 A2
Tempsford C Beds 29 C8
Ten Mile Bank Norf 38 F2
Tenbury Wells Worcs 26 B2
Tenby = Dinbych-y-Pysgod Pembs 22 F6
Tendring Essex 31 F8
Tendring Green Essex 31 F8
Tenston Orkney 95 G3
Tenterden Kent 13 C7
Terling Essex 30 G4
Ternhill Shrops 34 B2
Terregles Banks Dumfries 60 F5
Terrick Bucks 28 H5
Terrington N Yorks 52 B2
Terrington St Clement Norf 37 D11
Terrington St John Norf 37 D11
Teston Kent 20 F4
Testwood Hants 10 C2
Tetbury Glos 16 B5
Tetbury Upton Glos 16 B5
Tetchill Shrops 33 B9
Tetcott Devon 6 G2
Tetford Lincs 47 E7
Tetney Lincs 47 B7
Tetney Lock Lincs 47 B7
Tetsworth Oxon 18 A3
Tettenhall W Mid 34 E4
Teuchan Aberds 89 E10
Teversal Notts 45 F8
Teversham Cambs 29 C11
Teviothead Borders 61 C10
Tewel Aberds 83 E10
Tewin Herts 29 G9
Tewkesbury Glos 26 E5
Teynham Kent 20 E6
Thackthwaite Cumb 56 D3
Thainston Aberds 83 F8
Thakeham W Sus 11 C10
Thame Oxon 28 H4
Thames Ditton Sur 19 E8
Thames Haven Thurrock 20 C4
Thamesmead London 19 C11
Thanington Kent 21 F8
Thankerton S Lanark 69 G8
Tharston Norf 39 F7
Thatcham W Berks 18 E2
Thatto Heath Mers 43 C8
Thaxted Essex 30 E3
The Aird Highld 85 C9
The Arms Norf 38 F4
The Bage Hereford 25 D9
The Balloch Perth 75 F11
The Barony Orkney 95 F3
The Bog Shrops 33 F9
The Bourne Sur 18 G5
The Braes Highld 85 E10
The Broad Hereford 25 B11
The Butts Som 16 G4
The Camp Glos 26 H6
The Camp Herts 29 H8
The Chequer Wrex 33 A10
The City Bucks 18 B4
The Common Wilts 9 A11
The Craigs Highld 86 B7
The Cronk IoM 48 C3
The Dell Suff 39 F10
The Den N Ayrs 66 A6
The Eals Northumb 62 E3
The Eaves Glos 26 H3
The Flatt Cumb 61 F11
The Four Alls Shrops 34 B2
The Garths Shetland 96 B8
The Green Cumb 49 A1
The Green Wilts 9 A7
The Grove Dumfries 60 F5
The Hall Shetland 96 D8
The Haven W Sus 11 A9
The Heath Norf 39 C7
The Heath Suff 31 E8
The Hill Cumb 49 A1
The Howe Cumb 56 H6
The Howe IoM 48 F1
The Hundred Hereford 26 B2
The Lee Bucks 18 A6
The Lhen IoM 48 B3
The Marsh Powys 33 F9
The Marsh Wilts 17 C7
The Middles Durham 58 A3
The Moor Kent 13 D6
The Mumbles = Y Mwmbwls Swansea 14 C2
The Murray S Lanark 68 E5
The Neuk Aberds 83 D9
The Oval Bath 16 E4
The Pole of Itlaw Aberds 89 C6
The Quarry Glos 16 B4
The Rhos Pembs 22 E5
The Rock Telford 34 E2
The Ryde Herts 29 H9
The Sands Sur 18 G5
The Stocks Kent 13 D8
The Throat Wokingham 18 E5
The Vauld Hereford 26 D2
The Wyke Shrops 34 E3
Theakston N Yorks 58 H4
Thealby N Lincs 52 H4
Theale Som 15 G10
Theale W Berks 18 D3
Thearne E Yorks 53 F6
Theberton Suff 31 B11
Theddingworth Leics 36 G2
Theddlethorpe All Saints Lincs 47 D8
Theddlethorpe St Helen Lincs 47 D8
Thelbridge Barton Devon 7 E6
Thelnetham Suff 38 H6
Thelveton Norf 39 G7
Thelwall Warr 43 D9
Themelthorpe Norf 39 C6
Thenford Northants 28 D2
Therfield Herts 29 E10
Thetford Lincs 37 D7
Thetford Norf 38 G4
Theydon Bois Essex 19 B11
Thickwood Wilts 16 D5
Thimbleby Lincs 46 F6
Thimbleby N Yorks 58 G5
Thingwall Mers 42 D5
Thirdpart N Ayrs 66 B4
Thirlby N Yorks 51 A10
Thirlestane Borders 70 F4
Thirn N Yorks 58 H3
Thirsk N Yorks 51 A10
Thirtleby E Yorks 53 F7
Thistleton Lancs 49 F4
Thistleton Rutland 36 D5
Thistley Green Suff 38 H2

Upper Quinton Warks 27 D8
Upper Ratley Hants 10 B2
Upper Rissington Glos 27 G9
Upper Rochford Worcs 26 B3
Upper Sandaig Highld 85 G12
Upper Sanday Orkney 95 H6
Upper Sapey Hereford 26 B3
Upper Saxondale Notts 36 B2
Upper Seagry Wilts 16 C6
Upper Shelton C Beds 28 D6
Upper Sheringham Norf 39 A7
Upper Skelmorlie N Ayrs 73 G11
Upper Slaughter Glos 27 F8
Upper Soudley Glos 26 G3
Upper Stondon C Beds 29 E8
Upper Stowe Northants 28 C3
Upper Stratton Swindon 17 C8
Upper Street Hants 9 C10
Upper Street Norf 39 D9
Upper Street Norf 39 D9
Upper Street Suff 31 E8
Upper Strensham Worcs 26 E6
Upper Sundon C Beds 29 F7
Upper Swell Glos 27 F8
Upper Tean Staffs 34 B6
Upper Tillyrie Perth 76 G4
Upper Tooting London 19 D9
Upper Tote Highld 85 C10
Upper Town N Som 15 E11
Upper Treverward Shrops 33 H8
Upper Tysoe Warks 27 D10
Upper Upham Wilts 17 D9
Upper Wardington Oxon 27 D11
Upper Weald M Keynes 28 E4
Upper Weedon Northants 28 C3
Upper Wield Hants 18 H3
Upper Winchendon Bucks 28 G4
Upper Witton W Mid 35 F6
Upper Woodend Aberds 83 B8
Upper Woodford Wilts 17 H8
Upper Wootton Hants 18 F2
Upper Wyche Hereford 26 D4
Upperby Cumb 56 A6
Uppermill Gtr Man 44 B3
Uppersound Shetland 96 J6
Upperthong W Yorks 44 B5
Upperthorpe N Lincs 45 B11
Upperton W Sus 11 B8
Uppertown Derbys 45 F7
Uppertown Highld 94 C5
Uppertown Orkney 95 J5
Uppingham Rutland 36 F4
Uppington Shrops 34 E2
Upsall N Yorks 58 H5
Upshire Essex 19 A11
Upstreet Kent 21 E9
Upthorpe Suff 30 A6
Upton Cambs 37 H7
Upton Ches W 43 F7
Upton Corn 6 F1
Upton Dorset 8 F6
Upton Dorset 9 F8
Upton Hants 10 C2
Upton Hants 17 F10
Upton Leics 35 F9
Upton Lincs 46 D2
Upton Mers 42 D5
Upton Norf 39 D9
Upton Northants 28 B4
Upton Notts 45 E11
Upton Notts 45 G11
Upton Oxon 18 C2
Upton Pboro 37 E7
Upton Slough 18 D6
Upton Som 7 D8
Upton W Yorks 45 A8
Upton Bishop Hereford 26 F3
Upton Cheyney S Glos 16 E3
Upton Cressett Shrops 34 F2
Upton Cross Corn 4 D3
Upton Grey Hants 18 G3
Upton Hellions Devon 7 F7
Upton Lovell Wilts 16 G6
Upton Magna Shrops 34 D1
Upton Noble Som 16 H4
Upton Pyne Devon 7 G8
Upton St Leonard's Glos 26 G5
Upton Scudamore Wilts 16 G5
Upton Snodsbury Worcs 26 C6
Upton upon Severn Worcs 26 D5
Upton Warren Worcs 26 B6
Upwaltham W Sus 11 C8
Upware Cambs 30 A2
Upwell Norf 37 E10
Upwey Dorset 8 F5
Upwood Cambs 37 G8
Uradale Shetland 96 K6
Urafirth Shetland 96 F5
Urchfont Wilts 17 F7
Urdimarsh Hereford 26 D2
Ure Shetland 96 F4
Ure Bank N Yorks 51 B9
Urgha W Isles 90 H6
Urishay Common Hereford 25 E10
Urlay Nook Stockton 58 E4
Urmston Gtr Man 43 C10
Urpeth Durham 58 A3
Urquhart Highld 87 F8
Urquhart Moray 88 B2
Urra N Yorks 59 F6
Urray Highld 87 F8
Ushaw Moor Durham 58 B3
Usk = Brynbuga Mon 15 A9
Usselby Lincs 46 C4
Usworth T&W 63 H9
Utkinton Ches W 43 F8
Utley W Yorks 50 E6
Uton Devon 7 G7
Utterby Lincs 47 C7
Uttoxeter Staffs 35 B6
Uwchmynydd Gwyn 40 H3
Uxbridge London 19 C7
Uyeasound Shetland 96 C7
Uzmaston Pembs 22 E4

V

Valley Anglesey 40 C4
Valley Truckle Corn 4 C1
Valleyfield Dumfries 55 D9
Valsgarth Shetland 96 B8
Valtos Highld 85 B10
Van Powys 32 G5
Vange Essex 20 C4
Varteg Torf 25 H9
Vatten Highld 85 D7
Vaul Argyll 78 G3
Vaynor M Tydf 25 G7
Veensgarth Shetland 96 J6
Velindre Powys 25 E8
Vellow Som 7 C9
Veness Orkney 95 F6
Venn Green Devon 6 E2
Venn Ottery Devon 7 G9
Vennington Shrops 33 E9
Venny Tedburn Devon 7 G7
Ventnor IoW 10 G4
Vernham Dean Hants 17 F10
Vernham Street Hants 17 F10
Vernolds Common Shrops 33 G10
Verwood Dorset 9 D9
Veryan Corn 3 F8
Vicarage Devon 7 H11
Vickerstown Cumb 49 C1
Victoria Corn 3 C8
Victoria S Yorks 44 B5
Vidlin Shetland 96 G6
Viewpark N Lanark 68 D6
Vigo Village Kent 20 E3
Vinehall Street E Sus 13 D6
Vine's Cross E Sus 12 E4
Viney Hill Glos 26 H3
Virginia Water Sur 18 E6
Virginstow Devon 6 G2
Vobster Som 16 G4
Voe Shetland 96 E5
Voe Shetland 96 G6
Vowchurch Hereford 25 E10
Voxter Shetland 96 F5
Voy Orkney 95 G3

W

Wackerfield Durham 58 D2
Wacton Norf 39 F7
Wadbister Shetland 96 J6
Wadborough Worcs 26 D6
Waddesdon Bucks 28 G4
Waddingham Lincs 46 C3
Waddington Lancs 50 E3
Waddington Lincs 46 F3
Wadebridge Corn 3 B8
Wadeford Som 8 C2
Wadenhoe Northants 36 G6
Wadesmill Herts 29 G10
Wadhurst E Sus 12 C5
Wadshelf Derbys 45 E7
Wadsley S Yorks 45 C7
Wadsley Bridge S Yorks 45 C7
Wadworth S Yorks 45 C9
Waen Denb 42 F4
Waen Denb 42 F2
Waen Fach Powys 33 D8
Waen Goleugoed Denb 42 E3
Wag Highld 93 G13
Wainfleet All Saints Lincs 47 G8
Wainfleet Bank Lincs 47 G8
Wainfleet St Mary Lincs 47 G9
Wainfleet Tofts Lincs 47 G8
Wainhouse Corner Corn 4 B2
Wainscott Medway 20 D4
Wainstalls W Yorks 50 G6
Waitby Cumb 57 F9
Waithe Lincs 46 B6
Wake Lady Green N Yorks 59 G7
Wakefield W Yorks 51 G9
Wakerley Northants 36 F5
Wakes Colne Essex 30 F5
Walberswick Suff 31 A11
Walberton W Sus 11 D8
Walbottle T&W 63 G7
Walcot Lincs 37 B6
Walcot N Lincs 52 G4
Walcot Shrops 33 G9
Walcot Swindon 17 C8
Walcot Telford 34 D1
Walcot Green Norf 39 G7
Walcote Leics 36 G1
Walcote Warks 27 C8
Walcott Lincs 46 G5
Walcott Norf 39 B9
Walden N Yorks 50 A6
Walden Head N Yorks 50 A5
Walden Stubbs N Yorks 52 H1
Waldersey Cambs 37 E10
Walderslade Medway 20 E4
Walderton W Sus 11 C6
Walditch Dorset 8 E3
Waldley Derbys 35 B7
Waldridge Durham 58 A3
Waldringfield Suff 31 D9
Waldringfield Heath Suff 31 D9
Waldron E Sus 12 E4
Wales S Yorks 45 D8
Walesby Lincs 46 C5
Walesby Notts 45 E10
Walford Hereford 25 A10
Walford Hereford 26 F2
Walford Shrops 33 C10
Walford Heath Shrops 33 D10
Walgherton Ches E 43 H9
Walgrave Northants 28 A5
Walhampton Hants 10 E2
Walk Mill Lancs 50 F4
Walkden Gtr Man 43 B10
Walker T&W 63 G8
Walker Barn Ches E 44 E3
Walker Fold Lancs 50 E2
Walkerburn Borders 70 G2
Walkeringham Notts 45 C11
Walkerith Lincs 45 C11
Walkern Herts 29 F9
Walker's Green Hereford 26 D2
Walkerville N Yorks 58 G3
Walkford Dorset 9 E11
Walkhampton Devon 4 E6
Walkington E Yorks 52 F5
Walkley S Yorks 45 D7
Wall Northumb 62 G5
Wall Staffs 35 E7
Wall Bank Shrops 33 F11
Wall Heath W Mid 34 G4
Wall under Heywood Shrops 33 F11
Wallaceton Dumfries 60 E4
Wallacetown S Ayrs 66 D6
Wallacetown S Ayrs 66 F5
Wallands Park E Sus 12 E3
Wallasey Mers 42 C6
Wallcrouch E Sus 12 C5
Wallingford Oxon 18 C3
Wallington Hants 10 D4
Wallington Herts 29 E9
Wallington London 19 E9
Wallis Pembs 22 D5
Walliswood Sur 19 H8
Walls Shetland 96 J4
Wallsend T&W 63 G8
Wallston V Glam 15 D7
Wallyford E Loth 70 C2
Walmer Kent 21 F10
Walmer Bridge Lancs 49 G4
Walmersley Gtr Man 44 A2
Walmley W Mid 35 F7
Walpole Suff 31 A10
Walpole Cross Keys Norf 37 D11
Walpole Highway Norf 37 D11
Walpole Marsh Norf 37 D10
Walpole St Andrew Norf 37 D11
Walpole St Peter Norf 37 D11
Walsall W Mid 34 F6
Walsall Wood W Mid 34 E6
Walsden W Yorks 50 G5
Walsgrave on Sowe W Mid 35 G9
Walsham le Willows Suff 30 A6
Walshaw Gtr Man 43 A10
Walshford N Yorks 51 D10
Walsoken Cambs 37 D10
Walston S Lanark 69 F9
Walsworth Herts 29 E9
Walters Ash Bucks 18 B5
Walterston V Glam 14 D6
Walterstone Hereford 25 F10
Waltham Kent 21 G8
Waltham NE Lincs 46 B6
Waltham Abbey Essex 19 A10
Waltham Chase Hants 10 C4
Waltham Cross Herts 19 A10
Waltham on the Wolds Leics 36 C4
Waltham St Lawrence Windsor 18 D5
Walthamstow London 19 C10
Walton Cumb 61 G11
Walton Derbys 45 F7
Walton Leics 36 G1
Walton M Keynes 28 E5
Walton Mers 42 C6
Walton Pboro 37 E7
Walton Powys 25 C9
Walton Som 15 H10
Walton Staffs 34 B4
Walton Suff 31 E9
Walton Telford 34 D1
Walton W Yorks 51 E10
Walton W Yorks 51 H9
Walton Warks 27 C9
Walton Cardiff Glos 26 E6
Walton East Pembs 22 D5
Walton-in-Gordano N Som 15 D10
Walton-le-Dale Lancs 50 G1
Walton-on-Thames Sur 19 E8
Walton on the Hill Staffs 34 C5
Walton on the Hill Sur 19 F9
Walton-on-the-Naze Essex 31 F9
Walton on the Wolds Leics 36 D1
Walton-on-Trent Derbys 35 D8
Walton West Pembs 22 E3
Walwen Flint 42 E5
Walwick Northumb 62 F5
Walworth Darl 58 E3
Walworth Gate Darl 58 D3
Walwyn's Castle Pembs 22 E3
Wambrook Som 8 D1
Wanborough Sur 18 G6
Wanborough Swindon 17 C9
Wandsworth London 19 D9
Wangford Suff 39 H10
Wanlockhead Dumfries 60 B4
Wansford E Yorks 53 D6
Wansford Pboro 37 F6
Wanstead London 19 C11
Wanstrow Som 16 G4
Wanswell Glos 16 A3
Wantage Oxon 17 C10
Wapley S Glos 16 D4
Wappenbury Warks 27 B10
Wappenham Northants 28 D3
Warbleton E Sus 12 E5
Warblington Hants 10 D6
Warborough Oxon 18 B2
Warboys Cambs 37 G9
Warbreck Blackpool 49 F3
Warbstow Corn 4 B3
Warburton Gtr Man 43 D10
Warcop Cumb 57 E9
Ward End W Mid 35 G7
Ward Green Suff 31 B7
Warden Kent 21 D7
Warden Northumb 62 G5
Wardhill Orkney 95 F7
Wardington Oxon 27 D11
Wardlaw Borders 61 B8
Wardle Ches E 43 G9
Wardle Gtr Man 50 H5
Wardley Rutland 36 E4
Wardlow Derbys 44 E5
Wardy Hill Cambs 37 G10
Ware Herts 29 G10
Ware Kent 21 E9
Wareham Dorset 9 F8
Warehorne Kent 13 C8
Waren Mill Northumb 71 G10
Warenford Northumb 71 H10
Warenton Northumb 71 G10
Wareside Herts 29 G10
Waresley Cambs 29 C9
Waresley Worcs 26 A5
Warfield Brack 18 D5
Warfleet Devon 5 F9
Wargrave Wokingham 18 D4
Warham Norf 38 A5
Warhill Gtr Man 44 C3
Wark Northumb 62 F4
Wark Northumb 71 G7
Warkleigh Devon 6 D5
Warkton Northants 36 H4
Warkworth Northants 27 D11
Warkworth Northumb 63 C8
Warlaby N Yorks 58 G4
Warland W Yorks 50 G5
Warleggan Corn 4 E2
Warlingham Sur 19 F10
Warmfield W Yorks 51 G9
Warmingham Ches E 43 F10
Warmington Northants 37 F6
Warmington Warks 27 D11
Warminster Wilts 16 G5
Warmlake Kent 20 F5
Warmley S Glos 16 D3
Warmley Tower S Glos 16 D3
Warmonds Hill Northants 28 B6
Warmsworth S Yorks 45 B9
Warmwell Dorset 9 F6
Warndon Worcs 26 C5
Warnford Hants 10 B5
Warnham W Sus 11 A10
Warninglid W Sus 11 B11
Warren Ches E 44 E2
Warren Pembs 22 G4
Warren Heath Suff 31 D9
Warren Row Windsor 18 C5
Warren Street Kent 20 F6
Warrington M Keynes 28 C5
Warrington Warr 43 D9
Warsash Hants 10 D3
Warslow Staffs 44 G4
Warter E Yorks 52 D4
Warthermarske N Yorks 51 B8
Warthill N Yorks 52 D2
Wartling E Sus 12 F5
Wartnaby Leics 36 C3
Warton Lancs 49 B4
Warton Lancs 49 G4
Warton Northumb 62 C6
Warton Warks 35 E8
Warwick Warks 27 B9
Warwick Bridge Cumb 61 H10
Warwick on Eden Cumb 61 H10
Wasbister Orkney 95 E4
Wasdale Head Cumb 56 F3
Wash Common W Berks 17 E11
Washaway Corn 3 C9
Washbourne Devon 5 F8
Washfield Devon 7 E8
Washfold N Yorks 58 F1
Washford Som 7 B9
Washford Pyne Devon 7 E7
Washingborough Lincs 46 E4
Washington T&W 63 H9
Washington W Sus 11 C10
Wasing W Berks 18 E2
Waskerley Durham 58 B1
Wasperton Warks 27 C9
Wasps Nest Lincs 46 F4
Wass N Yorks 52 B1
Watchet Som 7 B9
Watchfield Oxon 17 B9
Watchfield Som 15 G9
Watchgate Cumb 57 G7
Watchhill Cumb 56 B3
Watcombe Torbay 5 E10
Watendlath Cumb 56 E4
Water Devon 5 C8
Water Lancs 50 G4
Water End E Yorks 52 F3
Water End Herts 19 A9
Water End Herts 29 G7
Water Newton Cambs 37 F7
Water Orton Warks 35 F7
Water Stratford Bucks 28 E3
Water Yeat Cumb 56 H4
Waterbeach Cambs 29 B11
Waterbeck Dumfries 61 F8
Waterden Norf 38 B4
Waterfall Staffs 44 G4
Waterfoot E Renf 68 E4
Waterfoot Lancs 50 G4
Waterford Hants 10 E2
Waterford Herts 29 G10
Waterhead Cumb 56 F5
Waterhead Dumfries 61 D7
Waterheads Borders 69 E11
Waterhouses Durham 58 B2
Waterhouses Staffs 44 G4
Wateringbury Kent 20 F3
Waterloo Gtr Man 44 B3
Waterloo Highld 85 F11
Waterloo Mers 42 C6
Waterloo N Lanark 69 E7
Waterloo Norf 39 D8
Waterloo Perth 76 D3
Waterloo Poole 9 E9
Waterloo Shrops 33 B11
Waterloo Port Gwyn 40 D6
Waterlooville Hants 10 D5
Watermeetings S Lanark 60 B5
Watermillock Cumb 56 D6
Waterperry Oxon 28 H3
Waterrow Som 7 D9
Water's Nook Gtr Man 43 B9
Waters Upton Telford 34 D2
Watersfield W Sus 11 C9
Waterside Aberds 89 F10
Waterside Blackburn 50 G3
Waterside Cumb 56 B4
Waterside E Ayrs 67 F7
Waterside E Ayrs 67 B7
Waterside E Dunb 68 C5
Waterside E Renf 68 E4
Waterstock Oxon 28 H3
Waterston Pembs 22 F4
Watford Herts 19 B8
Watford Northants 28 B3
Watford Gap Staffs 35 E7
Wath N Yorks 51 B9
Wath N Yorks 51 C7
Wath N Yorks 52 B2
Wath Brow Cumb 56 E2
Wath upon Dearne S Yorks 45 B8
Watlington Norf 38 D2
Watlington Oxon 18 B3
Watnall Notts 45 H9
Watten Highld 94 E4
Wattisfield Suff 31 A7
Wattisham Suff 31 C7
Wattlesborough Heath Shrops 33 D9
Watton E Yorks 52 D6
Watton Norf 38 E5
Watton at Stone Herts 29 G10
Wattston N Lanark 68 C6
Wattstown Rhondda 14 B6
Wauchan Highld 80 E1
Waulkmill Lodge Orkney 95 H4
Waun Powys 32 E4
Waun-y-clyn Carms 23 F9
Waunarlwydd Swansea 14 B2
Waunclunda Carms 24 E3
Waunfawr Gwyn 41 E7
Waungron Swansea 23 F10
Waunlwyd Bl Gwent 25 H8
Wavendon M Keynes 28 E6
Waverbridge Cumb 56 B4
Waverton Ches W 43 F7
Waverton Cumb 56 B4
Wavertree Mers 43 D6
Wawne E Yorks 53 F6
Waxham Norf 39 C10
Waxholme E Yorks 53 G9
Way Kent 21 E10
Way Village Devon 7 E7
Wayfield Medway 20 E4
Wayford Som 8 D3
Waymills Shrops 34 A1
Wayne Green Mon 25 G11
Wdig = Goodwick Pembs 22 C4
Weachyburn Aberds 89 C6
Weald Oxon 17 A10
Wealdstone London 19 C8
Weardley W Yorks 51 E8
Weare Som 15 F10
Weare Giffard Devon 6 D3
Wearhead Durham 57 C10
Weasdale Cumb 57 F8
Weasenham All Saints Norf 38 C4
Weasenham St Peter Norf 38 C4
Weatherhill Sur 12 B2
Weaverham Ches W 43 E9
Weaverthorpe N Yorks 52 B5
Webheath Worcs 27 B7
Wedderlairs Aberds 89 E8
Wedderlie Borders 70 E5
Weddington Warks 35 F9
Wedhampton Wilts 17 F7
Wedmore Som 15 G10
Wednesbury W Mid 34 F5
Wednesfield W Mid 34 E5
Weedon Bucks 28 G5
Weedon Bec Northants 28 C3
Weedon Lois Northants 28 D3
Weeford Staffs 35 E7
Week Devon 7 E6
Week St Mary Corn 4 B3
Weeke Hants 10 A3
Weekley Northants 36 G4
Weel E Yorks 53 F6
Weeley Essex 31 F8
Weeley Heath Essex 31 F8
Weem Perth 75 C11
Weeping Cross Staffs 34 C5
Weethley Gate Warks 27 C7
Weeting Norf 38 G3
Weeton E Yorks 53 G9
Weeton Lancs 49 F3
Weeton N Yorks 51 E8
Weetwood Hall Northumb 71 H9
Weir Lancs 50 G4
Weir Quay Devon 4 E5
Welborne Norf 39 E6
Welbourn Lincs 46 G3
Welburn N Yorks 52 A2
Welburn N Yorks 52 C3
Welbury N Yorks 58 F4
Welby Lincs 36 B5
Welches Dam Cambs 37 G10
Welcombe Devon 6 E1
Weld Bank Lancs 50 H1
Weldon Northumb 63 D7
Welford Northants 36 G2
Welford W Berks 17 D11
Welford-on-Avon Warks 27 C8
Welham Leics 36 F3
Welham Notts 45 D11
Welham Green Herts 29 H9
Well Hants 18 G4
Well Lincs 47 E8
Well N Yorks 51 A8
Well End Bucks 18 C5
Well Heads W Yorks 51 F6
Well Hill Kent 19 E11
Well Town Devon 7 F8
Welland Worcs 26 D4
Wellbank Angus 77 D7
Welldale Dumfries 61 G7
Wellesbourne Warks 27 C9
Welling London 19 D11
Wellingborough Northants 28 B5
Wellingham Norf 38 C4
Wellingore Lincs 46 G3
Wellington Cumb 56 F2
Wellington Hereford 25 D11
Wellington Som 7 D10
Wellington Telford 34 D2
Wellington Heath Hereford 26 D4
Wellington Hill W Yorks 51 F9
Wellow Bath 16 F4
Wellow IoW 10 F2
Wellow Notts 45 F10
Wellpond Green Herts 29 F11
Wells Som 15 G11
Wells Green Ches E 43 G9
Wells-Next-The-Sea Norf 38 A5
Wellsborough Leics 35 E9
Wellswood Torbay 5 E10
Wellwood Fife 69 B9
Welney Norf 37 F11
Welsh Bicknor Hereford 26 G2
Welsh End Shrops 33 B11
Welsh Frankton Shrops 33 B9
Welsh Hook Pembs 22 D4
Welsh Newton Hereford 25 G11
Welsh St Donats V Glam 14 D6
Welshampton Shrops 33 B10
Welshpool = Y Trallwng Powys 33 E8
Welton Cumb 56 B5
Welton E Yorks 52 G5
Welton Lincs 46 E4
Welton Northants 28 B2
Welton Hill Lincs 46 D4
Welton le Marsh Lincs 47 F8
Welton le Wold Lincs 46 D6
Welwick E Yorks 53 G9
Welwyn Herts 29 G9
Welwyn Garden City Herts 29 G9
Wem Shrops 33 C11
Wembdon Som 15 H8
Wembley London 19 C8
Wembury Devon 4 G6
Wembworthy Devon 6 F5
Wemyss Bay Invclyd 73 G10
Wenallt Ceredig 24 A3
Wenallt Gwyn 32 A5
Wendens Ambo Essex 30 E2
Wendlebury Oxon 28 G2
Wendling Norf 38 D5
Wendover Bucks 28 H5
Wendron Corn 2 F5
Wendy Cambs 29 D10
Wenfordbridge Corn 4 D1
Wenhaston Suff 39 H10
Wennington Cambs 37 H8
Wennington Lancs 50 B2
Wennington London 20 C2
Wensley Derbys 44 F6
Wensley N Yorks 58 H1
Wentbridge W Yorks 51 H10
Wentnor Shrops 33 F9
Wentworth Cambs 37 H10
Wentworth S Yorks 45 C7
Wenvoe V Glam 15 D7
Weobley Hereford 25 C11
Weobley Marsh Hereford 25 C11
Wereham Norf 38 E2
Wergs W Mid 34 E4
Wern Powys 32 D5
Wern Powys 33 D8
Wernffrwd Swansea 23 G10
Wernyrheolydd Mon 25 G10
Werrington Corn 4 C4
Werrington Pboro 37 E7
Werrington Staffs 44 H3
Wervin Ches W 43 E7
Wesham Lancs 49 F4
Wessington Derbys 45 G7
West Acre Norf 38 D3
West Adderbury Oxon 27 E11
West Allerdean Northumb 71 F8
West Alvington Devon 5 G8
West Amesbury Wilts 17 G8
West Anstey Devon 7 D7
West Ashby Lincs 46 E6
West Ashling W Sus 11 D7
West Ashton Wilts 16 F5
West Auckland Durham 58 D2
West Ayton N Yorks 52 A5
West Bagborough Som 7 C10
West Barkwith Lincs 46 D5
West Barnby N Yorks 59 E9
West Barns E Loth 70 C5
West Barsham Norf 38 B5
West Bay Dorset 8 E3
West Beckham Norf 39 B7
West Bedfont Sur 19 D7
West Benhar N Lanark 69 D7
West Bergholt Essex 30 F6
West Bexington Dorset 8 F4
West Bilney Norf 38 D3
West Blatchington Brighton 12 F1
West Bowling W Yorks 51 F7
West Bradford Lancs 50 E3
West Bradley Som 16 H2
West Bretton W Yorks 44 A6
West Bridgford Notts 36 B1
West Bromwich W Mid 34 F6
West Buckland Devon 6 C5
West Buckland Som 7 D10
West Burrafirth Shetland 96 H4
West Burton N Yorks 58 H1
West Burton W Sus 11 C8
West Butterwick N Lincs 46 B2
West Byfleet Sur 19 E7
West Caister Norf 39 D11
West Calder W Loth 69 D9
West Camel Som 8 B4
West Challow Oxon 17 C10
West Chelborough Dorset 8 D4
West Chevington Northumb 63 D8
West Chiltington W Sus 11 C9
West Chiltington Common W Sus 11 C9
West Chinnock Som 8 C3
West Chisenbury Wilts 17 F8
West Clandon Sur 19 F7
West Cliffe Kent 21 G10
West Clyne Highld 93 J11
West Clyth Highld 94 G4
West Coker Som 8 C4
West Compton Dorset 8 E4
West Compton Som 16 G2
West Cowick E Yorks 52 G2
West Cranmore Som 16 G3
West Cross Swansea 14 C2
West Cullery Aberds 83 C9
West Curry Corn 6 G1
West Curthwaite Cumb 56 B5
West Darlochan Argyll 65 F7
West Dean W Sus 11 C7
West Dean Wilts 10 B1
West Deeping Lincs 37 E7
West Derby Mers 43 C6
West Dereham Norf 38 E2
West Didsbury Gtr Man 44 C2
West Ditchburn Northumb 63 A7
West Down Devon 6 B4
West Drayton London 19 D7
West Drayton Notts 45 E11
West Ella E Yorks 52 G6
West End Bedford 28 C6
West End E Yorks 52 F5
West End E Yorks 53 F7
West End Hants 10 C3
West End Lancs 50 G3
West End N Som 15 E10
West End N Yorks 51 D7
West End Norf 38 E5
West End Norf 39 D11
West End Oxon 17 A11
West End S Lanark 69 F8
West End S Yorks 45 B10
West End Suff 39 G10
West End Sur 18 E6
West End W Sus 11 C11
West End Wilts 9 B8
West End Wilts 16 D6
West End Green Hants 18 E3
West Farleigh Kent 20 F4
West Felton Shrops 33 C9
West Fenton E Loth 70 B3
West Ferry Dundee 77 D7
West Firle E Sus 12 F3
West Ginge Oxon 17 C11
West Grafton Wilts 17 E9
West Green Hants 18 F4
West Greenskares Aberds 89 B7
West Grimstead Wilts 9 B11
West Grinstead W Sus 11 B10
West Haddlesey N Yorks 52 G1
West Haddon Northants 28 A3
West Hagbourne Oxon 18 C2
West Hagley Worcs 34 G5
West Hall Cumb 61 G11
West Hallam Derbys 35 A10
West Halton N Lincs 52 G5
West Ham London 19 C11
West Handley Derbys 45 E7
West Hanney Oxon 17 B11
West Hanningfield Essex 20 B4
West Hardwick W Yorks 51 H10
West Harnham Wilts 9 B10
West Harptree Bath 16 F2
West Hatch Som 8 B1
West Head Norf 38 E1
West Heath Ches E 44 F2
West Heath Hants 18 F2
West Heath Hants 18 F5
West Helmsdale Highld 93 H13
West Hendred Oxon 17 C11
West Heslerton N Yorks 52 B5
West Hill Devon 7 G9
West Hill E Yorks 53 C7
West Hill N Som 15 D10
West Hoathly W Sus 12 C2
West Holme Dorset 9 F7
West Horndon Essex 20 C3
West Horrington Som 16 G2
West Horsley Sur 19 F7
West Horton Northumb 71 G9
West Hougham Kent 21 G9
West Houlland Shetland 96 H4
West-houses Derbys 45 G8
West Huntington York 52 D2
West Hythe Kent 13 C10
West Ilsley W Berks 17 C11
West Itchenor W Sus 11 D6
West Keal Lincs 47 F7
West Kennett Wilts 17 E8
West Kilbride N Ayrs 66 B5
West Kingsdown Kent 20 E2
West Kington Wilts 16 D5
West Kinharrachie Aberds 89 E9
West Kirby Mers 42 D5
West Knapton N Yorks 52 B4
West Knighton Dorset 8 F6
West Knoyle Wilts 9 A7
West Kyloe Northumb 71 F9
West Lambrook Som 8 C3
West Langdon Kent 21 G10
West Langwell Highld 93 J9
West Lavington W Sus 11 B7
West Lavington Wilts 17 F7
West Layton N Yorks 58 F2
West Lea Durham 58 B5
West Leake Notts 35 C11
West Learmouth Northumb 71 G7
West Leigh Devon 6 F5
West Lexham Norf 38 D4
West Lilling N Yorks 52 C2
West Linton Borders 69 E10
West Liss Hants 11 B6
West Littleton S Glos 16 D4
West Looe Corn 4 F3
West Luccombe Som 7 B7
West Lulworth Dorset 9 F7
West Lutton N Yorks 52 C5
West Lydford Som 8 A4
West Lyng Som 8 B2
West Lynn Norf 38 C2
West Malling Kent 20 F3
West Malvern Worcs 26 D4
West Marden W Sus 11 C6
West Marina E Sus 13 F6
West Markham Notts 45 E11
West Marsh NE Lincs 46 A6
West Marton N Yorks 50 D4
West Meon Hants 10 B5
West Mersea Essex 31 G7
West Milton Dorset 8 E4
West Minster Kent 20 D6
West Molesey Sur 19 E8
West Monkton Som 8 B1
West Moors Dorset 9 D9
West Morriston Borders 70 F5
West Muir Angus 77 A8
West Ness N Yorks 52 B2
West Newham Northumb 62 F6
West Newton E Yorks 53 F7
West Newton Norf 38 C2
West Norwood London 19 D10
West Ogwell Devon 5 D9
West Orchard Dorset 9 C7
West Overton Wilts 17 E8
West Park Hrtlpl 58 C5
West Parley Dorset 9 E9
West Peckham Kent 20 F3
West Pelton Durham 58 A3
West Pennard Som 15 H11
West Pentire Corn 3 C6
West Perry Cambs 29 B8
West Putford Devon 6 E2
West Quantoxhead Som 7 B10
West Rainton Durham 58 B4
West Rasen Lincs 46 D4
West Raynham Norf 38 C4
West Retford Notts 45 D10
West Rounton N Yorks 58 F5
West Row Suff 38 H2
West Rudham Norf 38 C4
West Runton Norf 39 A7
West Saltoun E Loth 70 D3
West Sandwick Shetland 96 E6
West Scrafton N Yorks 51 A6
West Sleekburn Northumb 63 E8
West Somerton Norf 39 D10
West Stafford Dorset 8 F6
West Stockwith Notts 45 C11
West Stoke W Sus 11 D7
West Stonesdale N Yorks 57 F10
West Stoughton Som 15 G10
West Stour Dorset 9 B6
West Stourmouth Kent 21 E9
West Stow Suff 30 A5
West Stowell Wilts 17 E8
West Strathan Highld 93 C8
West Stratton Hants 18 G2
West Street Kent 20 F6
West Tanfield N Yorks 51 B8
West Taphouse Corn 4 E2
West Tarbert Argyll 73 G7
West Thirston Northumb 63 D7
West Thorney W Sus 11 D6
West Thurrock Thurrock 20 D2
West Tilbury Thurrock 20 D3
West Tisted Hants 10 B5
West Tofts Norf 38 F4
West Tofts Perth 76 D4
West Torrington Lincs 46 D5
West Town Hants 10 E6
West Town N Som 15 E10
West Tytherley Hants 10 B1
West Tytherton Wilts 16 D6
West Walton Norf 37 D10
West Walton Highway Norf 37 D10
West Wellow Hants 10 C1
West Wemyss Fife 70 A2
West Wick N Som 15 E9
West Wickham Cambs 30 D3
West Wickham London 19 E10
West Williamston Pembs 22 F5
West Willoughby Lincs 36 A5
West Winch Norf 38 D2
West Winterslow Wilts 9 A11
West Wittering W Sus 11 E6
West Witton N Yorks 58 H1
West Woodburn Northumb 62 E4
West Woodhay W Berks 17 E10
West Woodlands Som 16 G4
West Worldham Hants 18 H4
West Worlington Devon 7 E6
West Worthing W Sus 11 D10
West Wratting Cambs 30 C3
West Wycombe Bucks 18 B5
West Wylam Northumb 63 G7
West Yell Shetland 96 E6
Westacott Devon 6 C4
Westbere Kent 21 E8
Westborough Lincs 36 A4
Westbourne Bmouth 9 E9
Westbourne Suff 31 D8
Westbourne W Sus 11 D6
Westbrook W Berks 17 D11
Westbury Bucks 28 E3
Westbury Shrops 33 E9
Westbury Wilts 16 F5
Westbury Leigh Wilts 16 F5
Westbury-on-Severn Glos 26 G4
Westbury on Trym Bristol 16 D2
Westbury-sub-Mendip Som 15 G11
Westby Lancs 49 F3
Westcliff-on-Sea Southend 20 C5
Westcombe Som 16 H3
Westcote Glos 27 F9
Westcott Bucks 28 G4
Westcott Devon 7 F9
Westcott Sur 19 G8
Westcott Barton Oxon 27 F11
Westdean E Sus 12 G4
Westdene Brighton 12 F1
Wester Aberchalder Highld 81 A7
Wester Balgedie Perth 76 G4
Wester Culbeuchly Aberds 89 B6
Wester Dechmont W Loth 69 D9
Wester Denoon Angus 76 C6
Wester Fintray Aberds 83 B10
Wester Gruinards Highld 87 B8
Wester Lealty Highld 87 D9
Wester Milton Highld 87 F12
Wester Newburn Fife 77 G7
Wester Quarff Shetland 96 K6
Wester Skeld Shetland 96 J4
Westerdale Highld 94 E3
Westerdale N Yorks 59 F7
Westerfield Shetland 96 H5
Westerfield Suff 31 D8
Westergate W Sus 11 D8
Westerham Kent 19 F11
Westerhope T&W 63 G7
Westerleigh S Glos 16 D4
Westerton Angus 77 B9
Westerton Durham 58 C3
Westerton W Sus 11 D7
Westerwick Shetland 96 J4
Westfield Cumb 56 D1
Westfield E Sus 13 E7
Westfield Hereford 26 D4
Westfield Highld 94 D2
Westfield N Lanark 68 C6
Westfield Norf 38 E5
Westfield W Loth 69 C8
Westfields Dorset 8 D6
Westfields of Rattray Perth 76 C4
Westgate Durham 57 C11
Westgate N Lincs 45 B11
Westgate Norf 38 A4
Westgate Norf 38 A5
Westgate on Sea Kent 21 D10
Westhall Aberds 83 A8
Westhall Suff 39 G10
Westham Dorset 8 G5
Westham E Sus 12 F5
Westham Som 15 G10
Westhampnett W Sus 11 D7
Westhay Som 15 G10
Westhead Lancs 43 B7
Westhide Hereford 26 D2
Westhill Aberds 83 C10
Westhill Highld 87 G10
Westhope Hereford 25 C11
Westhope Shrops 33 G10
Westhorpe Lincs 37 B8
Westhorpe Suff 31 B7
Westhoughton Gtr Man 43 B9
Westhouse N Yorks 50 B2
Westhumble Sur 19 F8
Westing Shetland 96 C7
Westlake Devon 5 F7
Westleigh Devon 6 D3
Westleigh Devon 7 E9
Westleigh Gtr Man 43 B9
Westleton Suff 31 B11
Westley Shrops 33 E9
Westley Suff 30 B5
Westley Waterless Cambs 30 C3
Westlington Bucks 28 G4
Westlinton Cumb 61 G9
Westmarsh Kent 21 E9
Westmeston E Sus 12 E2
Westmill Herts 29 F10
Westminster London 19 D10
Westmuir Angus 76 B6
Westness Orkney 95 F4
Westnewton Cumb 56 B3
Westnewton Northumb 71 G8
Westoe T&W 63 G9
Weston Bath 16 E4
Weston Ches E 43 G10
Weston Devon 7 H10
Weston Dorset 8 G5
Weston Halton 43 D8
Weston Hants 10 B6
Weston Herts 29 E9
Weston Lincs 37 C8
Weston N Yorks 51 E7
Weston Northants 28 D2
Weston Notts 45 F11
Weston Shrops 34 C1
Weston Shrops 34 F1
Weston Staffs 34 C5
Weston W Berks 17 D10
Weston Beggard Hereford 26 D2
Weston by Welland Northants 36 F3
Weston Colville Cambs 30 C3
Weston Coyney Stoke 34 A5
Weston Favell Northants 28 B4
Weston Green Cambs 30 C3
Weston Green Norf 39 D7
Weston Heath Shrops 34 D3
Weston Hills Lincs 37 C8
Weston-in-Gordano N Som 15 D10
Weston Jones Staffs 34 C3
Weston Longville Norf 39 D7
Weston Lullingfields Shrops 33 C10
Weston-on-the-Green Oxon 28 G2
Weston-on-Trent Derbys 35 C10
Weston Patrick Hants 18 G3
Weston Rhyn Shrops 33 B8
Weston-Sub-Edge Glos 27 D8
Weston-super-Mare N Som 15 E9
Weston Turville Bucks 28 G5
Weston under Lizard Staffs 34 D4
Weston under Penyard Hereford 26 F3
Weston under Wetherley Warks 27 B10
Weston Underwood Derbys 35 A8
Weston Underwood M Keynes 28 C5
Westonbirt Glos 16 C5
Westoncommon Shrops 33 C10
Westoning C Beds 29 E7
Westonzoyland Som 8 A2
Westow N Yorks 52 C3
Westport Argyll 65 F7
Westport Som 8 C2
Westrigg W Loth 69 D8
Westruther Borders 70 F5
Westry Cambs 37 F9
Westville Notts 45 H9
Westward Cumb 56 B4
Westward Ho! Devon 6 D3
Westwell Kent 20 G6
Westwell Oxon 27 H9
Westwell Leacon Kent 20 G6
Westwick Cambs 29 B11
Westwick Durham 58 E1
Westwick Norf 39 C8
Westwood Devon 7 G9
Westwood Wilts 16 F5
Westwoodside N Lincs 45 C11
Wetheral Cumb 56 A6
Wetherby W Yorks 51 E10
Wetherden Suff 31 B7
Wetheringsett Suff 31 B8
Wethersfield Essex 30 E4
Wethersta Shetland 96 G5

Wetherup Street Suff 31 B8
Wetley Rocks Staffs 44 H3
Wettenhall Ches E 43 F9
Wetton Staffs 44 G5
Wetwang E Yorks 52 D5
Wetwood Staffs 34 B3
Wexcombe Wilts 17 F9
Wexham Street Bucks 18 C6
Weybourne Norf 39 A7
Weybread Suff 39 G8
Weybridge Sur 19 E7
Weycroft Devon 8 E2
Weydale Highld 94 D3
Weyhill Hants 17 G10
Weymouth Dorset 8 G5
Whaddon Bucks 28 E5
Whaddon Cambs 29 D10
Whaddon Glos 26 G5
Whaddon Wilts 9 B10
Whale Cumb 57 D7
Whaley Derbys 45 E9
Whaley Bridge Derbys 44 D4
Whaley Thorns Derbys 45 E9
Whaligoe Highld 94 F5
Whalley Lancs 50 F3
Whalton Northumb 63 E7
Wham N Yorks 50 C3
Whaplode Lincs 37 C9
Whaplode Drove Lincs 37 D9
Whaplode St Catherine Lincs 37 C9
Wharfe N Yorks 50 C3
Wharles Lancs 49 F4
Wharncliffe Side S Yorks 44 C6
Wharram le Street N Yorks 52 C4
Wharton Ches W 43 F9
Wharton Green Ches W 43 F9
Whashton N Yorks 58 F2
Whatcombe Dorset 9 D7
Whatcote Warks 27 D10
Whatfield Suff 31 D7
Whatley Som 16 G4
Whatlington E Sus 13 E6
Whatstandwell Derbys 45 G7
Whatton Notts 36 B3
Whauphill Dumfries 55 E7
Whaw N Yorks 57 F11
Wheatacre Norf 39 F10
Wheatcroft Derbys 45 G7
Wheathampstead Herts 29 G8
Wheathill Shrops 34 G2
Wheatley Devon 7 G8
Wheatley Hants 18 G4
Wheatley Oxon 28 H2
Wheatley S Yorks 45 B9
Wheatley W Yorks 51 G6
Wheatley Hill Durham 58 C4
Wheaton Aston Staffs 34 D4
Wheddon Cross Som 7 C8
Wheedlemont Aberds 82 A6
Wheelerstreet Sur 18 G6
Wheelock Ches E 43 G10
Wheelock Heath Ches E 43 G10
Wheelton Lancs 50 G2
Wheen Angus 82 F5
Wheldrake York 52 E2
Whelford Glos 17 B8
Whelpley Hill Herts 28 H6
Whempstead Herts 29 F10
Whenby N Yorks 52 C2
Whepstead Suff 30 C5
Wherstead Suff 31 D8
Wherwell Hants 17 G10
Wheston Derbys 44 E5
Whetsted Kent 20 G3
Whetstone Leics 36 F1
Whicham Cumb 49 A1
Whichford Warks 27 E10
Whickham T&W 63 G8
Whiddon Down Devon 6 G5
Whigstreet Angus 77 C7
Whilton Northants 28 B3
Whim Farm Borders 69 E11
Whimble Devon 6 F2
Whimple Devon 7 G9
Whimpwell Green Norf 39 C9
Whinburgh Norf 38 E6
Whinnieliggate Dumfries 55 D10
Whinnyfold Aberds 89 E10
Whippingham IoW 10 E4
Whipsnade C Beds 29 G7
Whipton Devon 7 G8
Whirlow S Yorks 45 D7
Whisby Lincs 46 F3
Whissendine Rutland 36 D4
Whissonsett Norf 38 C5
Whistlefield Argyll 73 D10
Whistlefield Argyll 73 D11
Whistley Green Wokingham 18 D4
Whiston Mers 43 C7
Whiston Northants 28 B5
Whiston S Yorks 45 D8
Whiston Staffs 34 D4
Whiston Staffs 44 H4
Whitbeck Cumb 49 A1
Whitbourne Hereford 26 C4
Whitburn T&W 63 G10
Whitburn W Loth 69 D8
Whitburn Colliery T&W 63 G10
Whitby Ches W 43 E6
Whitby N Yorks 59 E9
Whitbyheath Ches W 43 E6
Whitchurch Bath 16 E3
Whitchurch Bucks 28 F4
Whitchurch Cardiff 15 C7
Whitchurch Devon 4 D5
Whitchurch Hants 17 G11
Whitchurch Hereford 26 G2
Whitchurch Oxon 18 D3
Whitchurch Pembs 22 D2
Whitchurch Shrops 33 A11
Whitchurch Canonicorum Dorset 8 E2
Whitchurch Hill Oxon 18 D3
Whitcombe Dorset 8 F6
Whitcott Keysett Shrops 33 G8
White Coppice Lancs 50 H2
White Lackington Dorset 8 E6
White Ladies Aston Worcs 26 C6
White Lund Lancs 49 C4
White Mill Carms 23 D9
White Ness Shetland 96 J5
White Notley Essex 30 G4
White Pit Lincs 47 E7
White Post Notts 45 G10
White Rocks Hereford 25 F11
White Roding Essex 30 G2
White Waltham Windsor 18 D5
Whiteacre Heath Warks 35 F8
Whitebridge Highld 81 B6
Whitebrook Mon 26 H2
Whiteburn Borders 70 F4
Whitecairns Aberds 83 B11
Whitecastle S Lanark 69 F9
Whitechapel Lancs 50 E1
Whitecleat Orkney 95 H6
Whitecraig E Loth 70 C2
Whitecroft Glos 26 H3
Whitecross Falk 69 C8
Whitecross Staffs 34 C4
Whiteface Highld 87 C10
Whitefarland N Ayrs 66 B1
Whitefaulds S Ayrs 66 F5
Whitefield Gtr Man 44 B2
Whitefield Perth 76 D4
Whiteford Aberds 83 A9
Whitegate Ches W 43 F9
Whitehall Blackburn 50 G3
Whitehall W Sus 11 B10
Whitehall Village Orkney 95 F7
Whitehaven Cumb 56 E1
Whitehill Hants 11 A6
Whitehills Aberds 89 B6
Whitehills S Lanark 68 E5
Whitehough Derbys 44 D4
Whitehouse Aberds 83 B8
Whitehouse Argyll 73 G7
Whiteinch Glasgow 68 D4
Whitekirk E Loth 70 B4
Whitelaw S Ayrs 67 G6
Whiteleas T&W 63 G9
Whiteley Bank IoW 10 F4
Whiteley Green Ches E 44 E3
Whiteley Village Sur 19 E7
Whitemans Green W Sus 12 D2
Whitemire Moray 87 F12
Whitemoor Corn 3 D8
Whitemore Staffs 44 F2
Whitenap Hants 10 B2
Whiteoak Green Oxon 27 G10
Whiteparish Wilts 9 B11
Whiterashes Aberds 89 A9
Whiterow Highld 94 F5
Whiteshill Glos 26 H5
Whiteside Northumb 62 G3
Whiteside W Loth 69 D8
Whitesmith E Sus 12 E4
Whitestaunton Som 8 C1
Whitestone Devon 6 B3
Whitestone Devon 7 G7
Whitestone Warks 35 G9
Whitestones Aberds 89 C8
Whitestreet Green Suff 30 E6
Whitewall Corner N Yorks 52 B3
Whiteway Glos 26 G6
Whiteway Glos 26 G6
Whitewell Aberds 89 B9
Whitewell Lancs 50 E2
Whitewell Bottom Lancs 50 G4
Whiteworks Devon 5 D7
Whitfield Kent 21 G10
Whitfield Northants 28 E3
Whitfield Northumb 62 H3
Whitfield S Glos 16 B3
Whitford Devon 8 E1
Whitford Flint 42 E4
Whitgift E Yorks 52 G4
Whitgreave Staffs 34 C4
Whithorn Dumfries 55 E7
Whiting Bay N Ayrs 66 D3
Whitkirk W Yorks 51 F9
Whitland Carms 22 E6
Whitletts S Ayrs 66 D6
Whitley N Yorks 52 G1
Whitley Reading 18 D4
Whitley Wilts 16 E5
Whitley Bay T&W 63 F9
Whitley Chapel Northumb 62 H5
Whitley Lower W Yorks 51 H8
Whitley Row Kent 19 F11
Whitlock's End W Mid 35 H7
Whitminster Glos 26 H4
Whitmore Staffs 34 A4
Whitnage Devon 7 E9
Whitnash Warks 27 B10
Whitney-on-Wye Hereford 25 D9
Whitrigg Cumb 57 C8
Whitrigg Cumb 61 H8
Whitsbury Hants 9 C10
Whitsome Borders 71 E7
Whitson Newport 15 C9
Whitstable Kent 21 E8
Whitstone Corn 6 G1
Whittingham Northumb 62 B6
Whittingslow Shrops 33 G10
Whittington Glos 27 F7
Whittington Lancs 50 B2
Whittington Norf 38 F3
Whittington Shrops 33 B9
Whittington Staffs 35 E7
Whittington Staffs 34 G4
Whittington Warks 35 E7
Whittington Worcs 26 C5
Whittle-le-Woods Lancs 50 G1
Whittlebury Northants 28 D3
Whittlesey Cambs 37 F8
Whittlesford Cambs 29 D11
Whittlestone Head Blackburn 50 H3
Whitton Borders 70 H6
Whitton N Lincs 52 G5
Whitton Northumb 62 C6
Whitton Powys 25 B9
Whitton Shrops 26 A2
Whitton Stockton 58 D4
Whitton Suff 31 D8
Whittonditch Wilts 17 D9
Whittonstall Northumb 62 H6
Whitway Hants 17 F11
Whitwell Derbys 45 E9
Whitwell Herts 29 F8
Whitwell IoW 10 G4
Whitwell N Yorks 58 G3
Whitwell Rutland 36 E5
Whitwell-on-the-Hill N Yorks 52 C3
Whitwell Street Norf 39 C7
Whitwick Leics 35 D10
Whitwood W Yorks 51 G10
Whitworth Lancs 50 H4
Whixall Shrops 33 B11
Whixley N Yorks 51 D10
Whoberley W Mid 35 H9
Whorlton Durham 58 E2
Whorlton N Yorks 58 F5
Whygate Northumb 62 F3
Whyle Hereford 26 B2
Whyteleafe Sur 19 F10
Wibdon Glos 16 B2
Wibsey W Yorks 51 F7
Wibtoft Leics 35 G10
Wichenford Worcs 26 B4
Wichling Kent 20 F6
Wick Bmouth 9 E10
Wick Devon 7 F10
Wick Highld 94 E5
Wick S Glos 16 D4
Wick Shetland 96 K6
Wick V Glam 14 D5
Wick W Sus 11 D9
Wick Wilts 9 B10
Wick Worcs 26 D6
Wick Hill Wokingham 18 E4
Wick St Lawrence N Som 15 E9
Wicken Cambs 30 A2
Wicken Northants 28 E4
Wicken Bonhunt Essex 29 E11
Wicken Green Village Norf 38 B4
Wickenby Lincs 46 D4
Wickersley S Yorks 45 D8
Wickford Essex 20 B4
Wickham Hants 10 C4
Wickham W Berks 17 D10
Wickham Bishops Essex 30 G5
Wickham Market Suff 31 C10
Wickham Skeith Suff 31 B7
Wickham St Paul Essex 30 E5
Wickham Street Suff 30 C4
Wickham Street Suff 31 B7
Wickhambreaux Kent 21 F9
Wickhambrook Suff 30 C4
Wickhamford Worcs 27 D7
Wickhampton Norf 39 E10
Wicklewood Norf 39 E6
Wickmere Norf 39 B7
Wickwar S Glos 16 C4
Widdington Essex 30 E2
Widdrington Northumb 63 D8
Widdrington Station Northumb 63 D8
Wide Open T&W 63 F8
Widecombe in the Moor Devon 5 D8
Widegates Corn 4 F3
Widemouth Bay Corn 4 A3
Widewall Orkney 95 J5
Widford Essex 30 H3
Widford Herts 29 G11
Widham Wilts 17 C7
Widmer End Bucks 18 B5
Widmerpool Notts 36 C2
Widnes Halton 43 D8
Wigan Gtr Man 43 B8
Wiggaton Devon 7 G10
Wiggenhall St Germans Norf 38 D1
Wiggenhall St Mary Magdalen Norf 38 D1
Wiggenhall St Mary the Virgin Norf 38 D1
Wigginton Herts 28 G6
Wigginton Oxon 27 E10
Wigginton Staffs 35 E8
Wigginton York 52 D1
Wigglesworth N Yorks 50 D4
Wiggonby Cumb 56 A4
Wiggonholt W Sus 11 C9
Wighill N Yorks 51 E10
Wighton Norf 38 B5
Wigley Hants 10 C2
Wigmore Hereford 25 B11
Wigmore Medway 20 E5
Wigsley Notts 46 E2
Wigsthorpe Northants 36 G6
Wigston Leics 36 F2
Wigthorpe Notts 45 D9
Wigtoft Lincs 37 B8
Wigton Cumb 56 B4
Wigtown Dumfries 55 D7
Wigtwizzle S Yorks 44 C6
Wike W Yorks 51 E9
Wike Well End S Yorks 45 A10
Wilbarston Northants 36 G4
Wilberfoss E Yorks 52 D3
Wilberlee W Yorks 44 A4
Wilburton Cambs 29 A11
Wilby Norf 38 G6
Wilby Northants 28 B5
Wilby Suff 31 A9
Wilcot Wilts 17 E8
Wilcott Shrops 33 D9
Wilcrick Newport 15 C10
Wilday Green Derbys 45 E7
Wildboarclough Ches E 44 F3
Wilden Bedford 29 C7
Wilden Worcs 26 A5
Wildhern Hants 17 F10
Wildhill Herts 29 H9
Wildmoor Worcs 34 H5
Wildsworth Lincs 46 C2
Wilford Nottingham 36 B1
Wilkesley Ches E 34 A2
Wilkhaven Highld 87 C12
Wilkieston W Loth 69 D10
Willand Devon 7 E9
Willaston Ches E 43 G9
Willaston Ches W 42 E6
Willen M Keynes 28 D5
Willenhall W Mid 34 F5
Willenhall W Mid 35 H9
Willerby E Yorks 52 F6
Willerby N Yorks 52 B6
Willersey Glos 27 E8
Willersley Hereford 25 D10
Willesborough Kent 13 B9
Willesborough Lees Kent 13 B9
Willesden London 19 C9
Willett Som 7 C10
Willey Shrops 34 F2
Willey Warks 35 G10
Willey Green Sur 18 F6
Williamscot Oxon 27 D11
Willian Herts 29 E9
Willingale Essex 30 H2
Willingdon E Sus 12 F4
Willingham Cambs 29 A11
Willingham by Stow Lincs 46 D2
Willington Bedford 29 D8
Willington Derbys 35 C8
Willington Durham 58 C2
Willington T&W 63 G9
Willington Warks 27 E9
Willington Corner Ches W 43 F8
Willisham Tye Suff 31 C7
Willitoft E Yorks 52 F3
Williton Som 7 B9
Willoughbridge Staffs 34 A3
Willoughby Lincs 47 E8
Willoughby Warks 28 B2
Willoughby-on-the-Wolds Notts 36 C2
Willoughby Waterleys Leics 36 F1
Willoughton Lincs 46 C3
Willows Green Essex 30 G4
Willsbridge S Glos 16 D3
Willsworthy Devon 4 C6
Wilmcote Warks 27 C8
Wilmington Devon 8 E1
Wilmington E Sus 12 F4
Wilmington Kent 20 D2
Wilminstone Devon 4 D4
Wilmslow Ches E 44 D2
Wilnecote Staffs 35 E8
Wilpshire Lancs 50 F2
Wilsden W Yorks 51 F6
Wilsford Lincs 36 A6
Wilsford Wilts 17 F8
Wilsford Wilts 17 H8
Wilsill N Yorks 51 C7
Wilsley Pound Kent 13 C6
Wilsom Hants 18 H4
Wilson Leics 35 C10
Wilsontown S Lanark 69 E8
Wilstead Bedford 29 D7
Wilsthorpe Lincs 37 D6
Wilstone Herts 28 G6
Wilton Borders 61 B10
Wilton Cumb 56 E2
Wilton N Yorks 52 A4
Wilton Redcar 59 E6
Wilton Wilts 9 A9
Wilton Wilts 17 E9
Wimbish Essex 30 E2
Wimbish Green Essex 30 E3
Wimblebury Staffs 34 D6
Wimbledon London 19 D9
Wimblington Cambs 37 F10
Wimborne Minster Dorset 9 E9
Wimborne St Giles Dorset 9 C9
Wimbotsham Norf 38 E2
Wimpson Soton 10 C2
Wimpstone Warks 27 D9
Wincanton Som 8 B6
Wincham Ches W 43 E9
Winchburgh W Loth 69 C10
Winchcombe Glos 27 F7
Winchelsea E Sus 13 E8
Winchelsea Beach E Sus 13 E8
Winchester Hants 10 B3
Winchet Hill Kent 13 B6
Winchfield Hants 18 F4
Winchmore Hill Bucks 18 B6
Winchmore Hill London 19 B10
Wincle Ches E 44 F3
Wincobank S Yorks 45 C7
Windermere Cumb 56 G6
Winderton Warks 27 D10
Windhill Highld 87 G8
Windhouse Shetland 96 D6
Windlehurst Gtr Man 44 D3
Windlesham Sur 18 E6
Windley Derbys 45 H7
Windmill Hill E Sus 12 E5
Windmill Hill Som 8 C2
Windrush Glos 27 G8
Windsor N Lincs 45 A11
Windsor Windsor 18 D6
Windsoredge Glos 16 A5
Windygates Fife 76 G6
Windyknowe W Loth 69 D8
Windywalls Borders 70 G6
Wineham W Sus 11 B11
Winestead E Yorks 53 G8
Winewall Lancs 50 E5
Winfarthing Norf 39 G7
Winford IoW 10 F4
Winford N Som 15 E11
Winforton Hereford 25 D9
Winfrith Newburgh Dorset 9 F7
Wing Bucks 28 F5
Wing Rutland 36 E4
Wingate Durham 58 C4
Wingates Gtr Man 43 B9
Wingates Northumb 63 D7
Wingerworth Derbys 45 F7
Wingfield C Beds 29 F7
Wingfield Suff 39 H8
Wingfield Wilts 16 F5
Wingham Kent 21 F9
Wingmore Kent 21 G8
Wingrave Bucks 28 G5
Winkburn Notts 45 G11
Winkfield Brack 18 D6
Winkfield Row Brack 18 D5
Winkhill Staffs 44 G4
Winklebury Hants 18 F3
Winkleigh Devon 6 F5
Winksley N Yorks 51 B8
Winkton Dorset 9 E10
Winlaton T&W 63 G7
Winless Highld 94 E5
Winmarleigh Lancs 49 E4
Winnal Hereford 25 E11
Winnall Hants 10 B3
Winnersh Wokingham 18 D4
Winscales Cumb 56 D2
Winscombe N Som 15 F10
Winsford Ches W 43 F9
Winsford Som 7 C8
Winsham Som 8 D2
Winshill Staffs 35 C8
Winskill Cumb 57 C7
Winslade Hants 18 G3
Winsley Wilts 16 E5
Winslow Bucks 28 F4
Winson Glos 27 H7
Winson Green W Mid 35 G6
Winsor Hants 10 C2
Winster Cumb 56 G6
Winster Derbys 44 F6
Winston Durham 58 E2
Winston Suff 31 B8
Winston Green Suff 31 B8
Winstone Glos 26 H6
Winswell Devon 6 E3
Winter Gardens Essex 20 C4
Winterborne Clenston Dorset 9 D7
Winterborne Herringston Dorset 8 F5
Winterborne Houghton Dorset 9 D7
Winterborne Kingston Dorset 9 E7
Winterborne Monkton Dorset 8 F5
Winterborne Stickland Dorset 9 D7
Winterborne Whitechurch Dorset 9 D7
Winterborne Zelston Dorset 9 E7
Winterbourne S Glos 16 C3
Winterbourne W Berks 17 D11
Winterbourne Abbas Dorset 8 E5
Winterbourne Bassett Wilts 17 D8
Winterbourne Dauntsey Wilts 9 A10
Winterbourne Down S Glos 16 D3
Winterbourne Earls Wilts 9 A10
Winterbourne Gunner Wilts 17 H8
Winterbourne Monkton Wilts 17 D8
Winterbourne Steepleton Dorset 8 F5
Winterbourne Stoke Wilts 17 G7
Winterburn N Yorks 50 D5
Winteringham N Lincs 52 G5
Winterley Ches E 43 G10
Wintersett W Yorks 51 H9
Wintershill Hants 10 C4
Winterton N Lincs 52 H5
Winterton-on-Sea Norf 39 D10
Winthorpe Lincs 47 F9
Winthorpe Notts 46 G2
Winton Bmouth 9 E9
Winton Cumb 57 E9
Winton N Yorks 58 G5
Wintringham N Yorks 52 B4
Winwick Cambs 37 G7
Winwick Northants 28 A3
Winwick Warr 43 C9
Wirksworth Derbys 44 G6
Wirswall Ches E 33 A11
Wisbech Cambs 37 E10
Wisbech St Mary Cambs 37 E10
Wisborough Green W Sus 11 B9
Wiseton Notts 45 D11
Wishaw N Lanark 68 E6
Wishaw Warks 35 F7
Wisley Sur 19 F7
Wispington Lincs 46 E6
Wissenden Kent 13 B8
Wissett Suff 39 H9
Wistanstow Shrops 33 G10
Wistanswick Shrops 34 C2
Wistaston Ches E 43 G9
Wistaston Green Ches E 43 G9
Wiston Pembs 22 E5
Wiston S Lanark 69 G8
Wiston W Sus 11 C10
Wistow Cambs 37 G8
Wistow N Yorks 52 F1
Wiswell Lancs 50 F3
Witcham Cambs 37 G10
Witchampton Dorset 9 D8
Witchford Cambs 37 H11
Witham Essex 30 G5
Witham Friary Som 16 G4
Witham on the Hill Lincs 37 D6
Witham Halse Northants 28 C2
Withcall Lincs 46 D6
Withdean Brighton 12 F2
Witherenden Hill E Sus 12 D5
Witheridge Devon 7 E7
Witherley Leics 35 F9
Withern Lincs 47 D8
Withernsea E Yorks 53 G9
Withernwick E Yorks 53 E7
Withersdale Street Suff 39 G8
Withersfield Suff 30 D3
Witherslack Cumb 49 A4
Withiel Corn 3 C8
Withiel Florey Som 7 C8
Withington Glos 27 G7
Withington Gtr Man 44 C2
Withington Hereford 26 D2
Withington Shrops 34 D1
Withington Staffs 34 B6
Withleigh Devon 7 E8
Withnell Lancs 50 G2
Withybrook Warks 35 G10
Withycombe Som 7 B9
Withycombe Raleigh Devon 5 C11
Withyham E Sus 12 C3
Withypool Som 7 C7
Witley Sur 18 H6
Witnesham Suff 31 C8
Witney Oxon 27 G10
Wittering Pboro 37 E6
Wittersham Kent 13 D7
Witton Angus 83 F7
Witton Worcs 26 B5
Witton Bridge Norf 39 B9
Witton Gilbert Durham 58 B3
Witton-le-Wear Durham 58 C2
Witton Park Durham 58 C2
Wiveliscombe Som 7 D9
Wivelrod Hants 18 H3
Wivelsfield E Sus 12 D2
Wivelsfield Green E Sus 12 D2
Wivenhoe Essex 31 F7
Wivenhoe Cross Essex 31 F7
Wiveton Norf 38 A6
Wix Essex 31 F8
Wixford Warks 27 C7
Wixhill Shrops 34 C1
Wixoe Suff 30 D4
Woburn C Beds 28 E6
Woburn Sands M Keynes 28 E6
Wokefield Park W Berks 18 E3
Woking Sur 19 F7
Wokingham Wokingham 18 E5
Wolborough Devon 5 D9
Wold Newton E Yorks 52 B6
Wold Newton NE Lincs 46 C6
Woldingham Sur 19 F10
Wolfclyde S Lanark 69 G9
Wolferton Norf 38 C2
Wolfhill Perth 76 D4
Wolf's Castle Pembs 22 D4
Wolfsdale Pembs 22 D4
Woll Borders 61 A10
Wollaston Northants 28 B6
Wollaston Shrops 33 D9
Wollaton Nottingham 35 B11
Wollerton Shrops 34 B2
Wollescote W Mid 34 G5
Wolsingham Durham 58 C1
Wolston Warks 35 H10
Wolvercote Oxon 27 H11
Wolverhampton W Mid 34 F5
Wolverley Shrops 33 B10
Wolverley Worcs 34 H4
Wolverton Hants 18 F2
Wolverton M Keynes 28 D5
Wolverton Warks 27 B9
Wolverton Common Hants 18 F2
Wolvesnewton Mon 15 B10
Wolvey Warks 35 G10
Wolviston Stockton 58 D5
Wombleton N Yorks 52 A2
Wombourne Staffs 34 F4
Wombwell S Yorks 45 B7
Womenswold Kent 21 F9
Womersley N Yorks 51 H11
Wonastow Mon 25 G11
Wonersh Sur 19 G7
Wonson Devon 5 C7
Wonston Hants 17 H11
Wooburn Bucks 18 C6
Wooburn Green Bucks 18 C6
Wood Dalling Norf 39 C6
Wood End Herts 29 F10
Wood End Warks 27 A8
Wood End Warks 35 F8
Wood Enderby Lincs 46 F6
Wood Field Sur 19 F8
Wood Green London 19 B10
Wood Hayes W Mid 34 E5
Wood Lanes Ches E 44 D3
Wood Norton Norf 38 C6
Wood Street Norf 39 C9
Wood Street Sur 18 F6
Wood Walton Cambs 37 G8
Woodacott Devon 6 F2
Woodale N Yorks 50 B6
Woodbank Argyll 65 G7
Woodbastwick Norf 39 D9
Woodbeck Notts 45 E11
Woodborough Notts 45 H10
Woodborough Wilts 17 F8
Woodbridge Dorset 8 C6
Woodbridge Suff 31 D9
Woodbury Devon 5 C11
Woodbury Salterton Devon 5 C11
Woodchester Glos 16 A5
Woodchurch Kent 13 C8
Woodchurch Mers 42 D5
Woodcombe Som 7 B8
Woodcote Oxon 18 C3
Woodcott Hants 17 F11
Woodcroft Glos 15 B11
Woodcutts Dorset 9 C8
Woodditton Cambs 30 C3
Woodeaton Oxon 28 G2
Woodend Cumb 56 G3
Woodend Northants 28 D3
Woodend W Sus 11 D7
Woodend Green Northants 28 D3
Woodfalls Wilts 9 B10
Woodfield Oxon 28 F2
Woodfield S Ayrs 66 D6
Woodford Corn 6 E1
Woodford Devon 5 F8
Woodford Glos 16 B3
Woodford Gtr Man 44 D2
Woodford London 19 B11
Woodford Northants 36 H5
Woodford Bridge London 19 B11
Woodford Halse Northants 28 C2
Woodgate Norf 38 D6
Woodgate W Mid 34 G5
Woodgate W Sus 11 D8
Woodgate Worcs 26 B6
Woodgreen Hants 9 C10
Woodhall Herts 29 G9
Woodhall Invclyd 68 C2
Woodhall N Yorks 57 G11
Woodhall Spa Lincs 46 F5
Woodham Sur 19 E7
Woodham Ferrers Essex 20 B4
Woodham Mortimer Essex 30 H5
Woodham Walter Essex 30 H5
Woodhaven Fife 77 E7
Woodhay Aberds 89 E7
Woodhead Gtr Man 44 B3
Woodhey Gtr Man 50 H3
Woodhill Shrops 34 G3
Woodhorn Northumb 63 E8
Woodhouse Leics 35 D11
Woodhouse S Yorks 45 D8
Woodhouse W Yorks 51 F8
Woodhouse W Yorks 51 G9
Woodhouse Eaves Leics 35 D11
Woodhouse Park Gtr Man 44 D2
Woodhouselee Midloth 69 D11
Woodhouselees Dumfries 61 F9
Woodhouses Staffs 35 D7
Woodhurst Cambs 37 H9
Woodingdean Brighton 12 F2
Woodkirk W Yorks 51 G8
Woodland Devon 5 E8
Woodland Durham 58 D1
Woodlands Aberds 83 D9
Woodlands Dorset 9 D9
Woodlands Hants 10 C2
Woodlands Highld 87 G8
Woodlands N Yorks 51 D9
Woodlands S Yorks 45 B9
Woodlands Park Windsor 18 D5
Woodlands St Mary W Berks 17 D10
Woodlane Staffs 35 C7
Woodleigh Devon 5 G8
Woodlesford W Yorks 51 G9
Woodley Gtr Man 44 C3
Woodley Wokingham 18 D4
Woodmancote Glos 26 F6
Woodmancote Glos 27 F7
Woodmancote Glos 16 A6
Woodmancote W Sus 11 D6
Woodmancote W Sus 12 E1
Woodmancott Hants 18 G2
Woodmansey E Yorks 53 F6
Woodmansterne Sur 19 F9
Woodminton Wilts 9 B9
Woodnesborough Kent 21 F10
Woodnewton Northants 36 F6
Woodplumpton Lancs 49 F5
Woodrising Norf 38 E5
Wood's Green E Sus 12 C5
Woodseaves Shrops 34 B2
Woodseaves Staffs 34 C3
Woodsend Wilts 17 D9
Woodsetts S Yorks 45 D9
Woodsford Dorset 9 E6
Woodside Aberds 83 C11
Woodside Aberds 89 D10
Woodside Brack 18 D6
Woodside Fife 77 G7
Woodside Hants 10 E2
Woodside Herts 29 H9
Woodside Perth 76 D5
Woodside of Arbeadie Aberds 83 D9
Woodstock Oxon 27 G11
Woodstock Pembs 22 D5
Woodthorpe Derbys 45 E8
Woodthorpe Lincs 47 D8
Woodthorpe York 52 E1
Woodton Norf 39 F8
Woodtown Devon 6 D3
Woodtown Devon 6 D3
Woodvale Mers 42 A6
Woodville Derbys 35 D9
Woodyates Dorset 9 C9
Woofferton Shrops 26 B2
Wookey Som 15 G11
Wookey Hole Som 15 G11
Wool Dorset 9 F7
Woolacombe Devon 6 B3
Woolage Green Kent 21 G9
Woolaston Glos 16 B2
Woolavington Som 15 G9
Woolbeding W Sus 11 B7
Wooldale W Yorks 44 B5
Wooler Northumb 71 H8
Woolfardisworthy Devon 6 D2
Woolfardisworthy Devon 7 F7
Woolfords Cottages S Lanark 69 E9
Woolhampton W Berks 18 E2
Woolhope Hereford 26 E3
Woolhope Cockshoot Hereford 26 E3
Woolland Dorset 9 D6
Woollaton Devon 6 E3
Woolley Bath 16 E4
Woolley Cambs 37 H7
Woolley Corn 6 E1
Woolley Derbys 45 F7
Woolley W Yorks 45 A7
Woolmer Green Herts 29 G9
Woolmere Green Worcs 26 B6
Woolpit Suff 30 B6
Woolscott Warks 27 B11
Woolsington T&W 63 G7
Woolstanwood Ches E 43 G9
Woolstaston Shrops 33 F10
Woolsthorpe Lincs 36 C4
Woolsthorpe Lincs 36 B5
Woolston Devon 5 G8
Woolston Shrops 33 C9
Woolston Shrops 33 G10
Woolston Soton 10 C3
Woolston Warr 43 D9
Woolston Green Devon 5 E8
Woolstone M Keynes 28 E5
Woolstone Oxon 17 C9
Woolton Mers 43 D7
Woolton Hill Hants 17 E11
Woolverstone Suff 31 E8
Woolverton Som 16 F4
Woolwich London 19 D11
Woolwich Ferry London 19 D11
Wooperton Northumb 62 A6
Woore Shrops 34 A3
Wootten Green Suff 31 A9
Wootton Bedford 29 D7
Wootton Hants 9 E11
Wootton Hereford 25 C10
Wootton Kent 21 G9
Wootton N Lincs 53 H6
Wootton Northants 28 C4
Wootton Oxon 27 G11
Wootton Oxon 27 H11
Wootton Shrops 33 C9
Wootton Shrops 33 H10
Wootton Staffs 44 H5
Wootton Bridge IoW 10 E4
Wootton Common IoW 10 E4
Wootton Courtenay Som 7 B8
Wootton Fitzpaine Dorset 8 E2
Wootton Rivers Wilts 17 E8
Wootton St Lawrence Hants 18 F2
Wootton Wawen Warks 27 B8
Worcester Worcs 26 C5
Worcester Park London 19 E9
Wordsley W Mid 34 G4
Worfield Shrops 34 F3
Work Orkney 95 G5
Workington Cumb 56 D2
Worksop Notts 45 E9
Worlaby N Lincs 46 A4
World's End W Berks 17 D11
Worle N Som 15 E9
Worleston Ches E 43 G9
Worlingham Suff 39 G10
Worlington Suff 30 A3
Worlingworth Suff 31 B9
Wormald Green N Yorks 51 C9
Wormbridge Hereford 25 E11
Wormegay Norf 38 D2
Wormelow Tump Hereford 25 E11
Wormhill Derbys 44 E5
Wormingford Essex 30 E6
Worminghall Bucks 28 H3
Wormington Glos 27 E7
Worminster Som 16 G2
Wormit Fife 76 E6
Wormleighton Warks 27 C11
Wormley Herts 29 H10
Wormley Sur 18 H6
Wormley West End Herts 29 H10
Wormshill Kent 20 F5
Wormsley Hereford 25 D11
Worplesdon Sur 18 F6
Worrall S Yorks 45 C7
Worsbrough S Yorks 45 B7
Worsbrough Common S Yorks 45 B7
Worsley Gtr Man 43 B10
Worstead Norf 39 C9
Worsthorne Lancs 50 F4
Worston Lancs 50 E3
Worswell Devon 5 G6
Worth Kent 21 F10
Worth W Sus 12 C2
Worth Matravers Dorset 9 G8
Wortham Suff 39 H6
Worthen Shrops 33 E9
Worthenbury Wrex 43 H7
Worthing Norf 38 D5
Worthing W Sus 11 D10
Worthington Leics 35 C10
Worting Hants 18 F3
Wortley S Yorks 45 C7
Wortley W Yorks 51 F8
Worton N Yorks 57 G11
Worton Wilts 16 F6
Wortwell Norf 39 G8
Wotherton Shrops 33 E8
Wotter Devon 5 E6
Wotton Sur 19 G8
Wotton-under-Edge Glos 16 B4
Wotton Underwood Bucks 28 G3
Woughton on the Green M Keynes 28 E5
Wouldham Kent 20 E4
Wrabness Essex 31 E8
Wrafton Devon 6 C3
Wragby Lincs 46 E5
Wragby W Yorks 51 H10
Wramplingham Norf 39 E7
Wrangbrook W Yorks 45 A8
Wrangham Aberds 89 E6
Wrangle Lincs 47 G8
Wrangle Bank Lincs 47 G8
Wrangle Lowgate Lincs 47 G8
Wrangway Som 7 E10
Wrantage Som 8 B2
Wrawby N Lincs 46 B4
Wraxall Dorset 8 E4
Wraxall N Som 15 D10
Wraxall Som 16 H3
Wray Lancs 50 C2
Wraysbury Windsor 19 D7
Wrayton Lancs 50 B2
Wrea Green Lancs 49 F3
Wreay Cumb 56 B6
Wreay Cumb 56 D6
Wrecclesham Sur 18 G5
Wrecsam = Wrexham Wrex 43 G6
Wrekenton T&W 63 H8
Wrelton N Yorks 59 H8
Wrenbury Ches E 43 H9
Wrench Green N Yorks 59 H10
Wreningham Norf 39 F7
Wrentham Suff 39 G10
Wrenthorpe W Yorks 51 G9
Wrentnall Shrops 33 E10
Wressle E Yorks 52 F3
Wressle N Lincs 46 B3
Wrestlingworth C Beds 29 D9
Wretham Norf 38 G5
Wretton Norf 38 E2
Wrexham = Wrecsam Wrex 43 G6
Wrexham Industrial Estate Wrex 43 H7
Wrightington Bar Lancs 43 A8
Wrinehill Staffs 43 H10
Wrington N Som 15 E10
Writhlington Bath 16 F4
Writtle Essex 30 H3
Wrockwardine Telford 34 D2
Wroot N Lincs 45 B11
Wrotham Kent 20 F3
Wrotham Heath Kent 20 F3
Wroughton Swindon 17 C8
Wroxall IoW 10 G4
Wroxall Warks 27 A9
Wroxeter Shrops 34 E1
Wroxham Norf 39 D9
Wroxton Oxon 27 D11
Wyaston Derbys 35 A7
Wyberton Lincs 37 A9
Wyboston Bedford 29 C8
Wybunbury Ches E 43 H10
Wych Cross E Sus 12 C3
Wychbold Worcs 26 B6
Wyck Hants 18 H4
Wyck Rissington Glos 27 F8
Wycoller Lancs 50 F5
Wycomb Leics 36 C3
Wycombe Marsh Bucks 18 B5
Wyddial Herts 29 E10
Wye Kent 21 G7
Wyesham Mon 26 G2
Wyfordby Leics 36 D3
Wyke Dorset 9 B6
Wyke Shrops 34 E2
Wyke Sur 18 F6
Wyke W Yorks 51 G7
Wyke Regis Dorset 8 G5
Wykeham N Yorks 52 A5
Wykeham N Yorks 59 H10
Wyken W Mid 35 G9
Wykey Shrops 33 C9
Wylam Northumb 63 G7
Wylde Green W Mid 35 F7
Wyllie Caerph 15 B7
Wylye Wilts 17 H7
Wymering Ptsmth 10 D5
Wymeswold Leics 36 C2
Wymington Bedford 28 B6
Wymondham Leics 36 D4
Wymondham Norf 39 E7
Wyndham Bridgend 14 B5
Wynford Eagle Dorset 8 E4
Wyng Orkney 95 J4
Wynyard Village Stockton 58 D5
Wyre Piddle Worcs 26 D6
Wysall Notts 36 C2
Wythall Worcs 35 H6
Wytham Oxon 27 H11
Wythburn Cumb 56 E5
Wythenshawe Gtr Man 44 D2
Wythop Mill Cumb 56 D3
Wyton Cambs 29 A9
Wyverstone Suff 31 B7
Wyverstone Street Suff 31 B7
Wyville Lincs 36 C4
Wyvis Lodge Highld 86 D7

Y

Y Bala = Bala Gwyn 32 B5
Y Barri = Barry V Glam 15 E7
Y Bont-Faen = Cowbridge V Glam 14 D5
Y Drenewydd = Newtown Powys 33 F7
Y Fenni = Abergavenny Mon 25 G9
Y Ffôr Gwyn 40 G5
Y Fflint = Flint Flint 42 E5
Y Felinheli Gwyn 41 D7
Y Gelli Gandryll = Hay-on-Wye Powys 25 D9
Y Mwmbwls = The Mumbles Swansea 14 C3
Y Pîl = Pyle Bridgend 14 C4
Y Rhws = Rhoose V Glam 14 E6
Y Rhyl = Rhyl Denb 42 D3
Y Trallwng = Welshpool Powys 33 E8
Y Waun = Chirk Wrex 33 B8
Yaddlethorpe N Lincs 46 B2
Yafford IoW 10 F3
Yafforth N Yorks 58 G4
Yalding Kent 20 G3
Yanworth Glos 27 G7
Yapham E Yorks 52 D3
Yapton W Sus 11 D8
Yarburgh Lincs 47 C7
Yarcombe Devon 8 D1
Yard Som 7 C8
Yardley W Mid 35 G7
Yardley Gobion Northants 28 D4
Yardley Hastings Northants 28 C5
Yardro Powys 25 C9
Yarkhill Hereford 26 D3
Yarlet Staffs 34 C5
Yarlington Som 8 B5
Yarlside Cumb 49 C2
Yarm Stockton 58 E5
Yarmouth IoW 10 F2
Yarnbrook Wilts 16 F5
Yarnfield Staffs 34 B4
Yarnscombe Devon 6 D4
Yarnton Oxon 27 G11
Yarpole Hereford 25 B11
Yarrow Borders 70 H2
Yarrow Feus Borders 70 H2
Yarsop Hereford 25 D11
Yarwell Northants 37 F6
Yate S Glos 16 C4
Yateley Hants 18 E5
Yatesbury Wilts 17 D7
Yattendon W Berks 18 D2
Yatton Hereford 25 B11
Yatton N Som 15 E10
Yatton Keynell Wilts 16 D5
Yaverland IoW 10 F5
Yaxham Norf 38 D6
Yaxley Cambs 37 F7
Yaxley Suff 31 A8
Yazor Hereford 25 D11
Yeading London 19 C8
Yeadon W Yorks 51 E8
Yealand Conyers Lancs 49 B5
Yealand Redmayne Lancs 49 B5
Yealmpton Devon 5 F6
Yearby Redcar 59 D7
Yearsley N Yorks 52 B1
Yeaton Shrops 33 D10
Yeaveley Derbys 35 A7
Yedingham N Yorks 52 B4
Yeldon Bedford 29 B7
Yelford Oxon 17 A10
Yelland Devon 6 C3
Yelling Cambs 29 B9
Yelvertoft Northants 36 H1
Yelverton Devon 4 E6
Yelverton Norf 39 E8
Yenston Som 8 B6
Yeo Mill Devon 7 D7
Yeoford Devon 7 G6
Yeolmbridge Corn 4 C4
Yeovil Som 8 C4
Yeovil Marsh Som 8 C4
Yeovilton Som 8 B4
Yerbeston Pembs 22 F5
Yesnaby Orkney 95 G3
Yetlington Northumb 62 C6
Yetminster Dorset 8 C4
Yettington Devon 7 H9
Yetts o' Muckhart Clack 76 G3
Yieldshields S Lanark 69 E7
Yiewsley London 19 C7
Ynys-meudwy Neath 24 H4
Ynysboeth Rhondda 14 B6
Ynysddu Caerph 15 B7
Ynysgyfflog Gwyn 32 D2
Ynyshir Rhondda 14 B6
Ynyslas Ceredig 32 F2
Ynystawe Swansea 14 A2
Ynysybwl Rhondda 14 B6
Yockenthwaite N Yorks 50 B5
Yockleton Shrops 33 D9
Yokefleet E Yorks 52 G4
Yoker W Dunb 68 D4
Yonder Bognie Aberds 88 D5
York York 52 D1
York Town Sur 18 E5
Yorkletts Kent 21 E7
Yorkley Glos 26 H3
Yorton Shrops 33 C11
Youlgreave Derbys 44 F6
Youlstone Devon 6 E1
Youlthorpe E Yorks 52 D3
Youlton N Yorks 51 C10
Young Wood Lincs 46 E5
Young's End Essex 30 G4
Yoxall Staffs 35 D7
Yoxford Suff 31 B11
Yr Hôb = Hope Flint 42 G6
Yr Wyddgrug = Mold Flint 42 F5
Ysbyty-Cynfyn Ceredig 32 H3
Ysbyty Ifan Conwy 41 F10
Ysbyty Ystwyth Ceredig 24 A4
Ysceifiog Flint 42 E4
Yspitty Carms 23 G10
Ystalyfera Neath 24 H4
Ystrad Rhondda 14 B5
Ystrad Aeron Ceredig 23 A10
Ystrad-mynach Caerph 15 B7
Ystradfellte Powys 24 G6
Ystradffin Carms 24 D4
Ystradgynlais Powys 24 G4
Ystradmeurig Ceredig 24 B4
Ystradowen Carms 24 G4
Ystradowen V Glam 14 D6
Ystumtuen Ceredig 32 H3
Ythanbank Aberds 89 E9
Ythanwells Aberds 89 E6
Ythsie Aberds 89 E8

Z

Zeal Monachorum Devon 6 F6
Zeals Wilts 9 A6
Zelah Corn 3 D7
Zennor Corn 2 F3